KIERKEGAARD'S GO
AND THE GOOD LIFE

INDIANA SERIES IN THE PHILOSOPHY OF RELIGION

Merold Westphal, editor

KIERKEGAARD'S GOD
AND THE GOOD LIFE

Edited by Stephen Minister, J. Aaron
Simmons, and Michael Strawser

Indiana University Press

This book is a publication of

Indiana University Press
Office of Scholarly Publishing
Herman B. Wells Library 350
1320 East 10th Street
Bloomington, Indiana 47405 USA

iupress.indiana.edu

The paper used in this publication meets the minimum requirements of the American National Standard for Information Sciences—Permanence of Paper for Printed Library Materials, ANSI Z39.48-1992.

Manufactured in the United States of America

Library of Congress Cataloging-in-Publication Data

Names: Minster, Stephen [date], editor.
Title: Kierkegaard's God and the good life / edited by Stephen Minster, J. Aaron Simmons, and Michael Strawser.
Description: Bloomington : Indiana University Press, 2017. | Series: Indiana series in the philosophy of religion | Includes bibliographical references and index.
Identifiers: LCCN 2017005117 (print) | LCCN 2017033279 (ebook) | ISBN 9780253029485 (eb) | ISBN 9780253029249 (cl : alk. paper) | ISBN 9780253029362 (pr : alk. paper)
Subjects: LCSH: Kierkegaard, Søren, 1813-1855. | Religion. | Ethics.
Classification: LCC B4377 (ebook) | LCC B4377 .K5123 2017 (print) | DDC 198/.9—dc23
LC record available at https://lccn.loc.gov/2017005117

1 2 3 4 5 22 21 20 19 18 17

To our students, who contribute to the good life
by reminding us that standing before God
always means facing the others that we see.

Contents

Introduction

Stephen Minister, J. Aaron Simmons, and Michael Strawser

THE CONTRIBUTORS TO *Kierkegaard's God and the Good Life* offer new essays dealing with the complex questions that lie at the intersection of religion and ethics. These essays are timely since many people, both inside and outside of academia, now view the relationship between moral action and thinking about God as deeply problematic. This volume was conceived and organized to respond to two sites where this problematic relationship is evident in contemporary society.

First, within Kierkegaardian scholarship, there is a current trend to downplay the orthodox religious aspects of Kierkegaard's thought in order to make his philosophy more relevant to contemporary trends in philosophical inquiry and research in religious studies. For example, Jacques Derrida, Mark Dooley, Stephen Shakespeare, Mark C. Taylor, and John D. Caputo have in various ways suggested that Kierkegaard is more radical than is often realized by the Kierkegaard establishment. Instead of merely "bringing Christianity back to Christendom," as Kierkegaard said of his authorship, Kierkegaard's work stands as a challenge to theism, rejecting classical modes of transcendence, and offers new ways of inhabiting the world after the "death of God."

Second, in the contemporary nonacademic world there is an increasingly prominent intersection between religious existence and social life. Global Pentecostalism, renewed interest in Catholicism due to the influence of Pope Francis, increased attention to the dynamics of Islam, and emerging "religious" trends, some of which are even on display in certain strands of atheism, all refuse to be matters of merely theological interest; instead they impact social and political contexts.

In light of these two realities, this volume offers a sustained and multifaceted reflection on how the work of that peculiar Dane, Søren Kierkegaard (1813–1855), offers profound resources for contemporary existence, not despite his religious commitments, but precisely because of them. The contributors to this book do not aim to critique the work of Derrida, Shakespeare, Dooley, and so on, but instead they aim to think in conversation with such new directions in Kierkegaard scholarship and to offer reasons to think that there are no simple answers when it comes to understanding Kierkegaard's complex, theologically oriented authorship and its ethical impact. Similarly, this volume does not set out to offer a prescriptive vision for how to navigate the complicated intersection of religion and ethics in a globalized world. However, it does attempt to think about why such an intersection is so complicated, why it might be inevitable, and what a faithful and ethical response to it might involve.

Accordingly, this volume offers critical and constructive contributions by leading Kierkegaard scholars to contemporary philosophical debates in the philosophy of religion, moral philosophy, and epistemology while demonstrating that Kierkegaard continues to be an important resource for religious existence, public discourse, and social life. No single book can do everything, especially not when undertaking such complex issues of human embodied life. We do hope, though, that this volume makes a significant stride toward overcoming any facile view of Kierkegaard as being either irrelevant regarding such issues (due to the mistaken, but still widespread, interpretation of Kierkegaard as being an irrational fideist with no concern for social existence) or even dangerous for social life itself (due to the also mistaken, but still occasionally found, view of Kierkegaard as being an immoralist).

The book unfolds as follows.

The chapters that make up part 1, "Faith and Love," demonstrate collectively that without love, the good life is inconceivable, and that without God, humans would be unable to love. The authors of these chapters take Kierkegaard's *Works of Love* to be of utmost importance for this study, and the relevance of this text is shown morally, phenomenologically, and theologically. Along the way, Kierkegaard is brought into dialogue with Leo Tolstoy, Anders Nygren, Dietrich von Hildebrand, and Simone Weil. Two central themes from *Works of Love* emerge as dominant here. First, the contributors strive to illuminate Kierkegaard's view that "just as the quiet lake originates deep down in hidden springs no eye has seen, so also does a person's love originate even more deeply in God's love" (WL, 9). Second, they work to appreciate Kierkegaard's claim in the conclusion to *Works of Love* that "to love people is the only thing worth living for, and without this love you are not really living" (WL, 375), a claim that is directly addressed in the first two contributions.

In chapter 1, "Love As the End of Human Existence," Sharon Krishek argues for the centrality of love to human flourishing by considering Kierkegaard's *Works of Love* as a corrective to the life lived by Ivan Ilyich in Tolstoy's novella *The Death of Ivan Ilyich*. Specifically, Krishek applies Kierkegaard's metaphorical account of love as a quiet lake originating from a hidden spring to show that Ivan's life fails by not developing the love potential that exists within him and all human beings. In this way Krishek uses Tolstoy's text to identify the problem and Kierkegaard's text to identify the solution. Thus, our understanding of both texts is enhanced through this interpretation, as the problem of a wrongly lived life—even when on the surface everything seems fine—can be solved through actualizing the love-potential that is part of our human nature and originates, albeit mysteriously, from God. Using a Kierkegaardian lens, Krishek presents a detailed analysis of *The Death of Ivan Ilyich* to show readers how, even at the point of death, Ivan's life can be redeemed through realizing his relationship to God and fulfilling his potential to love.

The theme of love's primacy for the good life is continued by Michael Strawser in chapter 2, "Love Is the Highest Good." Here Strawser analyzes Kierkegaard's most specific analysis of "the good" in "An Occasional Discourse" in *Upbuilding Discourses in Various Spirits*. In this writing, Kierkegaard maintains that purity of heart involves willing only one thing, and that one thing to be willed is the good. Strawser reads this discourse together with *Works of Love* to argue that the good that makes one pure of heart should be understood as love. While acknowledging the hidden, and thus mysterious, origin of love in God, Strawser focuses on the relationship to the other and attempts to show how the problems of a theological reading can be avoided by considering the phenomenology of love. Thus Strawser argues against interpreting the good as somehow centrally involving the consciousness of guilt, as Louis Mackey holds, and instead views the good as the intentionality of love that is given through our experiences of loving other people in the world, such as when a loving mother teaches her child to walk. Strawser then considers the related notion of "the highest good" found in various places throughout Kierkegaard's authorship, and here too he argues that this notion should be interpreted as meaning the active love of others rather than "an eternal happiness," as this allows us to best account for the good life.

In chapter 3, "Erotic Wisdom: On God, Passion, Faith, and Falling in Love," Pia Søltoft further develops a phenomenological approach focused on the experienced interconnectedness of erotic love, specifically falling in love, and faith in God to show that our human experiences of love and Christian faith are inseparably linked. Søltoft starts by considering the notion of passion as described by Johannes Climacus in *Concluding Unscientific Postscript*, where she finds that this notion is understood both through the birth of eros as mythologically presented in Plato's *Symposium* and as that which relates the existing individual to Christianity. In this way the human (Greek) conception and the Christian conception are seen as complementary, rather than separate and distinct. Søltoft then turns to *Works of Love*, where she also finds significance in the metaphorical account of the quiet lake with hidden springs, as it shows how love should be understood as both dwelling within each human being and within God as the enigmatic source. Søltoft shows that Kierkegaard understands love as a double urge to love and to be loved, as an experience both natural and divine. This view counters the supposedly sharp divide between eros and agape, which is argued for most strongly by Anders Nygren. Søltoft shows Nygren's view to be problematic as she argues for a more nuanced view, one in which the passion of erotic love and the transformation of one's subjectivity in falling in love are seen as experientially connected to the passion involved in the Christian relationship of faith in God.

John Davenport continues the complex discussion surrounding the differing conceptions of special interhuman loves and divine neighborly love in chapter 4, "The Integration of Neighbor-Love and Special Loves in Kierkegaard and von Hildebrand." Considering Kierkegaard's and Nygren's writings initially, Davenport explains how these thinkers are read as maintaining that these kinds of love are contrary to each other. This should disturb us, Davenport explains, and he questions whether special "erosiac" loves should be viewed as inferior to agapic love. In agreement with Søltoft, Davenport argues that Kierkegaard does not invoke Nygren's strong dichotomy but instead opens space for bringing these two kinds of love together. How the human and divine expressions of love can be conceived as united is thus the central focus of Davenport's contribution to this volume. In explaining the "how," which is relevant to both Kierkegaard scholarship and moral psychology, Davenport argues for a normative ideal of special loves that involves an "agapic infusion." In developing his argument, Davenport examines Kierkegaard's treatment of special or preferential love in *Works of Love*, but he ultimately argues that Dietrich von Hildebrand's work in *The Nature of Love* offers a better and more systematic solution for this project. Davenport's detailed account demonstrates how the views of Kierkegaard and von Hildebrand can be fruitfully brought into dialogue, while also indicating where future work needs to be done.

The fifth and final chapter of part 1 is "Kierkegaard, Weil, and Agapic Moral Fideism" by Mark A. Tietjen. Here Tietjen addresses the question of whether our understanding of the good life requires the doctrine of Christian theism. In other words, does moral philosophy require a commitment to Kierkegaard's God? Tietjen starts by considering the problem that moral philosophers face when trying to justify their desire for equality, and he shows that the failure to provide such a foundational justification exposes the problem of cognitive limitation. To this is added the problem of sin by Christian thinkers, which further exposes our moral failure. According to Tietjen, Christian theism provides a compelling reason to trust our desire for equality, and this reason is love, or more specifically, the neighbor love that figures centrally in the thinking of both Kierkegaard and Simone Weil. Echoing the idea above that love connects the human and divine, Tietjen explains how love requires faith in both God and other people. In an elaboration of "love's faith," Tietjen considers the acts of creation and the incarnation as discussed in the writings of Weil and Kierkegaard, and he explains that these acts reveal God's loving character, which is the source of neighborly love. After exploring what it means to consider the source of love as mysterious, Tietjen explains what love's faith has to teach us with regard to the neighbor. For Weil this involves creatively attending to the other, and for Kierkegaard it involves presupposing love in the other. Ultimately, Tietjen's analysis of the concept of love in Kierkegaard and Weil leads him to argue for "agapic moral fideism," the position that belief and trust in God make possible love for one's neighbor, the other who is equal.

In part 2, "Moral Psychology and Ethical Existence," the focus shifts to the implications of Kierkegaardian moral psychology for ethical existence. The authors of these chapters explore the ways in which the virtues, passions, and faith commitments that Kierkegaard endorses shape our awareness of reality, our perceptions of goodness, and our capacities for ethical action. As such, these chapters demonstrate the value of Kierkegaard's work for personal moral development.

The first chapter in this section is John Lippitt's "Kierkegaard's Virtues? Humility and Gratitude as the Grounds of Contentment, Patience, and Hope in Kierkegaard's Moral Psychology." Building on recent work connecting Kierkegaard's thought with virtue ethics, Lippitt sketches the relationship between some of the key virtues in Kierkegaard's work. Lippitt takes as his central texts Kierkegaard's reflections on Jesus's comments about the lilies in the field and birds of the air. Based on these reflections, Lippitt argues that Kierkegaardian humility and gratitude are based on a faith in God's love and forgiveness. This faith provides a stable source of self-confidence and dignity independent of our fleeting accomplishments and comparisons of oneself with others. As such, humility is not an expression of self-abasement, despite Kierkegaard's occasional exaggerations to that effect. Instead, Lippitt suggests that humility is a disposition not to experience certain emotions, particularly emotions related to social status and competition. Humility and gratitude in turn create fertile ground for the development of further virtues such as contentment, joy, patience, and hope. Lippitt argues that contentment and joy can be thought of as a liberation, made possible by humility and gratitude, from the potentially overwhelming anxieties of this world. He characterizes hope and patience as expressions of ethical and epistemic humility, that is, as trust in a goodness that is beyond one's power to achieve and even one's ability to understand. Lippitt suggests that these virtues, grounded in faith in God, who loves and forgives, are essential both to individual flourishing and to loving others.

The next two chapters consider ways that our moral psychology is intimately connected to our attempts to know. As such, they offer Kierkegaardian-inspired ethical critiques of the ideal of objective, disinterested knowledge. In chapter 7, Rick Anthony Furtak examines how our moral psychology shapes our capacity for knowledge, while in chapter 8, Christopher Barnett investigates how contemporary knowledge-seeking shapes our moral psychology.

Furtak's chapter, "The Heart of Knowledge: Kierkegaard on Passion and Understanding," is centered on Kierkegaard's notion of impassioned understanding (*lidenskabelige Forstaaelse*). Drawing examples from throughout Kierkegaard's work, Furtak shows that our emotional dispositions deeply impact the ways we perceive ourselves and the world around us. Contrary to the dominant strands of modern philosophy that regard the impact of emotions on perception as an epistemic defect, Furtak offers a Kierkegaardian argument for the claim that passionate understanding is both inescapable and epistemically vital. Furtak defends Kierkegaard's claim that certain existential questions are so urgent for us that it is impossible to think about them truly without becoming passionate. Thus, far from this passion obscuring our pursuit of truth, Furtak argues that it is essential for perceiving significance and value in the world. Because of this, our ability to recognize meaning and goodness in life requires that we develop the right kind of affective receptivity. As an example of this link, Furtak considers Kierkegaard's discussion of the importance of gratitude and wonder in apprehending certain truths about our ethico-religious existence. Though Kierkegaard's connection between truth and subjectivity is well known, Furtak argues that scholarship on Kierkegaard has generally failed to appreciate the significance of the emotions for this linkage. Furtak's chapter is thus an attempt to get us to take seriously Kierkegaard's suggestion that "to love and to know" are "essentially synonymous."

Barnett's "From Hegel to Google: Kierkegaard and the Perils of 'the System'" complements Furtak's chapter by criticizing a contemporary conception of knowledge that is independent of love or any other passional investment. Specifically, Barnett takes aim at the conception of knowledge derived from the existence of Google and the influence that its ubiquitous search engine has on us. Barnett argues that Google's mission to "organize the world's information" recalls Kierkegaard's concerns about Hegelianism and "the system's" abstraction of knowledge from existence. Barnett reviews Climacus's critique of the system found in *Concluding Unscientific Postscript* and then applies these criticisms to Google, which he considers "the greatest information system" so far created. In addition to examining Google's design, Barnett also investigates the ways in which users relate to Google and are, in turn, shaped by that relationship. In his judgment, the influence of Google is generally negative, immersing users in indifferent knowledge rather than calling them to ethico-religious existence. Barnett argues that Kierkegaard's work, especially his upbuilding discourses, offers a much-needed antidote to this influence. In contrast to an immersion in abstract knowledge, these works encourage us to practice contemplation (*Betragtning*), which reengages us with individual, temporal existence. In the age of Google, Barnett suggests that this Kierkegaardian contemplation acts as therapy, making possible an earnest relationship with concrete existence and, through that, with God.

Whereas other chapters in this volume demonstrate the value of Kierkegaard's theological commitments for ethical thought and practice, the final chapter of part 2 serves as a reminder of the ethical risk that accompanies some of those commitments. In "An Ethics for Adults? Kierkegaard and the Ambiguity of Exaltation," Stephen Minister elucidates this risk by contrasting Kierkegaard's account of religious maturity with that of Emmanuel Levinas. Though Levinas is sympathetic to the possibility of a religious ethics, his vision of religious maturity includes a sharp ethical critique of certain Christian theological positions. The crux of Levinas's criticism is that Christianity's focus on the spiritual, transcendent, and eternal creates ambiguity about the significance of social, material, and historical existence. Minister argues that though Kierkegaard's account of religious maturity recognizes the significance of social, material, and historical existence, at times Kierkegaard traffics in precisely the sort of ambiguity about which Levinas is concerned. This is especially true with regard to Kierkegaard's conception of materiality and social existence. Minister's goal in this analysis is not to revive the rightly discredited interpretation of Kierkegaard as unethical and apolitical, but instead to point out ways in which the ambiguity of exaltation can become an obstacle to religiously mature ethical existence. Minister suggests that this realization is not necessarily inimical to Kierkegaard's work, but that it can be regarded as an extension of Kierkegaardian humility and self-critique.

In part 3, "Existence Before God," the focus shifts to the specifics of Christian life in light of Kierkegaard's account of God and human existence. The four chapters found here attend to different characteristics of such life, but taken together they speak to the way in which Kierkegaard's account of the divine is not abstracted from the realities of social engagement, understanding, and living well, but instead is deeply rooted in them.

Edward F. Mooney's chapter, "Difficult Faith and Living Well," starts off the final part of the volume with something of a Kierkegaardian manifesto for the relationship between the life of faith and the notion of a meaningful life. Mooney admits that such a task is not easy, given the frequency with which Kierkegaard's thought is oriented toward the struggle that faith represents and the difficulty that such faith presents for one's social engagements. Rather than giving in to an easy conception of faith as, for example, an algorithm of the right relationship with God or a set of propositional claims to be affirmed, Mooney poetically argues that faith is a matter of struggling appropriately with the mysteries with which life confronts us. Faith does not resolve the existential paradox so that living becomes easy, but rather it encourages boldness, trust, and openness in the face of the struggles of finitude. In *Fear and Trembling*, Mooney suggests, we find examples of what faith is not, but we also find a positive conception of what faith is when lived out in the world. This positive account does not shy away from the messiness of embodied existence, but rather it takes its impetus from such messiness in order to cultivate the virtues of what Mooney terms "giving up" and "giving back." For Kierkegaard, it is only in proper relation to God that one's dependency and desire can be appropriately oriented such that gratitude for and receptivity to the unforeseen can become habitual. As Mooney suggests in his conclusion, the importance of faith for a well-lived life is its ability to cultivate in us the strength to "weather disruptions" and the "ability to stay open to marvels."

The next chapter, by M. G. Piety, moves from Mooney's poetic register to a decidedly historical and epistemological one, all the while stressing the existential importance of Kierkegaard's thought. In "Kierkegaard and the Early Church on Christian Knowledge and Its Existential Implications," Piety provides a substantive account of Kierkegaard's conception of Christian knowledge. By tracing the remarkable similarities between Kierkegaard's position and that of Irenaeus and Clement of Alexandria, Piety contends that Kierkegaard must have been attempting to articulate an account that is consistent with early church doctrines. Importantly, however, Piety's argument is of more than merely historical interest. She shows that, as is the case for Irenaeus and Clement of Alexandria, Kierkegaard's Christian epistemology is one that cannot be detached from lived existence. Christian knowing is not merely about having true beliefs; it is primarily a matter of living out Christian truth as a way of life. Offering a wide-ranging engagement with Kierkegaard's authorship, Piety starts with Kierkegaard's account of knowledge of God, generally conceived, and then considers his Christian conception of epistemology, more specifically. Importantly, though, she explicitly notes that neither the two church fathers being considered, nor Kierkegaard himself, were epistemologists. As such, their account is less about providing a theory of knowledge for its own sake and more about articulating the role that knowledge plays in a life lived in relation to Christian truth as expressed maximally in God's grace, mercy, and love.

Staying with the theme of Christian truth understood as an existential task, Grant Julin's "Thunderstruck: Divine Irony in Kierkegaard's Job" offers an extended consideration of two Kierkegaardian texts from 1843: *Repetition* and *The Lord Gave, The Lord Took Away*. Attempting to think through the moral psychology of human suffering, Julin turns to Kierkegaard's Job not as an example of theodicy, but instead as an example of the role that rupture and irony play in the human attempt to deal with the messiness and difficulty of existence itself. Looking to the way in which Job has to live knowing, paradoxically, that both he and God are right, Julin extrapolates from this example to argue that Kierkegaard understands paradox not as merely an occasional fact in existence, but instead as attendant to the very fact of existence itself. Awareness of this deeper conception of paradox arises not from faith, Julin contends, but from irony. After working through different varieties of irony, Julin turns to Kierkegaard's own ironic take on the Job narrative. Rather than see the ultimate resolution in settling the paradox between God's rightness and Job's rightness, Julin contends that finally it is a matter of Job's relation to himself—whether he will see his own faith strengthened in trial or not. Drawing on the Young Man in *Repetition*, Julin concludes that the Young Man can only understand Job once the Young Man himself goes through a similar struggle. Similarly, Julin's account of Kierkegaard's Job helps us not only to better understand Kierkegaard, but also, through Kierkegaard's understanding of Job, to better understand ourselves.

The final chapter of the volume is by J. Aaron Simmons and focuses on two *Upbuilding Discourses* that have not received substantive attention in the literature: *Become Sober* and *It Is the Spirit Who Gives Life*. In "Kierkegaard and Pentecostal Philosophy," Simmons draws on the contemporary notion of "pentecostal philosophy," as developed by James K. A. Smith, to argue that Kierkegaard's account of God, faith, justice, and epistemology are productively understood in relation to pentecostalism. Simmons first looks at the five characteristics of pentecostal philosophy that Smith proposes: (1) radical openness to God, (2) an enchanted theology of creation and culture, (3) a nondualistic affirmation of embodiment and materiality, (4) an affective, narrative epistemology, and (5) an eschatological orientation to mission and justice. Then, turning to historical figures in Pentecostal theology, especially William J. Seymour, Simmons shows that Smith's account reflects a consistently progressive and substantive conception of what it means to live in a historical sociocultural context while maintaining a relationship with a relational, personal, and fully engaged God. With this framework in place, Simmons then turns to the *Upbuilding Discourses* (in which Kierkegaard addresses Pentecost) in order to show that they map well onto a framework of pentecostal philosophy. Though not claiming that Kierkegaard should be thought of as a Pentecostal, Simmons suggests that reading Kierkegaard as resonating with such a perspective is helpful not only for thinking differently about Pentecostalism, but also for making Kierkegaard's conception of God and the good life speak to a contemporary situation in which Pentecostalism is substantively gaining traction in the global South. Ultimately, then, Simmons provides good reason to think that Kierkegaard is a partner in the task that Smith names "thinking in tongues."

Despite significant similarities and points of contact across the chapters in this volume, the book itself does not present a unified stand on how to make theological sense of Kierkegaard's God. Further, it does not offer a static conception of what the good life means in light of that God. However, amid the dynamic proposals and pluralistic conceptions on offer, the volume does make a sustained case that to think about Kierkegaard's God requires thinking seriously about what the good life is and should be. In this way, the editors of this book hope that it stands as a substantive call to think anew about not only what Kierkegaard was saying or what he meant to say, but also about what we—here and now—can learn from Kierkegaard as we seek to live faithfully and responsibly in this moment. Ultimately, Kierkegaard's task to think well about what it means to "become a

Christian" is now understood as a moral task that involves becoming a faithful lover and living a life worthy of a human being. Importantly, "becoming" is never something one achieves; it is something one continually attempts to do; it is a matter of lived existence. The relation to God, far from being an abstract matter of merely propositional assent, is for Kierkegaard a call to engaged living. For all people who would read Kierkegaard, this call is transferred to us.

Abbreviations

(CA) *The Concept of Anxiety: A Simple Psychologically Orienting Deliberation on the Dogmatic Issue of Hereditary Sin.* Ed. and trans. Reidar Thomte and Albert B. Anderson. Princeton, NJ: Princeton University Press, 1980.

(CD) *Christian Discourses/A Crisis in the Life of an Actress.* Ed. and trans. Howard V. Hong and Edna H. Hong. Princeton, NJ: Princeton University Press, 1997.

(CI) *The Concept of Irony with Continual Reference to Socrates.* Ed. and trans. Howard V. Hong and Edna H. Hong. Princeton, NJ: Princeton University Press, 1989.

(*Crumbs*) *Philosophical Crumbs,* in *Repetition and Philosophical Crumbs.* Trans. M. G. Piety. Oxford: Oxford University Press, 2009.

(CUP) *Concluding Unscientific Postscript to Philosophical Fragments.* Vol. I. Ed. and trans. Howard V. Hong and Edna H. Hong. Princeton, NJ: Princeton University Press, 1992.

(EO I&II) *Either/Or.* Vols. I and II. Ed. and trans. Howard V. Hong and Edna H. Hong. Princeton, NJ: Princeton University Press, 1987.

(EUD) *Eighteen Upbuilding Discourses.* Ed. and trans. Howard V. Hong and Edna H. Hong. Princeton, NJ: Princeton University Press, 1990.

(*Fear and Trembling*) *Fear and Trembling.* Trans. Alastair Hannay. London: Penguin Books, 1986.

(FSE) *For Self-Examination,* in *For Self-Examination/Judge for Yourself!* Ed. and trans. Howard V. Hong and Edna H. Hong. Princeton, NJ: Princeton University Press, 1990.

(FT) *Fear and Trembling,* in *Fear and Trembling/Repetition.* Ed. and trans. Howard V. Hong and Edna H. Hong. Princeton, NJ: Princeton University Press, 1983.

(JC) *Johannes Climacus,* in *Philosophical Fragments/Johannes Climacus.* Ed. and trans. Howard V. Hong and Edna H. Hong. Princeton, NJ: Princeton University Press, 1985.

(JFY) *Judge for Yourself!,* in *For Self-Examination/Judge for Yourself!* Ed. and trans. Howard V. Hong and Edna H. Hong. Princeton, NJ: Princeton University Press, 1990.

(JN) *Journals and Notebooks.* Trans. Bruce H. Kirmmse et al. 8 volumes. Princeton, NJ: Princeton University Press, 2007–2015.

(JP) *Søren Kierkegaard's Journals and Papers.* Ed. and trans. Howard V. Hong and Edna H. Hong. Princeton, NJ: Princeton University Press, 1967–1978.

(M) *The Moment and Late Writings*. Ed. and trans. Howard V. Hong and Edna H. Hong. Princeton, NJ: Princeton University Press, 1998.

(*Papirer*) *Søren Kierkegaards Papirer*. Ed. Niels Thulstrup and N. J. Cappelørn. 2nd edition. Copenhagen: Gyldendal, 1968–1978.

(PC) *Practice in Christianity*. Ed. and trans. Howard V. Hong and Edna H. Hong. Princeton, NJ: Princeton University Press, 1991.

(PF) *Philosophical Fragments*, in *Philosophical Fragments/Johannes Climacus*. Ed. and trans. Howard V. Hong and Edna H. Hong. Princeton, NJ: Princeton University Press, 1985.

(PH) *Purity of Heart Is to Will One Thing*. Trans. Douglas V. Steere. New York: Harper & Row, 1938.

(PJS) *Papers and Journals: A Selection*. Ed. Alastair Hannay. New York, NY: Penguin, 1996.

(*Postscript*) *Concluding Unscientific Postscript*. Trans. Alastair Hannay. Cambridge: Cambridge University Press, 2009.

(*Provocations*) *Provocations: Spiritual Writings of Kierkegaard*. Ed. Charles Moore. Farmington, PA: Plough, 1999.

(R) *Repetition*, in *Fear and Trembling/Repetition*. Ed. and trans. Howard V. Hong and Edna H. Hong. Princeton, NJ: Princeton University Press, 1983.

(R 1946) *Repetition: An Essay in Experimental Psychology*. Trans. Walter Lowrie. Princeton, NJ: Princeton University Press, 1946.

(R 2009) *Repetition*, in *Repetition and Philosophical Crumbs*. Trans. M. G. Piety. Oxford: Oxford University Press, 2009.

(*Sickness*) *Sickness Unto Death*. Trans. Alastair Hannay. London: Penguin, 1989.

(SKS) *Søren Kierkegaards Skrifter*. Ed. N. J. Cappelørn et al. 4th edition. Copenhagen: Gads Forlag, 1997–2013.

(SLW) *Stages on Life's Way*. Ed. and trans. Howard V. Hong and Edna H. Hong. Princeton, NJ: Princeton University Press, 1988.

(SUD) *The Sickness unto Death: A Christian Psychological Exposition for Upbuilding and Awakening*. Ed. and trans. Howard V. Hong and Edna H. Hong. Princeton, NJ: Princeton University Press, 1980.

(TA) *Two Ages*. Ed. and trans. Howard V. Hong and Edna H. Hong. Princeton, NJ: Princeton University Press, 1978.

(TDIO) *Three Discourses on Imagined Occasions*. Ed. and trans. Howard V. Hong and Edna H. Hong. Princeton, NJ: Princeton University Press, 1993.

(UDVS) *Upbuilding Discourses in Various Spirits*. Ed. and trans. Howard V. Hong and Edna H. Hong. Princeton, NJ: Princeton University Press, 1993.

(WA) *Without Authority*. Ed. and trans. Howard V. Hong and Edna H. Hong. Princeton, NJ: Princeton University Press, 1997.

(WL) *Works of Love*. Ed. and trans. Howard V. Hong and Edna H. Hong. Princeton, NJ: Princeton University Press, 1995.

KIERKEGAARD'S GOD
AND THE GOOD LIFE

PART I
FAITH AND LOVE

1 Love as the End of Human Existence

Sharon Krishek

IN THIS CHAPTER I explore the crucial significance of love for human flourishing. I claim that according to Kierkegaard, love is a divinely inspired potential that humans must actualize for the purpose of living a good life. This has a two-fold reason: such an actualization is a fulfillment of one's nature, and it brings the human lover closer to God. I develop this thesis on the basis of a metaphorical picture that appears at the beginning of Kierkegaard's *Works of Love* and illustrate its existential implications by interpreting Tolstoy's novella "The Death of Ivan Ilyich" in light of it.

Love and Life

Often elusive and mysterious but always prevailing, love is undoubtedly central to human life. It pervades our existence, infusing it with meaningfulness and joy. Kierkegaard would doubtless have agreed with this observation, for as he writes at the conclusion of his *Works of Love* (1847), "to love people is the only thing worth living for" and "without this love you are not really living" (WL, 375).[1] What does it mean to live one's life while not *really* living it? Tolstoy's well-known novella "The Death of Ivan Ilyich" arguably presents an answer. The novella depicts the dark suffering of the dying Ivan Ilyich as he struggles with the threatening understanding "that he had not lived his life as he should have done."[2]

In this chapter I would like to present a reading of the novella in the light of a metaphorical passage that opens Kierkegaard's *Works of Love*. I believe that the two texts complement and enhance each other. The philosophical idea presented in Kierkegaard's text provides a productive framework for understanding the novella, and the human experience brought vividly to life in Tolstoy's text validates the Kierkegaardian idea. Thus, reading these two texts together, I hope to shed light both on the novella (and in particular its enigmatic ending) and on Kierkegaard's reflection regarding the wrongness of a life devoid of love. I begin by discussing what I take to be a key idea at the basis of Kierkegaard's understanding of love. According to my interpretation, the metaphorical picture at the opening of *Works of Love* (which depicts love as a quiet lake that originates in a hidden spring) presents love as a divinely inspired potential that we humans are required to actualize.[3] In light of this analysis, I offer a reading of Tolstoy's novella that, rather than emphasizing the role of death in revealing the (lack of) meaning in Ivan Ilyich's life,[4] focuses on the role of love in constituting such a meaning. By so doing, I hope to demonstrate how Kierkegaard's understanding of love provides the philosophical ground needed to explain the reason for Ivan Ilyich's sufferings, as well as his release from them. Seeing this, I hope that we can better understand why Kierkegaard claims that when one's life is devoid of loving, one is "not really living." This, in turn, will hopefully demonstrate the crucial significance of love to human flourishing.

The Love-Potential

In the first deliberation of *Works of Love*, a text devoted to a detailed exploration of the biblical duty to love one's neighbor, Kierkegaard offers a rather mysterious depiction of love:

> Just as the quiet lake originates deep down in hidden springs no eye has seen, so also does a person's love originate even more deeply in God's love. . . . Just as the quiet lake originates darkly in the deep spring, so a human being's love originates mysteriously in God's love. Just as the quiet lake invites you to contemplate it but by the reflected image of darkness prevents you from seeing through it, so also the mysterious origin of love in God's love prevents you from seeing its ground (WL, 9–10).

There are two forces in action here, God's love and a human being's love, which are likened to a spring and a quiet lake, respectively. The spring is hidden, lying deep, far beneath what the human eye can grasp. What we can see is a lake that flows out of it, but its accessibility must not mislead us: If we attempt to measure its depth and to look for its ground, we will find ourselves confused and disoriented. In the same way, human love—since it originates in God's love—is, in an important sense, unfathomable and elusive. However deeply one penetrates into "the life of love" (as Kierkegaard describes it), however seriously one contemplates it, there is still something mysterious left. By using this metaphor, then, Kierkegaard in effect is saying that human love cannot be fully explained in behavioral, sociological, psychological, or biological terms—nor can it simply be reduced to any of these humanly comprehensible phenomena.

The mystery of love is also mentioned in another metaphorical image that Kierkegaard presents a little earlier in the book: "There is a place in a person's innermost being; from this place flows the life of love. . . . But you cannot see this place; however deeply you penetrate, the origin eludes you in remoteness and hiddenness" (WL, 8). Putting these two images together (the one of the spring and the lake and the one of the secret place within us), I suggest that something like the following picture emerges. On the one hand, we have the ultimate source of all love, God's love. On the other hand, we have human love. And in between, somehow linking these two poles, is that hidden place within us, holding, as it were, God's love within us. What does this mean?

We can think of this picture as describing three levels of love. The upper level, somewhat external and in any case the most visible, is human love. We see this love, in all sorts of ways, around us. We read about it in novels and journals, see many representations of it on movie screens, hear about it, talk about it, and feel it ourselves—constantly. In short, we encounter it all the time, in various forms: romantic love, friendship, parental love, neighborly love.[5] In other words, human love, whether others' or our own, often forms part of our daily experience. The primary level—the deepest and most hidden—is God's love. We can imagine it as a colossal force that obviously transcends us and evades our "possession" (by not being subject to our understanding or will). However, this extraordinary force is also, in some mysterious way, within us. This brings us to the middle, intermediate level of love: the secret place within us that links the divine source of love with its visible human manifestations.

Given the metaphorical status of this picture, the "secret place" at issue is best understood (so I suggest) as a spiritual or mental *faculty* responsible for our capacity of loving. That is to say, it is a faculty, a power, that is "in ourselves" in the sense that it belongs to us and, more strongly, is essential to our human nature. Since God (according to Kierkegaard) has endowed us with the power to do what is most typical of him,[6] we may say that it is in *this* way that he has created us in his image. Thus, loving is the nature of humans due to their having been created by God. Moreover, although we are not the source of this capacity, and might not even be fully conscious or aware of it (hence its "secrecy"), having it "in us" (in the relevant sense) makes us nevertheless responsible for either fulfilling it or not. We may therefore call this intermediate level of love "the *potential* for loving" (or the love-potential): it is a crucial capacity, placed or implanted in us by God (to use Kierkegaard's words [see, for example, WL, 126, 163]) and responsible for whatever loving we realize in our lives.

Understanding the spring/lake metaphor in this way may also serve to explain the logic behind Kierkegaard's distinction between "love" and "works of love." As he states twice, his book is "not about *love* but about *works of love*" (WL, 3, 207, emphasis in the original). Against the background of our interpretation of the metaphor as depicting a unique potential belonging to human beings, we can say that "love" refers to the potential, while "works" refers to the enactment or actualization of that potential. Having the capacity to love, having this divinely inspired potential, is not enough. We have to work to bring this potential to light, to make it blossom, to give it form. Thus when Kierkegaard says that his discussion is not about "love" but rather about "works of love," what he means to say, I think, is that he is not interested in a metaphysical or conceptual inquiry regarding the nature of our love-potential (namely, the connection of this potential to God, its ontological status, its various characteristics). Rather, he is interested in the way in which one ought to actualize this potential, and thus in the nature of the *work* required for this. Let me say a few words about the nature of this work.

It seems that for Kierkegaard, the way to actualize one's love-potential into a genuine instance of love is by self-denial. Distinguishing between preferential love (which makes preferences and is directed only to a few) and neighborly love (which does not make any preferences and is directed equally to all), he claims that the first is nothing but self-love, and that only the latter is genuine. Thus, Kierkegaard holds that in order to love genuinely, we need to love in the neighborly way. Essentially, this means that we need to shape our preferential loves (for our romantic beloveds and close friends, for example)—which Kierkegaard does take to be legitimate—in the image and nature of neighborly love. This is a problematic thesis, however, as it is not clear how to make the exclusivity and self-attentiveness that are essential to preferential loves meet the demands of neighborly love for equality and self-denial. It is not my concern here to elaborate on this problem, so I shall only suggest briefly an alternative way of actualizing one's love-potential.[7] A major threat that neighborly love is meant to address (given its goal to morally purify natural and spontaneous—i.e., preferential—loves) is that of selfishness.[8] As preferential forms of love are motivated not only by a desire to address the needs of the beloved but also by a desire to address the needs of the *lover*, the risk that the latter motivation will blur the former is tangible. Hence Kierkegaard's demand for self-denial; however, love that is based on self-denial *alone* (as Kierkegaard indeed insists should be the case) cannot pay heed to self-regarding needs (mental and bodily alike). Yet without such heed being paid, it is not clear how preferential love (say, romantic love, which is essentially motivated by erotic desire) can exist at all. When it comes to shaping one's loves, then, self-denial is not enough. Thus, a different approach should be taken, and this, I suggest, should be the approach of Kierkegaardian faith. Faith, as Kierkegaard famously presents it in *Fear and Trembling*, is the ability to affirm one's attachment to some X (a son, a beloved, or more generally the world) while uncompromisingly renouncing X, accepting that X escapes one's secure hold.[9] Thus, renunciation ("infinite resignation," as Kierkegaard calls it) precludes "ownership": renouncing X, one cannot consider oneself as having any rights over X. Accordingly, renunciation of X necessarily precludes a conception of X as a means to satisfying one's needs (i.e., selfishness), since the latter assumes (even if only implicitly) some degree of ownership of X. In this sense renunciation is akin to self-denial. But faith goes further than self-denial, and having renounced X, it "returns" to X, allowing for a renewed attachment to it. Such an attachment to X is purified from selfishness (through renunciation) but also takes unreserved joy in it—joy that necessarily involves self-affirmation. Hence the double movement of faith permits a realization of love such that the needs of the lover are met, but without compromising the demands of self-denial.

Returning now to the main point of our discussion, Kierkegaard is asking us, then, to take as a given that love is a divine force placed within us, one that drives us toward what we experience as the "life of love." According to my interpretation, this "force" is crucially embedded within us only as a potential, which can be actualized or not, and, if the former, can be actualized in various forms and to different degrees. Let us now go a step further. Underlying Kierkegaard's project is the assumption that it is *desirable* to actualize our love-potential by performing works of love. It seems that for Kierkegaard, there is a strong connection between loving well and living well. Or, to put it differently, the failure to love properly results, in his view, in an unhappy life. We will shortly see how this proves to be true in Tolstoy's novella, but first we need to ask: why does Kierkegaard find it desirable for us to carry out works of love?

One possible way to answer this question is by an appeal to the Aristotelian theory of happiness. According to this theory, as presented in Aristotle's *Nico-machean Ethics,* the realization of one's nature, which amounts to a full actu-alization of one's essential potentialities, is a condition for the good life.[10] If we agree with this basic outline of the Aristotelian conception of what constitutes the good life, then we can easily see why Kierkegaard, given our interpretation of the spring/lake metaphor, considers the undertaking of the work of love to be a desirable project. As sketched above, my claim is that the Kierkegaardian distinc-tion between love and its works can be understood as referring to a distinction between the *potential for loving* (which is essential to our nature as God's created) and the *actualization* of this potential (through the works of love). Against the background of the Aristotelian theory, we can see why carrying out the work of love—which, after all, amounts to an actualization of our nature—is crucial for our happiness.

However, we must not disregard the significant fact that the potential that Kierkegaard focuses on is the *love*-potential. Namely, it is meaningful that the human capacity in need of realization is not just one human capacity among others but specifically the capacity for *loving.* What is so unique about loving? As we already said, this is the major characteristic of God, so that having this capacity is part of being created in God's image.[11] Accordingly, we may claim that a realization of the capacity for loving—more than a realization of any other human capacity—is what brings us closest to God. In this sense, to love is not only to fulfill one's nature but also to enter into a relationship with God.[12] Being in such a relationship is, from Kierkegaard's point of view, a necessary condition for a good, satisfying, joyful life.[13] Thus, if to love is to fulfill a relationship with God, and fulfilling a relationship with God is what makes one's life satisfying and meaningful, we see yet again the vital connection between loving and living well, between loving and happiness.

Therefore, in terms of both structure (the realization of one's potentialities as a condition for the good life) and content (the realization of one's potential for *loving* in particular as a condition for the good life), we see why according to Kierkegaard loving is essential for a worthy life—or, to use his words again, why *not* loving amounts to "not really living." Having these thoughts in mind, it is now time to turn to Tolstoy's novella, to see how these Kierkegaardian insights regarding the essentiality of *loving* for the desirable kind of *living* throw light on the life, and death, of Ivan Ilyich.

The Love of Ivan Ilyich

Tolstoy's novella "The Death of Ivan Ilyich," which was published in 1886, is considered one of the heights of his writing. The novella tells the story of its protagonist's dying, and by this it tells the gloomy tale of a life that was "ordinary and dreadful in the extreme,"[14] the wasted life of someone who could easily be one of our acquaintances (not to mention one of us). At the same time, the novella ends quite enigmatically: having gone through a physical and mental ordeal, and having reached painful conclusions about the emptiness and worthlessness of his life, Ivan Ilyich dies in a state of joy. How could this be? To answer this question, let us take a closer look at the novella and begin by asking: What kind of life did Ivan Ilyich lead?

On the face of it, nothing seemed to be wrong with Ivan Ilyich's life. Having family and friends, living in a lovely house, and working in a respectable job, Ivan Ilyich was confident that he was living a good life. To be sure, now and again something like a feeling of frustration or boredom interrupted the pleasant course of his life (a growing alienation from his wife, for example, or a feeling of bitterness when he was not promoted in his job), but then Ivan Ilyich found a new task to be preoccupied with (a new house to decorate, a new job to apply for), and life was good again. But then one day he fell ill, and as the days went by, it turned out that he was terminally ill. At first he was consumed by his physical suffering, but slowly a more profound suffering—a "suffering in spirit," as Tolstoy calls it—came over him: "His spiritual suffering took the form of a thought that had suddenly struck him that night . . . 'What if I really have been *wrong* in the way I've lived my whole life . . . ?'"[15]

What was it that made Ivan Ilyich, in the face of his impending death, doubt the goodness of his life? What was there, in the event of his dying, that made him suspect that he had been wrong in the way he lived his life? To begin with, his coming death forced him to ask the question about the correctness or wrongness of his life. During his lifetime Ivan Ilyich submitted himself to the flow of life, as it were. He simply lived, without asking himself what counted as meaningful for him, and with the false, even unconscious, confidence that he would always have "the future" waiting for him to address his changing needs. This state of mind allowed him to absorb himself in daily duties and small pleasures: a lifeless routine of family life and uninspiring social goals (such as achieving a better job or forming connections with members of high society). In other words, he lived his life without giving any thought to the fact that one day it would come to an end. But now that his life *was* ending, he was forced to reflect upon it and give himself the account he never did before: Did he like his life? Now that he was looking back at his life with the grim knowledge that there was no time left for him to do anything differently, did he feel satisfied?

While "running out of time" forces Ivan Ilyich to ask the question, it does not in itself explain why he has reached (reluctantly, obviously) the dark answer that he has lived wrongly. Something else, which is also connected to his death, has led him to this unhappy answer. It is the way everybody around him (except for his servant) treats the fact of his dying. Tolstoy calls it "the lie":

> Ivan Ilyich's worst torment was the lying—the lie, which was somehow maintained by them all, that he wasn't dying, he was only ill. . . . And this lie was a torture for him—he was tortured by their unwillingness to acknowledge what they all knew and he knew. . . . All this lying to him, lie upon lie, on the eve of his death, lying that was inexorably reducing the solemn act of his death to the same level as their social calls, their draperies, the sturgeon for dinner . . . it was all a terrible torment for Ivan Ilyich.[16]

Thus we may say that the wrongness of his life made itself perceptible quite silently. "The lie" about his situation, embraced so easily by all those around him, revealed that he was alone in his misery. The gap between people's understanding of the severity of his situation and their unwillingness to at least acknowledge it showed Ivan Ilyich how little his tragedy meant to them. Now, there may, of course, be many reasons for people surrounding a dying person to avoid acknowledging and focusing on his impending death. In the case of Ivan Ilyich, however, it was very clear that the reason his family and friends were avoiding his situation was that they were not willing to make the effort that it took to confront it: "He could see that the awful, terrible act of his dying had been reduced by those around him to the level of an unpleasant incident. . . . He could see that no one had any pity for him because no one had the slightest desire to understand his situation."[17]

Such a lack of desire is not surprising: it is, after all, very difficult to face a situation of this kind. It is not easy to face the agony of a person who knows he is about to depart from this world, to face his fears, to face your fears. One needs to really *care* in order to become honestly and wholeheartedly involved in such a demanding situation. And thus, during the long days of his suffering, Ivan Ilyich slowly came to the understanding that made him suffer most of all. He realized that there was nobody among those he counted as close to him who really cared about his suffering, who really cared about his dying, who really cared, as a matter of fact, about *him*. The reader, who learns at the very beginning of the novella how those surrounding Ivan Ilyich reacted to his death, knows that he had quite an accurate understanding of the situation. This is what we are told about his colleagues' thoughts when they learned about Ivan Ilyich's death:

> So, the first thought that occurred to each of the assembled gentlemen on hearing the news of his death was how this death might affect his own prospects, and those of their acquaintances, for transfer or promotion. . . . Apart from [such] speculations . . . the very fact of the death of someone close to them aroused in all who heard about it, as always, a feeling of delight that he had died and they hadn't. . . . But his closest acquaintances, Ivan Ilyich's so-called friends, couldn't help thinking that they would now have to fulfill some tedious social obligations such as attending the funeral and calling on the widow to express their condolences.[18]

The unloving thoughts of his friends after his death, as well as those of his wife (who was immersed in self-pity and preoccupied with the discomfort his dying and death caused *her*[19]), reflect what Ivan Ilyich felt very vividly before his death. He did not need to read their thoughts; it was enough for him to perceive the state of mind of those closest to him. Rather than feeling sorrow, such as one would expect of a loving person when he witnesses the approaching loss of the one he loves, they quite effortlessly succeeded in ignoring his impending death.

And so, the indifference and the unloving way in which those surrounding him treated his imminent death made Ivan Ilyich understand that he had lived an entire life without forming a single meaningful relationship—his life, he understood, was devoid of love. This was entirely consistent with his desire (presented in the novella more than once) for a pleasant life. At first glance there is nothing wrong with such a desire. However, turning *this* into the goal of one's life reflects an improper desire to avoid difficulties. Of course, in themselves difficulties are not desirable, and there are indeed difficulties that one should desire to avoid (those involving ill health or poverty, for example). At the same time, meaningful attachments and valuable achievements cannot be attained without difficulty. To become truly involved in anything whatsoever requires effort and often involves discomfort, frustration, and suffering (namely, difficulties). Thus, Ivan Ilyich's sole desire for a pleasant life in effect led to a detached life. And a detached life, obviously, cannot afford significant love relationships. At the end of his life, however, love became his strongest desire—this was what he needed the most. This understanding is expressed explicitly by Tolstoy,[20] and Ivan Ilyich gained it through his relationship with his devoted servant, Gerasim, the only person who treated him with compassion and care.[21] By his direct, unpretentious, neighborly love, Gerasim's attitude was a living example of how different things could, and should, have been:

> Gerasim was the only one who did understand his situation, and he was sorry for him. This was why Ivan Ilyich felt comfortable only with Gerasim. . . . Apart from all [the] lying, or perhaps because of it, the most tormenting thing of all for Ivan Ilyich was the fact that no one showed him any pity in the way he wanted them to . . . what he wanted was for someone to take pity on him as if he were a sick child. . . . And his relationship with Gerasim offered something close to this, which was why the relationship with Gerasim gave him comfort.[22]

At the end of his life, Ivan Ilyich, for the first time in his life, is in a position to value the importance of a loving relationship. Accordingly, the absence of such relationships forces upon him a new, very painful understanding. All along he was aiming in the wrong direction: his achievements, goals, desires, and satisfactions blinded him to what is really valuable. This tragic understanding took shape in one of the nights before his death, in the course of a dialogue with himself: "What is it that you want?" he asked himself, and when the answer "Staying alive" came up automatically, his inner voice insisted, "Staying alive? How?" and Ivan Ilyich answered, "'Oh, life like it used to be. Happy and good.' 'Life like it used to be? Happy and good?' came the voice. And in his imagination he started to run through the best times of his happy life. But what was strange was that all the best times of his happy life . . . melted away now before his eyes and turned into something trivial and often disgusting."[23]

During the course of his life, Ivan Ilyich had been driven by the desire to accomplish all kinds of goals that he believed would endow his life with meaning. He never gave much thought to the value of the things he wanted, and he acted in accordance with normative expectations. Thus he succeeded in attaining a respected job, an honorable wife, a decorated house, and a circle of honorable friends. But now, forsaken in his agony, he realizes that his life has been nothing but a desert of loneliness, deceptively concealed behind empty goals and the (ultimately) "melting" pleasures accompanying them.

But Tolstoy does not let his protagonist die in this dreadful situation; he does afford him a saving revelation. This was the moment in which Ivan Ilyich felt a bond of care tying him to his family. He saw *their* suffering and wanted to do something about it; for the first time in his life he felt the urge to perform an act purely focused on the good of the other, an act of caring, an act—a *work*—of love:

> He opened his eyes and looked at his son. He felt sorry for him. His wife came over. He looked at her. . . . He felt sorry for her. 'Yes, I'm hurting them,' he thought. . . . 'Must *do* something.' . . . And suddenly everything was clear to him: what had been oppressing him and would not go away *was* now going away, all at once, on two sides, ten sides, all sides. He felt sorry for them, and he must do something to stop hurting them.[24]

When he experienced this new, liberating feeling, the pain and the fear that until that moment had dominated his soul were defeated. Ivan Ilyich died in a state of joy: "There was no fear whatsoever because there was no death. Instead of death there was light. 'So that's it!' he said suddenly, out loud. 'Oh, bliss!'"[25]

What is the source of this happy peacefulness? What is its reason? First, if we identify the cause of Ivan Ilyich's greatest suffering as the realization that he wasted his life, and if he felt that he wasted his life because it was devoid of love, then the experience of loving at the end of his life is indeed a response to that waste. His life is saved (from being a complete waste) by achieving at its end the only thing that might give it valid meaning. Second, and more directly, Ivan Ilyich dies with a feeling of blissfulness *because* he experiences the joy of loving. The reason for *this* joy is not explained by Tolstoy, but it can be explained by the Kierkegaardian understanding of love presented above. If Kierkegaard is right in suggesting that love is both a fulfillment of one's nature and a realization of one's relationship with God, then Ivan Ilyich indeed had two strong reasons to feel joyful when he finally felt love.[26]

Love as the End of Life

"Hell," Dostoevsky tells us (in the voice of Father Zosima), "is the suffering of no longer being able to love."[27] In this chapter I tried to show how love—and in particular lov*ing*—is indeed a necessary condition for human flourishing. Focusing on a key idea in Kierkegaard's view of love, I have claimed that humans have a potential for loving, and that its realization is crucial for the fulfillment of the good life for two reasons: first, because happiness is conditioned by one's realization of one's nature (the Aristotelian picture of the good life), and love is central to that nature; and second, because a joyful life (that is, one devoid of despair and meaninglessness, for example) is conditioned upon fulfilling one's relationship with God, and loving one's human fellows is one way, perhaps the only way, to do so.[28]

Using Tolstoy's novella to amplify Kierkegaard's view and demonstrate it existentially, we saw that it can serve to explain why Ivan Ilyich, who devoted his life to the kind of things that have nothing to do with the work of love, indeed lived unhappily. Ignoring his love-potential, he betrayed his nature and failed to attain the only thing that lasts when dying makes so many of the struggles and accomplishments of everyday living irrelevant—namely, a loving relationship. Such a relationship draws its strength and endurance from its mysterious origin, God's love, and not only fulfills one's nature but also brings one into a relationship with God. This understanding of love also explains the enigmatic ending of the novella. The joy of the *loving* Ivan Ilyich is the joy of realizing one's nature, and of realizing a relationship with God that is inherent in this nature. By carrying out the work of love, then, Ivan Ilyich fulfilled the highest condition for the good life, and he died peacefully.

Having this in mind, we are in a better position to understand Kierkegaard's assertion with which we opened this chapter: "To love people is the only thing worth living for, and without this love you are not really living" (WL, 375).

SHARON KRISHEK is a lecturer in the philosophy department at the Hebrew University of Jerusalem. She is author of *Kierkegaard on Faith and Love*.

Notes

1. Kierkegaard was often judged as a hostile critic of the forms of love that dominate human life, such as romantic love and friendship, because their preferential nature seems to distort the demand for equality presented by neighborly love. Recent studies, however, have done a great deal to refute this problematic judgment and present a more sympathetic interpretation of Kierkegaard's view of love. See, in particular, Sylvia Walsh, "Forming the Heart: The Role of Love in Kierkegaard's Thought," in *The Grammar of the Heart*, Richard H. Bell, ed. (New York: Harper & Row, 1988), pp. 234–56; M. Jamie Ferreira, *Love's Grateful Striving: A Commentary on Kierkegaard's* Works of Love (Oxford: Oxford University Press, 2001); M. Jamie Ferreira, "The Problematic Agapeistic Ideal–Again," in *Ethics, Love, and Faith in Kierkegaard: Philosophical Engagements*, Edward F. Mooney, ed. (Bloomington, IL: Indiana University Press, 2008), pp. 93–110; M. Jamie Ferreira, "Love," in *The Oxford Handbook of Kierkegaard*, John Lippitt and George Pattison, eds. (Oxford: Oxford University Press, 2013), pp. 328–343; C. Stephen Evans, *Kierkegaard's Ethic of Love: Divine Commands and Moral Obligations* (Oxford: Oxford University Press, 2004); John Lippitt, *Kierkegaard and the Problem of Self-Love* (Cambridge: Cambridge University Press, 2013); and Michael Strawser, *Kierkegaard and the Philosophy of Love* (Lanham, MD: Lexington Books, 2015).

2. Leo Tolstoy, "The Death of Ivan Ilyich," in *The Death of Ivan Ilyich and Other Stories*, trans. Ronald Wilks, Antony Briggs, and David McDuff (London: Penguin Classics, 2008), p. 213.

3. I discuss this idea elsewhere as well. See Sharon Krishek, *Kierkegaard on Faith and Love* (Cambridge: Cambridge University Press, 2009); and Sharon Krishek, "The Enactment of Love by Faith: On Kierkegaard's Distinction between Love and Its Works," *Faith and Philosophy* 27.1 (2010): 3–21.

4. As Heidegger famously does, for example, in his discussion of death. See Martin Heidegger, *Being and Time*, trans. John Stambaugh (Albany: State University of New York Press, 1996), p. 254, n.12.

5. One might object to the inclusion of neighborly love here, claiming that it has a different status than the other forms of human love mentioned. I present my justification for considering neighborly love to be a form of love ranking at the same level with other forms of love elsewhere. See my article "In Defence of a Faith-Like Model of Love: A Reply to John Lippitt's 'Kierkegaard and the Problem of Special Relationships: Ferreira, Krishek, and the "God Filter",'" *International Journal for Philosophy of Religion* 75.2 (2014): 155–166.

6. In various places in his authorship, and particularly in *Works of Love*, Kierkegaard (in accordance with the Christian tradition) declares that "God is love." It is not my purpose here

to explore the meaning of this rather enigmatic claim, but the very least that we can say about it is that it considers the main characteristic of God to be love: namely, what is most typical of divine activity (and presence) is that it is *loving*.

7. I discuss this problem extensively—as well as the alternative understanding of love that I offer as a solution: love in the structure and image not of neighborly love but rather of faith—in my *Kierkegaard on Faith and Love*.

8. Another major threat is that of inequality, that unlike the threat of selfishness—which mostly pertains to those neighbors who are *loved* preferentially—pertains to those neighbors who are *not loved* preferentially. Due to space limitations, I will not discuss this threat, and what I consider the best way to address it, in the present context.

9. In the interest of not digressing from the topic of the present discussion, I refrain from defending this interpretation and explaining how I take faith to reconcile renunciation with affirmation. For such a defense and explanation, see chapters 2 and 3 in my *Kierkegaard on Faith and Love*.

10. See Aristotle, *Nicomachean Ethics*, trans. Terence Irwin (Indianapolis and Cambridge: Hackett, 1985): books I–II. Obviously, there is much to say about this influential theory, both in its praise and as a criticism, but for my purpose here, it is sufficient to focus only on the basic idea underlying it, that was stated briefly above.

11. See note 6 above.

12. In the same way, for example, that a child who consciously fulfills a trait of character that he identifies with his parent is entering into a meaningful relationship with the parent (even if it is not necessarily tangible, if the parent is dead or away, for example). In other words, by adhering to the parent's character, the child is following the parent's way, thinks about him, contemplates the parent's will, and so forth. He thus eo ipso sustains a meaningful relationship with the parent.

13. The connection between being in a relationship with God and living a correct, worthy life is a theme that recurs in different forms throughout Kierkegaard's writings. To give one prominent example, in *The Sickness unto Death* (1849), Kierkegaard specifically defines being in a relationship with God as the cure for despair, namely, as the "formula" for living the good life (SUD, 14, 49).

14. Tolstoy, "The Death of Ivan Ilyich," p. 166.

15. Tolstoy, "The Death of Ivan Ilyich," p. 213, emphasis in the text.

16. Tolstoy, "The Death of Ivan Ilyich," p. 199.

17. Tolstoy, "The Death of Ivan Ilyich," p. 199.

18. Tolstoy, "The Death of Ivan Ilyich," pp. 158–159.

19. See Tolstoy, "The Death of Ivan Ilyich," p. 163.

20. Tolstoy writes that all he wanted was "to be kissed and cuddled and have a few tears shed over him in the way that children are cuddled and comforted" ("The Death of Ivan Ilyich," p. 200).

21. Importantly, however, Gerasim's attitude is not in itself sufficient to make Ivan Ilyich perform the work of love *himself* (without which love relationships, and therefore the good life, cannot be achieved). Gerasim, in treating Ivan Ilyich with neighborly love, demonstrates that there is an alternative to the empty relationships that filled his life. But in order for love to be truly present in his life, Ivan Ilyich must himself find a way to treat others with love—something that he does, as we will shortly see, just before he dies.

22. Tolstoy, "The Death of Ivan Ilyich," p. 199.

23. Tolstoy, "The Death of Ivan Ilyich," p. 208.

24. Tolstoy, "The Death of Ivan Ilyich," p. 216, emphasis in the original.

25. Tolstoy, "The Death of Ivan Ilyich," p. 217.

26. Gordon Marino's "A Critical Perspective on Kierkegaard's *At a Graveside*" in *Kierkegaard and Death*, Patrick Stokes and Adam J. Buben, eds. (Bloomington: Indiana University Press, 2011) presents a rather different confluence between Tolstoy's novella and Kierkegaard's ideas. While also reading the novella as expressing the centrality of love to a worthy life, and as demonstrating the way that one's imminent death has the power to reveal love's importance, Marino appeals to the novella to make a different point. Tolstoy's profound insight, he claims, is completely missed by Kierkegaard: "In Tolstoy's masterpiece it is the relationship with others that is front and center. For Kierkegaard, in contrast, there is scarcely a word about the relationship between our death awareness and the ties that bind us" (p. 158). Marino's paper as a whole is critical of Kierkegaard's view of love, so that the appeal to Tolstoy's novella functions to highlight the shortcomings of Kierkegaard's view, which is quite the opposite of the thesis I present here. This is not the place for a debate with Marino's understanding of Kierkegaard's view of love, but at the very least, I hope that the present paper succeeds in showing that an alternative convergence between Kierkegaard's philosophy and Tolstoy's story should be taken seriously.

27. Fyodor Dostoevsky, *The Brothers Karamazov*, trans. David McDuff (London: Penguin Classics, 2003), p. 417.

28. Due to the theological assumption that love is not just one capacity among other human capacities but rather a *divine* capacity: a capacity that somehow, mysteriously, is related to the essence of God. An explanation and justification of this profound theological assumption is of course a goal for a different project.

2 Love Is the Highest Good

Michael Strawser

> It is certain that love is the highest good—something surely no one doubts.
>
> Søren Kierkegaard[1]

Wнат is it that forms a heart? It is love. What is it that makes a heart pure? It is love. What is the highest good that alone should be willed? It is love. What is both the source and the substance of the good life? It is love.

Love is the answer. It is the answer to the questions above, and it is the answer that follows, I shall argue, from a questioning of Kierkegaard's God and the good life. Such a questioning must no doubt include an investigation of the notion of "the good"—especially when expressed as "the highest good" throughout Kierkegaard's writings—although the meaning of this notion is sometimes ambiguous or vague. How are we to understand the highest good, and how should it unfold in our lives? Or better, how can we allow the highest good to manifest itself in human existence? This is the key question of the present study.

Kierkegaard's most direct and sustained reflection on the good can be found in "An Occasional Discourse" in *Upbuilding Discourses in Various Spirits* (most commonly known as "Purity of Heart" after the first English translation in 1938), where we learn that "purity of heart is to will one thing" and "the person who in truth wills only one thing can will only the good, and the person who wills only one thing when he wills the good can will only the good in truth" (UDVS, 24). Consequently, a reading of this discourse is of primary importance in this paper. Within Kierkegaard's "An Occasional Discourse," however, the good is not directly identified. Thus I suggest that it makes sense to take important cues from *Works of Love*, the work that followed the publication of *Upbuilding Discourses in Various Spirits* by about six months in 1847, and to identify the good, the highest good that makes one pure of heart, as love.[2] These two works are not very commonly read together; thus I am also suggesting that they ought to be, for their historical proximity within Kierkegaard's authorship itself lends weight to the interpretation of the highest good as love.[3]

According to Eduard Geismar, a Danish Kierkegaard scholar writing in the early twentieth century, "anyone who really wants to understand Kierkegaard does well to begin with [*Upbuilding Discourses in Various Spirits*]," since "nothing of what he has written is to such a degree before the face of God."⁴ This is an interesting opinion and one that seemingly contrasts with the contemporary view of George Pattison that *Works of Love* is "the central work in Kierkegaard's entire authorship"⁵ and consequently the place that readers should start developing their understanding of Kierkegaard. While I am inclined to agree more with Pattison, the focus of this essay involves a closer reflection on "An Occasional Discourse" than on *Works of Love*, for as already indicated, an inquiry into the (highest) good is more explicitly addressed in the former text.⁶ "An Occasional Discourse" should be read through the eyes of love, however, and we do better to seek the face of love, as this provides a clearer, more accountable pursuit.⁷

For Kierkegaard, as I wish to argue, the good life is defined by love, but how can love be defined? How love is to be understood is definitely a complicated matter, and Kierkegaard indicates in the preface of *Works of Love* that love is "essentially indescribable" and "essentially inexhaustible" (WL, 3). Ultimately, of course, Kierkegaard believes that God is love, but this equivalence is problematized by language and does not aid us in defining love. Perhaps it is because love is that which defines the good life that it is beyond any all-encompassing definition. Perhaps it is because love is that which defines who I am, my individuality, that it cannot be subject to a definition itself. As Jean-Luc Marion writes in *The Erotic Phenomenon*, we are "defined neither by the *logos*, nor by the being within [us], but by this fact that [we] love."⁸ Thus it is precisely because love conditions and defines my ipseity and the good life I strive to achieve, that any attempt to define it is misguided and must ultimately fail. Ultimately, when our focus is on loving, on living the good life and not simply theorizing about it, then we must agree with Kierkegaard's pseudonym Vigilius Haufniensis that "whoever loves can hardly find joy and satisfaction, not to mention growth, in preoccupation with a definition of what love properly is" (CA, 81).

This means, no doubt, that any attempt to define God, who is love, is equally wrongheaded. But with this claim comes the accompanying corollary that any conception of God that does not express love is false. It is a divine madness that fails to grasp the eternity of love. Further, it appears that the highest good, like God and love, cannot be defined in any straightforward manner, and to seek as one's goal a definition in thought is to misunderstand that which is being sought in life.

Is our discussion of love, God, and the good life thus doomed to futility? Nothing could be further from the truth, for defining the highest (which cannot be done) is not the highest, but rather living a life structured by the highest, just as Kierkegaard writes that "Christ does not speak about knowing the neighbor but about becoming a neighbor oneself, about showing oneself to be a neighbor just as the Samaritan showed it by his mercy" (WL, 22). Further, when speaking about the life of love involved in marriage, the wise Judge William counsels, "We are not to read about or listen to or look at what is the highest and the most beautiful in life, but are, if you please, to live it" (EO II, 138–139).

The highest good, again we affirm, is love, and love calls us into relation with the neighbor, what philosophers call the other (WL, 89). Kierkegaard believes this, as he opens *Works of Love* with a call to believe in love, and he embraces the idea that we can all realize the value of love. Although a reflection on "the highest" or "the highest good" is not central in *Works of Love*—just as a reflection on love is not central in "An Occasional Discourse"—the impression readers get is clear: fulfilling the command "You shall love" is the highest good, and loving people is the highest and only thing to be valued in life.[9] More directly, in *Works of Love* Kierkegaard expresses two key insights regarding the highest good that must continually inform this study: (1) we have an intuitive understanding of the highest, and (2) the highest requires a relation to the other. Let us consider these insights more closely.

Even though love itself is essentially inexhaustible and indescribable, it can still be known by its fruits, if not also phenomenologically through experience and the kind of saturated intuition that the experience of love yields. Interestingly, it appears that for Kierkegaard, "the highest" is grasped in this latter way, for as he writes, "In the quiet hour's remoteness from the confusion of life and the world, every person understands what the highest is" (WL, 88). So, following Kierkegaard, we all intuitively understand the highest, which is that we shall love, and that love is the highest good. This implies that the highest good is made manifest through the love-relation to another, and even more interestingly, Kierkegaard clearly indicates that the highest cannot be achieved by one's self alone, as the self-relation denoted by self-love cannot manifest the highest good. Self-love is a deception; it cannot lead us to the highest good. In *Works of Love*, Kierkegaard explains that the highest good is something held in common with another: "Certainly the highest good shall not be booty; you shall not selfishly have it for yourself, for what you can have only for yourself alone is never the highest good" (WL, 43). In other words, the highest good cannot be related to self-love, a view that is quite contrary to the position of Harry Frankfurt, who argues in his influential *Reasons of Love* that the purest form of love is self-love and thereby seemingly implies that the highest may be grasped through a self-relation alone. Frankfurt's view, as I have argued elsewhere,[10] is not without its problems, and overall it fails to compel. Nevertheless, it is interesting that Frankfurt finds reason to refer to Kierkegaard's view that "purity of the heart is to will one thing,"[11] thus providing an opening for a comparison; but nothing that Frankfurt writes suggests a careful consideration of Kierkegaard's discourse, so there is little reason to reflect further on the contents of Frankfurt's text here.

Instead, let us advance our analysis by considering one reading of "An Occasional Discourse" that presents a conception of the good that is different from the one being argued for here. Only relatively recently have Kierkegaard scholars begun to emphasize the significance of the concept of love for reading Kierkegaard, and the prominent Kierkegaard scholar Louis Mackey shows in his chapter "The Analysis of the Good in Kierkegaard's *Purity of Heart*" how Kierkegaard's argument regarding the good can be read in the absence of a deliberation of love.[12] According to Mackey, "the good" is understood quite counter-intuitively as remorse and penitence, but is this right? If our focus is refined by an interpretation of the good as love, and if we view Kierkegaard as a phenomenologist of love (as I have argued at length elsewhere),[13] then should not the interpretation of the good as remorse and penitence manifesting itself in the consciousness of guilt be replaced by the intentionality of love? I shall argue for the interpretation that love is the highest good, but let us now consider Mackey's presentation of his argument.

While acknowledging the extreme and likely deliberate vagueness of the term "the Good,"[14] Mackey starts by identifying the equivalence of the good and God: "In *Purity of Heart* Kierkegaard argues that the only adequate understanding of the Good is religious: the Good is really known only when it is experienced as God. The power of the Good (=God) is effective for a human individual in the situation of remorse and the act of penitence."[15] Consequently even Mackey, who was well known for promoting an interpretation of Kierkegaard as "a kind of poet,"[16] emphasizes a religious reading of the good for Kierkegaard, and the good life becomes one in which the individual consciousness is pervaded by guilt, remorse, and penitence. "The only 'purity of heart'," Mackey writes, "is the penitent confession of one's own irrefragable *impurity*."[17] But is this really so?—which is a question Mackey himself will ask later[18]—and why should we accept this? While we can agree that the good is a power—and if you want to equate this power with God, that is fine, provided that the fear of God does not result in loving others less—as already indicated, an alternative reading is possible in which the good is best understood as love, and the only purity of heart is to will to love.

Mackey explains how Kierkegaard differs from the majority of philosophers who strive to define the good: "Kierkegaard's explicit rejection of this conviction [i.e., that 'the good' can be defined] makes his discussions of ethical problems virtually unique. He is persuaded that the Good cannot be known nor its possibility apprehended except by *individuals*, each in the context of his personal exigence."[19] This view is significant, as it shows that Kierkegaard emphasizes action—or better, works and deeds—over arguments, and thus ethics is conceived as more primordial than epistemology and ontology. The good is not something that can be abstractly defined; instead, it is to be lived and manifested in lived relations with others. When we understand that for Kierkegaard, the good is love, and that his first philosophy is an ethics of love, then we recognize the need to qualify Mackey's explanation. For it is not isolated individuals who come to know the good, but rather lovers in relation to their beloveds, for it is the good (or love) that conditions their coming to know themselves as individuals. It is precisely because the good is primary that it cannot be defined, for it serves as both the condition or occasion of knowledge and the truth of knowledge. Consequently, as Mackey points out through an importantly qualified exception, the good can be known within a context, and this context is the experience of love. For this reason it is clearer to speak of the equivalence of the good with love over its equivalence with God, for if God is "defined" as the absolute unknown, then this leads to an absolute impasse that cannot be overcome.

Although Kierkegaard explains that "*there must be repentance and remorse*" (PH, 38),[20] he is clear that the "*essential* moral task is: to will the Good with purity of heart."[21] This leads Mackey to claim that "the fundamental moral phenomenon is the consciousness of guilt,"[22] even though he questions this fundamentality as a "theological prejudice" one paragraph later. But he seeks to explain away this prejudice, rather than show how it clashes with the philosophy of love developed throughout Kierkegaard's writings and most fully articulated in *Works of Love*, where we instead come to understand that it is the phenomenon of love that yields the fundamental moral consciousness. A careful examination of Kierkegaard's phenomenology of love, which must of course involve a deliberation of the intentionality of love that hides a multitude of sins,[23] leads away from the supposedly Kierkegaardian view unraveled by Mackey in which morality is said to consist in a recognition of guilt and repentance, two phenomena characterized correctly as negative emotions by Spinoza, who understood repentance as being "doubly wretched."[24] A contrasting view to this one sees the good through the eyes of love, and as Kierkegaard writes in his earliest edifying discourse on love, "When love lies in the heart, the eye has the power to love forth the good in the impure, but this eye sees not the impure but the pure, which it loves and loves forth by loving it" (EUD, 61). Thus, it is not a stretch to see that for Kierkegaard, morality consists essentially in loving the neighbor and hiding his multitude of sins, in which case the highest good is the eternal shall. Therefore it is not guilt that morality demands. Contrary to Mackey's interpretation that "the highest moral achievement possible for a man is the everlasting recollection of guilt,"[25] the highest moral achievement possible for human beings is to will to love only. This view is expressed most powerfully in the conclusion to *Works of Love*, where Kierkegaard reflects on the words of the apostle John to come to a full realization of the power of love, such that it is as if it never needed to be commanded in the first place: "The commandment is that you shall love, but ah, if you will understand yourself and life, then it seems that it should not need to be commanded, because to love people is the only thing worth living for, and without this love you are not really living" (WL, 375). Here Kierkegaard clearly affirms the view that loving human beings is the highest good—it is "the only thing worth living for"—and it is that which makes possible the good life, for without loving others, Kierkegaard reasons, you are not even really living a life. In other words, while one might say, in contrast to Kierkegaard here, that life is defined by biological functions, such that if you are breathing you are alive, Kierkegaard's response would have to be that what is intended is that *a good life* is not defined by biological functions, but rather only meaningful loving relations with other people.

Consider now what Kierkegaard writes in *Purity of Heart*: "The Good without condition and without qualification, without preface and without compromise, is absolutely the only thing that a person may and should will, and is only one thing" (PH, 54). What, then, is the good? The best way to add substance to this notion is to consider the good as love. The *only thing* that a person can and should will is to love others, as this is the only thing that makes life worth living. Nevertheless, the equivalence of the good with God seems to emerge as Kierkegaard further develops this passage in "An Occasional Discourse" and personalizes the good through speaking of it as a "Thou": "For as the Good is only a single thing, so all ways lead to the good, even the false ones: when the penitent one follows the same way back. Oh, Thou the unfathomable trustworthiness of the Good! Wherever a man may be in the world, whichever road he travels, when he wills one thing, he is on a road that leads him to Thee" (PH, 54).

Mackey further explains that "this exposition of the Good, which is the Good itself in its existential epiphany, is penitence." He goes on to say, "It is the necessarily absolute *how* of the willing."[26] While we can understand relating the good to the *how*, it is not penitence that is the good, even if it happens to tend toward the good. For penitence, a negative emotion, is based on a passive intentional state, not the active intentionality of love that "loves forth the pure in the impure" and "loves up" (*elske op*) love (EUD, 6)—an expression used both in the early *Edifying Discourses* and in *Works of Love*, where the "upbuilding" is ultimately explained as the "uploving" (WL, 217). Thus, insofar as one successfully loves forth love by presupposing the ground of love that enables edification and hides a multitude of sins, penitence will remain at best a derivative phenomenon occasioned by a return to the natural attitude and the inability to maintain the proper *how*. For it is only love that is the *how*, the way, in which one wills the good for the other—the stranger, the neighbor, and the beloved.

Mackey also argues that Kierkegaard's message in *Purity of Heart* is to be "sharply distinguished from the romantic thesis that anything a man does is good if only he does it wholeheartedly and with passion."[27] This invokes a position of moral relativism, but for Kierkegaard the good is absolute and the same for all persons. It is interesting to see how this interpretation contrasts with Frankfurt's more recent view that equates self-love with wholeheartedness: "To be whole-hearted *is* to love oneself. The two are the same."[28] But as we have already seen, the highest good cannot be a form of self-love, for it is not something that one can have for oneself alone. Mackey then writes that "the Good itself is reality and power"[29] and "remorse and penitence are the Good exercising its claim on the human will."[30] This, for Mackey, is Kierkegaard's central point. But if the good is power, then it cannot be equivalent to guilt and penitence, which are negative expressions of a lack of power. Therefore, we are far better to equate it with love, which is indeed a positive power or force.

Mackey quotes Kierkegaard: "For as only one thing is necessary, and as the theme of the talk is the willing of only one thing: hence the consciousness before God of one's eternal responsibility to be an individual is that one thing neces-sary" (PH, 197–198). But rather than recognizing the "eternal responsibility" as the eternal will to love the neighbor, Mackey offers an extreme interpretation centered on the consciousness of guilt rather than the intentionality of love. He writes: "It is the self-accusation of conscience that is the revelation of the Good in its reality and its power. But the reality and power of the Good so revealed is *God*."[31] Here Mackey explains his interpretation: "What Kierkegaard has tried to show is that the moral situation of man is the situation of remorse, and that this situation, existentially apprehended, transforms itself dialectically into the *religious* situation, the situation in which the Good manifests itself as God. The existential analysis of the experience of remorse leads to the being of God as the presupposition and the meaning of that experience. The experience of remorse is dialectically the experience of the Good which imparts itself in the very act of annihilating every effort to achieve it."[32] Although Mackey would seemingly wish to avoid a theological interpretation, this is precisely what he offers, and it is an interpretation that misses the mark, as it fails to account for the experience of love and the phenomenological conception of love, which can be seen as a corrective to what appears to be a weighty experience of remorse that is anything but good. Remarkably, Mackey writes, "Life is good when it is accepted as guilty before God."[33] This is not to say that guilt and remorse can-not ever lead one to will the good, but they are not the manifestation of the good, which is what Mackey takes as Kierkegaard's claim. Further, Mackey sug-gests ultimately that there is an absolute difference between a person and the good (i.e., God),[34] thus making any attempt to actualize the good within one's life problematic at best and impossible at worst. While it cannot be denied that within Kierkegaard there is the propensity toward fear and trembling and guilt and remorse, these existential experiences are distinguishable from the lived experience of the good as the will to love, which after all is the only thing worth living for.

Love is a positive power that can be enacted in a multitude of ways in a mul-titude of contexts, but it is clearly distinct from an experience of guilt, remorse, and fearful trembling. Only a modicum of self-reflection is needed to grasp this point, but if you want a poignant illustration of the comedy and horror involved in a failure to recognize this, see Flannery O'Connor's *Wise Blood*. None of this is meant to imply, however, that one will not experience guilt, fear, and suffering throughout what may be a good life, but these experiences are not experiences of the good itself or the highest good, for this is love, and only when we are in the moment of willing love are we truly living the good life.

Some might object that this is a weakening of the conception of the good and the good life in Kierkegaard, but this is not the case. Is it not actually more strenuous to will to love out of an abundance of power and positive strength, rather than because one feels guilty (i.e., bad) about oneself? Is not the former an expression of willing the good in truth, as the latter involves the double-mindedness involved in wanting to remove the consciousness of guilt?

Mackey writes, "In a word, the Good is God; and the reality of God in human existence is remorse, contrition and repentance."[35] How he could not see that, in a word, the good is love—that, in a word, God is love—is hard to understand, for is not the reality of God in human existence love? Consequently, Mackey offers us a view that fails to account for the philosophy of love in Kierkegaard's writings and thereby also fails to account for the highest good. Surprisingly, none of Mackey's readings in *Points of View: Readings of Kierkegaard* considers the significance of love as even marginally related to a point of view for interpreting Kierkegaard. Even more astonishing is the fact that Kierkegaard's *Works of Love*—the major work published in the same year and only about six months later than "An Occasional Discourse"—is not found among the thirty entries by Kierkegaard listed in Mackey's bibliography, and the term "love" is not found in the index. In my view, "An Occasional Discourse"—or, if you prefer, *Purity of Heart*—should be read as thematically linked to *Works of Love*, for the former work develops in more general terms the intentional pursuit of the good, while the latter work explores the specific actions involved in the good life (although they are not exhaustively stated).

As I have argued, "An Occasional Discourse," in which the purity of heart is identified and explained, should be read through the eyes of love. Granted, a direct focus on love is not central in this work, but it is not the case that there is no reflection of love here. Consider this important passage in which love is used to illustrate the good, thus suggesting their equivalence:

> Only the good is one thing in its essence and the same in every one of its expressions. Let love illustrate it. The person who truly loves does not love once and for all; neither does he use a portion of his love now and then in turn another portion, because to exchange it is to make a changeling. No, he loves with all his love; it is totally present in every expression; he continually spends all of it, and yet he continually keeps it all in his heart. What marvelous wealth! When the miser has amassed all the world's gold—in grubbiness—he

has become poor; when the lover spends all his love, he keeps it whole—in purity of heart. If a person is in truth to will one thing, the one thing he wills must indeed be of such a nature that it remains unchanged amid all changes; then by willing it he can win changelessness. (UDVS, 30)

What does Kierkegaard communicate here? If the good is "one thing in its essence and the same in every one of its expressions," and if love illustrates this because "it is of such a nature that it remains unchanged amid all changes," then are we not entirely justified in concluding that the good and love are one and the same thing? Like Spinoza's expression "*Deus sive Natura*," in which God and nature are held to be one and the same thing, for Kierkegaard we can state, "*Summum bonum sive amor*"—in other words, *love* is *the good*, the highest good, as these two terms share the same essence or nature.[36] On a more practical level, why wouldn't we conceive love as the highest good? This does not have to be motivated deductively or theologically, for we all already understand that it is not fame and fortune but rather love that is the highest good. This is given to us through our experience of ourselves in the world, which is to say it is given phenomenologically, as we understand that loving others is the only thing worth living for.

Kierkegaard links love with the good in a few other places in "An Occasional Discourse." For example, Kierkegaard suggests that "an honest erotic love is also an upbringing to the good" (UDVS, 35), although he also writes that "falling in love is still not the good" (UDVS, 35). Although there is not the space here to develop a thorough exposition of Kierkegaard's concept of love and to consider the knotty question of whether there are multiple, essentially distinct kinds of love (e.g., erotic love and neighborly love), I have attempted to argue for a unified conception of love elsewhere,[37] and the first quotation above points toward a unified conception, as erotic love is said to educate one on the good (i.e., love, which is to will the good for another). Falling in love, however, indicates a passive state, which may become "a formative educator . . . in truth to will one thing and to will the good" (UDVS, 35), but it is not love's fullest active expression. One can fall in or out of love, but insofar as the lover remains steadfast in the willed advance of love, then love works to help the other person. Again linking the good and love, Kierkegaard illustrates the point that "the good is only one thing, so it wants to be alone in helping a person" (UDVS, 49) with the example of a loving mother (who has no doubt become a loving mother after falling in love):

The good teaches the one who is striving, helps him, yet only in the way the loving mother teaches the child to walk alone. The mother is far enough in front of the child so that she cannot actually hold onto the child, but she stretches out her arms; she imitates the child's movements. . . . The most loving mother can do no more if there is to be any truth in this matter of the child's walking alone. And yet she does do more, inasmuch as her face, her countenance—indeed, it is beckoning like the reward of the good and the encouragement of eternal happiness. So the child is walking alone, with its eyes fixed on its mother's face, not on the difficulty of the way, supporting itself by the arms that do not hold onto it. (UDVS, 49)

In this beautiful passage designed to illustrate the work of the good, we find a rich expression of the power of love, involving a mother and a child gazing at each other, a face-to-face encounter that may be understood phenomenologically as a crossed phenomenon culminating in the glorification of the face.[38] What is also interesting is that here readers find a connection between the good and eternal happiness, which is how Kierkegaard will define the highest good elsewhere. Thus let us now leave "An Occasional Discourse" to consider the concept of the highest good in Kierkegaard's other works.

In a recent analysis, Roe Fremstedal remarks that Kierkegaard uses the concept of the highest good rather cryptically throughout his writings,[39] and thus we can see that viewing love as the highest good can be productive in a more comprehensive interpretation of Kierkegaard's writings. In addition to a rather cryptic usage, it must be admitted that Kierkegaard also uses the concept ambiguously. For example, in the pseudonymous *Concluding Unscientific Postscript*, which according to Fremstedal contains arguably the most explicit discussion of the term,[40] the highest good is equated with eternal bliss or blessedness (*Salighed*), while in *Christian Discourses* it is identified as blessedness (CD, 222), grace (CD, 65), faith (CD, 191), and love of God (CD, 200). It seems problematic, or at the least unhelpful, to maintain that all these terms are equivalent, although they may still be related. Why is Kierkegaard so slippery in this regard? Is he playing with readers to get them to seek the love of God, which may be seen as the ultimate culmination of grace and faith, as well as the source of the meaningfulness of these terms? We must also keep in mind that for Kierkegaard, faith without love is dead, and blessedness is loving people, for as he writes in the conclusion of *Works of Love*, "To love people is the only blessed comfort both here and in the next world; and to love people is the only true sign that you are a Christian— truly, a profession of faith is not enough either" (WL, 375). Nevertheless, given the variety of terms used, one would almost think that there are several high goods, and that we must struggle to find which one is the highest. But it seems unlikely that this is the case. Or perhaps with the right theological explanations, all these concepts can be aligned into a single unified good. But this is surely problematic. What then, specifically, shall we understand as the single highest good in Kierkegaard's writings? Of course, we all already know the answer.

Although there has not been much research on the highest good in Kierkegaard's writings, Fremstedal argues that "the concept of the highest good is of systematic importance in Kierkegaard."[41] Fremstedal focuses on Climacus's identification of the highest good (*det høieste Gode*) with eternal bliss (*Salighed*) in *Concluding Unscientific Postscript* and suggests that this is the absolute telos, which "consists in the realisation of virtue and happiness."[42] Throughout his careful work, Fremstedal shows how Kierkegaard's position basically agrees with Kant's view, in which "the highest good is the single most important concept in [his] philosophy of religion."[43] For Kant the highest good is explicitly identified as the Kingdom of God, thus adding another notion to the cluster of terms held to be the highest good. Contrary to some readers of Kierkegaard, Fremstedal argues that "Kierkegaard interprets the highest good as the Kingdom of God and that this important point has been overlooked by previous scholarship."[44] While there is no great leap involved in aligning the Kingdom of God with eternal bliss, as Fremstedal does, readers may wonder whether or how love is aligned with this, and why the transcendent concepts of the Kingdom of God and eternal bliss are accentuated rather than the practical and phenomenological concept of love.

Although the concept of love is not prominent in Fremstedal's article, it does appear toward the end of the discussion of the Kingdom of God. Here a passage is cited from *Works of Love* where Kierkegaard says that the highest good and the greatest blessedness (*største Salighed*) is "truly to love, and next truly to be loved" (WL, 239).[45] To this Fremstedal adds the following comment: "In my view, this passage can be taken to say that universal neighbor love is the highest good. Arguably, this is what constitutes the Kingdom of God. Put in Kantian terms: the realisation of the highest good involves universal respect or practical love."[46] While we can wholeheartedly agree with this rather late comment and the identification of the highest good with love (*Kjerlighed*), it must be admitted that this is clearly not the focus of Fremstedal's argument, which includes no explanation of how love constitutes the Kingdom of God. Further, when we come to the conclusion of Fremstedal's article, the main purpose of which is "to clarify the meaning and importance of the highest good in Kierkegaard,"[47] there is no reference at all to love. Instead, the highest good is claimed to involve "the following three elements: (A) virtue, (B) happiness or bliss, and (C) a society or kingdom,"[48] and Kant and Kierkegaard are held to agree on this.[49] Now, arguably, love may very well be connected to these three elements, but claiming this does not amount to the same thing as claiming that love, and love alone, is the highest good. Of course, it cannot be denied that Kierkegaard's writings include characterizations of the highest good as a future transcendent state, but it also cannot be denied that Kierkegaard powerfully calls for an enactment of the highest good, here and now, through works of love. Thus, I maintain, the highest good is best conceived as an active state—as a verb that refers to working or doing—that expresses love for another person. Whether love leads to an eternal bliss in heaven is at best a secondary concern, however beautiful it may be to conceive that it does. That love leads to the good life on Earth must be our primary affirmation.

As Kierkegaard suggests in *Works of Love*, we all know that love is the highest, the greatest, and to maintain the importance of these others concepts without explicit connection to love—as we must admit Kierkegaard himself does at times—can be misleading. Perhaps Kierkegaard struggled himself with the concept of the highest good—how could he not have?—and perhaps he also wanted his readers to come to the realization for themselves that "surely [to love God] is the highest good" (CD, 200). In a passage from *Christian Discourses* that firmly demonstrates this point while also showing the relation that love has to life, Kierkegaard writes:

> To love God is to live. *To live!* When the words are used this way with special emphasis, one indicates the full, rich life that is in possession of the conditions for living, indicates a life that is truly worth living, a life that so to speak, overflows with a blissful sense of life. One lives this way only when one possesses the highest good, but the highest good is to love God. But in that case, no matter what happens to him, the one who loves God indeed possesses the highest good, because to love God is the highest good. Oh, is this not true! If you will permit me for the sake of a pious jest to make fun just once of this demonstrating conceit, I shall add: *quod erat demonstrandum* [which was to be demonstrated]! (CD, 200)

What it means "to love God" is clearly not self-evident, especially a God who is unknown, hidden, and mysterious, a God whose face is unseen and whose flesh remains uncrossable. It may also happen that in one's attempt at loving God, one conceives of God within one's own image and gently veers down the lonesome path of self-love.[50] This, of course, would be a grave mistake, so it is fortunate that Kierkegaard emphasizes rather the requirement of loving the neighbor in order to be like God.[51] In the above passage, Kierkegaard again writes of a life that is truly worth living, a life that is experienced as an overabundant fullness, and as already explained, such a life is lived by loving people. From a phenomenological point of view, it makes sense to maintain the focus solely on the love of the neighbor or what philosophers call the other, for this task is analyzable[52] and has more than enough to concern itself with each and every day. What is more, when this task is accomplished, we may believe that the love of God has already taken care of itself.

MICHAEL STRAWSER is Chair of the Department of Philosophy and Professor of Philosophy at the University of Central Florida. He is author of *Both/And: Reading Kierkegaard from Irony to Edification* and *Kierkegaard and the Philosophy of Love.*

Notes

1. This quotation is from a passage deleted from the final manuscript of *Works of Love* (see WL, 452).

2. Although Kierkegaard writes about "the good" in "An Occasional Discourse" and "the highest good" elsewhere, it is my view that "the good" of "An Occasional Discourse" can clearly be understood as the highest good, for there is no indication within this work that there is some other good higher than "the good." Although one may wish to draw distinctions when considering Kierkegaard's usage more broadly—and, as we shall see, Kierkegaard is not globally consistent throughout his authorship—I would argue that focusing on the concept of love provides a way of unifying these two expressions.

3. *Upbuilding Discourses in Various Spirits* was published on March 13, 1847, and *Works of Love* was published on September 29, 1847, while "the writing of the First Series of *Works of Love* was finished in April 1847" (WL, ix).

4. Eduard Geismar, *Søren Kierkegaard, hans Livsudvikling og Forfattervirksomhed* [Søren Kierkegaard, The Development of His Life and Activity as an Author] I–VI (Copenhagen: Gads Forlag, 1927), V, p. 11. Quoted in UDVS, xiv.

5. George Pattison, "Foreword," in *Works of Love* (New York: Harper Perennial, 2009), p. ix.

6. For a closer and more substantive reflection on *Works of Love*, see Michael Strawser, *Kierkegaard and the Philosophy of Love* (Lanham, MD: Lexington, 2015).

7. Throughout this study of the notions of the good and love, our thoughts necessarily will also converge upon the notion of God. This convergence is undoubtedly complicated. Throughout his authorship Kierkegaard affirms over and over that God is love; it appears from his early dissertation *The Concept of Irony* (CI, 45) to *Works of Love* (WL, 62) to the late *The Moment*. Surprisingly, however, the view that God is love does not prevent Kierkegaard from also claiming that God hates and is our "mortal enemy." See *The Moment*, where Kierkegaard writes, "God is indeed a human being's most appalling enemy, your mortal enemy. Indeed, he wants you to die, to die to the world; he hates specifically that in which you naturally have your life, to which you cling with all your zest for life," and "the minor premise in the statement 'God is love' is: he is your mortal enemy" (M, 177–178). Preferable to this late view is the view in which Johannes Climacus expresses that God is the unknown or the absolutely other (PF, 39), and this aligns with Kierkegaard's view that love's source is hidden and mysterious (see WL, 8–9), for while we may hold that this source is God, the meaning of this is undetermined— after all, it is hidden and impenetrable and thus has to be believed. This convergence is thus problematic because of the unclear relation between God and love. Is the relation one of identity or attribution? Ultimately, we cannot know, and this fact suggests that we would do well to focus our attention centrally on love alone, which arguably can be known phenomenologically with certainty. Thus, in contrast to many of the contributions in this collection, in this essay I focus more on Kierkegaard's understanding of the good (life) than his understanding of God, while nevertheless offering a consideration of what it may mean to affirm the claim that God is love.

8. Jean-Luc Marion, *The Erotic Phenomenon*, trans. Stephen E. Lewis (Chicago: University of Chicago Press, 2007), p. 7.

9. Kierkegaard importantly concludes *Works of Love* with the claim that "loving people is the only thing worth living for" (WL, 375).

10. See the section "Frankfurt on Self-Love" in my *Kierkegaard and the Philosophy of Love* (Lanham, MD: Lexington, 2015), pp. 154–159.

11. Harry Frankfurt, *The Reasons of Love* (Princeton, NJ: Princeton University Press, 2004), pp. 95–96.

12. This is the second chapter of Louis Mackey's *Points of View: Readings of Kierkegaard* (Tallahassee: Florida State University Press, 1986), which was the first text published in the *Kierkegaard & Postmodernism* series with Mark C. Taylor as general editor and Louis Mackey and E. F. Kaelin as associate editors.

13. See Michael Strawser, *Kierkegaard and the Philosophy of Love*. In a sense, this paper can be seen as a further development of the argument provided in my book that Kierkegaard can be read as, first and foremost, a philosopher of love who offers readers a first phenomenology of love, for in my larger work, "An Occasional Discourse" and *Christian Discourses* are not discussed as they are here.

14. Mackey, "The Analysis of the Good in Kierkegaard's *Purity of Heart*," p. 25.

15. Mackey, "The Analysis of the Good in Kierkegaard's *Purity of Heart*," p. 23.

16. See Louis Mackey, *Kierkegaard: A Kind of Poet* (Philadelphia: University of Pennsylvania Press, 1971).

17. Mackey, "The Analysis of the Good in Kierkegaard's *Purity of Heart*," p. 23.

18. Mackey, "The Analysis of the Good in Kierkegaard's *Purity of Heart*," p. 29.

19. Mackey, "The Analysis of the Good in Kierkegaard's *Purity of Heart*," p. 24.

20. This is Steere's translation, which reads rather differently than the Hongs' more recent one, especially given that Steere inserted "fifteen sectional divisions and headings" (PH, 24) that give the text quite a different look than the original.

21. Mackey, "The Analysis of the Good in Kierkegaard's *Purity of Heart*," p. 25.

22. Mackey, "The Analysis of the Good in Kierkegaard's *Purity of Heart*," p. 26.

23. For this argument see my article "Kierkegaard's Erotic Reduction and the Problem of Founding the Self," in *Narrative, Identity and the Kierkegaardian Self*, edited by John Lippitt and Patrick Stokes (Edinburgh, Scotland: Edinburgh University Press, 2015), pp. 78–94. The section "Kierkegaard's Phenomenology of Love" (pp. 90–93) is especially relevant.

24. See Benedict de Spinoza, *Ethics*, edited and translated by Edwin Curley (New York: Penguin, 1996), where he writes, "Repentance is not a virtue, or does not arise from reason; instead, he who repents what he has done is twice wretched, or lacking in power" (Part IV, proposition 54; p. 144). Nevertheless, in the scholium to this proposition, Spinoza explains that insofar as we are affected by negative emotions, this one is more beneficial than others, as it brings more good than harm.

25. Mackey, "The Analysis of the Good in Kierkegaard's *Purity of Heart*," p. 28.

26. Mackey, "The Analysis of the Good in Kierkegaard's *Purity of Heart*," p. 30.

27. Mackey, "The Analysis of the Good in Kierkegaard's *Purity of Heart*," p. 30.

28. Frankfurt, *The Reasons of Love*, p. 95.

29. Mackey, "The Analysis of the Good in Kierkegaard's *Purity of Heart*," p. 30.

30. Mackey, "The Analysis of the Good in Kierkegaard's *Purity of Heart*," p. 31.

31. Mackey, "The Analysis of the Good in Kierkegaard's *Purity of Heart*," p. 31.

32. Mackey, "The Analysis of the Good in Kierkegaard's *Purity of Heart*," p. 33.

33. Mackey, "The Analysis of the Good in Kierkegaard's *Purity of Heart*," p. 33. He cites *Concluding Unscientific Postscript* and also the *Gospel of Suffering* as support for this claim.

34. Mackey, "The Analysis of the Good in Kierkegaard's *Purity of Heart*," p. 33.

35. Mackey, "The Analysis of the Good in Kierkegaard's *Purity of Heart*," p. 37.

36. Spinoza's fifth proposition in Part I of his *Ethics* provides this argument: "There cannot exist in the universe two or more substances having the same nature or attribute."

37. See Strawser, *Kierkegaard and the Philosophy of Love*, especially pp. 116–122.

38. On the "crossed phenomenon" and the "glorification of the face," see Marion, *The Erotic Phenomenon*, pp. 103 and 126–127. Also, it is highly noteworthy that in the very next paragraph of "An Occasional Discourse," Kierkegaard illustrates how fear has no part of the good ("Fear,

on the other hand, is a dry nurse for the child—it has no milk" [UDVS, 49]), which consequently also shows the radical separation between the concepts of love and fear. This is a good reason for being wary of the love/fear of God. For further discussion see chapter 7, "Love's Fear," in Strawser, *Kierkegaard and the Philosophy of Love.*

39. See Roe Fremstedal, "The Concept of the Highest Good in Kierkegaard," *International Journal for Philosophy of Religion* 69 (2011): p. 155. Note that Fremstedal's discussion of this topic also appears in chapter 5 of his book *Kierkegaard and Kant on Radical Evil and the Highest Good: Virtue, Happiness, and the Kingdom of God* (London: Palgrave Macmillan, 2014).

40. Fremstedal, "The Concept of the Highest Good in Kierkegaard," p. 156

41. Fremstedal, "The Concept of the Highest Good in Kierkegaard," p. 155.

42. Fremstedal, "The Concept of the Highest Good in Kierkegaard," pp. 156, 165.

43. Fremstedal, "The Concept of the Highest Good in Kierkegaard," p. 166.

44. Fremstedal, "The Concept of the Highest Good in Kierkegaard," p. 169.

45. Fremstedal, "The Concept of the Highest Good in Kierkegaard," p. 169; see also J. D. Glenn Jr., "'A Highest Good . . . An Eternal Happiness': The Human Telos in Kierkegaard's *Concluding Unscientific Postscript*," in *International Kierkegaard Commentary, Vol. 12*, Concluding Unscientific Postscript to "Philosophical Fragments," R. L. Perkins, ed. (Macon, GA: Mercer University Press, 1997), p. 261. I would note that the word "next" is highly significant here, for it clearly shows that "to love" and "to be loved" are separate experiences.

46. Fremstedal, "The Concept of the Highest Good in Kierkegaard," p. 169.

47. Fremstedal, "The Concept of the Highest Good in Kierkegaard," p. 170.

48. Fremstedal, "The Concept of the Highest Good in Kierkegaard," p. 170.

49. This is obviously a debatable point, and it seems to me that a developed understanding of love as the highest good shows more agreement between Kierkegaard and Plato than between Kierkegaard and Kant.

50. Note that in *Works of Love*, Kierkegaard claims that "to love God is to love oneself truly" and "to love God is true self-love" (WL, 107). In this context, where the focus is on love of the neighbor (which is also equated with the love of God) and self-love is primarily being considered negatively, it must be admitted that Kierkegaard's claim is ambiguous, just as is his concept of self-love. In *Kierkegaard and the Problem of Self-Love* (New York: Oxford University Press, 2013), John Lippitt finds these to be "rather gnomic remarks" (p. 45). For a more detailed discussion of the problematic notion of self-love, see chapter 6, "Love's Fall," in Strawser, *Kierkegaard and the Philosophy of Love.*

51. The relevant passage in Kierkegaard's *Works of Love* is this: "But God is Love, and therefore we can be like God only in loving, just as we also, according to the words of the apostle, can only be God's co-workers—in love" (WL, 62).

52. To say that it is analyzable does not mean that it is completely analyzable, nor does it deny the transcendence involved in love of the other. It affirms, rather, that we can find within our experience an encounter with the other, which no doubt involves a face-to-face encounter and at least a potential crossing of the flesh, and this saturated phenomenon allows for analysis. Further, Kierkegaard's *Works of Love* provides solid analyses of the love of the other involving a specific intentionality and a perspective of eternity, which is further discussed in my *Kierkegaard and the Philosophy of Love.*

3 Erotic Wisdom: On God, Passion, Faith, and Falling in Love

Pia Søltoft

In THIS CHAPTER I will discuss two basic questions concerning Kierkegaard's notion of faith regarded as a loving relationship to God and the interaction between these two questions. First, I would like to address the question: How are we to understand Kierkegaard's notion of passion? And secondly: What is the relation between existence as a passionate interest that resembles erotic love and faith as a passionate relation to God that also resembles erotic love? I will suggest that the interconnection between Kierkegaard's descriptions of faith and of falling in love can shed light over this question. In what follows I shall argue for a tight connection between our human experiences of love and our relation to God in faith. Finally, I will reach the conclusion that to Kierkegaard, faith can only be "understood" through our human passion, our "erotic wisdom"—and that in this way, Christianity and humanity are linked inseparably.

What Is Passion?

In *Concluding Unscientific Postscript*, Johannes Climacus describes the only true relation between a person and Christianity as an infinite passionate interest. He calls this interest "subjectivity." In the first small part of *Postscript,* only sixty-four pages, Climacus totally denies that the truth of Christianity could ever be of an objective kind. Therefore, the second part and the last five hundred pages of this work deal with the relation between subjectivity and Christianity. In this part Climacus often refers to Socrates, and especially to the myth on the birth of Eros that Socrates was told by the wise woman Diotima in Plato's *Symposium.*

Climacus draws a parallel and states that the way Eros is described resembles the way he himself thinks of existence as a passionate striving that bridges the gap between the finite and the infinite, the temporal and the eternal. Existence, like Eros, is double-bound: "According to Plato, Poverty and Plenty begot Eros, whose nature is made up of both. But what is existence? It is that child who is begotten by the infinite and the finite, the eternal and the temporal, and is therefore continually striving. This was Socrates' view—therefore love is continually striving, that is, the thinking subject is existing" (CUP, 92). When defining both existence and love, Kierkegaard combines Christianity with Plato's notion of both concepts, and this is why Kierkegaard can state that his definitions are valid for every human being, no matter which religious setting one is in. This is exactly why he refers to Plato and the connection between the birth of Eros and our human passion, for Climacus also states that it is not possible to exist in truth without passion. There is no objective system for existence. Therefore, Climacus says that to understand oneself as a single existing individual is *both* the Greek *and* the Christian principle (CUP, 99). There is no either/or here. The passion that is interconnected with human existence has already been discovered by Plato as love, and therefore Kierkegaard states that it has always been the task for human beings, Christian or not, to relate passionately to themselves and to what interests them infinitely and what they love.

This means that when we talk about existence, the opposition is not between our human experiences on the one side and Christianity on the other side. To relate in subjectivity to Christianity is to relate through the passion that we know and experience through our existence. The true relation to Christianity is the true humanity—but of course not the other way round.

Mythologically speaking, passion occurs with the birth of Eros. Let us now look a little deeper into this connection between love, passion, and faith in Kierkegaard.

What Is Love?

When Kierkegaard speaks of love, he always speaks of it as a given facticity in the world. And he always ties the givenness of love to a religious premise that, quite simply, states that love is given in the world because it is given by God.[1] But although Kierkegaard undoubtedly grounds the origin of love in God, it is also clear that he places this religious premise, which he does not hesitate to call "Christian," together with our universal human experience of love.

This connection between the religious and the human is due to Kierkegaard's understanding of love as both a divine gift and a fundamental human condition. In *Works of Love*, he writes, "Where does love come from, where does it have its origin and its source, where is the place it has its abode from which it flows? Yes, this place is hidden or is secret. There is a place in a person's innermost being; from this place flows the life of love . . . . Just as the quiet lake originates deep down in hidden springs no eye has seen, so also does a person's love originate even more deeply in God's love" (WL, 8–9). That love both dwells in the foundation of every person and in God means, quite simply, that love constitutes the basis of a person's humanity. Kierkegaard is therefore able to speak about the relationship between love and a person's self in the following way: "You shall preserve love, and you shall preserve yourself and by and in preserving yourself preserve love" (WL, 43). The idea that love dwells *in the foundation* of a person already involves a presupposition that *no person is without love*. To be able to love and be loved constitutes, to a certain extent, the very definition of what a person is.

In *The Erotic Phenomenon*, Jean-Luc Marion defines humans as loving animals, and on the basis of the idea of foundational love, one can almost hear Kierkegaard in this definition by Marion: "Man is defined neither by the logos, nor by the being within him, but by this fact that he loves (or hates), whether he wants to or not. In this world, only man loves, for animals and computers, in their own way, think just as well as he, indeed better than he; but one cannot affirm that they love. But man does—the loving animal."[2] Marion's definition of man as a loving animal resembles Kierkegaard's notion of man as a passionate creature. When we truly relate to something, we either hate or love what we relate to. The opposite of such a "true" passionate relation is an *apathetic* mood. In apathy no relation is possible, and it is precisely because love is an inalienable part of a person's humanity that Kierkegaard can maintain that when we relate to something, we always relate in passion. If we are apathetic, we do not relate, and then we lose our self, because we neglect the love that is implanted in us and shows itself through our passion: "To defraud oneself of love is the most terrible, is an eternal loss, for which there is no compensation either in time or in eternity" (WL, 6). The loss of love is the loss of oneself.[3] Kierkegaard therefore understands love as *the* basic human condition, which defines, on a very fundamental level, what a person is.

Rick Anthony Furtak describes Kierkegaard's view of the fundamental significance of love for human life as follows: "Love is the enigmatic power at the base of the psyche, and the deepest ground of human existence. This, Kierkegaard says, is the explanation that we crave in our inner being, which explains the meaning of life 'in the God who holds everything together in his eternal wisdom.' This God of infinite wisdom, manifest in the experience of love, is the 'source of all love' so that, as emotional beings, we are what we are only by virtue of being in love."[4] Being a fundamental property, love defines a person as a *relational* being, and Kierkegaard therefore stresses that love is "not a being-for-itself quality but a quality by which or in which you are for others" (WL, 223).

Love as a foundational character is therefore the precondition for all our relations: our relations to our friends, partners, children, neighbors, and our self, *and our relation to God*. Hereby one must suspect some similarities between all these different ways of loving, and in what follows, I shall try to classify some of the similarities between faith and falling in love, as I argue that not only do the two relations have the same origin, namely God, but they also share many of the same characteristics.

Love as a Double Urge

In *Works of Love*, Kierkegaard again and again calls love an urge. But to Kierkegaard love is an urge in a double sense. On the one hand, love is an urge in the sense that we need to *be loved*. We need to *have* love. In this sense the urge to love springs from a *lack*. Love is something that we long for. But love is also an urge in the sense of a *surplus*. It is also an urge to give shape and direction to one's love, an urge to cast one's love on another person. In a longer quotation from *Works of Love*, Kierkegaard explains the doubleness of this urge:

> How beautiful it is that the same thing that signifies the utmost misery also signifies the greatest riches! Urge, to have need, to be a needy person—how reluctant a person is to have this said about him! Yet we are saying the utmost when we say of the poet, "He has a urge to write;" of the orator, "He has an urge to speak;" and of the young woman, "She has an urge to love." Ah, how rich was even the neediest person who has ever lived, but who still has had love, compared with him, the only real pauper, who went through life and never felt a need for anything! This is precisely the young woman's greatest riches, that she needs the beloved; and this is the devout man's greatest and his truest riches, that he needs God. (WL, 10–11)[5]

This double-bound urge to love is by Kierkegaard considered *universal*. No man or woman is without this urge. It means that a person is not the source of his or her love: "It is God, the Creator, who must implant love in each human being, he who himself is Love" (WL, 216). Insofar as God has implanted this double urge in every person, each of us is created with the possibility of being able to love by actualizing this fundamental urge to love as a longing for love *and* as love-for-another.

In creation, love as a double-bound urge is implanted in every human being. And before creation, it is even implanted in Christ:

> How deeply the urge [*Trang*] of love is rooted in human nature! . . . So deeply is this urge [*Trang*] rooted in human nature that since the creation of the first human being there has been no change, no new discovery has been made . . . . So deeply is this urge rooted in human nature, and so *essentially* does it belong to being human, that even he who was one with the Father and in the communion of love with the Father and the Spirit, he who loved the whole human race, our Lord Jesus Christ, even he felt this urge *to love and be loved* by an individual human being. (WL, 154, my italics)

When mentioning Christ, Kierkegaard explicitly describes the urge to love as a double motion: not only does Christ have an urge to love, but he also has an urge to receive love. Kierkegaard explains this tricky interpretation by elaborating on the biblical story about Christ who three times asks Peter, "Do you really love me?" Christ has an urge to be loved—and, of course, an urge to give love. This double-directed universal urge is thus described as a unity of lack and surplus, and Kierkegaard again directly quotes Socrates's retelling of the myth of the birth of Eros from Plato's *Symposium*, stating, "Love is a son of Affluence and Poverty" (WL, 175).

Eros and Agape

As shown, Kierkegaard describes love as a deeply felt *urge* to love and be loved, an urge that in a fundamental way is characteristic of every person and lies at the heart of what is often, somewhat misleadingly, called a person's *natural love*, understood as the passionate desire and inclination that we are *immediately* driven by when we love. In what follows, I will not be using the term "natural" love, but rather I will speak of our *immediate experience* of what it is to love and be loved.

Kierkegaard further defines love as an intermediate entity between God and humans, and thereby further stresses that love is a fundamental human condition that has a divine origin. This, along with the double-bound notion of the urge to love, immediately places Kierkegaard outside the traditional theological distinction between two types of love—one human, the other divine—a distinction that is often mentioned as the distinction between eros and agape.

Ever since Anders Nygren (1890–1978) published in 1938 his study *Den kristna kärlekstanken genom tiderne* [The Christian Idea of Love through the Ages], with the well-known subtitle *Eros and Agape*, it has been a challenge to combine the naturally lived human experiences of love (such as falling in love, friendship, and parental love) with the Christian notion of neighbor-love. *Den kristna kärlekstanken* appeared for the first time in a small publishing house in Lund, Sweden, but the book immediately became a systematic success and was quickly translated into all main languages, and in a few years the division between eros and agape became the one and only way to think and talk about love.

To Nygren eros is a love that desires something; he finds this notion of love very clearly in Plato's concept of eros. But Nygren argues that this conception of eros-love is found long before Plato and continues to have a strong impact on the notion of love long after Plato, as eros in the later history of love affiliates with Christian thinking, first and foremost in the theology of Augustine, which Nygren rejects.

Agape, on the other hand, is a strictly Christian form of love. Agape is a love that does not need anything but gives itself away. To Nygren Christ is the pure incarnation of agape. This means that to Nygren, true Christian love is agape-love, a love that loves out of a surplus and demands nothing in return. According to Nygren, one of the great contributions of Luther was to see this love in the notion of the divine love as pure grace. But this also led Nygren to mistrust any kind of love relation that does not resemble agape but also implies a desire, a need to be loved.

There is still a vivid but wrong tradition of interpreting Søren Kierkegaard as a thinker who does not allow for a bridge between human and Christian love.[6] C. S. Lewis also had a problem with such a harsh distinction between these two different forms of love.

Need-Love and Gift-Love

In his small book from 1960 *The Four Loves*, C. S. Lewis (1898–1963) contrasts four different forms of love: affection, friendship, eros, and charity. Lewis's thoughts are developed as a critical corrective to Nygren's very sharp differentiation between eros and agape. In his study Lewis wants to show which of these forms of love has a resemblance to Christian love. To do that, he develops two ways of describing a love relation. It could be a relation of "need" or a relation of "gift." A relation of need is one in which we love something that we lack and therefore desire. A relation of gift is a relation where we love out of a surplus and want to give our love to somebody else. From what I have already shown, it is already clear that Kierkegaard does not make this separation, as he speaks of love both as a lack and as a surplus.

Lewis does not agree with Nygren's very sharp differentiation between gift and need, which lies at the bottom of Nygren's division of eros and agape. And therefore Lewis performs an analysis of the four just-mentioned kinds of love, to see what is characteristic in the way we love. As a tool for this investigation, he invents the terms "Need-Love" and "Gift-Love." Lewis's point of departure is that God's love is solely Gift-Love. To Nygren this would mean that if we should call human love "true," it would have to "look like" God's love and therefore be pure Gift-Love, if we use Lewis's vocabulary. But that leads Lewis to the important question: Does this mean that Need-love is not love at all? This is the question Lewis is trying to answer in his study of the four loves beginning with the following statement: "I cannot now deny the name love to Need-Love."[7] To substantiate his rejection, he continues to analyze each of the four mentioned forms of love to show how need and gift work together in most of them.

Affection is the kind of love that human beings share with animals. Affection is the kind of love parents show their children; and in a broad sense, it is the love that we show people we are familiar with. Friendship is of course the love among friends. Eros, to Lewis, is not the Greek concept; it is his way of naming being-in-love, or the kind of love that lovers are "in." Charity is Lewis's notion of neighbor-love. The point is that in the first three forms of human love, there is both a need-motive and a gift-motive present. Only charity proves itself to be solely a gift. But unlike Nygren, Lewis will not go as far as to say that affection, friendship, and eros then are not love at all. Instead he stresses that the love of a human being will always be both Need-Love and Gift-Love and only God's love can be purely Gift-Love. But that, of course, forms a very broad gap between the love of the Creator and the love of the created.

Human Love versus Divine Love?

It is almost a tradition in Kierkegaard research to view Kierkegaard's notion of love in the rather anachronistic light that Nygren's just-mentioned differentiation between eros and agape seems to have shed over any later discussion of the phenomenon of love. In this tradition there seems to be a consensus in interpreting Kierkegaard's view of "true" love as a straightforward agapistic view, while his relation to erotic love is said to be a little bit tense, if not directly unsympathetic.

In the line of this interpretation, Kierkegaard is most often accused of denying and disowning "natural" love, as he refuses to confess the fundamental importance of erotic love. In what follows I wish to argue against this widely accepted interpretation of Kierkegaard's notion of erotic love.

Consequently, I will argue for a more nuanced view on the relation between erotic love and religious love in the sense of faith. Due to the notion of love as a God-given and double-bound urge that was even present in Christ, it is possible for Kierkegaard to combine human love with divine love, eros with agape, and Need-Love with Gift-Love. Love is simply what bridges the human and the divine: "What is it, namely, that connects the temporal and eternity, what else but love, which for that very reason is before everything and remains after everything is gone" (WL, 6).

For Kierkegaard there is thus only one love, and this single love is established in every human being by God, who is himself love. This is why this one love must be able to find expression through all the varied ways in which a person is capable of loving. Fundamentally there is therefore no inconsistency between divine love and our human way of loving. Divine love is simply the origin of human love, just as it is the origin of itself.

Love as Preferential

As just mentioned Kierkegaard only rarely speaks of *natural* love, but he does often talk about *immediate* love. Immediate love is, as the term suggests, the love we immediately, and therefore without prior reflection and decision, have for a beloved, a friend, a child. The term "immediate love" covers infatuation, friendship, parental love, and even self-love. When it concerns such matters, love is characterized as "immediate" because all of these love-experiences arise from an immediate urge to love that no person is without and that immediately expresses itself when we love in all the ways just mentioned.

But immediate love is not *unconscious*. It is indeed always *consciously directed* at one person or a very few other persons. Hence Kierkegaard describes immediate love as *preferential* love. The term "preferential" shall capture the distinctive aspect of immediate love: that it is *exclusive*. When we love, it is always the case that we immediately cast our love upon a particular few: a lover, a friend, a child. And even if there were several lovers, friends, or children, it is still a matter of exclusive love, insofar as we love these few in a special way compared to our relation to all others. That our immediate love always manifests itself as preferential love means that it is a matter of loving those we love especially. Immediate love is therefore *always conscious* that it loves this other or these others; it is conscious of its *direction*. Immediate love is thus immediately conscious of itself and of whom it loves, even though no one who loves can explain why she loves precisely this beloved. The immediate love imposes itself as an urge without any prior decision, but nonetheless it is conscious exclusively in its directedness toward the beloved, whether this is a lover, friend, or child.

Immediate love is preferential love, and preferential love is not by itself negative. Kierkegaard says that it is only in the way "the poet" treats immediate love as the highest, as the one and only form of love, that it becomes a hidden self-love. In itself preferential love is the basic form of all other loves. And when we love, we are always very aware whom we love.

In this strict sense, *no love* is *unconscious*. It may be immediate, but it is always directed and therefore *intentional*. When we talk of faith as love of God, it is often claimed that this love is opposed to immediate love. But if we consider immediate love as intentional love, then faith as the love of God must be considered preferential and thereby also immediate and intentional. It is consciously directed toward God, and in this sense, faith as the love of God is also to be considered as preferential love, both according to its directedness toward a certain object, which I just have called love's intentionality, and according to its passion.

Love of God, faith, is intentional and preferential because it is not just love but exactly love of a specific God. And in the same way as the relation to the beloved, the child, or the friend awakens preferential love as erotic, parental, or friendly, it is the relation to God that awakens love as faith. It is in this sense that we can understand God as the creator of faith.

Preferential love is a specific way of loving. Indeed, preferential love is the most natural way of loving, because it is how we love immediately, when we direct the urge to love and to be loved (which arises from foundational love) toward a determinate other person or toward God. In this way, preferential love builds upon the exclusivity of passion, and thereby its object, the one who is loved, comes into focus for preferential love.

Passion always only wants one thing. It is impossible to be in love with two persons at the same time, and it is impossible to love two gods at the same time.

Either you hate the one and love the other, or you love the one and hate the other. Passion is always one-sided, and passionate love is therefore always exclusive.

Hereby it becomes clear that being in love and faith share the same whole-heartedness of passion. The wholeheartedness of passion is to will one thing. But it is also to will not to try to reshape the beloved, in the belief that the beloved simply is what he or she is. In the discourse "Our Duty to Love the People We See" from *Works of Love*, we find precisely this theme, and in *Concluding Unscientific Postscript*, it is regarded as a distortion of love and offensive in relation to the beloved if the lover is ashamed of his beloved. And it is just as disheartening when a believer is ashamed of his or her faith: "When faith, however, begins to feel ashamed of itself, when, like a young woman in love who is not satisfied with loving but subtly feels ashamed of the beloved and consequently must have it substantiated that he is something exceptional, that is, when faith begins to lose passion, that is, when faith begins to cease to be faith, then the demonstration is made necessary in order to enjoy general esteem from unbelief" (CUP, 30–31). Passion in willing one thing and willing the beloved as the beloved is similar in faith and in falling in love. The same similarity is striking when we compare the double-bound urge that is present in both faith and in falling in love.

The Two Sides of Love

Preferential love always has two sides. As explained, Kierkegaard understands love as an urge that presents itself as a surplus, a desire to cast one's love onto another as an overflow of life, desire, and passion. But love is also an urge in the sense of a longing or a lack—a desire to be loved. This bidirectional desire constitutes the basic precondition for a person being able to direct his or her love toward a concrete other person or toward God. This double-sided urge, which arises from the God-given foundational love, thereby constitutes the wondrous precondition of both faith and falling in love.

In falling in love, the dialectic between surplus and longing in the urge to love turns into a dialectic between love's two directions: the inward direction within the lover and the outward direction toward the beloved. In *A Literary Review*, Kierkegaard describes being in love in the following way: "Being in love is the culmination of a person's purely human existence, which is a double existence, and for that very reason being in love is simultaneously just as much inwardness as it is a relation directed outward to actuality. Happy erotic love is the equilibrium of the relation. Less inwardness and a dominant relation to actuality is a less beautiful love; a dominant inwardness and a lesser relation to actuality tends toward unhappy love" (TA, 49). That being in love is described as "the culmination of a person's purely human existence" shows just how radically transformative a power Kierkegaard takes love to be—even when it appears in the form of falling in love. That this transformative aspect is especially characteristic of falling in love is due to the fact that we are here concerned with a love-experience in which one is particularly aware of her love. Being in love is experienced as a power that sovereignly imposes itself and changes both of the lovers. In the above quotation, Kierkegaard describes being in love as a two-sided love, and he stresses the equilibrium between the two directions I have just laid out. The inward direction and the outward direction underpin being in love. If the direction is mostly oriented outwardly and is thereby preoccupied with what one can receive from the other—indeed, perhaps even most concerned with how the relation appears to others—the love is, we are told, less beautiful. If the inward direction in the lover is dominant in the relationship, the love will tend to be unhappy, because there is no corresponding movement in the other person—a reciprocation of one's love. If, however, both parties are in love, then the relationship is mutual and thereby happy, because each relationship of preferential love rests upon a wish to be loved in return. The nature of reciprocal love is determined by the form of preferential love. If we are in love, we wish that our love be reciprocated with love (in the sense of "being in love") and not, for example, with friendship.

The same goes for faith as love of God. In faith we also have this longing to love and to be loved by the beloved. In faith we love God, but we also long to be loved by God, and being in faith, we believe that we are loved by God. Also, faith is therefore characterized by the same double structure, the same double-sidedness as is characteristic of falling in love. A well-known passage from *Philosophical Fragments* shows this very clearly: "If the paradox and the understanding meet in the mutual understanding of their difference, then the encounter is a happy one, like erotic love's understanding—happy in the passion to which we as yet have given no name" (PF, 215). Of course, the name is faith, and another characteristic shared by both faith and falling in love is constituted by the strange notion of a first-time event that goes along with both forms of passionate love.

A First-Time Experience

Kierkegaard makes the further point that the first time a person falls in love, something decisively new happens to him or her. The same experience is characteristic of faith. Kierkegaard understands falling in love for the first time as a momentous event, one that leaves its mark on the lover; and it is this mark that we will pursue in what follows. With the help of Zygmunt Bauman, one can describe the first-time character of falling in love as follows: "Neither love nor death can be entered twice; even less so than Heraclitus' river. They are, indeed, their own heads and tails, being dismissive and negligent of all others. Love and death have no history of their own. They are events in human time—each one a separate event, not connected (let alone connected causally) to other 'similar' events . . . . And so you cannot learn to love; nor can you learn to die."[8] And neither can you learn to believe one could continue. Kierkegaard's praise of the first time you fall in love is not the result of some prudish attempt to guard against promiscuity and capriciousness. Rather, it is an attempt to pinpoint the moment in a person's history when the urge to love effects a radical change in a person's consciousness. This change in consciousness takes place in the moment when a person first casts her love onto another person and thereby experiences, in body and soul, what it is to fall in love. The first-time love awakens as consciously being in love with another person, and something completely new happens. The urge to love acquires an outward direction, and the desire for companionship that is grounded in love's relational character becomes actualized. In this sense, the first love has a one-off character, as this awakening, and the consequent change in consciousness, can only happen once.

Every subsequent falling in love is also experienced as being the first of its kind, because preferential love is always felt as the first of its type. Every falling in love therefore has this character of a first-time experience, because it is a matter of being in love with a specific other person, who thus becomes irreplaceable, and the experience of being in love becomes unique. This will happen each time one falls in love, because as has been shown, falling in love is characterized as preferential and intentional, whereby each love relation of this kind will be experienced as a first-time event. In actuality, it is of course just a case of a repetition of the first love, which thereby remains the first in temporal terms; but as Baumann indicates, it is a repetition without causality, and one therefore cannot learn to be in love.

Hence the significance of the first love does not lie in its being quantitatively the first in a long line, but rather in that its being qualitatively the first of its kind brings about a new recognition in the individual. The first love thus establishes a new quality. In the same way, Adam's first sin must not be understood as the first in an infinitely long lineage of sins, but instead as the first of its kind; it is the sin that brings Adam to a new consciousness, just as every subsequent individual's first sin has the same decisive and transformative significance for that individual's subsequent self-understanding. In the same way, the first love is the love that comes to itself as love for another. This only happens once, even if one falls in love many times.

This change in consciousness is a product of the fact that it is foundational love, the God-created love in every person, that first makes itself known when a person falls in love. This renewed transformation has the character of being a one-off event, though each time we fall in love, we experience it as being the first event of its kind. Faith also brings about this radical transformation in a person. In faith everything becomes new. Faith is a relation to God in which you only enter once in *the moment* (PF, 28). In faith the moment has decisive significance, just as in falling in love for the first time, and the transformation of a person in faith is also by Kierkegaard described as a first-time experience. You only enter into faith once, even though faith can—and must—be kept alive as a continuous, vivid love of God. We have to do with a kind of daily repetition. The first-time character of both faith and falling in love points to another similarity between a lover and a believer. Let us now consider another possible point of resemblance.

Silence and Secrecy

In *Christian Discourses* silence is posited as the opposite of the attempt to justify one's faith or one's love, just as in *Fear and Trembling* Abraham's silence is emphasized as being precisely the decisive element in the unconditional obedience that makes him the father of faith. Silence thus seems to constitute a common mark of both being in love and faith.

Silence is not the same as being mute or lacking the ability to speak. That was not the case with Abraham either. Silence comes from refraining from justifying your being in love (or your faith, as in Abraham's case): "The one whom falling in love does not make silent is not in love, and so also with the true resolution" (CD, 245). Silence and the stillness that follows from it show precisely the fact that the person in love is at one with herself and does not need to explain herself or ask others for advice: "But the person who truly made up his mind, that person is in stillness" (UDVS, 20), as is said in the long confessional discourse that introduces *Upbuilding Discourses in Various Spirits*. This stillness also constitutes a point of similarity between the lover and the believer. Furthermore, this silence is attended by a certain secrecy:

> Is there perhaps something lacking in faith since in this way it is and remains and ought to be a secret? Is this also the case with erotic love, or is it not just the transient emotions that become manifest immediately and therefore in turn immediately vanish, while the deep impression always keeps the secret, so that we even say, and rightly so, that the falling in love that does not make a person secretive is not real falling in love. Secret falling in love can be an image of faith. (WL, 28)

It is important to stress that when silence is asserted to be a mark of being in love, this does not mean that the lover must not express his love to the beloved or to others. In a certain sense, one cannot refrain from doing so (WL, 11). Love impresses itself not just via bodily expressions but also verbally. Silence, stillness, and secrecy are thus marks of both being in love and of faith. They are not invisible marks but in fact are visible through the way passion manifests itself in a person.

Conclusion

I have put forward above some points of resemblance between a lover and a believer. These points of resemblance allow us to see that there are no watertight boundaries between our religious and human experiences when it comes to love. Being in love and having faith are two phenomena that are experienced in the same way: both faith and being in love are preferential forms of love. They are conscious and intentional forms of love. Both falling in love and faith are two-sided relations that are characterized by silence and secrecy, but at the same time, both faith and falling in love are visible through a wholehearted passion in the lover or the believer. It is passion that has the character of a first-time experience that constitutes a radical transformation of the believer and the lover and combines these to create passionate experiences: "Behold, erotic love is a qualification of subjectivity . . . behold, faith is indeed the highest passion of subjectivity" (CUP, 132).

In this short study, I have tried to argue for this interaction between faith and falling in love, but of course this connection is not a rational structure; instead it is an experienced interconnection that only makes itself known through what I (with Marion) would like to call "the erotics of wisdom."[9] The passion of faith and falling in love can never be explained, but it has its own form of rationality, a certain structure that I have tried to show by this analysis of faith and falling in love.

Of course, Kierkegaard shares the view that love is inexplicable and enigmatic. But that love cannot be explained and rationally justified does not mean that it cannot be described and felt. This is due to love's passionate dimension, and to the fact that there is an intimate connection between love and the body. It is a connection that simply allows the urge to love to be noticeable in and through the body of a person.

A person's interior is thus the source of love's life, of its expressions. The body forms the basis for these expressions. For this reason, we can even speak of love making itself known within a person, and this is the reason why we, on a purely phenomenological level, can become acquainted with love's life. In *The Erotic Phenomenon*, Jean-Luc Marion suggests that we have a universal human experience of love's strength and transforming power, and he attacks what he calls "the erotic blindness of metaphysics."[10] Instead, Marion wants to develop a concept of love that can contain the experience of love as an erotic phenomenon. In this short study, I have argued that Kierkegaard's view of love as a double-bound urge—a surplus and a need that manifests itself through a person's body—in some sense anticipates the phenomenological insights of Marion. It is my contention that Marion's insistence on love as an erotic engagement is a very accurate description of the way Kierkegaard describes existence, erotic love, and faith as a passionate interest. This interest we can use as an erotic wisdom that combines our immediate experiences with love with the relation to God that we normally call faith.

Of course faith and falling in love are not the same forms of love. But they share the same passion and a lot of the same characteristics, and Kierkegaard even states that falling in love could lead a person in the direction of faith:

> For example, sometimes erotic love has probably helped a person along the right road. He faithfully willed only one thing, his love; for it he would live and die, for it he would sacrifice everything; in it alone he would have his happiness. In the deepest sense, however, falling in love is still not the good but possibly became for him a formative educator that finally led him, by winning the beloved or perhaps by losing her, in truth to will one thing and to will the good. Thus a person is brought up in many ways; an honest erotic love is also an upbringing to the good. (UDVS, 35)

Therefore there is no need to cast off erotic love as a secondhand love compared to Christian love. Instead we should learn from the passion of erotic love what it feels like to be passionate in faith.

PIA SØLTOFT is Associate Professor of Systematic Theology at the University of Copenhagen. She is author of *Kunsten at vælge sig selv: Om Kierkegaard, coaching og lederskab* and *Kierkegaard og kærlighedens skikkelser.*

Notes

1. Love is God's finest gift to humanity, for "what gift of God is comparable to love, which he implanted in the human heart?" (WL, 163.)

2. Jean-Luc Marion, *The Erotic Phenomenon*, trans. Stephen E. Lewis (Chicago: University of Chicago Press, 2007), p. 7.

3. In *The Sickness Unto Death*, despair is defined precisely as a form of loss-of-self, and one could say that in this work, Kierkegaard investigates the various ways in which a person can lose himself or herself. This leads to an analysis of the various forms of despair and their symptoms, "but all its symptoms are also dialectical, and therefore the superficial view is very easily deceived in determining whether or not despair is present" (SUD, 24). In *Works of Love*, Kierkegaard investigates the various forms of love and their symptoms, so as to be able to say on this basis what the correct understanding of love is.

4. Rick Anthony Furtak, *Wisdom in Love: Kierkegaard and the Ancient Quest for Emotional Integrity* (Notre Dame, IN: University of Notre Dame Press, 2005), p. 96.

5. Note that here and below, I have altered the Hongs' translation of *Trang* from "need" to "urge."

6. This misinterpretation may have to do with a statement in the historical introduction to the English translation of *Works of Love*, where it is suggested that not only does the Danish word *elskov* (translated as "erotic love") cover a different form of love than Christian love,

which is of course true, but *elskov*/erotic love is also said to be in contrast to Christian love, which is not at all the case, as I will show in the following analysis (WL, xi).

7. C. S. Lewis, *The Four Loves* (Orlando, FL: Harcourt Brace, 1960), p. 2.

8. Zygmunt Bauman, *Liquid Love: On the Frailty of Human Bonds* (Cambridge: Polity, 2003), p. 3.

9. Marion, *The Erotic Phenomenon*, p. 3.

10. Marion, *The Erotic Phenomenon*, p. 7.

4 The Integration of Neighbor-Love and Special Loves in Kierkegaard and von Hildebrand

John J. Davenport

Recent Debates about Kierkegaard on Love and the Root of the Tensions

In recent Kierkegaard scholarship, there has been a vigorous and fascinating discussion of the relation between neighbor-love and the other forms of interhuman love. The topic is important in its own right beyond work on Kierkegaard, because all plausible ethical outlooks must grapple with the question of how attention to particular loved ones and "significant others" can and should ideally integrate with more universally directed benevolence or care for humanity in general. This problem is also existentially crucial because the various forms of love help to give shape to our purposes and meaning to our lives. Among them, romantic love that may be consecrated in marriage, deep affection among family members, close bonds with a few dear friends, and wider relations of care for one's associates are central to our lives in contemporary cultures. Such personal relations seem to be found in cultures around the world and through time, although arguably Western cultures are especially influenced by the romantic tradition dating from the courtly love genre.[1] We do not think of these "special loves" as especially self-interested,[2] because their authentic or primary forms include concern for the loved person's well-being for his or her own sake (while love of friend, child, or erotic partner as a mere means to one's other ends are *deficient* versions of such loves, at best). But we commonly recognize that these special loves are distinct from a rarer form of love that is held up in biblical religions as the central virtue: namely, the agape that names God's pure love for creatures beyond anything they can merit, deserve, or reciprocate, and its human expression as "love of neighbor." Unlike the special loves, love of neighbor is described by its adherents as a duty that should extend to all persons. In this respect, love of neighbor should be like universal benevolence in Stoic and Buddhist traditions but with special appreciation for the uniqueness of each human person as a center of free will capable of responding to human and divine love and of loving others in turn.

Thus it should disturb us that some nineteenth- and twentieth-century philosophers and theologians, starting with the famous Danish existential thinker Søren Kierkegaard, have argued that this morally required form of neighbor-love is contrary in most respects to the motives that constitute human special loves, which Kierkegaard seems to characterize as self-interested and possessive by contrast (e.g., WL, 53, 267). After Kierkegaard, though arguably independent of his influence,[3] the Swedish theologian Anders Nygren drove the wedge deeper in an influential work titled *Agape and Eros*. There he developed Plato's account of love in the *Symposium* as a sense of *lack-seeking-completion*, or a feeling that we need some good that the loved person promises to add to our being. Broadening this model of eros, Plato had argued that all human motives have this "erosiac" form—an idea taken up and developed throughout the eudaimonist tradition.[4] Nygren argued that agapic love does *not* seek the lover's fulfillment through unification with the beloved or loved object, but instead projects from the agapic lover toward the neighbor without regard to the lover's gains or the neighbor's merits, qualities, or features.[5] In this, Nygren seems to follow Luther's view that there is no right form of self-love as desire for *eudaimonia*.[6] Contrast this with Aristotle's account of noble friendship (philia) as a love that indeed seeks the friend's good, but out of admiration for his virtuous dispositions. As a result, some commentators like Daphne Hampson have compared Luther, Kierkegaard, and Nygren as all denying "that God takes up and transforms human love[s]" with agape.[7]

This dichotomy has deeply marked twentieth-century philosophical work on love. Although he denies that eros and agape are incompatible, C. S. Lewis famously contrasts them in a way that parallels Nygren: while "Need-love," as Plato saw, is "the son of poverty" or lack, "the primal love is Gift-love. In God there is no hunger that needs to be filled."[8] The American analytic philosopher Alan Soble makes Nygren's dichotomy the basis of his analyses, dividing forms of love into those that are responsive to properties of their objects versus those that are not property-based.[9] And a series of continental thinkers from Martin Buber to Emmanuel Levinas, Gabriel Marcel, and now Jean-Luc Marion have conceived agapic love as a self-donating response to the other's "alterity," difference, or independent uniqueness (which transcends the other's iterable properties) that is totally without regard for the lover's self—although Buber, like Gene Outka, allows a legitimate hope for reciprocation.

Are we then stuck with the conclusion that the special loves are always distorted by self-interest because of their erosiac interest in self-actualization, their neediness, or their possessiveness? The evidence for this view in Kierkegaard's *Works of Love* is puzzling, because in his pseudonymous *Either-Or*, the younger Kierkegaard actually defended romantic love as consecrated in marriage. In the voice of Judge William, he argued that conjugal love is upbuilding, propelling the

nascent spirit toward the ethical "stage" of existence, in which eternal moral considerations provide a firmer basis for a personal identity defined by commitments
that can last over time.[10] As Michael Strawser puts it, in the Judge's conception
(with its clear debts to Hegel), "both romantic love and marital love are faithful,"
as the lover wills them to endure on an eternal basis.[11]

This apparent tension between the Dane's earlier and later texts has been
explored in several recent works, starting with M. Jamie Ferreira's master-
ful monograph on *Works of Love*, which argues that Kierkegaard's considered
view is actually that the special loves can be made consistent with the duties of
neighbor-love when they are checked by "conscience," understood as a moral
sense that limits what we may legitimately do for (or to) the persons whom we
love as family members, friends, romantic partners, etc.[12] Sharon Krishek has
responded by arguing in effect that this solution leaves us in "infinite resignation" in Kierkegaard's sense: while Ferreira's interpretation may be generally
correct, *Works of Love* still fails to appreciate the full value and potential of the
special-love relationships, because it fails to affirm the value of earthly, temporal
goods in the robust way that these are affirmed in Abrahamic faith according
to *Fear and Trembling*.[13] A rich discussion has emerged from this interchange,
including rejoinders from Ferreira and Krishek,[14] and contributions by Sylvia
Walsh and John Lippitt,[15] who reconsider the role of proper (or agapic) self-love
that Ferreira introduced.[16] Several essays in a recent collection on love according to Kierkegaard and Harry Frankfurt also bear on my theme by clarifying
Kierkegaard's conception of neighbor-love and the form of special loves.[17] While
I am generally sympathetic with Krishek's position in these recent debates, I
will argue that Kierkegaard is not committed to Nygren's dichotomy; instead, he
leaves open the possibility of bringing agapic and special loves together.

Beyond Kierkegaard, the crucial question in moral psychology concerns how
we should conceive an ideal relation between the different kinds of love as a theoretical goal, or as a measure of the most adequate conception of the loves. The
recent developments in Kierkegaard scholarship are especially significant in this
context, because the conundrum of how to connect special loves and agapic love
has been largely ignored in the (otherwise rich) revival of work on love in analytic
philosophy, and the problems that Kierkegaard encountered in addressing this
conundrum are symptomatic of its deepest difficulties. For example, one solution
might be to lower expectations for the special loves. Soble focuses on the worry
that property-responsive special loves would be objectifying, valuing the beloved
simply for qualities that can change. He responds that we should bite this bullet,
arguing that "personal love is adequately understood within the eros tradition,
that we need not appeal to elements of the agape tradition to salvage personal
love . . . [and] that personal love should not be pictured as constant, exclusive,
and reciprocal"—aspects that are harder to justify on property-responsive

views—although he argues that agape also cannot support exclusive love for any one person.[18]

My initial ideal for the personal or special loves is almost the opposite of Soble's. I hold that the best outcome would be that neighbor-love is not only *compatible* with the special loves but can also be expressed *in and through* the other loves (including even romantic love)—even if such transformed special loves have lost the naive confidence in our capacities that they have in the natural attitude.[19] Of course, this is not proposed as part of a definition of the special loves; rather, it is a *normative* ideal, which I call "agapic infusion" of the special loves, that has been implicit in the recent Kierkegaard debates. Note that this has nothing directly to do with virtues "infused" by grace: the question is whether any conception of agapic and personal loves that is true to their most evident aspects can explain the possibility of agapic care living within the special loves. Ferreira recognizes this goal in Kierkegaard's *Works of Love*, specifically in his idea that "neighbor-love, *Kjerlighed*, is not a 'higher' love that should replace or be added to erotic love and friendship ([WL] pp. 45, 58). Kierkegaard says quite straightforwardly that the goal is to preserve love for the neighbor in erotic love and friendship ([WL] p. 62). Nonpreferential [agapic] love is to 'permeate' all expressions of love—to transform them—yet not in the sense of adding something to them . . ." ([WL] p. 112).[20] Yet in her interpretation, Kierkegaard's solution is mainly to say that all the particularized ways in which we may love those few persons with whom we have special relations, attending to their concrete needs and circumstances, should pass the test of "conscience." This means that the same ethical obligations we have to all other persons also apply to our family members, friends, and romantic partners—that we are first and foremost neighbors means that everyone deserves "the fundamental respect appropriate to our equality before God."[21] It also means that the extra attentions we give to those persons whom we love in the special ways should not prevent our doing our duty to strangers. Aside from questions about how this balance is defined, though, this resolution makes neighbor-love mainly into a *negative check* on the "preferential" loves, as Kierkegaard calls them: it does not provide an adequate sense in which agapic regard can be positively expressed in differentiated ways *within and by* the types of caring that are essential to the preferential loves, as infusion requires. Ferreira repeatedly notes textual evidence that Kierkegaard only means to reject the "selfishness" in (unmodified) preferential loves (including self-love), but without fully explaining how the special loves can *remain* in some respects "preferential" or limited to a few persons without being "selfish."[22]

This understandable focus on a negative checking function reappears in John Lippitt's view that not all specific forms of preferential love can "pass this test" of being in accordance with the good, which he later calls "the God filter" (this is "part of what is meant by God being the 'middle term'" in all proper special love-relationships).[23] While such filtering is surely part of the answer, it cannot be the whole of it, because Kierkegaard in *Either/Or* II clearly also imagines God as inspiring infinite commitment in romantic love (and by extension in other special loves), giving it the stamp of "eternity." In this respect, God plays a positive role more consistent with infusion: we can see the special beloved as a gift related to our unique calling or divinely given vocation. Lippitt rightly stresses (against Krishek) that Kierkegaard's insistence on the equality of (constitutive ontological) value in all persons need not imply "an equality of treatment which makes it impossible to distinguish my love for my beloved from my love for the stranger."[24] But if the reasons for different treatment of others in various special relations are just *extra* to agapic regard, we do not have positive expression of agapic love *in these tailorings* of our responses to distinct persons. Then whatever justification my preferences for particular others (or perhaps my particular awareness of their distinguishing merits) provide for treating my special beloveds differently—which often includes legitimately giving them deeper sorts of attention—these special cares and attentions operate merely *over and above* my agapic recognition of equal inherent value in my child, brother, wife, and stranger. The two are not interwoven in such a way that the special cares also express agapic devotion in their very distinctness.

Hence I judge that Krishek was on the right track in looking for an agapic way to affirm the concrete particulars valued within the special loves: the main problem with her critique of Kierkegaard's *Works of Love* is that she does not quite pin down the need for infusion as the root of the other problems she identifies. She says that Kierkegaard's conception of neighbor-love is inadequate because he limits it to an equal empathetic care or compassion for all persons (given their equal inherent value), to which other kinds of attitudes and valuations that distinguish the special loves are merely tacked on:

> Accordingly, when Kierkegaard requires that our preferential loves be manifestations of neighbourly love—a love that should be equally directed at everybody—the implicit conclusion is that elements that cannot be directed equally at everybody (like passionate longing, emotional affinity, spiritual kinship, exclusive intimacy, and so on) become inessential to love. . . . [E]quality, which is essential to neighbourly love, cannot include elements that are *precisely the constituents of preferential love*. Thus, taking neighbourly love . . . as the model for all love means that these elements are wiped aside as something superfluous.[25]

So Krishek thinks that Kierkegaard's difficulties stem from conceiving neighbor-love as the authentic form of all love, which makes the special loves count as *loving at all* only in virtue of their including agapic respect and empathy that is equally directable to all, and *not* insofar as they are preferential. In other words, the non-universal attention in special loves has no ultimate value, and the lover's

own desires and needs (which might pick out particular beloveds) play no positive role. There are plenty of passages that suggest this problem. For example, in
the Second Series, Kierkegaard argues that the one who truly loves cannot be
deceived by a sly seducer seeking love, given that the ideal agapic lover "loves
him because the true lover loves all" (WL, 240). Kierkegaard sometimes seems to
conflate not demanding reciprocal love from those we love (WL, 237–241) with
loving all persons in the same way.

Yet in my view, this alleged demotion of special loves to a merely secondary
role, adding nothing to authentic "loving," is only a symptom of the deeper problem: the distinctive motives and intentions that vary among special loves must
themselves be able to express agapic care; more strongly, they might be part of the
only way to show adequate neighbor-love to particular others in some situations.
This synthesis suggests that in certain cases, the only adequate way to love the
other *as neighbor* might be to love that person precisely *as* one's parent, friend, or
even romantic partner as well; and it is only when we have an account that can
support this sort of conclusion that we have fully resolved the apparent conflict.
Call this goal *robust infusion*. One might propose alternatives for Kierkegaard's
approach that meet Krishek's conditions without adequately resolving this underlying issue.[26] On the other hand, it should be evident that an account of neighbor-
love that supported robust infusion would necessarily satisfy Krishek's worries.[27]

Krishek's diagnosis of the problem thus leads her to a solution that "allows for
the coexistence" of agapic and special loves; they are compatible because special
loves add to a basis or kernel provided by neighbor-love.[28] But this relation remains
only additive, as when a friend with whom we shared committed philia also happens to hire us for a monthlong job, briefly adding another aspect to our relation;
the two motives are not fused or interwoven. By emphasizing the need for a conception of love that supports robust infusion or internal integration of agapic and
special loves, I hope to build on insights that emerged in the Ferreira–Krishek–
Lippitt–Walsh dialogues, and to suggest a better way forward. In what follows,
I first break down the various problems in Kierkegaard's account of agapic and
special loves in a way that clarifies why the issue of infusion lies at their root. Part
of the goal here is to detail the logic of the problem with greater rigor that should
help in articulating solutions. Then I argue that Dietrich von Hildebrand's work
on love offers better steps toward a fully satisfactory set of solutions.

Kierkegaard's Erosiac Conception of "Preferential Loves" in Their Natural Forms

I begin with three notes on Kierkegaard's treatment of special loves in his influential *Works of Love*. First, this book supports much of what is said about ethical life in his other texts, such as the pseudonymous *Either/Or* vol. II, *Fear and
Trembling*, and the occasional discourse on "Purity of Heart" (Ferreira rightly

emphasizes the links between this discourse and *Works of Love*). Second, like Aquinas, Kierkegaard treats the agapic ideal of religious faith as a revealed command that "did not arise in any human being's heart" (WL, 24), and he holds that loving in this way requires grace—although not necessarily special grace to particular individuals, as Kierkegaard says more than once that God's love is the secret, hidden wellspring of all human loves (WL, 8, 146).[29] I will call this the "unified-source thesis." Third, as if to emphasize this, Kierkegaard does not refer to "agapic" love but instead uses a word for spiritual love (*Kjerlighed*) that is more neutral in connotation (implying affection and even fondness): as Carl Hughes notes, this term has a more general sense in Danish, including *Elskov* among other types of love as its species.[30] This serves Kierkegaard's apparent desire to indicate how spiritual love can inform the other types of interhuman love—although positing a unitary source only stipulates infusion without explaining how it is could work psychologically.[31] However, I will still use "agape" as synonymous with neighbor-love for Kierkegaard because, as we will see, he describes its motive-structure in ways that fit several (if not all) features of agape as conceived in Lutheran thought.

As I have noted, what von Hildebrand calls the "natural categories of love" for family members, friends, spouse, and the like,[32] which contemporary theorists refer to as "special loves," Kierkegaard terms "preferential loves" to emphasize that they single out particular people: "to love this one person above all others, to love him in contrast to all others" (WL, 19). He seems to have "best friends" and romantic partnerships especially in mind in choosing the "preferential" label to contrast with neighbor-love's universal directedness toward all neighbors without distinction or exception. In hindsight, though, this way of naming the difference between agapic and natural/special loves may have been a rhetorical mistake, for it may appear to conflate focusing on particular individuals, or even preferring them *comparatively* to others (WL, 19), with loving people *for* their bodily, psychic, social, and historical properties (both intrinsic and relational), when these are not obviously equivalent. Moreover, it may obscure rather than clarify Kierkegaard's main objection to familiar interhuman loves. As most recent commentators agree, his complaint is really that the special loves are (at least partly?) self-interested: such loves prefer certain individuals because of their particular properties, to which the loving agent desires to relate (bodily, emotionally, or cognitively), given their apparent value for the lover's life. Thus the loves that poets celebrate are "secretly self-love" (WL, 19). The lover is drawn to these distinguishing properties in the beloved because relating to their goodness promises to enrich his or her being in some way, or to bring fulfillment. This is why Kierkegaard asserts that "passionate preferential love is another form of self-love" (WL, 53), as if all special loves are subsumed under our desire for our own *eudaimonia*. This self-interest in the special loves might not always lead the lover to *selfish* or illegitimate ways of pursuing his own good in the special relations, but it opens up this risk.

Call this the "preference-implies-self-interest" thesis. Most of the issues in the recent debates depend on how this claim is interpreted; the main strategy of Kierkegaard's defenders, such as Ferreira and Lippitt, has been to argue that Kierkegaard really means that preference *plus something else*—something that can be removed from special loves—entails self-interest, which always taints the *purity* of such loves, even if it does not become selfishness that pursues the lover's own good to a morally suspect extent. Though *Works of Love* is not sufficiently clear on Kierkegaard's reasons for this key thesis, we can find clues in several places. It is not just that in erotic love and friendship, we are self-loving by indulging our personal tastes, or perhaps by only loving people similar to ourselves (as his reference to "the pagans" suggests [WL, 21]). The deeper problem is that such devotions, at least in their default or natural-aesthetic forms, are not based on anything higher, any objective good to which they respond for its own sake (WL, 29–30). Instead, "this [preferential] love actually gives itself the significance by which it swears" (WL, 30), or tries to, anyway; we see this when two lovers "swear by their love to love each other forever, instead of swearing love to each other by eternity" (WL, 31). This point directly repeats Judge William's critique of the aesthete who wants to bind himself to an exclusive romantic relation with his beloved by swearing on the moon or some similar symbol of romantic pathos itself, rather than by devotion to any eternal ethical ideal that could justify enduring commitment and thereby operate as a middle term or "third power" (EO II, 55–56). This suggests that the deeper problem with special loves is that they can be shallow: they may only love the other person for a constellation of superficial traits that have no eternal significance. In such cases, as a loving agent, I respond to no other values in the friend, family member, or erotic beloved except those that are *conferred* by my prior inclinations (or dispositions), which themselves derive from no objective justification. Such Humean loves, as we might call them, thus lack "enduring continuance"; their motivating power can disappear quickly if my appetites alter or the beloved loses those properties that my extant inclinations happen to light up as good (WL, 31, 36).

On this reading, the main problem with special loves is not that they only or primarily *aim* at the lover's own gain; although Kierkegaard suggests that what we call "love" is sometimes only an instrumental interest in another person (WL, 7), this is obviously not true in all special love-relations. Rather, shallowness results from my love being too dependent on passive aspects of my own psyche (which is why it can look narcissistic for the lover to insist too strongly on pursuing her merely accidental preferences). The possessive aspect that makes some special loves prone to jealous preoccupation similarly derives from too much dependence on "spontaneous" desires that are both contingent and passive rather than controlled by authoritative sources of agency (WL, 34–35). Thus, underlying Kierkegaard's distinction between preferential and agapic loves is "the difference there is between the play of feelings, drives, inclinations, and passions, in short that play of the powers of immediacy . . . in desire or in want—what a difference between this and the earnestness of eternity, the earnestness of the commandment" (WL, 25; compare WL, 50).

In other words, the appetites of our "immediate" nature are passively acquired or given by our animal form, whereas neighbor-love "is a matter of conscience and thus is not a matter of drives and inclinations" (WL, 143). Neighbor-love displays a different *motivational relation* between agent and end/goal: it aims at the well-being of the neighbor for her own sake, but the agent *actively sets* this end rather than merely being *drawn* toward the neighbor's good, as might occur if she saw the neighbor's good as part of her own happiness or perfection. Thus we have "*to will* to love the neighbor" against the grain of human nature, instinctive inclination, social mores, and peer pressure (WL, 81, my italics). Like Kantian "good will," then, agape is a volitional motive that must be actively worked up by the agent, rather than caused by the magnetic appeal of the goal, given our natural desire for happiness or completion: it is free of "natural determinants" (WL, 56), including even the general desire for eudaimonia.

Call this the "volitional thesis": agapic love is more autonomous because it is grounded on freely accepted obligation (WL, 37) and requires a choice of attitude (WL 234); we *will* our commitment to the other as neighbor, beyond any passively occurring motive within our psyche. Thus neighbor-love is not dependent on the loved one in the way that acquisitive desire is (WL 38): because it flows from the agent's will rather than from given attraction, it "does not depend on the object of love" retaining its attractive qualities (WL, 39). Here is the true link between Kierkegaard's conception and Nygren's: Kierkegaard agrees that neighbor-love is a *non-erosiac* type of motive. Love actively "forms the heart" rather than being formed by "fleeting feelings" of inclination (WL, 12), and thus it is necessarily earnest (WL, 15, 25).[33] In that sense, agapic love is a work, an effort (WL, 14) involving continued striving, as we see in one who perseveres in "repaying evil with good over a long period of time" (WL, 334). Kierkegaard thus repeats Judge William's argument that an aesthetic love is heteronomous, having "the law of its existence outside itself," rather than "relating itself" back to itself in relating to its beloved (WL, 38)—which means freely willing the emotions and affections directed outward to the beloved.

This idea that neighbor-love is a motive with a non-erosiac structure helps to explain several other related theses that Kierkegaard adds soon after introducing his main distinction, including the following:

THE EQUALITY THESIS: Unlike preferential loves, neighbor-love shows *equal regard* for all other persons without distinction because it is not based on their (contingent or distinctive) features (WL, 19).

GOD AS MEDIATOR (OR GOD AS MIDDLE-TERM): Interhuman agapic love is founded on the eternal basis of God's equal creative relation to each person. God binds the lover and loved person together, and love of God is involved in the capacity of human beings to show neighbor-love to other human persons.

MISAPPROPRIATION: The (natural or pre-transfigured) preferential loves tend toward undue *possessiveness* (WL, 33–35); for example, jealousy lurks in friendships, and especially in the desire for exclusive or distinctive regard from the other, as Othello famously illustrated (WL, 54–55). Unchecked, this tendency can make special loves too controlling or can lead the lover to objectify the loved person.

NO RECIPROCATION-CONDITION: By contrast, agapic love does not demand reciprocation from the other (WL, 16) and thus does not aim at an exclusive relationship with the human other or God (WL, 27); the loving agent can hope that the beloved will freely reciprocate, but this can never be a condition for showing agapic regard (WL, 39–40).

These theses clarify the senses in which neighbor-love is free from types of self-interest that can sometimes distort our special loves (even if there are also legitimate forms of self-interest). Agapic caring does not intend to receive love in return (or to demand reciprocation), it does not possessively control the other to secure the loving agent's own good, and it does not give excessive authority to the agent's own contingent predilections.

If this is the correct interpretation, then Kierkegaard's claim that preferential loves tend toward selfishness does not mean what it first appears to say. The problem with preferential loves is that they are too beholden (in contemporary parlance) to *brute preferences*: they tend not to be responsive to "duty" or eternal requirement (WL, 33), and thus they lack the autonomy and staying power of agapic commitments. His "preferential" versus "nonpreferential" distinction thus derives mainly from an underlying implicit contrast between two adverbial *modes of motivation* (rather than different goal-contents involving our own good as opposed to the other's good) that is similar to Nygren's contrast between eros and agape. Moreover, in some passages, Kierkegaard seems to anticipate Nygren's contentious premise that if love is *property-based*, or responds to contingent features of the beloved that vary between people, then this love must be erosiac in form (a lack-seeking-completion) and so formally self-interested. It is apparently for this reason that God's love for us cannot be property-based (WL, 65).

So Kierkegaard is sometimes read as suggesting a Nygren-style argument that agapic love cannot respond to features of the loved person(s):

The First Nygren-Soble Argument That Agapic Love Is Not Property-Based[34]
E = erosiac love or form of attraction
P = property-based attention or response to loved person's/object's valuable traits
A = agapic love or regard (which must be active rather than drawn by attraction)
F = fungibility; the object of love is replaceable by another that is just as good or better
x = any instance of love
1. If Ex → Px (the premise that Nygren and Alan Soble draw from Plato's conception of eros-love)
2. If Px → Ex (a more controversial premise of Nygren's [and probably Soble too])
3. Hence, if not-Ex → not-Px (from 2 by transposition)
4. But if Ax → not-Ex (by definition of A above)
5. So Ax → not-Px (by hypothetical syllogism from 3 and 4)

I have previously called the second premise "Nygren's fallacy": he assumes that the only way to respond to attributes of the beloved (or object of love) is to feel a need of them for one's completion (and so to be drawn toward them). This is incorrect, since it is also possible to take the object's relevant properties as a justification for willed love of that object. So understood, agapic love is a species of "projective volition," or motivation that is worked up in response to objective or desire-independent practical grounds.[35] While erosiac love responds to its object's properties in a self-fulfillment-seeking way, as per premise 1, the converse (2) does not follow from this.

This suggests that rejecting premise 2 is a promising way forward. But Alan Soble has offered a slightly different way of arguing that agapic love cannot be responsive to properties of the beloved, which is also relevant for considering Kierkegaard's account:

The Second Nygren-Soble Argument
6. If Px → Fx (a Nygrenian premise conceiving value-properties as comparative)[36]
7. If Ax → not-Fx (common desideratum for an adequate conception of agapic love)
8. So if not-Fx → not-Px (from 6 by transposition)
9. Hence, if Ax → not-Px (by hypothetical syllogism from 7 and 8)

The problem with this argument lies in its first premise (6), which *generalizes* Nygren's idea that erosiac love has fungible objects because it loves these objects *for* their properties, while other potential objects could have the same properties or an even better array of them. This is false if there is another way of understanding the properties of a beloved person as a unique gestalt. For example, we may focus on the *particular historical way* that a single individual instantiates or combines her features, or include among the relevant properties our unique historical relation to the object.[37] In line with these responses to Nygren and Soble, I will argue that (despite appearances in some passages) Kierkegaard does not agree with Nygren that the only way for love to respond to features of the beloved is by way of erosiac attraction toward them; rather, he ultimately accepts that neighbor-love responds to a transcendent value found in each individual's uniqueness. Yet von Hildebrand will improve on Kierkegaard's efforts to avoid the fallacy that drives Nygren and Soble to deny responsiveness to loved ones' properties in agapic love.

The Infusion Thesis: How Can Agapic Love Inform/Transform Preferential Loves?

The basic problem now appears in a new light. Kierkegaard's unitary source-thesis implies that all human forms of love at least have some potential relation to *Kjerlighed* and ultimately to God's creative love as their source; this is one of his reasons for holding that agapic love demands giving people the benefit of the doubt, awakening their capacity to love by giving them every chance, and even showing our enemies agapic love that could inspire them to reconcile with us. Yet Kierkegaard's erosiac conception of the motives constituting special loves distinguishes them from agapic love. If preferential loves are erosiac and neighbor-love is non-erosiac in basic structure, they could only be co-present as distinct motives for the same act; they could not combine or synthesize. Even if it is only the natural or spontaneous forms of special loves that are entirely erosiac, adding agapic care to such erosiac motives merely results in having two different motives side by side (with the higher correcting the lower). Just as I might file an honest tax return both because it is morally right to do so and because it protects my financial interests, I might have more than one motive for benevolent action toward my friend or spouse.

Conceiving agapic duty as a kind of "filter" for the preferential loves works in just this way, via dual motives: conscience, through awareness of our obligations for neighbor-love, asks whether we are treating our friends, spouse, child, or coworker (and even ourselves) *also* as our neighbor, and whether we are attending sufficiently to strangers in need while devoting our special loves to these significant others on a preferential basis.[38] As Kierkegaard says, the husband may love "his wife in particular, but he must never love her in particular in such a way that she is an exception to being the neighbor that every human being is" as well (WL, 141–142); for example, he should respect her basic human rights. Yet, while agapic duty must always operate this way as a check on excesses of natural-preferential loves, this solution leaves us with two distinct loves, which Kierkegaard rejects: we cannot defend Christianity by saying that it "does indeed teach a higher love but *in addition* praises erotic love and friendship" (WL, 45). Moreover, a filter cannot tell us that we sometimes show *too little* of the relevant special-relationship love to certain persons, or explain how agapic love may be expressed *in and through* a given form of natural-preferential love. Sometimes what certain others need from us is to be distinguished from strangers, to be the object of special forms of attention as our child, friend, romantic partner, or fellow community member; perhaps that is even part of what we ought to give them *as neighbors*. This "infusion thesis" seems to be what Lewis meant in claiming that "the natural loves are summoned to becomes modes of Charity while also remaining the natural loves they were," rather than simply being replaced by agapic or divine love.[39]

There are several passages in *Works of Love* that could be read either in terms of the filtering/additive relation or as indicating Kierkegaard's intention to support infusion. For example, he says that Christianity demands that conscience spread to all the other loves, and that the neighbor-love commanded by Christianity "now takes possession of every other form of love"; thus it has made even "erotic love a matter of conscience" (WL, 140). In every special relationship, "in loving the beloved, we are first to love the neighbor"; so "your wife must first and foremost be to you the neighbor; that she is your wife is then a more precise specification of your particular relationship to each other. But what is the eternal foundation must be the foundation of every expression of the particular" (WL, 141).

A "foundation" seems to be different from a separate, higher motive that trumps or regulates the operation of other motives, as in Kant's idea that whatever first-order personal goals we pursue for ourselves and for our loved ones should conform to the second-order end of pursuing them only in morally legitimate ways (that are fair to each individual as a final end). Instead, Kierkegaard's language suggests that agapic love can operate within and transform all the natural forms of preferential love, so that erotic love, friendship, love of children, and even natural self-love are enhanced in their modes of special attention by awareness of the other person's transcendence and participation in divinity. As Kierkegaard puts it, agapic love willed by the human spirit and inspired by God's love "can lie at the base of and be present in every other expression of love" (WL, 146). He says that erotic love and friendship can be taught to "preserve love for the neighbor" within them. Thus Christianity does not ask us to give up the natural or preferential loves: "No, love the [romantic] beloved faithfully and tenderly, but let love for the neighbor be the sanctifying element in your union's covenant with God. Love your friend honestly and devotedly, but let love for the neighbor be what you learn from each other in your friendship's confidential relationship with God" (WL, 62).[40] This suggests that neighbor-love can contribute *positively* to all the other kinds of love, in which case it must enhance love of an other precisely *qua* sibling, parent, child, friend, partner in a vocation or good cause, or romantic beloved, enhancing what we will do for these others in light of what is special or distinctive about them in their concreteness and in our factical relation to them.[41] This means loving them as they are, rather than loving a false image of them (WL, 164), and recognizing that their personhood, which makes them equal to all other persons in deserving agapic regard, involves their ineffable, property-transcending uniqueness as well (WL, 68–69).

We find this point emphatically confirmed in the importance of preserving the other's "distinctiveness" according to the crucial section titled "Love Does Not Seek Its Own." This fits well with Anti-Climacus's pietist doctrine that each person is destined to a distinct identity defined by her or his unique God-given tasks, if only he or she will accept this divine vocation—as opposed to defiantly willing a different shape for himself or being "ground down smooth" into non-distinctiveness by mass aesthetic banality (SUD 33–34). This uniqueness, achieved by the agent's will working on the factical aspects of her embodied personality, is thus the correlate of existing in faith "before God": even the person who seems most insignificant in worldly terms, "if he has the courage to be himself before God, then he has distinctiveness" (WL, 271). Thus agapic love must aim to encourage and preserve this unique potential in the other, while the "domineering person" tries to impose his own arbitrary vision of the other's ideal shape on this other. Neighbor-love has *two* moments: "First, it makes no distinction," just as the equality thesis requires; but "next, which is just like the first, it infinitely distinguishes itself in loving the diverse," like the God who treasures the uniqueness of even the smallest flower (WL, 270). The combination of these movements is infusion.

Moreover, it is easier to see how agape can work positively within the special loves in this light. While the tyrannical erotic lover wants "to crush the other person's distinctiveness or torment it to death" in order to mold her according to his own aesthetic ideal, the agapic romancer treasures her beloved for his unique calling, the mystery of his alterity. While the "small-minded" person uncomfortable with her own distinctiveness will not befriend another who does not fit the narrow typology that she idolizes, the agapic friend does not try to make his companion into a "likeness" of himself, but instead cherishes his friend for her special gifts and surprising individuality (WL 271–273). Similarly, the truly loving parent tends the infant even when she does not cry to demand attention and without repayment by gratitude (WL 349–352), and must have the authority that is "grounded in truly willing, with eternal responsibility, the best for the child" (WL, 236). So it seems that agapic love not only can keep us from doing wrong in the name of our special loves, but it can also inspire the best kinds of special loves.

Yet if the preferential loves are all primarily erosiac, then the lover will always be aiming at his own perfection through the special relation with the loved ones rather than aiming at the loved person's good, or at encounter with her uniqueness, simply for the loved one's own sake. One way we might avoid this result is to explain the flaw in special loves in terms of their tendency towards *possessiveness* (e.g., jealous desire to exclude third parties from friendship with our friend [WL, 54], or insistence that no other man can even see our wife's face). This kind of possessiveness is a clear indication that our love for the other consists partly in our interest in how (some of) their features contribute to our own material or psychic well-being, e.g., by enhancing our pleasures, status, sense of special privileges, prospects of healthy children, flattering self-image, or even by the envy of others.[42] This interpretation locates the conflict with agapic regard in a contingent aspect of the special loves, rather than in their essential form. Then, even if they naturally begin with a possessive cast, infusion with agape can rid the special loves of possessiveness, thus allowing the lover to appreciate for himself or herself the freedom, mystery, or *alterity* of the other—a term from Levinas that I use to stand for all that makes it wrong and ultimately impossible to possess another person. While there are many hints in this direction in *Works of Love*, Kierkegaard seems to explain the possessive tendency largely in terms of the erosiac structure of special loves: we insist on following our arbitrary "natural predispositions" (WL, 55). Still, as we have seen, the willfulness that inspires possessive attitudes may also arise from the agent's domineering insistence that others "be trimmed according to his pattern for human beings," which is at bottom a defiant rejection of the distinctiveness that God intends for them (WL, 270).[43]

This diagnosis points toward a better solution found in Kierkegaard's argument that the love-command is a duty to "love the people we see" in their concrete particularity, despite all their flaws. In this section, he suggests that we can *will* devotion to our "beloved" or "friend" as that individual person who underlies all their features and traits, and remains the same even when these change (WL, 164–165). That kind of love expresses faith in the beloved individual beyond all of his or her imperfections, and thus it recognizes his or her ultimate potential. For example, consider the nephew in Dickens's famous story who remains loyal to his uncle Scrooge in the conviction that within him, a better man is struggling to get out. Or consider, even more poignantly, Cordelia's abiding love for her errant father King Lear (in Shakespeare's greatest work). In these examples, love operates within the bond of close kinship but is infused with a saving hope; it clearly transcends any natural or non-willed kind of human affection. Kierkegaard envisions this kind of unconditional commitment being given within a special relation to particular people, so that we view imperfections in our lovers, relatives, or friends not as reasons to withdraw, but instead as tests to *overcome together* (WL, 166–167). Such solidarity is possible within special loves in our experience, and it illustrates another positive relation between agapic and natural-preferential loves.

This route has two promising features. First, it accepts that in special relations, our motive *can* become pure of self-interest:[44] we can love the other person for his or her own sake, apart from our anticipated benefits from the other (or from loving interaction with the beloved)—which is the purity most exemplified in Christ's love (WL, 100). The test Kierkegaard sets out for such purity is that the "person aflame with erotic love" would "give up the erotic love if the beloved required it" (WL, 21)—or in general, if the loved person's good could only be secured by resignation that gave up cultivation of the special relation. Kierkegaard repeats this test in discussing the importance of valuing the other's God-given uniqueness. "Erotic love and friendship love the beloved and the friend according to his distinctiveness," but only within this limit: "they can give up all things for the other's distinctiveness, but not themselves." By contrast, the romantic lover or friend inspired by agape should be able to let the beloved or friend go, if that is the only way to avoid warping or ruining their destined identity (WL, 273).

Second, on this approach, special loves can include this kind of pure care for the other's good without becoming nothing more than (what we might call) the bare agapic regard owed even to complete strangers, because the purified special love focuses on the other as *unique and irreplaceable*. This uniqueness thesis is often occluded in *Works of Love*, because Kierkegaard stresses the equality of all neighbors with its correlate universality thesis so much: "the other human being is every other human being . . . . *Love for the neighbor is therefore the eternal equality in loving*, but the eternal equality is the opposite of preference" (WL, 58). Yet, like Buber and Levinas after him, Kierkegaard still holds that no person-*qua*-neighbor can be exchanged for any other, for *each* is infinitely valuable as a distinct individual: "The neighbor is the utterly unrecognizable dissimilarity between persons or is the eternal equality before God" (WL, 68). God loves and judges each person as a unique individual (WL, 69–70, compare 97), but this individuation is largely invisible to ordinary sight, because it is not determined by distinguishing earthly traits: as we saw, it instead flows from being "before God," or from being created capable of self-direction (WL 274). The paradox that makes agapic infusion possible is that all are equally unique: "distinctiveness is not mine but is God's gift by which he gives being to me, and he indeed gives it to all" (WL 271).

This combination of equality and uniqueness has an ontological basis. God can give being in such a way that the created person "does not become nothing"

(WL 271–272) or a mere part of God's being, but instead is free in relation to God. In other words, God is the unique source of personal alterity, and alterity is equal in all persons, not in virtue of properties that constitute merits or demerits, but rather in being unique as free sources of response to given facticity, with the capacity for commitment and potential to love. Moreover, within the human species, "each individual is the essentially different or distinctive" because God relates to each in a way that transcends the application of universal moral standards to all of them (WL 230)—for example, by assigning tasks to each person beyond what shared ethical standards require, as *Fear and Trembling* argued. The "common watermark" that they all share (WL, 89) is thus not a *property* in the ordinary sense of a multiply instantiable universal: persons are all equally "spirit," but that is precisely what transcends rational comparisons between them and makes each irreplaceable.

If this is right, then loving all equally as persons requires treasuring their non-fungibility, which provides a possible point of convergence between agapic and special loves.[45] While our agapic love for our neighbor cannot be based on any critical assessment of her merits, we serve the neighbor as a particular person (WL, 165–167), not as an instance of persons collectively; our more particular relations with that person must then matter in a loving response to them. Agape-infused love of children, friends, or romantic partners would then value their traits (in some cases, even as merits) but also look beyond such properties to the "spirit" or individual center of agency that *lives out* these features, and that is always more than its present traits, given both freedom and future potential. The loving agent who values the individual for his or her distinctive traits should also treasure the radically individual spirit "behind" those traits as well, thus profoundly *deepening* the special relation itself. Classical accounts of eros and philia make them *entirely* property-based and thus render their objects fungible, but we are not forced to stop at this level. *Essentially particularistic* versions of the "preferential" loves value more than a set of traits; they also break the link between property-focus and possessiveness, because they value the other for her own sake, *beyond* whatever they value in her present features.[46]

I believe that this solution is on the right track, because it provides a clear way of explaining why special loves are not *essentially* self-interested: the lover (X) can move beyond focusing only on features (F) of the loved person (Y) that can benefit him (X), both by valuing F *apart* from their likely benefit to X (i.e., valuing F as admirable in an agent-neutral sense), and by valuing Y as *transcending* F. It thus explains how Kierkegaard can describe the natural loves positively as a "noble fire" that can be infused with agape (WL, 62). As we will see, von Hildebrand effectively pursues this idea. But in working out how agapic attention to uniqueness interacts with the attitudes and motives that constitute special loves, we have to avoid a pitfall: while the agapic aspects add willed commitment into X's prior attraction to Y's features, X should not view these natural attractions or psychic bonds to Y as a *mere occasion* for focusing his volitional energy on this particular person. If Y is seen as a mere occasion in this sense, then X will not really express agapic love to Y *through* his special responses to her intrinsic and relational features as a family member, friend, or erotic beloved, which infusion requires.

Von Hildebrand is sensitive to this distinction. Like Kierkegaard, he is not a eudaimonist; he implicitly recognizes what I have called projective motivation; and he also aims to justify the infusion thesis. Thus, comparing their accounts may help move the recent debates forward.

Von Hildebrand's Solutions on Different Levels

Works of Love was written to be edifying, not as an analytical treatise. The more systematic work of Dietrich von Hildebrand on love offers us possible ways to solve the problems that Kierkegaard faces in explaining how transformed versions of special loves can embody neighbor-love within them. Relying primarily on chapters 6–7 and 9–10 of von Hildebrand's *The Nature of Love*, I will briefly explain four key points in his account of the different kinds of love and relations between them, and I will note how each of these points improves on Kierkegaard's picture. Until the last point, I ignore the subtle distinction that he draws between *caritas* and love of neighbor, which is not found in Kierkegaard (although Nygren also emphatically distinguishes them).

The Priority of the Beloved in Authentic Natural Loves as I–Thou Relations

Von Hildebrand's account of the natural loves is superior because it insists that their relation to my "subjectivity," including my concern for my own happiness through these loves (NL, 209), does not make them simply egoistic—either in the Hobbesian sense of looking for relations with material benefit to me, or in the sense of Platonic eros as "an appetitus" for the lover's own perfection (NL, 123). Against this, von Hildebrand argues that in natural loves, the push toward union with the beloved has the character of Martin Buber's I–Thou encounter with another person in all her alterity (NL, 125), which he says is achieved by an "interpenetration of looks" (NL, 126—clearly a Buberian idea).[47] So the anticipated union with my beloved, which I fully hope will contribute to my own happiness when completed in the beloved's reciprocation, is still *secondary* to my concern for the "objective good" of the beloved for her own sake (NL, 147). In fact, he argues that all authentic value-response aims simply to appreciate and express objective value "as important in itself," quite apart from the "subjective needs and appetites" of the responding agent.[48] On this more Catholic account, my primary response in authentic special loves is to the other's unique value that arises "in the realm" of other values associated with her (NL, 129).

Such loves retain their eudaimonist aspect: in agreeing with Kierkegaard that *Eigenleben* (or proper self-concern for one's subjective personality) is crucial for a good human life, von Hildebrand argues that this right self-love is a necessary basis for the other special loves (NL, 215). Yet in such loves, "the happiness and salvation of the beloved person rank higher than the happiness of my union with him" (NL, 212); so my happiness through close relation with the beloved is also intended, but *only secondarily*.[49] Von Hildebrand here recovers an insight from Aristotle's account of friendship, namely that we can care about another person's good for its own sake while also hoping for happiness through union with them. And beyond this, for von Hildebrand, the happiness I derive from completion of a loving relation is at least partly a *by-product* of my devotion to the values manifested by my beloved and to the beloved's good for their own sake (NL, 132).[50] Relative to my primary goal in loving actions toward my beloved, my happiness from the union is an unintended side-effect (even if I expect it); but at a secondary level, it is also thematic for me and intended, though only equally to my hope that the union will also contribute to my beloved's happiness in turn (NL, 132).[51] Thus in natural loves, I am concerned for the loved one *for her own sake*, but I am also concerned about achieving and sustaining my particular relation with her.

A strict Kierkegaardian might respond that this is a very optimistic picture of the special loves that describes their ideal state when they avoid the many types of possessiveness, distortion by interest in our own perfection, and concern for material benefits that the beloved brings, along with the side benefit that I get to ignore needy others—the ills that Kierkegaard stresses in his critiques of real-life preferential loves, for which "self-denial" is the antidote.[52] In fact, von Hildebrand does distinguish authentic natural loves from their "baptized" state infused with *caritas* (NL, 252), as we will see later. But he gives a convincing description of special loves which shows that in their authentic form, they are not simply possessive or selfish. Most importantly, by adding the Buberian I–Thou union with the other treasured as irreplaceable and unpossessable, von Hildebrand develops the crucial idea that special loves can focus on the *uniqueness* of the other (behind and beyond her traits). As we saw with Kierkegaard, this focus in turn can involve agapic regard: "The penetration of all other categories of love with this stream of *caritas*" that comes from awareness of God's universal love actually "brings to perfection" the natural loves (NL, 259).

In particular, von Hildebrand's Buberian interpretation of the *intentio unionis* in perfected natural loves suggests a kind of attention to the other that, while valuing her traits and her distinctive way of embodying them or synthesizing them in the process of living,[53] also pushes beyond these features to the very personhood that transcends them, the individual freedom of the other who can *turn* to me in the I–Thou relation. It was primarily from Buber that von Hildebrand developed the idea that love of the other's alterity at the core of her being can transfigure the various special loves as well. While this may be insufficient to show that agapic love is expressed through von Hildebrand's authentic special loves, it at least gives us an *alterity-focused* version of the special loves, which can no longer properly be called "preferential" in Kierkegaard's sense. For this form of the special loves is not primarily erosiac in Plato's sense; at most, only its secondary concern for the loving agent's happiness (equal with the beloved's happiness through their union) is erosiac. Thus one essential feature of preferential love in Kierkegaard's account does not apply to von Hildebrand's special loves in their authentic forms.

Neighbor-Love Distinguished by Transcending Affective Subjectivity

Von Hildebrand shares with Kierkegaard an emphatic distinction between the special loves and agapic love (NL, 238–239), but he draws this distinction carefully. He insists on the primacy of agapic duty (and obedience to God) over the value-responses in each of the special loves (NL, 215), and so he agrees with Kierkegaard that "there is a fundamental moral difference between . . . love of neighbor and the other natural categories of love" that involve erosiac motivation in their *intentio unionis* (NL, 235). In addition to being the highest moral imperative, neighbor-love is built on "love for God, whereas the natural kinds of love are not" (NL, 237). Moreover, while there is a "tendency to love with one's whole being" in the natural loves (as their I–Thou aspect implies), one can still be less than wholehearted in natural loves. By contrast, neighbor-love can *only* be wholehearted. This is related to Kierkegaard's point that real agapic love must continue in the face of difficulties in special relations (WL 305). Similarly, von Hildebrand holds that loving one person as friend, child, parent, or romantic partner (for instance) while hating others involves no contradiction, while neighbor-love must be universally welcoming to all others (NL, 239)—a thesis taken up below.

Thus the command to love our neighbors is challenging. Von Hildebrand argues that "in loving my neighbor I step out of my subjectivity" or familiar perspective in a way that I typically do not in loving my friends, spouse, or children, because these natural loves (even in their best form) still concern my well-being secondarily. By contrast, loving the other as neighbor does not concern my happiness: I do not apprehend the other *qua* neighbor as "a source of happiness for me" (NL, 209) (even if by luck, loving this neighbor happens to be rewarding). Agapic devotion moves me more out of my comfort zone, but is not about intimacy: it "does not establish any lasting personal union" (NL, 250).

At most, in neighbor-love there is a weak *intentio unionis* through hope for fellowship in the hereafter: "It does not aim, as in the [natural] human loves, at union with the beloved person but rather at unity in the kingdom of Christ" (NL 270). This does not mean that agapic love is self-abasing: like Kierkegaard, von Hildebrand stresses that willing the good of the neighbor is not the same as total self-abnegation, detachment, denial of one's own value, or loss of any interest in one's own good (NL, 213–217). Similarly, Kierkegaard preserves a role for agapic self-love as authentic concern for the loving quality of one's own character.[54] So there is close agreement between them on motives constituting neighbor-love and the importance of attending to the uniqueness of each neighbor.

For von Hildebrand, then, agapic love is distinguished by its pure concern for the good of the neighbor without aiming at direct present union with the loved one. This might make it sound like the neighbor must be a stranger to us, someone whose good is not already bound up with our own happiness by some shared community or special love-relation. If that were right, how could the light of agapic care shine through particular aspects of other human relations? But probably, von Hildebrand only means that *the form* of care for the other that constitutes neighbor-love is not concerned with my contingent relations to her. Moreover, he holds that special loves involve "an intimate personal self-donation that is not found in love of neighbor" by itself (NL, 212); that is, when it is not combined with any of the special-love relations. This intimacy is found, for example, in the erotic and philial aspects of spousal love, in the tenderness of parents toward a child, in a young child's adoration of an older sibling, and in the spontaneous empathy of close friends who know what each other is thinking. Such intimacy is a sign of strong emotional attachment and the I–Thou encounter involved in such special love-relations. Although arguably there must also be a volitional element of commitment to the other in these loves if they are more than passively arising erosiac attraction, the volitional element in the special loves is bound up with complex and often intense affective responses that are not under direct volitional control.

Thus von Hildebrand's point is that in the special loves, caring for the other produces certain emotional processes that call forth and respond to the other's responding emotions in turn; part of what I must do to love the other rightly in these cases is to open my own heart to him or her, making "a gift of my subjectivity" (NL, 220). Yet this kind of complex affective interchange need not be involved in love of the neighbor, who after all *can* be a complete stranger in the ordinary sense. In cases where I know the person to whom I must show agapic love, at least *qua neighbor* they are not in such an intimate union with me. Von Hildebrand is surely correct that neighbor-love cannot generally require affection or any similar intimate emotional response that is psychologically possible only in relation with a few others. Thus he concludes that willed donation of self-to-other in neighbor-love does not involve the affective intimacy of special loves.

Wholeheartedness and Independence of Contingent Values in the Neighbor

While von Hildebrand agrees with Kierkegaard that agapic love is distinguished by being a direct expression of a will to moral rightness (NL, 236), he explains how universality and non-preferentiality in agapic caring link up with valuing each neighbor as unique and irreplaceable. Consider his point—which Kierkegaard would certainly endorse—that hating person A detracts from showing agapic love to person B in a way that we do not find in the natural loves (NL, 238–239). This follows from the idea that agapic love must express one's whole being and express the "goodness dwelling in the soul of the one who loves" (NL, 239). Kierkegaard would phrase the point this way: one can only love the neighbor with one's *whole heart*; to be divided in one's will through hating even one person detracts from the agape that I may try to show to anyone else. Kierkegaard famously argued in his "Purity of Heart" discourse that only the good could be willed with absolute wholeheartedness. If the good is loving one's neighbor as oneself, then his formula says that wholeheartedness entails agapic love. Von Hildebrand adds the converse of this thesis, along with the Kierkegaardian point that loving one person as neighbor rationally commits us to loving all persons this way, since we respond to "the same" alterity in each (the paradox of equal and universal uniqueness).

This potential to expand neighbor-love universally is due, von Hildebrand says, to its response to value in the loved other being more "anticipatory," recognizing only the other's potential (beyond any contingent merit or demerit) as a person and inherent sanctity as someone loved by God. Thus in contrast to the benevolent caring for the other in special loves,

> with Christian love of neighbor the *intentio benevolentiae* is not the result of affirming my neighbor in a[n affective?] value-responding way; it is rather an actualization of the goodness dwelling in the soul of the one who loves. Although this goodness can only be actualized in a value-response to my neighbor, it does not arise from *taking delight* in him or her. The one who loves another with love of neighbor is good to the other on the basis of the goodness and fundamental attitude of love that reigns in him; he brings this to the encounter with the other. (NL, 239; italics added)

This might sound like an endorsement of Nygren's view that in agape, (a) there is no response to antecedent perception of values in the person-as-neighbor (because that would be attraction to what delights us); but (b) instead all the value that the agapic lover discerns in the neighbor results from his devotion to her—what Soble calls the "bestowal" theory of the loved person's value. As I noted, Kierkegaard also sounds like this when he appears to say that agapic love cannot be property-based: whereas erotic love and friendship are "defined by [their] object," only "love for the neighbor is defined by love" (WL, 66); and its need to express its overflowing love is so great that "it seems as if it might almost be able to produce its object" (WL, 67)—a reference to the idea of divine agape as creative. If we go too far down this road, it can make the gap between natural loves and agape unbridgeable, as Nygren intended.

Yet I think von Hildebrand only means that neighbor-love does not depend on the kind of affective or erosiac value-responses that are essential to the special loves; he does not mean to imply that the will of the person who loves her neighbor responds volitionally to *nothing* that is already in the other-*qua*-neighbor. For he also writes, "There is a beauty and worth that inheres in every human person for as long as he lives, even if he is stained by the worst qualitative disvalues" (including moral wrongs); this is the "image of God" in each (NL, 237), which Kierkegaard calls the divine "watermark." Thus the generalized benevolence of a warmhearted person differs not only from the natural loves (as it lacks their response to the individualized values in the loved one) *but also* from "love of neighbor," because generalized benevolence does not respond "to the dignity that each person has as an image of God and as a being who is loved and redeemed by Christ" (NL, 269). Although the neighbor-loving agent is drawing on goodwill already in her soul, much as the benevolent person is drawing on his warmhearted sentiments, "love of neighbor also has the element of value response" (NL, 269). As a result, the charity within the loving agent also has a different quality from that of natural sympathy: it is an expression of the love of God, a response to the miraculous transcendent value in each person (NL, 270–271).

Hence agapic love does respect something about the other; there is a distinct kind of value found in the capacity for free will, independent life, and potential to love that are standard for human persons. The willed effort of agapic love can be grounded or justified on this basis: it is inspired by a transcendent value, although this value does not attract like the objects of erosiac inclinations. The value of personhood transcends the kind of values that can appeal to my subjectivity as potentially part of my fulfillment, or in ways that draw on my personal affinities for certain goods rather than others in the world—those to which my emotions and affects respond more readily, for example.[55] Thus in agape, "it is my neighbor who stands at the center of my attention and not my personal union with him or her;" this implies "a certain independence of the neighbor from me" (NL, 240). In fact we might say that the alterity involved in the other's freedom is most fully thematized in agapic regard. So in neighbor-love, the "primacy that the beloved person possesses" in all authentic cases of the natural loves (in von

Hildebrand's view) is radicalized in agape; I focus entirely on the neighbor rather than on cultivating my special relation(s) with him.

This is a convincing way of avoiding the arbitrariness and gratuity of agape in Nygren's construal, similar to the alternative I attributed to Kierkegaard.[56] But I suggest one revision based on Kierkegaard's acknowledgement that we may at least hope that the other reciprocates in agapic love, both for us and for others in turn. This suggests to me the possibility of an I–Thou relation via neighbor-love. The transcendent value to which neighbor-love responds is found in the neighbor's radical individuality as a free spirit, which subtends all of her actual and potential traits, living in their interstices, animating the developing relations among them, giving her singular individuality. Thus when I love the other as neighbor, I am loving him as radically unique, as Buber's account of I–Thou relations requires. This may not always be a fulfilled relation with reciprocation, but it communicates something to the neighbor—at least that someone else is capable of loving him just for being a person with the potential to love in his turn. This message may be rebuffed or barely recognized; yet it is enough for a fleeting anticipation of a kind of encounter, though without the affectionate intimacy of the natural loves. While the natural loves focus more on the beloved's iterable properties, they can also approach the alterity that subtends these traits—from the "other side," as it were.

Infusion with Caritas *versus Neighbor-Love*

This brings me to von Hildebrand's steps toward infusion, which are aided by his intriguing distinction between *caritas* as a *qualitative aspect* of loves and the formal category of neighbor-love. He defends this distinction on the grounds that *caritas* is found in authentic human love for God, which he follows Aquinas in conceiving as the ultimate desire for union born of infinite value-response (NL, 241–242). Likewise, Christ's love for human persons has the quality of *caritas* but involves a will to ultimate union with the individual that interhuman neighbor-love lacks (NL, 249–250—though I just suggested a type of union that may be felt in agape). Von Hildebrand does not fully clarify what defines the quality of *caritas* that also appears in neighbor-love, but he seems to equate it with a "holy substantial goodness and kindness" that expresses pure care for the unique other, apart from any self-concern (NL, 244). For example, he says, "Caritas is constituted in love for God, and neighbor-love is the fruit of caritas" (NL, 243). But apart from its inspiration from God and dependence on grace, this quality looks like the privileging of the other's good that we find in all the authentic loves.

Could this distinction help to solve Kierkegaard's problem? It may help at this point to sum up von Hildebrand's subtle distinctions between different kinds

Table 4.1. Relations between kinds of love according to von Hildebrand

Categorical structure: Motive quality ↓	Strong *intentio unionis* and intimate self-donation	Weak *intentio unionis* without intimate self-donation	Scope of focus
Caritas as a generous and kind quality of motivation projecting beyond the agent's own happiness	1. Human love for God; Christ's love for us; *"Baptized" natural loves [right subjectivity]	2. *Interhuman neighbor-love [desubjectivizing, except in proper agapic self-care?]	Universal concern
Benevolent care for the other without *caritas*	3. Untransfigured but authentic natural loves [right subjectivity]	4. Detached benevolence (as in utilitarianism) [desubjectivizing]	Particularistic concern and preference for few persons
Egoistic priority given to agent's own goods	5. Distorted natural loves [perverse subjectivity]	6. Lack of natural loves, egoistic independence [perverse subjectivity]	Concern primarily or only for oneself as agent

Note: The aspect of subjectivity as a third dimension is indicated in square brackets.

of love, values to which loves respond, and qualities of motivation in a tentative table indicating their conceptual relations.

If table 4.1 is correct in its essentials, it suggests that von Hildebrand sees neighbor-love proper and the agape-infused special loves (both marked by * in the table) as *two species of caritas*. What this table cannot depict is how *caritas* interacts with the other motives involved in special loves, transfiguring them into a genus of type-1 love.

Technically speaking then, *neighbor-love* (type 2) cannot be expressed within the natural loves even in their authentic forms for von Hildebrand (because these loves always aim in part at special union with the beloved—a union with intimacy that to some extent takes our attention and the beloved's away from third parties, as Kierkegaard stresses). But this is partly an artifact of his terminology, for the quality of *caritas* can and should infuse all the natural loves (NL, 252). It does this by removing the danger of "egoism for the beloved person" or preference for them beyond the bounds of justice to others (NL, 252–253). It also brings us back to the other person's interests and values, away from the excessive focus on our own agendas that can result from any serious commitment (NL, 255; compare Kierkegaard's critique of domineering lovers). When love for God is present within our natural interhuman loves, it inspires us to remember others who could be wronged by our preferences for special beloveds if preference for them extends beyond legitimate bounds.

This seems to be very close to an ideal solution: what we need is to isolate an agapic quality that can be present in special love-relations, and even expressed within their preferential focus and (in some types) their need for an exclusive relation. While there must be a kind of "bare" neighbor-love that transcends all such natural loves, because it can operate beyond the bounds of all special relations (universally), what makes it agapic in motive-structure might be a motivational quality (*caritas*) that can combine fruitfully with the patterns of motive and affect that are essential to special loves. Yet the way that von Hildebrand explains the entry of *caritas* into the other loves looks too much like the corrective or filtering relation we found in Kierkegaard's account, according to which neighbor-love *checks* the natural loves with moral demands. Von Hildebrand says that *caritas* provides more than "the protective wall erected by the fundamental moral attitude against the dangers of natural love," and his idea seems to be that *caritas* avoids all forms of egoism more spontaneously, without the pain of conscientiousness; it is a virtue beyond dutifulness (NL, 262). But we may need to spell out the positive motivation within *caritas* a bit further to specify how the special attentions given to certain others in the different natural loves can *themselves* become (in part) expressions of the spirit of *caritas*.

Conclusion

Our comparison suggests that for both thinkers, agapic and special loves can converge in appreciating the uniqueness of the loved person, while remaining responsive to different aspects of the one loved. Still, von Hildebrand might doubt Kierkegaard's volitional thesis as a way of explaining infusion, because *caritas* for him seems to be partly a special emotional attitude, rather than a pure will to care about the other. This raises the question of how the closeness with another that we offer in natural loves can be strengthened by an agapic volitional effort to sustain emotions of intimacy and commitment never to abandon the other, given the transcendent value of his alterity. Here is a suggestion: our special attentions within natural loves can eventually communicate to the other not only that we prize her happiness above our own, or appreciate her good qualities beyond our own delight in them, but also that we do this partly because it can express our absolute gratitude *for the very existence of this other as a person*. For example, beyond communicating to our spouse that we adore her beauty and value all the good qualities of her character, we also express—"between the lines," as it were, of our special-love statements—that we prize, above all of these, her very being and potentials because of her basic independence and sanctity as a person. We then love all of her changeable qualities partly for the sake of that in her which cannot change, because she is constituted as a person with the telos of moral responsibility and love.

This is not to lace romance with Kantian duty but rather to indicate that we fully appreciate the deeper mystery behind the physical and psychical traits, or underlying the shared experiences and historical relationship we have developed. Although we might sometimes express this by being unwilling to do injustices for the good of our spouse or friend or child, verifying that our love for them ultimately endorses the same reality that is the basis of our duties to third parties, we also express more directly, in intimate attentions shown to them (rather than to strangers), that our love for them is more than duty and more than aesthetic appreciation: we love them not only for the values to which the special loves naturally respond, *but even more* for the inner glory of their being as a center of mystery that we could never possess, whose being and freedom is given by God. So von Hildebrand is right that *caritas* here involves a love for God, a thanks to God for giving me the chance to know this person, for as brief or as long a time as may be (given our efforts and fortunes)—which includes my gratitude to God for loving them better than I can.

This is not to divorce the process of *caritas* infusing special loves from the moral quality of neighbor-love that is well-expressed by the filter model, which extends even to respect for basic rights. Rather, in the fully positive relation, I hold that the legitimately bounded expressions of the natural loves are part of *what* those who stand in certain special relations with me need from me, and thus part of what I ought to give to them (to the extent that I legitimately can). To reach this conclusion requires the additional premise that *what* concretely is due to each as neighbor is mediated to an extent by other layers of relations that vary between persons, and so are not universal—relations of community, law, shared history, and bonds of natural love-relations as well. That might be a controversial thought today, but it is one that we could defend by looking back to Aquinas, among others.[57] However, this may only show that a completely satisfying resolution to the problem of infusion is impossible without a more adequate and fairly detailed account of the *content* of our agapic duties according to the best agapic ethics. I have largely set this question aside here, because Kierkegaard does not try to work out detailed agapic norms, and neither does von Hildebrand (in *The Nature of Love*); but this is a substantive normative topic that deserves more serious attention.

JOHN J. DAVENPORT is Professor of Philosophy and Director of Peace and Justice Studies at Fordham University. He is author of *Narrative Identity, Autonomy, and Mortality: From MacIntyre and Frankfurt to Kierkegaard*, and coeditor with Anthony Rudd of *Love, Reason and Will: Kierkegaard After Frankfurt*

Notes

1. A classic work in this genre is C. S. Lewis's *The Allegory of Love*. While the medieval European debates were complex, there was a definite strengthening of romantic norms through the centuries. For example, the highly influential poet Edmund Spenser defended romantic love as the root of all virtues in his massive epic poem, *The Faerie Queene* (see the introduction to Book 4).

2. The term "special loves" is not very articulate or clear, but it is largely neutral (unlike "preferential loves") and now commonly used in philosophical literature.

3. See Michael Strawser's helpful discussion of this issue in his *Kierkegaard and the Philosophy of Love* (Lanham, MA: Lexington, 2015), pp. 115–119.

4. As I have argued at length in *Will as Commitment and Resolve* (New York, NY: Fordham University Press, 2007), chs. 4–8.

5. Anders Nygren, *Agape and Eros*, trans. Philip Watson (New York, NY: Harper and Row, 1969), p. 77: "Agape is 'indifferent to value'" in the loved person. He also seemingly agrees with Augustine that God "needs nothing outside Himself" because he is perfection (in Plato's sense) (p. 479).

6. Nygren, *Agape and Eros*, p. 711; this makes agape "spontaneous in contrast to all activity with a eudæmonistic motive" (p. 726). Although Nygren is describing Luther's views in this section, they agree well with his own claims that "agape . . . is a social idea which as such has nothing in common with individualistic and eudæmonistic ethics" (p. 45). Because this sounds a lot like Kierkegaard's critiques of eudaimonism, it suggests a link through their common debts to Luther. However, Kierkegaard's insistence that a person rightly maintains an infinite interest in salvation as her Highest Good suggests a more Kantian view that is less extreme than Luther's view that even human desire for "fellowship with God . . . is polluted by the egocentricity which is inherent in everything human" (p. 714).

7. See Daphne Hampson, *Kierkegaard: Exposition and Critique* (Oxford, UK: Oxford University Press, 2014), p. 185.

8. C. S. Lewis, *The Four Loves* (New York: Harcourt Brace Jovanovich, 1988), p. 2 and p. 126. He adds that "natural Gift-love" built into human nature is "always directed to objects which the lover finds in some way intrinsically loveable," while supernatural or "Divine Gift-love" granted by special grace enables us to "love what is not naturally loveable; lepers, criminals, enemies, morons, the sulky," etc. (p. 128).

9. Alan Soble, *The Structure of Love* (New Haven, CT: Yale University Press, 1990). In fact, Soble labels any love paradigmatically "erosic" if it responds to (real or apparent) properties in the loved person, and "agapic" if it does not (pp. 11–13). Also see Alan Soble, ed., *Eros, Agape, and Philia: Readings in the Philosophy of Love* (St. Paul, MN: Paragon House, 1998), which includes key selections from Nygren. I add an "a" to his term "erosic" (making it "erosiac") just so the difference from "erotic" is harder to miss.

10. On this theme, see my essay "Romantic Marriage as a Model for Ethical Will," forthcoming in *Klassiker Auslegen: Søren Kierkegaards Entweder-Oder*, Hermann Deuser and Marcus Kleinert, eds. (de Gruyter, 2017). I argue in this essay that the positive view of romantic love as upbuilding is not merely an artifact of Judge William's limited perspective, but instead it fits with central elements of several works in Kierkegaard's "second authorship."

11. Strawser, *Kierkegaard and the Philosophy of Love*, pp. 121–122.

12. M. Jamie Ferreira, *Love's Grateful Striving: A Commentary on Kierkegaard's* Works of Love (Oxford, UK: Oxford University Press, 2001), pp. 43–47; ch. 6 on conscience, especially

pp. 90–94; and pp. 112–114 (discussing difference and commonality, which correspond to special relations and universal love, respectively).

13. Sharon Krishek, *Kierkegaard on Faith and Love* (Cambridge, UK: Cambridge University Press, 2009), especially ch. 4, and pp. 142–145, pp. 152–160.

14. See M. Jamie Ferreira, "Review of Krishek, *Kierkegaard on Love and Faith*," *Notre Dame Philosophical Reviews* (January 21, 2010), http://ndpr.nd.edu/news/kierkegaard-on-faith-and-love/, pp. 3–4. And see Sharon Krishek, "In Defense of a Faith-Like Model of Love: A Reply to John Lippitt's 'Kierkegaard and the Problem of Special Relationships: Ferreira, Krishek, and the "God-Filter," '" *International Journal of the Philosophy of Religion* 75.2 (April 2014; online June 2013): 155–166, esp. pp. 158–161.

15. See John Lippitt, *Kierkegaard and the Problem of Self-Love* (Cambridge, UK: Cambridge University Press, 2013), especially ch. 4 on "The Problem of Special Relationships" (responding in part to Krishek), and ch. 6 on the limits of self-denial (responding in part to Sylvia Walsh, *Living Christianly: Kierkegaard's Dialectic of Christian Existence* [State College, PA: Penn State University Press, 2005], esp. ch. 3).

16. Ferreira, *Love's Grateful Striving*, ch. 2, especially p. 35; and ch. 8, pp. 124–136 on Levinas and Gene Outka's "blank check" objection.

17. See especially the essays by Sylvia Walsh, John Lippitt, and Troy Jollimore in *Love, Reason, and Will: Kierkegaard after Frankfurt*, Anthony Rudd and John Davenport, eds. (New York and London: Bloomsbury, 2015).

18. Soble, *The Structure of Love*, pp. 17–18. He considers but rejects the idea of trying to add property-responsiveness to the agapic model.

19. This is what Sylvia Walsh means in arguing that Kierkegaard affirms the place of human loves in Christian existence, but only as transformed by a dying-to-oneself; see *Living Christianly*, p. 80.

20. Ferreira, *Love's Grateful Striving*, p. 94.

21. Ferreira, *Love's Grateful Striving*, pp. 90–93.

22. Ferreira, "Review of Krishek, *Kierkegaard on Love and Faith*," p. 4.

23. See Lippitt, *Kierkegaard and the Problem of Self-Love*, p. 77 and p. 82.

24. Lippitt, *Kierkegaard and the Problem of Self-Love*, p. 84.

25. Krishek, "In Defense of a Faith-Like Model of Love," pp. 159–160.

26. For example, Krishek's own proposed solution is that agapically qualified romantic love can be described as a caring for the beloved that is (a) self-denying or resigned (non-possessive and accepting the possibility of losing the beloved or the beloved's love) while also (b) making the second movement that characterizes faith by affirming the concrete or "idiosyncratic" aspects of the lover's self that ground the "self-focused concerns" that figure into her preferences for a particular romantic beloved (see Krishek, "In Defense of a Faith-Like Model of Love," pp. 162–163). While I agree with her account of Kierkegaardian faith, making faith in this sense essential to agape-infused particularistic (or "preferential") loves may seem to pass too quickly over the problem of how exactly agapic regard can be expressed within the particular affirmative attitudes of the special loves.

27. I am effectively saying that Krishek's conditions for a solution are not *demanding enough*, and thus she is actually not *critical enough* of Kierkegaard's account.

28. Krishek, "In Defense of a Faith-Like Model of Love," p. 164.

29. Still it is not clear that Kierkegaard would agree with Duns Scotus that a human analog of agapic love (perhaps something like MacIntyre's "just generosity") is possible for us through the power of our wills prior to grace.

30. Carl S. Hughes, "Anders Nygren: Influence in Reverse?" in *Kierkegaard's Influence on Theology*, tome II, Jon Stewart, ed. (Aldershot, UK: Ashgate, 2012), p. 212.

31. Hughes cites Rick Furtak and Sylvia Walsh on this point about the unitary hidden source of all loves, to conclude, "For Kierkegaard, Christian love is not a rejection of preferential love or eros but their purification; it infinitizes them through the mediation of love for God" ("Anders Nygren: Influence in Reverse?" p. 213). I agree that this is Kierkegaard's goal, which involves overcoming Nygren's dichotomy. But I think Kierkegaard has inherited enough of the Lutheran contrast between agape and the special loves that he has a hard time reaching this implied goal.

32. Dietrich von Hildebrand, *The Nature of Love*, trans. John F. Crosby with John H. Crosby (South Bend, IN: St. Augustine's Press, 2009), p. 237. Hereafter cited parenthetically throughout this chapter using the abbreviation "NL."

33. This is not "autonomy" in the sense of absolute independence, Stoic autarky, or the willful self-assertion of a person who want to "steer on his own" and take credit for "all his achievement." Rather, when Kierkegaard says that neighbor-love should help the other become "free, independent, his own master . . . [or] help him stand alone," he has in mind a modest, creaturely autonomy compatible with accepting a divinely given vocation, or being "an instrument in the hand of Governance" (WL, 86). Similarly, in *The Heart*, von Hildebrand argues that the true self is not only free will but also the person's affective facticity (see *The Heart: An Analysis of Human and Divine Affectivity*, ed. John Henry Crosby, South Bend, IN: St. Augustine's Press, 2007, pp. 67–68)—a view that arguably agrees with Kierkegaard's account of the self in *Sickness Unto Death*.

34. I present this argument and the next informally (without the full apparatus of predicate logic). In my view, Soble (in responding to Irving Singer) errs in making "bestowal" or "love's not being property-based" essential to the agapic paradigm (*The Structure of Love*, p. 23). It is possible instead to make projective (non-erosiac) motivation, which is responsive to properties without being attracted to them, a necessary condition of the agapic paradigm. Soble's account forces him to regard agape (and all loves with agapic form) as irrational, or not reason-dependent. Thus he calls any sort of neighbor-love that does respond to features of the loved neighbor "a universal erosic love" (p. 195), which is at least terminologically awkward.

35. For my critique of Nygren's fallacy and argument that Levinas's conception of agapic love and duty depends on it, see my *Will as Commitment and Resolve*, ch. 9.

36. See Soble, *The Structure of Love*, p. 27 (on Plato); pp. 32–33 on Gellner's paradox; and ch. 9 on exclusivity (especially §7).

37. Drawing on Jeffrey Blustein's *Care and Commitment*, I explore this solution in *Narrative Identity, Autonomy, and Mortality: From Frankfurt and MacIntyre to Kierkegaard* (New York: Routledge, 2012), pp. 113–114. Also see my *Will as Commitment and Resolve*, ch. 14, pp. 513–519.

38. Again see John Lippitt on the "God Filter" in *Kierkegaard and the Problem of Self-Love*, in ch. 4, "The Problem of Special Relationships," pp. 82–85.

39. Lewis, *The Four Loves*, p. 133.

40. The idea of God as the "middle term" is thus closely related to the infusion thesis throughout Kierkegaard's work. For example, he implies that having God as the middle term in loving one's spouse involves helping one's spouse come to love God, though this may imply actions that are not what the spouse wanted (WL, 107). Knud Løgstrup's famous criticism of *Works of Love* is related to this idea; see Løgstrup, *The Ethical Demand*, trans. Jensen and Puckering, Hans Fink and Alasdair MacIntyre, eds. (Notre Dame, IN: University of Notre Dame Press, 1997). I think Løgstrup errs by failing to see that "helping the beloved to love God" is a formal paradigm that is meant to include all sorts of more specific goods. Kierkegaard does not think that helping the other become more religious is all that neighbor-love requires. But in this essay, I am largely setting aside issues about *the content of what* we should give the neighbor.

41. Strawser similarly finds examples where Kierkegaard portrays familial or romantic love without much indication of possessiveness or self-love; see *Kierkegaard and the Philosophy of Love*, p. 57 and p. 121.

42. Kierkegaard frequently suggests that God's love is not envious, that God does not want us to love God *rather than* other human beings; on the contrary, God insists that we love him through loving human persons (WL, 160)—an idea taken to its extreme in Levinas.

43. Focusing on possessiveness is also unpromising, because it requires a premise to the effect that if we love X for X's properties, then we seek to possess or own X's properties: our focus on the beloved's distinguishing features results from our aiming to keep these features *related to us*, rather than to respect or express their inherent value for their own sake. But there may be other ways of valuing the preferred other for her distinguishing traits, including some that see *through* the traits to the beloved who bears them, as an individual with further trait-transcending value. Robert Adams rightly moves in this direction in his argument against Nygren that agapic love need not be arbitrary; see Adams, *Finite and Infinite Goods* (New Haven, CT: Yale University Press, 1999), pp. 163–166.

44. Harry Frankfurt has defended this claim about special loves in detail in his *Reasons of Love*, but only at the price of accepting that authentic special loves are not property-based, or even (in their core motives) responsive to the loved person's features. This attests to Nygren's influence on Frankfurt, as I have argued elsewhere. Thus while Frankfurt defends the unselfish purity of essentially particularistic love of individuals, he does not actually resolve our main conundrum at all; instead, he simply reduces special loves to particularistic versions of Nygrenian agape.

45. Soble accepts that this reconciliation will work if the uniqueness thesis is defensible. But he rejects it, critiquing several attempted arguments for it (see *The Structure of Love*, ch. 3). In particular, he argues against Anthony Quinton that uniqueness in narrative identity (in part due to unique memories) is too trivial to serve as a basis for essentially particularistic love (p. 55). But he misses the idea that such narratival uniqueness accrues to the adverbial modification of valuable (non-unique) first-order properties in the beloved, and this second-order gestalt is *not* trivial. Lewis also holds that eros (or romantic love) sees through the beloved's traits to her uniqueness as a precious individual; see *The Four Loves*, pp. 94–95.

46. This idea is worked out in detail in Richard White's rather Buberian conception of friendship in his *Love's Philosophy* (Lanham, MA: Rowman & Littlefield, 2001), pp. 28–32.

47. Compare Lewis's point that romantic love at its purest rises to such a focus on the beloved as unique individual that the lover desires an inarticulable form of ontological union with the beloved (*The Four Loves*, pp. 94–95). Yet von Hildebrand also argues that the other is not pure subject for us, but also an object, in the sense of an objective reality outside our minds that is not constituted by our consciousness.

48. This point is especially clear in von Hildebrand's better-known book, *The Heart* (op. cit), p. 37. Thus even the *intentio unionis* that that such value-response inspires is, in a sense, primarily "selfless" for von Hildebrand.

49. In *Will as Commitment and Resolve* (chs. 7–8), I put it much this way by saying that friendship involves two ends, the primary one being the good of the friend, and the secondary one being the good of cultivating my relationship with him.

50. Again, compare Lewis, who says that eros at its height "has the air of regarding pleasure as a by-product" (*The Four Loves*, p. 96). Von Hildebrand adds, "Such goods are in no way a means for my happiness; it is rather the case that I am made happy in a superabundant way by giving myself to them and letting their intrinsic value stand at the center of my attention" or become "thematic" for me (NL, 132).

51. Similarly, in *The Heart*, von Hildebrand says that the lover wants to fill the heart of the beloved with happiness that is based in part on affective response to the lover (p. 67).

52. At one point von Hildebrand suggests that the "opposite of this self-donation" or seeking I–Thou union in the special loves is the "egocentricity that expresses itself in a person never being so happy as when he is independent of others and able to live out his desires without being bothered by them" (NL, 212). This makes egocentricity a state without special loves even in their deficient forms, whereas Kierkegaard recognizes these deficient forms as partly egocentric. Elsewhere von Hildebrand recognizes the deficient forms, such as when he diagnoses an inauthentic simulacrum of love that is only concerned about its agent's own happiness as a "will to possess" the other (NL, 135).

53. In past work, I have stressed this point that the other will have an empirically unique set of second-order adverbial properties realized in the ways he embodies, lives, expresses, and combines his first-order properties. I develop this idea from insights in Jeffrey Blustein's and Neera Badhwar's work on caring; see Davenport, *Narrative Identity, Autonomy, and Mortality* (op. cit), pp. 113–114.

54. On this point, see Lippitt's insightful analysis (building on Ferreira's analysis of proper self-love) in his *Kierkegaard and the Problem of Self-Love*, chs. 3 and 6, along with his own proposals in chs. 7–9; compare Lippitt, "Giving the 'Dear Self' its Due: Kierkegaard, Frankfurt, and Self-Love," in *Love, Reason, and Will*, Rudd and Davenport, eds. (op. cit.), ch. 6 (responding in part to Walsh's essay on "Self-Love, Redoubling, and Self-Denial" in this same collection).

55. Still, von Hildebrand may be correct that such a volitional response to the neighbor and concern for his good without relation to myself presupposes a "substantial goodness" infused into the loving agent by God (NL, 242). Without this, perhaps we cannot love the neighbor in what he calls the "anticipatory" way that does not respond to the beloved's merits.

56. I have also defended this claim that neighbor-love is responsive to transcendent value in the neighbor (even if that is not precisely "*property*-responsiveness") in "Frankfurt and Kierkegaard on BS., Wantonness, and Aestheticism," in *Love, Reason and Will*, pp. 73–113, especially pp. 74–76.

57. For this I am indebted to Eleanore Stump's discussion of *caritas* differentiated by different social "stations" in her presidential address to the APA: "Love, By All Accounts," *Proceedings and Addresses of the American Philosophical Association* 80.2 (November 2006): 25–43. Also see von Hildebrand, NL, ch.12.

5   Kierkegaard, Weil, and Agapic Moral Fideism

Mark A. Tietjen

> These kinds of love are supernatural, and in that sense they are absurd. They are the height of folly. So long as the soul has not had direct contact with the very person of God, they cannot be supported by any knowledge based either on experience or reason. They cannot therefore rest upon any certainty, unless the word is used in a metaphorical sense to indicate the opposite of hesitation.
>
> Simone Weil, "Forms of the Implicit Love of God"[1]

Some Problems of Moral Philosophy

A philosopher once told me he considered himself a moral Christian but not a metaphysical Christian. I thought the claim was a joke, as it was offered in a humorous way (and in an inebriated state), but the philosopher was perfectly serious. He was on the whole compelled by the moral vision of Christianity—especially the ideals of love for one's neighbor and justice for the poor; he was compelled by the importance of virtues like honesty, self-control, and peacemaking; mostly he was compelled by the notion that all human life possesses equal value, worth, and dignity. Yet he was not at all compelled by the religious doctrine behind that moral vision: the existence of a benevolent, almighty God who maintains a claim on human existence (to say nothing of the incarnation of that God in the person of Jesus Christ). The linkage between the two was by no means necessary. This philosopher believed—as we can be sure many others believe—that one does not need the doctrines of Christian theism (or any religion, for that matter) to arrive at a rich and robust view of the moral life.[2]

Two problems quickly come into view that inform attempts by atheists and theists alike to think hard about morality and specifically the beliefs that undergird moral understanding. We might call these the *problem of desire* and the *problem of cognitive limitation*. First, contemporary moral philosophers, themselves part of the post–Enlightenment West, generally *desire* to find justification for what they believe deeply to be true—that all humans ought to be treated equally or at least as though they have equal dignity by virtue of their being human. This desire for equality, not far beneath the surface of many modern and contemporary ethical theories, can be found in the fundamental moral beliefs that undergird important documents such as the United Nations Declaration of Human Rights, which inform international laws and regulations. Though not all people share the desire for equality—sociopaths and racists come to mind—many (perhaps most) do, and we do in such a way that we think those who disagree do not just have a different, though equally (or decently) justified position, but are in fact wrong, somehow morally deficient. They are wrong in some deep sense—not quite like one is wrong about who won the game (where one can obviously be wrong), but far closer to that than being wrong about which suit is better to wear on a date. Most often we tend to explain cases of moral wrongness like this in terms of upbringing, though sometimes in terms of physiological malfunction; in either case we could call it a failure of moral perception and conviction, a kind of blindness or ignorance—sometimes willful—to moral truth.

It is this desire for equality that stands behind the Enlightenment project of trying to find a rational justification for morality—a justification that would allow those who otherwise disagree with one another about religion to agree that all people are of equal worth and ought to be treated as ends in themselves, as Kant says. It is this deep desire that also explains why evolutionary accounts of morality, however fascinating, fail fully to explain morality. As George Mavrodes hinted decades ago,[3] while evolutionary ethics might explain why humans are the kinds of beings that possess moral convictions—and they are doing this more and better every day—it has not explained, cannot explain, and likely could not in the future explain that those moral convictions are veridical, that they are true regardless of or independent of convictions about them, or that they are true all the way down, as it were. Evolutionary ethics cannot help us with the question of whether there actually are such things as moral obligations. To think evolutionary ethics could do so would be a kind of category mistake, along the lines of the attempt to show that a human being is God, to take an example from Kierkegaard. But many moral philosophers do not simply want everyone to agree to treat each other equally (this would be good enough for heads of state or schoolmasters); as moral *philosophers* they want to know that this agreement is founded upon something more than wishful thinking, if possible in some facts about the universe. They want their desire—this deep-seated conviction—somehow supported by evidence, justified. This is why the claim that moral truth is simply a brute fact of the universe is not just a non-starter but in fact a scandal to the philosophical mindset. It seems like an ad hoc throwing in the towel on one of the most interesting and pressing questions of human existence.

The failures of ethical theories to provide compelling justification or evidence that would satisfy the desire for equality (among other moral claims) clearly explains why more than one philosopher has turned away from the project alto-gether, whether to some form of anti-realism, anti-theory, or nihilism. Despite those options, though, the desire for equality and the companion desire I have been discussing, *the desire to justify the desire for equality*, are strong impulses that seem not to have disappeared despite the surface appeal of relativism. Nev-ertheless, these failures lead to a second problem facing moral philosophers: cog-nitive limitation. What does one do when one believes something to be the case but is unable or ill-equipped to prove or to demonstrate that something is the case? How does the philosopher proceed when her ability to support rationally a position fails to match her commitment to and conviction about that position?

Contemplating cognitive limitations is an age-old philosophical practice, maybe *the* age-old philosophical practice. One observes this in Socrates's confes-sion about the limits of his own knowledge and his undermining the knowledge claims of his interlocutors. One seems to find it in many of Socrates's philosophi-cal progeny, including the classical skeptics, who attempted to subject all propo-sitions to questioning, resisting to the best extent they could claims to certain knowledge. One finds a theological version of this in the philosophical theol-ogy of apophatic thought. Finite beings contemplating an infinite being know negatively if they know at all. Modern philosophy, in a variety of different ways, seeks to raze the foundation of knowledge in an attempt at epistemic honesty and with the hope of rebuilding that knowledge basis. Contemporary philosophy has located cognitive limits in mistaken views about language, which assumed without argument that language carried unaltered, pure meaning between two parties. Since the dawn of the twentieth century, more than a few philosophers have followed the skepticism of modernity to its natural end by altogether dis-missing truth (or certain kinds of truth) as an intelligible concept. What could be a stronger (if unintended) statement of cognitive limit!

With the exception, perhaps, of Socrates, the limits of knowledge noted in the schools above were tied either to the natural constraints of one's cognitive apparatus or to one's finite perspective on the world. Our minds hit a wall in their quest for knowledge, and our situatedness in the world prevents us from discov-ering as much as we would like. But Socrates (and Aristotle), and then Christian philosophers like Augustine, add to these types of limit an additional problem for knowledge that gets introduced by moral shortcoming, namely *sin* in Christian terminology. It is not just Augustine's knowledge of God (which he has at least some intellectual version of before his full conversion) but also his knowledge of the world, of others, and of himself that is rotted by sin, by his slavery to the "mad master"[4] of lust. In other words, it is not just God's infinity and humans' finitude that make God a difficult concept and being to grasp, but it is the love of created things over the Creator, as Augustine would put it, or the human desire to live autonomously, without the input, conviction, or assistance of God, that damages one's ability to *know* God and the things of God. And that autonomy gets in the way of knowing others, the world, and oneself properly. To take a nonreligious example, my ability to learn the needs (and thus act to address those needs) of the physical environment where I live is hindered by my greed to make money off the land in a way that damages that land. Or my seeking to learn more deeply the injustices faced by factory workers in China is hindered by my desire to have an affordable, trendy piece of technology. What I can know (and subsequently what I can do) cannot move forward because of a moral problem.

Cognitive limitation is thus of two kinds: one strictly related to my inability to know as much as I would like (including maintaining perspectives other than my own) and one related to the phenomenon of moral failure, where vices such as greed block my capacity to know things. Tied specifically to moral knowledge, then, we face difficulties discerning moral truth, both because our brains are too small but also because our hearts are too corrupt. Keeping in mind the initial distinction between moral and metaphysical Christianity posed by my philosopher friend, the claim I will put forward in the next section is that despite the variety of limits to discerning moral knowledge, Christian theism offers good reason to trust the desire for equality that many of us find within ourselves, and that atheism, conversely, either promotes this desire at the risk of being charged with wishful thinking or leaves us wanting in providing a compelling explanation of where to locate moral truth. Thus, although for Christian theism belief that all humans are equal and should be treated as such rests on faith in God, this could be a more favorable epistemic position than the atheistic view, which wants to believe these truths but cannot locate them anywhere. (Thus, I am leaving to the side a few options that others might find attractive: moral relativism and nihilism, anti-theory, and the grounding of morality found in other religions.)

Christian theism offers good reason to trust the desire for equality, in part because equality is situated in the rich moral concept of Christian (agape) love, sometimes called neighbor-love. Few Christian thinkers present a more compelling picture of Christian love than Søren Kierkegaard and Simone Weil. Importantly, while both Kierkegaard and Weil understand this kind of love, which views all humans as equal, as dependent upon Christian doctrine, they also grant that loving in this way is a risk. Christianly loving others is a risk because it is difficult to do, because it will sometimes occasion the scorn and mistrust of others, but also because it requires deep faith—both in God and in those one would love. We turn, then, to a discussion of love's faith, which refers both to the faith that love has *in God* as the basis for loving others and to the faith that love has *about* the neighbor or other, the object of love.

Love's Faith *in God*

For Weil and Kierkegaard, the source of love for the neighbor is God, and thus "since God is not present to the soul," as Weil writes, love drawn from God comes through faith and trust in God.[5] Specifically, the love for neighbor that comes from God is a love that originates in God's own loving character. For Weil God's loving character is disclosed especially in creation and in the Incarnation. Weil identifies Christian love with what she terms "the supernatural virtue of justice," which she defines as "behaving exactly as though there were equality when one is the stronger in an unequal relationship."[6] Creation, Weil argues, demonstrates this attribute in God, an infinitely powerful being that creates *out of nothing* something with no value apart from itself. The creation of the world, she claims, does not reflect God's "self-expansion" but rather God's "restraint and renunciation," a kind of "diminution," a "voluntary effacement:"[7] She argues further that "God causes this universe to exist, but he consents not to command it, although he has the power to do so. Instead he leaves two other forces to rule in his place. On the one hand there is blind necessity attaching to matter, including the psychic matter of the soul, and on the other the autonomy essential to thinking persons."[8]

The idea that God expresses love by the act of creation, and specifically by the act of creating free creatures, is maintained also by Kierkegaard in discourse III from "What We Learn from the Lilies in the Field and from the Birds of the Air": "Do you know of any more overwhelming and humbling expression for God's condescension and extravagance towards us human beings than that he places himself, so to say, on the same level of choice with the world, just so that we may be able to choose; that God, if language dare speak thus, woos humankind—that he, the eternally strong one, woos sapless humanity?" (UDVS, 206)[9] Human freedom, and specifically the capacity to choose God among other competing goods, serves as a sign of God's loving orientation toward his human creation. Had God created only orchids, amoebas, and automatons, one could not deduce this attribute. The idea of a God who self-restrains in the act of creation and in its interaction with humans forms Weil's criterion for distinguishing true from false religion: "The religions which represent divinity as commanding wherever it has the power to do so seem false," while those in which God interacts with humans (or anything other than God) as though there were some equality, bear truth.

The Incarnation also demonstrates the character of God's love. As a Trinitarian, Weil affirms not just the biblical claim that "God is love" (I John 4:8) but also what follows from this claim: that, from eternity past, "God loves himself."[10] Though two lovers might be nearer to one another than almost any other human couple, in the Triune God "there is infinite nearness or identity."[11] But this means that when God became human, dwelt among us, and suffered in a manner common to all people, the result was "infinite distance" between God and God.[12] For Weil, this expression of love and the Father's abandonment of Christ to the cross represent the divine source of love that motivates human love for the other. Never one to shy from the difficulties of human existence, she comments on the abandoned Christ: "There cannot be a greater good for us on earth than to share in it."[13] To share in Christ's sufferings is to share in God's love for the world. It is to fathom the distance God went for no other reason than love.

Weil's claims here call to mind Kierkegaard's pseudonym Johannes Climacus's thinly veiled discussion of the Incarnation in *Philosophical Fragments.* Working his way through a thought experiment from which he has deduced the concept of a god who alone provides truth to humans, Climacus likens the god of his postulation to Aristotle's unmoved mover, but he points out that since the god does not act out of necessity, the best explanation for the god's action in the world is love: "What moves him then but love, for love does not have the satisfaction of need outside itself but within" (PF, 24). However, the love is unhappy[14] since it is love that cannot be realized, due to the absence of equality among the lover and beloved. The unhappiness of this love prompts the king in Climacus's tale to take on a lowly form, to become as equal to the maiden. The biblical texts behind this passage are obvious: the suffering servant passages (e.g., Isaiah 53) and the second chapter of Philippians (vv. 5–8). Climacus beautifully summarizes the love of the Incarnation:

> It is love that gives rise to all this suffering, precisely because the god is not zealous for himself but in love wants to be the equal of the most lowly of the lowly. When an oak nut is planted in a clay pot, the pot breaks; when new wine is poured into old leather bottles, they burst. What happens, then, when the god plants himself in the frailty of a human being if he does not become a new person and a new vessel! But this becoming—how difficult it really is, and how like a difficult birth! (PF, 34)

Love of neighbor thus originates in God's loving character. Because the source of human love for others is God, and because God is not present to the soul (or the senses), God is the "hidden source" of love, Kierkegaard writes. "Just as the quiet lake originates deep down in hidden springs no eye has seen, so also does a person's love originate even more deeply in God's love" (WL, 9). Kierkegaard says further that this genesis is "mysterious" (WL, 10). To speak of God as the mysterious source of love implies two things. First, at least in a qualified sense, such love does not proceed naturally from humans. Whereas romantic and parental loves come naturally, love for the neighbor does not. The first of the two "dangers" Kierkegaard associates with neighbor-love in *Works of Love* (see WL, p. 192ff) specifically addresses the challenge of love's self-denial to what he calls the "inner being"; that is, the natural human desire to determine what constitutes one's own happiness and fulfillment. Weil similarly notes how "the sympathy of the strong for the weak" in the specific case of loving the afflicted goes "against nature."[15] Just like the second of Kierkegaard's two dangers concerns how society will misunderstand and possibly scorn the one who loves this way, so too will those who operate only with what Weil calls a natural conception of justice find such love scandalous. She quotes Thucydides's retelling of how the Athenians justified to themselves the destruction of the little island of Melos; they said, "We know quite well that you also, like all others, once you reached the same degree of power, would act in the same way."[16] Just as natural justice only obtains where two parties are equal, so does natural (or preferential) love extend only as far as it wants to, as it likes, as it considers the other worthy. Put a different way, might makes right—Thrasymachus's position in *The Republic* is the natural or default position of human existence, not the treatment of all others as equals.

Calling the source of love mysterious, second, points to the supernatural transaction that Weil and Kierkegaard believe occurs in neighbor love. Such love is not a heightening of natural powers, to use Aquinas's language, but rather it is a divine gift. In the discourse "Love Builds Up," Kierkegaard describes how love for one's neighbor depends entirely on God's unique loving activity of placing love within a human heart. "But can one human being implant love in another human being's heart? No, this is a suprahuman relationship . . . . It is God, the Creator, who must implant love in each human being, he who himself is Love" (WL, 216). Likewise, Weil notes, "The love of our neighbor is the love which comes down from God to man."[17] She goes a step further by claiming that the love that proceeds from God's implantation *remains* God's love. "The soul does not love like a creature with created love. The love within it is divine, uncreated; for *it is the love of God for God* that is passing through it."[18] Thus, it seems consistent for Weil to claim that the love of a neighbor "has the virtue of a sacrament."[19] Looking ahead to the next section, rooting the human love of others in God's gift of love means that God is credited and glorified through humans' love for one another rather than through the human lover himself or herself, and thus we will see why one appropriate image for conveying the human role in love involves little more than a particular kind of *looking* to God when one *sees* the neighbor.

Love's Faith *about the Neighbor*

For both Kierkegaard and Weil, the very concept of neighbor-love itself owes entirely to God's special revelation: "With Christianity came the divine explanation of what love is" (WL, 110). Thus, to situate love's faith about the neighbor in love's faith in God is to understand ethics as rooted in a broader faith perspective that interprets the world in a way that may have internal consistency yet appear absurd from the outside. Weil has a particularly idiosyncratic faith perspective that entirely colors her understanding of how to love the neighbor. In her 1942 letter to Father Perrin concerning her hesitations about baptism, Weil lays out three domains of will in the world: the first domain is "that which is independent of us," which more or less includes all that has happened in the past or things that are happening or will happen over which we have no control.[20] She includes all evils here, and she claims that all of these things are the will of God and accordingly should be loved. The second domain "is that which is placed under the rule of the [human] will."[21] Specifically, she seems to be thinking here about the normative values that come with the regulations of religious and civil law. We are free to follow such law, she claims. The third domain is not "under the empire of the will" and yet includes that which is "not entirely independent of us."[22] The operative concept of this domain she calls the "pressure of God," which can be experienced through the first domain and what we think of as the mechanical laws of nature. If we are to love these laws, as she suggests, then while we cannot exert our will successfully against them, we can—much like Epictetus tells us—change our judgments about nature when it presses upon us or those we love. Weil believes that this third domain involves our faithful turning to God with attention and with love. While we may be helpless to act or to move, the posture of lovingly looking toward God, of abandoning "ourselves to the pressure," eventually leads to our perfection.[23] The scripture behind the scenes here is undoubtedly John 3:14–15.[24]

It is within this framework of faith that Weil then speaks of how and what love believes about the neighbor. "Love," she writes, "is a direction," both toward God but in turn toward the neighbor.[25] Specifically, love is an attending-to that is creative, a *looking at* that brings to life, that humanizes, and therefore that participates in the divine action of creation. In short, she calls such love "creative attention." We noted above how in God one finds what Weil calls the supernatural virtue of justice by which God *acts* as though equality is present when in fact it is not. In its human form, such treatment of others is present among those who care for "the least of these"—the hungry and thirsty, the stranger, the naked, the sick, and the imprisoned (Matthew 25:34–36). Love's *faith* about the neighbor is the intellectual corollary of such action, and thus creatively to look at or to attend to one's neighbor accompanies the imitation of God, as one *acts* justly. "He who treats as equals those who are far below him in strength really makes them a gift of the quality of human beings, of which fate had deprived them. As far as it is possible for a creature, he reproduces the original generosity of the Creator with regard to them."[26] Such love that "sees what is invisible" thus requires faith.[27] And the faith to see humanity where there is ugliness, evil, burnout, affliction, ignorance, or displacement recalls, for Weil, Hebrews 11:1: "Faith is the evidence of things not seen" (KJV). Addressing the interdependence of faith and love, she concludes that in the moment of "giving our attention to what does not exist," "faith is present as much as love."[28] She illustrates faith's love in the story of the Good Samaritan in Luke 10. Those who did not help the beaten man *did not see* him, and thus they lacked love's and faith's creative sight: "Those who pass by this thing scarcely notice it, and a few minutes afterward do not even know that they saw it."[29] The nonhuman antecedent "thing" and neuter pronoun "it" convey the blindness of those who pass by. By contrast, the one who *attends* to the beaten man in effect brings the man to new life and *creatively* imitates the work of God.

But Weil states it more strongly: one does not simply imitate God when creatively attending to another; one becomes a vessel of God and is nearly passive. "God alone has this power, the power really to think into being that which does not exist. Only God, present in us, can really think the human quality into the victims of affliction."[30] Weil would thus read the messianic Hebrew epithet *Emmanuel* as literally the case, when it comes to love. God is *with us* when we love: "In true love it is not we who love the afflicted in God; it is God in us who loves them."[31] To call this treatment of others "creative attention" also, then, is literal, according to Weil. When one loves the lowly, one gifts them humanity; one actually participates in the divine activity of creation (or perhaps re-creation). This does not entail that every apparently loving act is indeed that. When one acts toward the lowly not out of the faith of creatively attending to "what is invisible" but only "as an occasion for doing good," "God is not present."[32] In other words, if God acts toward humans out of love and not out of mere pity, then humans can be sure they are to act out of love (faith or creative attention) rather than pity. Weil stops short of filling in the details of creative attention to the other; primarily she wants to argue that love humanizes those who have lost their humanity, which is why love is divinely creative. At this point it is helpful to turn to Kierkegaard to supplement the faith involved in Christian love.

The following words of Job summarize where we are and direct us toward Kierkegaard's ethic:

> If I have rejected the cause of my male or female slaves when they brought a complaint against me, what then shall I do when God rises up?
> When he makes inquiry, what shall I answer him?
> Did not he who made me in the womb make them?
> And did not one fashion us in the womb? (Job 31:13–15, NRSV)

Job seeks to act justly toward his servants when equality is lacking, because he faithfully construes them as children of God and thereby equal in humanity to himself. That is, all people—even slaves—are creatures of a creator god, who therefore are to be valued as such. Of course Job has no more proof of this than he has proof that God has created him.[33] Rather, he trusts the one claim to be true as he trusts the other. Similarly, Kierkegaard's conception of love's faith affirms an *assumption of love* in the other based in common creation. *"The one who loves presupposes that love is in the other person's heart"* (WL, 216). As we saw above, Kierkegaard believes that love's source is hidden, and it is hidden not only in the one who loves but in all people—it has been implanted by God. Thus, the action of loving one's neighbor requires trust in God that this is the case. To presuppose love is to see what is the truth about the other, which is very often invisible, as Weil says. By truth we mean a number of things. First, as Job says, each human is related to God as a loving creation to creator. This is a truth obscured not simply by the self-deception of atheism, but also by the shame brought about by afflic-tion or trauma, or the willfulness of autonomous beings, theistic or atheistic, to determine their own destiny. This is a transformative, life-giving, and life-affirming truth, and thus it is utterly compatible with Weil's language of *cre-atively attending* to the other.

The presupposition of love in the other notices a second truth about the neighbor. Not only is the neighbor deserving of love, but also the neighbor is capable of love. Kierkegaard does not mean to suggest that one loves so that one can get loved back, but instead that the very activity of love *calls forth* love from the other. Love "loves forth" or draws love out of the other (WL, 217). Love empowers the other—the lowly or afflicted—to love. When someone is loved, he or she is spurred on toward love. It is as though there is a magnetic attraction between love and love, what Kierkegaard calls the "like for like." This attraction is similar to the principle underlying the proverb, "A gentle answer turns away wrath, but a harsh word stirs up anger" (Proverbs 15:1, NIV). Gentleness begets gentleness; love begets love. Weil gets at the magnetism of love through the virtue of gratitude in the one who is loved. Only when justice takes on its supernatural form of love is the dignity of the one loved respected, and only when that occurs can the one loved love in return by expressing gratitude. Of course it can be dif-ficult for one who is loved to love in return, especially if one feels like a char-ity case, or if one's pride has been wounded. Thus Weil specifies "supernatural gratitude" as the virtue where one is glad "to be the recipient of supernatural compassion."[34] Such gratitude is possible only when self-respect is left intact, she writes, but of course that is far more likely when one is loved appropriately—as an image-bearing child of God. Supernatural gratitude reflects the love of a restored soul that, once human again, can then participate in the full activity of creatively attending to, or loving, his or her neighbor.

Love's presupposition does a number of things, then. (1) It expresses faith in God's creative, implanting work; (2) it participates in that work—Kierkegaard calls love "sheer action" (WL, 98); (3) it points the neighbor to the truth of love that is in the "heart" of the neighbor, as Kierkegaard says; and therefore (4) it humanizes, dignifies, and restores the neighbor. Importantly, the restoration of the one loved is none other than their being empowered to love others back, as they have been loved. And Kierkegaard views neighbor-love as transformative not just of relationships with enemies, neighbors, or the afflicted, but also with all others—family, lover, friend. "Each one individually, before he relates in love to the beloved, the friend, the loved ones, the contemporaries, must first relate to God" (WL, 112). Thus, central to the restoration of selfhood that results from being loved is viewing all others as themselves loving creatures of a loving God. Kierkegaard calls God the "middle term," that which links two human parties and thus that which gives security and fulfillment to human relationships.

If all of this were not enough to show that the faith love has in love's treatment of the other is rooted in faith in God, Kierkegaard's summation of neighbor-love's content leaves no room for dispute: "The essentially Christian is this: truly to love oneself is to love God; truly to love another person is with every sacrifice . . . to help the other person to love God" (WL, 114). The two great commandments—to love God and to love one's neighbor—are thus inseparable. Likewise, faith in God cannot be distinguished from love's faith about the neighbor, and vice versa. This is not just a controversial claim to provoke the atheist on the part of Kierkegaard; it is a serious warning to misanthropic (neighbor-hating) Christians.

Agapic Moral Fideism

Kierkegaard and Weil claim that faith in God justifies, enables, and requires one to have appropriate faith in the other, who is to be treated as equal. Put differently, faith in God allows one to love one's neighbor. It is in light of love's dependence on faith that Weil claims it "cannot be supported by any knowledge based either on experience or reason."[35] That is, how one ought to treat the other, in this view, cannot be deduced through philosophical argument. Let us call this position "moral fideism." If fideism, construed most charitably, is the view that truly to know God, one must first believe certain things about God and trust God, even though one cannot know with apodictic certainty those things to be true, then moral fideism is the view that truly to act as one ought to act in relation to others, one must do so trustingly, even though one cannot know with apodictic certainty that one is acting as one ought (or that there is a way that one ought to act in the first place). And since in our preceding discussion, the faith to act as one ought is rooted in divine love and in turn produces neighborly love, let us call this position "agapic moral fideism" (where agape is the type of Christian love that Kierkegaard and Weil explore).

Of course fideism is an "ism" without advocates, a school with no students, but since the thesis I have presented is scandalous enough, it seems fit to use the term because the term fits. And, ironically, there is some good *reason* for taking a more friendly view toward fideism than we might think at first glance. In the course of considering the views of faith held by a number of figures including Aquinas, Kant, Kierkegaard, and Wittgenstein, C. Stephen Evans makes the case that some forms of fideism can be responsibly held.[36] Evans argues that the kinds of fideism that absolutely dismiss or are impervious to reason, as represented, for example, by Cornelius van Til or Ludwig Wittgenstein, are—as critics tend to ascribe to all forms of fideism—irrational and therefore irresponsibly held. But these are not the only options for the religious believer. Based upon the work of William James and Alvin Plantinga, Evans suggests that fideism does not entail an outright rejection of reason at all, but simply the claim that knowledge of God comes primarily through faith. "Responsible fideism" allows for faith to be rationally scrutinized, but it also affirms that at times, faith is *above* or even *against* reason. If one grants that what counts as reason is socially or culturally conditioned and thus strongly reflects the prevailing "logic" of a particular society, including the prevailing moral opinions of the day (*Sittlichkeit*), then it follows that a faith that promotes certain moral beliefs and behavior might conflict with modes of thought that go by the name of reason. This does not entail that faith is necessarily irrational, but rather that it may offend a standard of rationality presupposed in the culture. And clearly not every philosophical position, let alone cultural viewpoint, that has proclaimed itself rational has been so according to all other conceptions of rationality. As Merold Westphal writes, "When human thought calls itself 'Reason,' this is all too often little more than self-congratulation and even self-deception."[37]

That knowledge of God comes primarily through faith rather than reason, through God's initiation rather than humans', is the classical Christian position, and it is a position supported by the second problem introduced above—that of cognitive limitation. Given the limits on human reason derived from the human cognitive makeup and moral shortcomings, it is reasonable that one has to rely upon God to know God, and this reliance takes the shape of faith. My position is that the same is true for moral knowledge, if one is to allow that such a thing exists and is knowable in the first place. The "reason" lacking from agapic moral fideism is not, importantly, reasonableness; it is simply a recognition that, in the words of Alasdair MacIntyre, "there is no presuppositionless point of departure," and likewise, those presuppositions of Christian theism will appear unreasonable to many people.[38] Thus responsible fideism, when combined with moral inquiry, adds to that moral inquiry the idea that some amount of trust (and humility, modesty, honesty, and so on) in one's assumptions is requisite and that philosophical argument ultimately fails to justify the moral life.[39] When the moral beliefs that one trusts are true find as their basis the love of God as in Kierkegaard and Weil, we have agapic moral fideism. The question left for the moral—not metaphysical—Christian is whether, in a world without a benevolent, almighty

God, the faith required to affirm the truth that all humans are of equal worth, value, and dignity is more reasonable than the Christian theistic picture. Either way, some measure of some kind of faith seems required. One way to describe the position of both the atheist and theist is "fideistic."

MARK A. TIETJEN is chaplain and Grace Palmer Johnston Chair of Bible at the Stony Brook School in Stony Brook, New York. Tietjen is author of *Kierkegaard, Communication, and Virtue: Authorship as Edification* (Indiana University Press, 2013), and *Kierkegaard: A Christian Missionary to Christians.*

Notes

1. Simone Weil, *Waiting for God*, trans. Emma Craufurd (New York: Harper Perennial Classics, 2000), pp. 137–138.
2. "To arrive at" is ambiguous language. It could indicate that one does not need to *know* Christian doctrine to *know* one's duty to others, for example; this is an epistemic issue. Our issue concerns the metaphysics of morality and so is altogether different from the epistemic issue. The claim here is that—regardless of how one comes to moral knowledge—religion does not ground morality. Moral truths are independent of religion.
3. "Religion and the Queerness of Morality," in *Rationality, Religious Belief, and Moral Commitment*, William Wainwright and Robert Audi, eds. (Ithaca, NY: Cornell University Press, 1986), pp. 213–226.
4. Plato, *The Republic*. in *Complete Works*, edited by John M. Cooper (Indianapolis, IN: Hackett, 1997), 329d.
5. Weil, *Waiting for God*, p. 83.
6. Weil, *Waiting for God*, p. 87. Cf. Psalm 98:9b: "He [the LORD] will judge the world with righteousness, and the peoples with equity."
7. Weil, *Waiting for God*, p. 83.
8. Weil, *Waiting for God*, p. 99.
9. I have here chosen the translation from Søren Kierkegaard, *Provocations: Spiritual Writings of Kierkegaard*, Charles Moore, ed. (Farmington, PA: Plough, 1999), pp. 9–10.
10. Weil, *Waiting for God*, p. 74.
11. Weil, *Waiting for God*, p. 74.
12. Weil, *Waiting for God*, p. 74.
13. Weil, *Waiting for God*, p. 75.
14. Weil also describes Jesus's love as unhappy love.
15. Weil, *Waiting for God*, pp. 90, 91.
16. Weil, *Waiting for God*, p. 86.
17. Weil, *Waiting for God*, p. 93.
18. Weil, *Waiting for God*, p. 80.
19. Weil, *Waiting for God*, p. 84.
20. Weil, *Waiting for God*, p. 3.
21. Weil, *Waiting for God*, p. 4.
22. Weil, *Waiting for God*, p. 4.
23. Weil, *Waiting for God*, p. 4.

24. "And just as Moses lifted up the serpent in the wilderness, so must the Son of Man be lifted up, that whoever believes in him may have eternal life" (NRSV).

25. Weil, *Waiting for God*, p. 81.

26. Weil, *Waiting for God*, p. 88.

27. Weil, *Waiting for God*, p. 92.

28. Weil, *Waiting for God*, p. 92.

29. Weil, *Waiting for God*, p. 90.

30. Weil, *Waiting for God*, pp. 92–93.

31. Weil, *Waiting for God*, pp. 93–94.

32. Weil, *Waiting for God*, pp. 92, 93.

33. "*By faith* we understand that the universe was formed at God's command, so that what is seen was not made out of what was visible" (Hebrews 11:3, NIV).

34. Weil, *Waiting for God*, p. 91.

35. Weil, *Waiting for God*, p. 137.

36. C. Stephen Evans, *Faith Beyond Reason: A Kierkegaardian Account* (Grand Rapids, MI: Eerdmans, 1998).

37. Merold Westphal, *Whose Community? Which Interpretation?* (Grand Rapids, MI: Baker Academic, 2009), p. 151.

38. Alasdair MacIntyre, *Dependent Rational Animals: Why Human Beings Need the Virtues* (Chicago: Open Court, 1999), p. 77.

39. In *Ethics and the Limits of Philosophy*, Bernard Williams seems to affirm this view by claiming that confidence, not certainty, is what we are seeking in the development of a moral outlook (Cambridge, MA: Harvard University Press, 1985), pp. 170–171.

.

PART II

Moral Psychology and Ethical Existence

6 Kierkegaard's Virtues? Humility and Gratitude as the Grounds of Contentment, Patience, and Hope in Kierkegaard's Moral Psychology

John Lippitt

In RECENT YEARS, a growing body of work has connected Kierkegaard with discussions of the virtues. While some have objected to this move,[1] I think this scepticism can legitimately be resisted, provided we understand what connecting Kierkegaard with the virtues does—and does not—necessarily commit us to. Robert C. Roberts has perhaps been the most powerful advocate of the idea that Kierkegaard can profitably be read as exploring various character traits that we should not balk at calling "virtues."[2] Roberts sees Kierkegaard as part of a tradition he labels "virtuism," which emphasizes such features as our having a common human nature or telos, and developing enduring character traits that hinder or help in the pursuit of that telos. Such traits—something we are, rather than just something we do or passively undergo—are dispositions to act, feel, perceive, and so on, in particular ways. An excellent trait—a virtue—tends to be endorsed, confirmed, and consolidated by the choices of the one possessing it. These traits operate not in isolation, but are interconnected in various ways, such that they tend either to support or undermine each other (virtue tending to beget virtue, and vice to beget vice). Virtues (or vices) tend to make for (or fail to make for) the well-being of their possessor, and to an extent that of their associates. And finally, "virtuists" are committed to ethical and spiritual education or "upbuilding," including the formation of proper concerns and dispositions to emotions, perceptions, and actions.

We should perhaps distinguish such "virtuism" from "virtue ethics" as that term is often used, for at least two reasons. First, as Roberts himself notes, the traits in question are not necessarily "ethical" in any narrow sense that would exclude such spiritual qualities as hope or faith.[3] Second, Kierkegaard's interest in virtues obviously does not arise from seeing "virtue ethics" as an approach more promising to solving theoretical problems in ethics than are deontology or consequentialism.[4] (Such a view constitutes what has been called "routine" as opposed to "radical" virtue ethics, Kierkegaard having more in common with the latter.[5]) As Gregory Beabout has noted, this distinguishes both Kierkegaard and the classical virtue tradition from "virtue ethics" as that term is often used in contemporary parlance.[6] Rather, both Kierkegaard and the classical virtue tradition aim primarily at "upbuilding."

A further distinction to be made between Kierkegaard and several key thinkers in the mainstream tradition of "virtuism" is that some of the latter (such as Plato, Aristotle and Aquinas) see virtues as being perfections of specific faculties. But for Kierkegaard, virtues are features of the whole person, and it is the whole person who needs to be "built up."[7] Secondly, consider the possible worry that virtues are often thought of as *achievements of an individual*, such that sin—and its roots in the human will—is overlooked.[8] But there is no obligation to view virtues in such a way. In Augustine's critique of pagan virtue, for instance, the criticism is not of virtues per se, but instead of the aspiration to self-sufficiency.[9] Anyone who achieves what "virtuism" calls a virtue could quite consistently hold that this is not their own achievement, but rather a gift of which they are merely a steward, responsible for using it for good. As I have suggested elsewhere, concerns about meritoriousness can be avoided if such a person operates with what Mark Tietjen has suggested as a working definition of virtues according to Kierkegaard: "dispositions to be achieved by works that one must strive to do in response to God's grace, with the help of God's grace."[10] This central focus on grace derails the tacit assumption of the proud person who thinks that divine favor results from his own merits. In summary, therefore, I think it is quite reasonable to describe as "virtues" the spiritual qualities I shall focus upon in this essay.

But if such qualities are interconnected, how do they hang together, for Kierkegaard? Part of the answer is obvious, insofar as most such "Kierkegaardian virtues" are either expressions of faith or in some other way related to faith. But can we say more than this? In this paper, inspired in part by an approach taken by Roberts in his *Spiritual Emotions*, I explore the prospects for understanding three such notions—the contentment beyond anxiety that Kierkegaard sometimes calls "joy," patience, and hope—as rooted in underlying attitudes of *humility* and *gratitude*. I explore what kind of humility and gratitude is in play, before going on to consider how these attitudes might support that species of *contentment* that seems integral to several of Kierkegaard's discourses on the lilies and the birds. How, in turn, might this give rise to *patience* and *hope*, and of what sort? The paper thus seeks to sketch something of the internal dynamics of the relations between several virtue-terms—including how, for Kierkegaard, they are all rooted in an image of a God of forgiveness. In this sense, I think my view differs somewhat from that of Roberts, who sees hope, humility, and gratitude (among others) as "auxiliary" to faith and love in Kierkegaard.[11] By contrast, I see these virtues as part of the very structure of Kierkegaardian faith and love.

Humility and Gratitude as a "Moral Project"

I propose approaching Kierkegaard's discussion under the heading of humility and gratitude "as a moral project," to borrow Roberts's phrase.[12] Roberts's task is to outline a background against which he can usefully unpack several "emotion-virtues." He understands emotions as "concern-based construals." They are construals insofar as they have "an immediacy reminiscent of sense perception. They are impressions, ways things appear to the subject; . . . not just judgements or thoughts or beliefs."[13] They differ from other construals in being based on the subject's *concerns*: their desires, aversions, interests, and so on. So, for example, fear is the construal of its object as threatening in some way. As we shall see, this allows for a view of emotion-virtues as, *inter alia*, certain *ways of seeing* that can be encouraged by cultivating certain *ways of looking*.[14] The view of "humility as a moral project" is a key part of the background against which Roberts discusses six "fruits of the spirit"—contrition, joy, gratitude, hope, peace, and compassion—all of which he treats as Christian "emotion-virtues." I want to explore whether some similar picture will ground Kierkegaard's discussion of some other virtue-terms.

Humility[15]

On the face of it, humility seems a plausible central candidate, given Kierkegaard's repeated focus on such notions as "dying to the self" and "self-denial." I have argued elsewhere that Kierkegaard in places over-eggs the importance of self-denial, on occasion failing to distinguish between humility and self-abasement, and that this can deafen us to a gentler Kierkegaardian voice that has much of "upbuilding" value to say to us.[16] One of the places in which this voice is perhaps clearest is the 1847 discourses on the lilies and the birds (the second part of *Upbuilding Discourses in Various Spirits*). I think we can better understand what is valuable about the "dying to the self" talk by asking, first, how might this be an expression of humility? And second, humility of what sort?[17]

Whatever it turns out to be, Kierkegaard sees humility as necessary for faith and Christian practice. Indeed, the intriguing phrase "humble courage [*Ydmyge Mod*]" used to describe the faith of Abraham in *Fear and Trembling* (FT, 49; SKS 4:143), reappears in *The Sickness Unto Death* as that which is needed to be able to bear the offence of Christianity's incarnational claims (SUD, 85; SKS 11:199). Similarly, in *For Self-Examination*, humility is presented as central to being able to accept the doctrine of salvation by grace alone: "Your life should express works as strenuously as possible; then one thing more is required—that you humble yourself and confess: But my being saved is nevertheless grace" (FSE, 17; SKS 13:46). Moreover, this humility is in a sense an attitude of *divine imitation*: in the *Postscript*, for instance, humility is presented as how love has expressed itself in "the form of the absolute difference" between God and humanity, and we are called to imitate this in loving our neighbors (CUP, 492; SKS 7:446). *Works of Love* goes on to discuss loving acts in terms of a *mutual humbling that is nevertheless not humiliating*, thanks to the dexterity of love: "The one who loves humbles himself before the good, whose lowly servant he is, and, as he himself admits, in frailty; and the one overcome does not humble himself before the loving one but before the good. But when in a relationship between two people both are humbled, then there of course is nothing humiliating for either one of them" (WL, 340; SKS 9:335).

Robert Puchniak has suggested that humility (as Kierkegaard understands it) makes it possible for one to suffer patiently, deepen Christian faith, experience peace, and love others.[18] He adds, "If one is overly troubled by the thought of one's insignificance or is too preoccupied with worldly status, genuine humility will be impossible."[19] There is surely something right about this, but as with self-denial, I think to talk of our "insignificance" is potentially misleading. Hence the need for our questions: how should we best think about humility? Does this show us to be "insignificant"? Is this the best way to construe what becoming "nothing" before God means in this context, or should we construe it in a different way?

In addressing these questions, I turn first to Kierkegaard's 1847 discourses on the lilies and the birds. They serve as a commentary on Matthew 6:24–34 (part of the Sermon on the Mount), a passage that so intrigued Kierkegaard that he returned to it on numerous occasions.[20] Part of the message here seems to be the possibility of opposing potentially overwhelming, debilitating worry with a certain kind of contentment that Kierkegaard sometimes labels "joy" [*Glæde*].[21] This is especially true of those many cases where we ourselves are the ultimate cause of our worries.[22]

Kierkegaard describes the lilies and the birds as our "divinely appointed teachers," and the discourses go on to consider what they teach (UDVS, 157; SKS 8:258).[23] The theme of the first discourse is "to be contented with being a human being," and both it and the biblical passage on which it reflects address *the worried* (UDVS, 159, 162; SKS 8:261–262). The first thing we are to learn from the lilies and the birds is their *silence*,[24] through which we humans might learn a kind of positive self-forgetfulness that counteracts the destructive self-centeredness and self-absorption that is, for Kierkegaard, at the heart of so many human ills. Kierkegaard argues that the distressed person can achieve this by contemplating the lilies and the birds and in so doing at least temporarily forgetting himself—and yet he, "unnoticed . . . learns something about himself" (UDVS, 161–162; SKS 8:261). What does he learn?

Kierkegaard's overall argument here is for a parallel between the beauty or value of a lily and that of a human being (UDVS, 165; SKS 8:265). The sheer wonder of being alive, and of being human, is typically forgotten through the "worried inventiveness of comparison" (ibid.). *Comparison* now becomes a crucial theme in the discourse, and the kind of damaging self-focus that it encourages inspires one of the most moving passages in the discourse literature, on "the worried lily."

In this parable, the life of a beautiful, carefree lily is complicated by the arrival of a small bird. Instead of delighting in the lily's beauty, the bird stresses its difference (its freedom of movement) and—worse still—waxes lyrical about the beauty of other lilies it has encountered on its travels. It typically ends its chatter with the remark that "in comparison with that kind of glory the lily looked like nothing—indeed, it was so insignificant that it was a question whether the lily had a right to be called a lily" (ibid.). But note—for this will become important—that Kierkegaard *rejects* the bird's claim of the lily's insignificance.

The lily becomes worried, and its self-doubts disturb its previously carefree existence. Its static life starts to seem restrictive, and, influenced by the bird's destructive chatter, it starts to feel *humiliated*, wishing it was a Crown Imperial, which the bird has told it is the most gorgeous of all lilies, envied by all others (UDVS, 168; SKS 8:267). Now comes a subtle twist in the tale. The lily convinces itself that its desire is not so unreasonable, since it is not "asking for the impossible, to become what I am not, a bird, for example. My wish is only to become a gorgeous lily, or even the most gorgeous" (UDVS, 168; SKS 8:267–268).

Eventually, the lily confesses its worries to the bird, and together they hit upon a solution. The bird will peck away the soil restricting the lily to its spot and uproot it, and together they will fly to where the most gorgeous lilies grow, in the hope that with the change of location, the lily might succeed in realizing what it has convinced itself is its full "potential."

Such ambition is the root of its destruction: once uprooted, of course, the lily withers and dies. The moral Kierkegaard draws is that while the lily is the human being, the "naughty little bird" is "the restless mentality of comparison, which roams far and wide, fitfully and capriciously, and gleans the morbid knowledge of diversity" (UDVS, 169; SKS 8:268). While the diversity it notes between human beings is not a falsehood, "the poetic"—a mixture of truth and untruth—"consists in maintaining that diversity . . . is the supreme, and this is eternally false" (UDVS, 169; SKS 8:269). The problem arises from stressing the *diversity* that results from the spirit of comparison more than our *common humanity*.[25] Relatedly, the lily's key mistake seems to be to fail to recognize its earthbound nature, to refuse to be what it was intended to be (UDVS, 170; SKS 8:269). Hence Kierkegaard concludes, "If a human being, like the lily, is contented with being a human being, he does not become sick with temporal worries, and if he does not become worried about temporal things, he remains in the place assigned to him;

and if he remains there, then it is true that he, by being a human being, is more glorious than Solomon's glory" (ibid.).

Human freedom is *rooted*. From the lilies, we can learn a certain kind of *self-acceptance*: to be contented with being a human being, and to recognize that *our common humanity transcends the diversity between us*.[26] We can already start to see how the *contentment* being offered in these discourses is rooted in humility, gratitude to God, and placing all one's worries on God. But talk of our "insignificance" does not do justice to what Kierkegaard wishes us to glean here: as we saw, *that the lily (and thus the human being) is insignificant is explicitly rejected*. Somewhat counterintuitively, to say that I am "nothing" is *not* to say that I am insignificant.

I suggest that Roberts's account of humility sheds further light on this. Rejecting some familiar accounts of non-virtuous "humility"—Uriah Heep's deviously strategic display of "being 'umble" for personal advantage in Dickens's *David Copperfield*; the excessive self-abasement of some medieval monastic literature—Roberts claims that humility, as he wishes to valorize it, is "a transcendent form of self-confidence"[27] (in a sense to be explained shortly). In line with our discussion above, such humility stems from a worldview in which everyone is viewed as ultimately equal.[28] This enables us to transcend the demands of the "restless mentality of comparison," in which we live in perpetual anxiety about how we compare to others. (Yes, you once won the Booker Prize, but are those smart young novelists a generation younger than you now about to eclipse your achievements? Yes, I have abased myself before all and sundry, but insofar as I have to admit that I took a certain pride in this self-abasement, should I not be abasing myself all over again for that?) This is not anxiety as the gateway to freedom; it is anxiety as the tool of an endlessly competitive—because comparative—ego. Is a key part of what we should understand by "dying to the self" a dying to this competitive ego, and the self-obsession that it sponsors? Roberts suggests that such humility is consistent not only with self-confidence but also with "initiative, assertiveness, and self-esteem."[29] If by self-esteem he means self-acceptance, I agree. Such humility is "a psychological principle of independence from others"—I don't need to go one better than them in order to feel at ease with myself—"and a necessary ground of genuine fellowship with them."[30] The ideal here, which Roberts discusses in the context of raising a child in a healthily loving environment, is as follows: "This implicit and inarticulate sense of his own worth, if carried into adulthood by becoming articulated in a definite life view, would *be the radical self-confidence that Christians call humility*: a self-confidence so deep, a personal integration so strong that all comparison with other people, both advantageous and disadvantageous, slides right off him."[31] He has a sufficient sense of his own worth neither to be distressed by the fact that others are in several respects ahead of him in the "games of life," nor to take a sense of glee in the respects in which he is himself ahead.[32] Such an attitude manifests both a humility rooted in considering our common humanity as more important than the differences highlighted by "comparison," and a self-acceptance that enables one to keep anxiety or worry in its place.[33]

Roberts suggests that such humility is not an emotion per se, but rather "an emotion-disposition—primarily a negative one, a disposition *not* to feel the emotions associated with caring a lot about one's status."[34] Such a person's sense of self-worth does not depend upon any kind of ranking (in terms of money, power, intelligence, etc.). Insofar as such a person resists what Roberts calls "a spiritually cannibalistic appetite,"[35] he resists the snares of the "spirit of comparison" against which Kierkegaard warns.[36]

Roberts draws two important implications from this. First and most obviously, in order to cultivate such a virtue, we would require a view that requires us to see our neighbors as our valued equals (rather than "the competition"). And second, it requires some alternative basis for our self-acceptance than success in competitive ranking or the esteem of others. Christianity, in which our ultimate value derives from being loved by God, provides such a worldview (though not, as Roberts notes, uniquely so).[37] The same self-confidence described above is, he suggests, the "psychological structure of the kingdom of God," in which we are each aware of being so surrounded by love that the kind of comparison and competitiveness that induce such worry do not impact upon our self-evaluation.[38]

Gratitude

Gratitude seems a fairly natural companion virtue to humility as sketched above.[39] Most of Kierkegaard's references to gratitude are to be found in signed works and journal entries rather than pseudonymous writings.[40] In the signed works, the focus tends to be on how Christians are to be grateful for temporal gifts, whereas in the journals the focus is more specific: on the Christian's gratitude for the forgiveness of his sins, and how such gratitude should be the spur toward imitation of Christ. A famous 1851 journal entry puts this clearly: "*Christianly* the emphasis does not fall so much upon to what extent or how far a person succeeds in meeting or fulfilling the requirement, if he actually is striving, as it is upon his getting an impression of the requirement in all its infinitude so that he rightly learns to be humbled and to rely upon grace . . . infinite humiliation [in the sense of "learning to be humbled"] and grace, and then a striving born of gratitude—this is Christianity" (JP § 1993; SKS 24).[41]

This quote alone suggests how humility and gratitude are central (and both rooted in the God who forgives). Corey Tutewiler gives a plausible account of the basic Lutheran logic of this picture. "Infinite humiliation" relates to consciousness of my own sin, which I am unable to atone for through my own works or merits. "Grace" is the forgiveness of my sins, which taken seriously inspires an extraordinary feeling of gratitude, which is the catalyst for my "striving" and imitation of Christ. As Kierkegaard puts it in another journal entry, "Imitation or discipleship does not come first, but 'grace'; then *imitation follows as a fruit of gratitude*, as well as one is able" (JP § 1886/SKS 24, NB 22:52, my emphasis). "Works" are then simply a "stronger expression of gratitude" than the merely verbal giving of thanks (JP § 4524; SKS 24, NB 22:122). For all that Kierkegaard is on this point a card-carrying Lutheran, "works" needs to be stressed to a complacent Christendom that, lacking Luther's anguished conscience, has signed up to the doctrine of *sola gratia* justification in such a way as to let themselves off the hook of bothering with "works" at all (ibid.).[42] In further journal entries, Kierkegaard claims that "Christ has desired only one kind of gratitude: from the individual, and as practically as possible in the form of imitation" (JP § 1518; SKS 25, NB 30:7; see also JP § 1892; SKS 24, NB 22:144). In this way, Tutewiler notes that gratitude for Kierkegaard is both "causal and consequential."[43] In other words, as well as being the consequence of grace (akin to the joy that results from receiving a gift), it is the "cause" of—it might be better to say "catalyst for"—imitation and works. Tutewiler also describes gratitude for Kierkegaard as a "disposition of receptiveness."[44] But again, I think we can draw on Roberts to shine further light on this.

In a discussion of the virtuously grateful person, Roberts argues that such a person is disposed to see the loving motive in her benefactor, and to discount the less noble.[45] This is rooted in humility. Roberts's chief literary example of humility is Esther Summerson in Dickens's *Bleak House*, and—supporting my general hypothesis as to the importance of connecting humility with gratitude—it is to Esther that he returns in discussing the virtue of gratitude. Gratitude *qua* virtue "has a kind of generosity built into it, a generosity in attributing motives."[46] (We might think of this as a manifestation of how love presupposes love in the other, *à la Works of Love*.) But Roberts makes a second point, which interestingly suggests *how* such humility can be a source of strength that bears its fruit in gratitude. Consider two views of dignity. In contrast to the person whose sense of dignity requires "constant maintenance and defense"[47]—such as he who tends to see slights where none were intended—Esther's sense of dignity (a view of herself as a creature loved and forgiven by God) is more secure. Her "generous disposition to see the best in givers' motives and to overlook their foibles is possible because she does not feel that she needs constantly to be defending or re-establishing her dignity."[48] This is "*dignity as a creature and as a fellow-creature . . .* the sense of one's own importance [an importance shared by all one's neighbors] that derives from and is qualified by thinking of oneself as *fundamentally* a recipient of grace"; that one's very life is a divine gift. This gloss on dignity in terms of an importance that each individual shares is a useful corrective, I submit, to the kind of focus on humility and gratitude that talks about them in terms of our "insignificance." Central to this is a particular way of seeing: in line with his view of emotions as concern-based construals, Roberts presents gratitude as a kind of *seeing* that we can practice by *looking* (such as for blessings in adversity).[49] The secure sense of dignity that stems from construing oneself as loved and forgiven by God gives rise to gratitude, and it disposes Esther both to see—and actively look for—the best in people and the world.[50]

Both *immediate seeing* and *active looking* are important here. On one level, things tend to *strike* the grateful person as undeserved gifts. Yet on another level, man cannot live on such ecstatic epiphanies alone. So not only must grace always be *actively chosen*,[51] this needs to be done in *repetition*: there is typically an element of continual struggle needed to maintain such a way of seeing. So in this sense, both humility and gratitude are indeed moral *projects*.[52]

Contentment, Joy, Patience, and Hope

Next, I want to consider the implications of the above for the kind of contentment that Kierkegaard sometimes calls "joy," patience, and hope. The dignity we just discussed typically expresses itself in a kind of contentment that we already encountered in our discussion of the lilies and the birds. I want now to connect this both to Paul's mention of contentment in his letter to the Philippians and to Kierkegaard's discussion of joy.

Contentment and Joy

Joy [*Glæde*] is a central concept for Kierkegaard.[53] To the Anglophone reader, the etymological link to the English word "glad" is worth noting, as in English "joy" is potentially misleading. The word "joy," to my ear, has a certain *effervescence* that is not, as far as I can see, a necessary requirement for what Kierkegaard means by his usage of the term.[54] I submit that we might better understand joy or gladness as stemming from addressing one's worry through grace.[55] And it is in this sense similar to what Paul (or his NIV translators) means by *contentment*, when in his letter to the Philippians, he writes: "I am not saying this [that is, giving thanks] because I am in need, for I have learned to be content whatever the circumstances. I know what it is to be in need, and I know what it is to have plenty. I have learned the secret of being content in any and every situation, whether well fed or hungry, whether living in plenty or in want. I can do all this through him who gives me strength" (Phil 4:11–13).

If we are honest, I think this will at first strike most of us as an extraordinary claim. Content in *any and every* situation?[56] Yet Paul clearly roots this claimed ability in his faith. The ideas expressed a few verses earlier[57]—how to deal with anxiety, and how the peace of God may be attained—are central to Kierkegaard's discussions of joy, particularly in the "lilies and birds" discourses. Hence my suggestion that one way joy can be understood is as *the feeling of liberation from the power that worry has over us*. Depending on the circumstances, this might be either a feeling of effervescent ecstasy or a quieter sense of relief and rest combined with a sense that one has been graced with the ability to persevere, whatever life throws at one. In the latter kind of case, just as earlier we considered humility as primarily a "negative" disposition—a disposition *not* to feel certain emotions—perhaps joy (or contentment) can be seen as a "negative" disposition in the sense that it is a disposition *not* to let the cares, sorrows, and vicissitudes of life overwhelm you.[58] As Paul implies, and I think Kierkegaard agrees, such a disposition would be rooted in faith, humility, and gratitude. This freedom from worry—achieved by casting all our sorrow upon God (WA, 41; SKS 11:45)[59]—is what enables creatures like us, who understand ourselves at least partially as temporal beings, to live contentedly in "today": not denying the burdens of "tomorrow," but not overwhelmed or debilitated by them.[60] Kierkegaard seems to rank qualitatively different kinds of joy, from the relatively superficial joy of the aesthete—regarded as self-deceptive (EO II, 252; SKS 3:240)—to the "unconditional joy" embodied in the lilies and the birds, from whom we can learn to be *properly* joyful.[61] In the "lilies and birds" discourses, joy is explained as being "present to oneself," which in turn is unpacked as "truly *to be today*" and to view as irrelevant "tomorrow" (WA, 38–39; SKS 11:42–43).[62] The joy that the lilies and birds teach puts "the whole emphasis on: *the present time*" (WA, 39; SKS 11:43). In a related discourse, "The Worry [*Bekymring*] of Self-Torment," Kierkegaard describes "the next day" as "the grappling hook [*Entrehagen*] with which the huge mass of worries seizes hold of the single individual's little ship" (CD, 72; SKS 10:81, translation adjusted); thus "if a person is to gain mastery over his mind, he must begin by getting rid of the next day" (CD, 71; SKS 10:80). The *silence* that the lily and bird also teach human beings is explicitly linked to *forgetting oneself and one's plans* (WA, 19; SKS 11:24).[63] What makes this possible, on this account, is the kind of joyful "self-confidence" that is rooted in trust in God, he upon whom all sorrows can be cast (WA, 41–42; SKS 11:45).[64]

But joy need not be otherworldly. In Kierkegaard's view, one can legitimately take a religious joy in the world, take joy in the "good and perfect gifts" bestowed upon us. Life itself, the changing of the seasons (WA, 39–40; SKS 11:43–44), erotic love (EUD, 43; SKS 5:419), and even wealth are mentioned among these goods (CD, 32; SKS 10:43). Yet what really matters is what he calls "unconditional joy" as manifested by the lilies and the birds, who fundamentally *are* joy and are thus best placed to teach it (WA, 36–38; SKS 11:40–42). The lilies and birds' joy is a matter of being freed from regret about the past and worry about the future. Again, one way of achieving this—as in some forms of stoicism—is to rid oneself of desire, cultivating passionless detachment. But Kierkegaard is again critical of this, associating such an attitude—"wanting to kill the wish"—with animality and describing it as "spiritual suicide" (UDVS, 100; SKS 8:203). The lilies and birds, present as they are to themselves, teach us to cast all our sorrows upon

God; their message for human beings is "worshipfully to dare to believe 'that God cares for you.' The unconditional joy is simply joy over God, over whom and in whom you can always unconditionally rejoice" (WA, 43; SKS 11:46). Elsewhere this is connected with "the only joyful thought," namely that each of us is loved by God (UDVS, 274; SKS 8:370). Thus we can see that this joy or contentment is meant to follow from the sense that God loves us and forgives our sins. Perhaps it is to be thought of as an expression of our *gratitude* for this.

Patience and Hope

In what space remains, I want briefly to suggest how patience—the cultivation of which is made easier by such contentment as sketched above—is related to the hope that Kierkegaard calls "expectancy" [*Forventning*]. Both are exemplified by Simeon and especially Anna, figures briefly mentioned in Luke's gospel.[65] Kierkegaard picks up from his predecessors[66] the significance of Anna's fidelity to the memory of her dead husband as well as to God, throughout a long widowhood following a relatively short marriage.[67] This twin fidelity schools her in patience, perseverance, and hope, and the 1843 and 1844 discourses in which she appears make much of these themes.

Though surprisingly underdiscussed, once one starts to look for it, the centrality of hope in Kierkegaard's thought is hard to exaggerate. He describes all life as being "one nightwatch of expectancy" (EUD, 206; SKS 5:207). Similarly, the *Works of Love* deliberation "Love hopes all things" tells us that "the whole of one's life should be the time of hope" (WL, 251; SKS 9:251). There Kierkegaard defines hoping as relating oneself in expectancy to the possibility of the good (WL, 249; SKS 9:249). We are concerned here not merely with hope that arises episodically, but rather a hopefulness that is a "formed disposition of the person of faith."[68] All this recalls the 1843 discourse "The Expectancy of Faith."

There, Kierkegaard views the ability to occupy oneself with the future as "a sign of the nobility of human beings" (EUD, 17; SKS 5:27). Our ability to project ourselves imaginatively into the future is something that separates us from the animals (or the birds . . .)—but as we have already seen, it is precisely this that threatens us with worry about "the next day." Faith has already been presented in this discourse as "the only power that can conquer the future," which we by now might suspect relates to these worries (EUD, 16; SKS 5:25).[69] And sure enough, Kierkegaard goes on to add that this battle with the future is really a battle with oneself, insofar as the only power the future has over us is that which we give it (EUD, 18; SKS 5:27). One conquers the future—that is, one's worries about "tomorrow"—by means of something constant, "the eternal." But the "eternal power in a human being" (EUD, 19; SKS 5:28) is precisely faith: trust in the eternal God, treated as our lodestar. And faith expects "victory," interpreted as that God is working all things together for good.[70]

Strikingly, Kierkegaard claims that one important contrast between the hope or expectancy of the person of faith, and alternative notions of hope, is that genuine hope cannot be disappointed (EUD, 23; SKS 5:32; cf. WL, 262; SKS 9:261). How can this be? He explains it thus: "There is an expectancy that the whole world cannot take from me; it is the expectancy of faith, and this is victory. I am not deceived, since I did not believe that the world would keep the promise it seemed to be making to me; my expectancy was not in the world but in God. This expectancy is not deceived; even now I sense its victory more gloriously and more joyfully than I sense all the pain of loss." (EUD, 24; SKS 5:32.)

Consider this in light of the 1844 discourse in which Kierkegaard glosses being victorious as *God* being victorious (in line with the Lutheran idea of one's "center of gravity" being transferred to God).[71] Such hope is not mere wishing—it *expects* victory (which it construes as *God's* victory). But what makes it unshakable? Crucial here is the distinction Kierkegaard makes between such hope and one way of not having faith, namely expecting *something particular [noget Enkelt]*. He claims, "Not only the person who expects absolutely nothing does not have faith, but also the person who expects something particular or who bases his expectancy on something particular" (EUD, 27; SKS 5:35).

I suggest that we can best understand Kierkegaard's meaning here by connecting what he says about hope with what Jonathan Lear has called "radical hope."[72] Lear's key exemplar of radical hope is Plenty Coups, the last chief of the North American Crow Nation, who according to Lear manifested this hope in the context of the impending collapse of the entire civilization and way of life the Crow had hitherto known. In brief, such hope is radical insofar as one "needed some conception of—or commitment to—a goodness that transcended one's current understanding of the good."[73] (Compare the New Testament idea that "everything is new in Christ.") Lear imagines Plenty Coups reasoning as follows: "God . . . is good. My commitment to the genuine transcendence of God is manifest in my commitment to the goodness of the world transcending our necessarily limited attempt to understand it. My commitment to God's transcendence and goodness is manifested in my commitment to the idea that *something good will emerge even if it outstrips my present limited capacity for understanding what that good is.*"[74]

It is this attitude of extreme openness to the future that makes such hope "radical," and that differs from hope for "something particular." Significantly, John Macquarrie notes this as a feature of hope in both the Old and New Testaments. Macquarrie remarks that human promises tend to be "sufficiently specific" to know whether or not they have been kept. However, he adds,

> No such simple criteria seem to operate when we are thinking of the promises of God. His basic promise is to give us more abundant life. But we cannot

specify the conditions of such a life in advance. It is only in the unfolding of history and the actual deepening of human life that we can say whether the promise is being fulfilled. This could well mean that it is fulfilled differently from the way we had at one time expected, for our expectation could be framed only in terms of what we had experienced up to that point, whereas the fulfilling of the promise might bring with it something new.[75]

To bring us full circle, *such hope is a manifestation of humility*, not only in the sense that it has transferred the center of gravity from self to God, but also because it recognizes the limits of one's imaginative capacities *qua* finite creature. We have here both *an ethical and an epistemic humility*.[76] What such hope amounts to, in part, is a commitment to a goodness beyond its understanding. This sounds like what it means to "cast all one's worries upon God"—to turn the whole situation over to God in faith, trust, and hope (cf. CD, 77; SKS 10:86).

So how is hope—which is essentially about the future—compatible with what Kierkegaard says about getting rid of "the next day"—that is, the future? The answer, I think, is simply that one is urged to limit one's tasks to the challenges of today, and that the attitude one should take toward the troubles of tomorrow is one of faithful and trusting hope.[77] In this sense, perhaps casting all one's worries upon God is simply another term for hope.

All this makes a difference to the connected account of patience. Such hope or "expectancy" is not a natural disposition but instead a "hard-won achievement," an achievement won "in patience."[78] Anna's patience amounts to a persistence in sustaining an attitude of expectant hope in the face of tribulations that militate against it.[79] Her faith makes her especially resilient; fulfilment can never come too late, and so there is no need for impatience. And note that this is itself a concern-based construal: Anna construes the coming of the Messiah as so important that nothing could constitute "waiting too long" for it (EUD, 215–216; SKS 5:215–216). Note, though, that this connects with a more general point about our having both a temporal and an eternal nature. Because the self is what it is through being *acquired* (in part through lived, *repeated* self-choice as self-receptivity), it is never "completed" in time. And this simply underlines the importance of hope.[80]

Summary

In light of the question of how various virtue-terms discussed by Kierkegaard hang together, I have tried to offer a preliminary sketch of how contentment beyond worry, patience, and hope are rooted in dispositions of humility and gratitude, which are in turn, for Kierkegaard, rooted in a picture of a God who forgives. Cultivating the dispositions of humility and gratitude is for Kierkegaard part of a moral project necessary for faith and Christian practice. The

1847 discourses on the lilies and the birds invite us to be contented with being a human being: here our common humanity is judged more important than the differences between us, and I have suggested reading the "silence" the lilies and birds teach as silencing the ceaseless demands of the comparative and competitive ego. But this is not the same thing as teaching that we are "insignificant," a view that is explicitly rejected. I have suggested that such a view of humility dovetails nicely with Roberts's account of humility as a kind of "self-confidence" that transcends the comparative ego; judges others as valued equals (rather than "the competition"); and derives a sense of self-acceptance from being valued, loved, and forgiven by God. Such humility is inextricably linked to a gratitude that is both consequential upon grace and a catalyst for "works" and the imitation of Christ. I connected this gratitude with a certain generosity of spirit in relation to others that is itself rooted in humility and a sense of dignity or self-worth that is not dependent upon competitive ranking, thereby suggesting that humility is a source of strength that bears its fruit in gratitude. I then tried to sketch the implications of this for contentment, patience, and hope. Contentment—one dimension of Kierkegaardian joy—I treated as a feeling of liberation from the power that worry has to overwhelm us. The key to achieving this is seeing ourselves as "eternal" as well as temporal beings. This further impacts upon patience and hope, conceived of in terms of trust in the eternal God. Such hope is "radical" in the sense that what "the good" amounts to may outstrip our capacity, at any given point, to conceptualize it. In this way we come full circle, insofar as such hope is one manifestation of both epistemic and ethical humility.[81]

JOHN LIPPITT is Professor of Ethics and Philosophy of Religion at the University of Hertfordshire, UK, and Honorary Professor of Philosophy at Deakin University, Australia. He is author of the *Routledge Guidebook to Kierkegaard's Fear and Trembling*, *Kierkegaard and the Problem of Self-Love*, and *Humour and Irony in Kierkegaard's Thought*.

Notes

1. See for instance Bruce H. Kirmmse, "Kierkegaard and MacIntyre: Possibilities for Dialogue," in *Kierkegaard After MacIntyre: Essays on Freedom, Narrative and Virtue*, John J. Davenport and Anthony Rudd, eds. (Chicago: Open Court, 2001).

2. See Robert C. Roberts, "The Virtue of Hope in *Eighteen Upbuilding Discourses*," in *International Kierkegaard Commentary, Vol. 5*, Eighteen Upbuilding Discourses, Robert L. Perkins, ed. (Macon, GA: Mercer University Press, 2003); "Kierkegaard, Wittgenstein and a Method of Virtue Ethics," in *Kierkegaard in Post/Modernity*, Martin J. Matustik and Merold Westphal, eds. (Bloomington: Indiana University Press, 1995); and "Existence, Emotion and Character: Classical Themes in Kierkegaard," in *The Cambridge Companion to Kierkegaard*, Alastair

Hannay and Gordon D. Marino, eds. (Cambridge: Cambridge University Press, 1998). See also C. Stephen Evans and Robert C. Roberts, "Ethics," in *The Oxford Handbook of Kierkegaard*, John Lippitt and George Pattison, eds. (Oxford: Oxford University Press, 2013).

3. Roberts, "The Virtue of Hope," p. 184, n. 6.

4. It seems clear to me that there are deontological, teleological, and virtues-based elements in Kierkegaard's thought.

5. David Solomon, "Virtue Ethics: Radical or Routine?" in *Intellectual Virtue: Perspectives from Ethics and Epistemology*, Michael DePaul and Linda Zagzebski, eds. (New York: Oxford University Press, 2003). For a brief yet helpful discussion of Kierkegaard in light of this distinction, see Mark A. Tietjen, *Kierkegaard, Communication and Virtue: Authorship as Edification* (Bloomington: Indiana University Press, 2013), pp. 130–134.

6. Gregory R. Beabout, "The Silent Lily and Bird as Exemplars of the Virtue of Active Receptivity," in *International Kierkegaard Commentary, Vol. 18*, Without Authority, Robert L. Perkins, ed. (Macon, GA: Mercer University Press, 2007), pp. 138–139.

7. For further discussion on this, see Beabout, "The Silent Lily and Bird," especially pp. 141–142.

8. I suspect that it is ultimately some such worry that underlies Kirmmse's scepticism about the very idea of talk of Christian virtues, and his insistence that it is *faith* rather than virtue that Kierkegaard offers as Christianity's response to sin (Kirmmse, "Kierkegaard and MacIntyre," p. 198).

9. This point is made by Jennifer A. Herdt, *Putting on Virtue: The Legacy of the Splendid Vices* (Chicago: University of Chicago Press, 2008), p. 52.

10. Mark A. Tietjen, "Kierkegaard and the Classical Virtue Tradition," in *Faith and Philosophy*, vol. 27 no. 2, p. 163. (For further discussion on this general point, see John Lippitt, *Kierkegaard and the Problem of Self-Love* (Cambridge: Cambridge University Press, 2013), pp. 6–7.) Tietjen offers an effective response to Kirmmse, as well as a fuller account of the prospects of thinking of Kierkegaard in light of the virtue tradition, both here and—in a slightly revised form—in *Kierkegaard, Communication and Virtue*, pp. 117–134.

11. See Evans and Roberts, "Ethics," pp. 224–225.

12. Robert C. Roberts, *Spiritual Emotions: A Psychology of Christian Virtues* (Grand Rapids: Eerdmans, 2007), pp. 78–93.

13. Robert C. Roberts, *Emotions: An Essay in Aid of Moral Psychology* (Cambridge: Cambridge University Press, 2003), p. 75.

14. In a similar way, I would argue that Kierkegaard's is to a significant extent a "vision" view of love (cf. Troy Jollimore, *Love's Vision* [Princeton: Princeton University Press, 2011]), one that warrants comparison with Iris Murdoch and Jollimore under this aspect. For more on this, see my "Love's Perception: Søren Kierkegaard," in *The Oxford Handbook of the Philosophy of Love*, Christopher Grau and Aaron Smuts, eds. (Oxford: Oxford University Press, forthcoming).

15. My focus here on humility is, I believe, consistent with the brief coda in support of a qualified notion of pride that I offered in *Kierkegaard and the Problem of Self-Love*, pp. 181–189. I still think that the Christian tradition's worries about pride have led to several healthy babies being thrown out with the bathwater. But the precise relationship between the kinds of pride and the kinds of humility that I consider to be both commendable and compatible is a topic beyond the scope of this article.

16. See Lippitt, *Kierkegaard and the Problem of Self-Love*, especially chapters 6–8.

17. On the varieties of humility, see Robert C. Roberts, "Gratitude and Humility," in *Perspectives on Gratitude: An Interdisciplinary Approach*, David Carr, ed. (London: Routledge,

2016); and "Learning Intellectual Humility," in *Intellectual Virtues and Education: Essays in Applied Virtue Epistemology*, Jason Baehr, ed. (London: Routledge, 2016).

18. Robert B. Puchniak, "Humility," in *Kierkegaard Research: Sources, Reception and Resources, Vol. 15, Kierkegaard's Concepts, Tome III: Envy to Incognito*, Steven M. Emmanuel, William McDonald, and Jon Stewart, eds. (London: Ashgate, 2014), especially p. 174.

19. Puchniak, "Humility," p. 174.

20. In fourteen discourses in all: the three in part 2 of *Upbuilding Discourses in Various Spirits*; seven in *Christian Discourses* (Part 1, "The Worries of the Pagans"); the three in *The Lily in the Field and the Bird of the Air: Three Devotional Discourses* (in the collection known in English as *Without Authority*); and one in *Judge for Yourself!*

21. On the intriguing history of the concept of joy, including its importance in Luther and post-Reformation thought, see Adam Potkay, *The Story of Joy: From the Bible to Late Romanticism* (Cambridge: Cambridge University Press, 2007). See also *Kierkegaard and Joy*, Edward F. Mooney and Carson Webb, eds., unpublished manuscript.

22. Such a case is astutely diagnosed and offered such a Kierkegaardian therapy in Matias Møl Dalsgaard, *Don't Despair: Letter to a Modern Man*, trans. Patrick Stokes (London: Pine Tribe, 2014). Within Kierkegaard's corpus, see especially the discourse "The Worry [*Bekymring*] of Self-Torment," in *Christian Discourses* (CD, 70–80; SKS 10:79–88).

23. The next few paragraphs are developed from John Lippitt, "What Can Therapists Learn from Kierkegaard?" in *Therapy and the Counter-Tradition: The Edge of Philosophy*, Manu Bazzano and Julie Webb, eds. (London: Routledge, 2015).

24. Kierkegaard returns to this theme in later discourses on the lilies and the birds (see WA, 1–45, especially 1–20; SKS 11:7–48, especially 7–25).

25. This seems to speak to all kinds of issues about "status anxiety." As the psychotherapist Rollo May later put it, in a book influenced by Kierkegaard, "We are no longer prey to tigers and mastodons but to damage to our self-esteem, ostracism by our group, or the threat of losing out in the competitive struggle. The form of anxiety has changed, but the experience remains relatively the same" (*The Meaning of Anxiety*, revised edition [New York: Norton, 1977], p. xiv).

26. It is worth noting here that Kierkegaard's focus is on the common lilies of the field, not those "rare plants" raised by a gardener and "looked at by experts" (UDVS, 162; SKS 8:262).

27. Roberts, *Spiritual Emotions*, p. 81.

28. Roberts, *Spiritual Emotions*, p. 83.

29. Roberts, *Spiritual Emotions*, p. 83.

30. Roberts, *Spiritual Emotions*, p. 83. Does this mean there are no grounds for comparing ourselves with others? After all, I have known friendships between students that seem to be based in part on a healthy competition between them. I don't say that this is *necessarily* problematic (though I suspect it might very easily become so). What would be key to its remaining healthy, I believe, would be that one's overall, "global" sense of one's value does not derive from the kind of success that is the heart of what the competition is about.

31. Roberts, *Spiritual Emotions*, p. 90, my emphasis.

32. Someone who most decidedly lacks this particular virtue is an acquaintance of a relative of mine, an elderly lady who enjoys checking the death announcements in the local paper in order to see how many more people of her own generation she has managed to outlive.

33. For a further account of humility that well complements the one discussed here, see Joseph Kupfer, "The Moral Perspective of Humility," in *Pacific Philosophical Quarterly*, vol. 84 (2003), pp. 249–269. The four dimensions of this "moral perspective of humility" are (1) a recognition of one's radical dependence on others (e.g., that our achievements are never ours

alone); (2) a focus on the morally exemplary that helps keep our "technical" (e.g., professional, academic, or sporting) achievements in perspective; (3) a recognition of and focus on the infinite nature of the ethical demand, such that even for the morally exemplary, there is always more to be done; and (4) an orientation toward things of value in the world apart from their instrumental value to ourselves. The upshot of this is that humble people are disposed not to dwell upon themselves. For a more detailed discussion of this in relation to Kierkegaard, see my "Joy Beyond Worry: On Learning Humility from the Lilies and the Birds," in *Kierkegaard and Joy*, Mooney and Webb, eds., unpublished manuscript.

34. Roberts, *Spiritual Emotions*, p. 88. I take it that Kupfer's position, not discussed by Roberts, could serve as a gloss upon this point.

35. Roberts, *Spiritual Emotions*, p. 88.

36. Roberts extends this view in a later paper (Roberts, "Learning Intellectual Humility"). See the discussion of humility as a "family of lacks" and the idea that the most perfect humility does not *aim* at humility.

37. Roberts, *Spiritual Emotions*, p. 89.

38. Roberts, *Spiritual Emotions*, p. 90. This "self-confidence" puts me in mind of the attitude Kierkegaard sometimes calls "jest" [*Spøg*], which often accompanies his discussions of the crucial category of "earnestness" [*Alvor*]. For more on this, see my "Jest as Humility: Kierkegaard and the Limits of Earnestness," in *Humor, Comedy, and Laughter in 19th-Century Philosophy*, Lydia L. Moland, ed. (New York: Springer, forthcoming).

39. Kupfer, "The Moral Perspective of Humility," pp. 260–263, also makes this connection.

40. Cf. Corey Benjamin Tutewiler, "Gratitude," in *Kierkegaard Research: Sources, Reception and Resources, Vol. 15, Kierkegaard's Concepts, Tome III: Envy to Incognito*, Steven M. Emmanuel, William McDonald, and Jon Stewart, eds. (London: Ashgate, 2014), p. 125. He notes that the main pseudonymous exceptions are the second volume of *Either/Or* and the *Postscript*.

41. For more on this theme, see FSE, 152–154; SKS 16:202–203, where Kierkegaard compares "the unconditioned requirement" to a weight that, if I had to lift it myself, would crush me. However, he claims, the gospel's intention is precisely the opposite: Humbled by the requirement, and responding in faith and worship, I become "light as a bird," "the thought of God's grace" (FSE, 153; SKS 16:203) lifting me up in a way that the thought of my own deeds never could. This "lightness" seems to me one way of describing that sense of "self-confidence" rooted in God that is a feature of Christian humility.

42. Cf. David Coe, "Asceticism," in *Kierkegaard Research: Sources, Reception and Resources, Vol. 15, Kierkegaard's Concepts, Tome I: Absolute to Church*, Steven M. Emmanuel, William McDonald, and Jon Stewart, eds. (London: Ashgate, 2013), p. 107.

43. Tutewiler, "Gratitude," p. 127.

44. Tutewiler, "Gratitude," p. 127.

45. Roberts, *Spiritual Emotions*, p. 142.

46. Roberts, *Spiritual Emotions*, p. 142.

47. Roberts, *Spiritual Emotions*, p. 141.

48. Roberts, *Spiritual Emotions*, p. 142.

49. Roberts, *Spiritual Emotions*, p. 146.

50. However, this perhaps only begins to capture the radical nature of Kierkegaard's view of gratitude, if we take seriously the implications of the *Postscript*'s claim that we cannot just give thanks to God for what we *know* to be a good, since this would amount to "transforming God in likeness to me" (CUP, 178; SKS 7:164). A fuller discussion of thankfulness for all things would need to consider the first three of the *Four Upbuilding Discourses* of 1843 (EUD, 109–158; SKS 5:113–158), but such a discussion is beyond the scope of the present article.

51. George Pattison suggests that this applies both to the grace offered "in the God-relationship of creation" and—more decisively—"in the Christ-relationship of redemption" ("The Joy of Birdsong, or Lyrical Dialectics," in *International Kierkegaard Commentary, Vol. 18, Without Authority*, Robert L. Perkins, ed. [Macon, GA: Mercer University Press, 2007], p. 125).

52. I don't think this is inconsistent with talking in terms of construals *qua* impressions, since as Roberts explicitly suggests, one can work at aiming to see things in a particular way, perhaps to rediscover the way one has previously been struck. As an example from Kierkegaard, consider the 1850 journal entry in which he discusses how a person who lacks a *concrete impression* of God's love can nevertheless cling on to the *thought* that God is love, and claims that this is part of a "rigorous upbringing" in faith that will eventuate in a concrete God-relationship (CA Suppl. 172–173 [JP § 1401] *Papirer* X 2 A 493). This sounds precisely like a *looking* that aims hopefully at an eventual *way of seeing*.

53. The most substantial discussions all involve the lilies and the birds: in UDVS, CD, and the 1849 discourses on the lilies and the birds in WA. See also Benjamin Miguel Olivares Bøgeskov, "Joy," in *Kierkegaard Research: Sources, Reception and Resources, Vol. 15, Kierkegaard's Concepts, Tome IV: Individual to Novel*, Steven M. Emmanuel, William McDonald, and Jon Stewart, eds. (London: Ashgate, 2014).

54. I do not mean, of course, that everything Kierkegaard puts under the heading of *Glæde* can be described as contentment—and there are passages where this sense of joy (in response to a specific religious experience) does seem more effervescent. See for instance the discussion in George Pattison, *Kierkegaard's Upbuilding Discourses: Philosophy, Literature and Theology* (London: Routledge, 2002), pp. 56–57.

55. I develop this claim in more detail in Lippitt, "Joy Beyond Worry: On Learning Humility from the Lilies and the Birds."

56. Cf. Paul's admonition to give thanks in all circumstances at 1 Thess. 5:18, Kierkegaard's version of which idea we touched upon in note 50 above.

57. "Rejoice [Dan: *glæde sig*] in the Lord always. I will say it again: Rejoice! . . . Do not be anxious about anything, but in every situation, by prayer and petition, with thanksgiving, present your requests to God. And the peace of God, which transcends all understanding, will guard your hearts and your minds in Christ Jesus" (Phil. 4:4, 6–7 NIV).

58. This quieter sense comes out in "The Joy of It" discourses in part 2 of *Christian Discourses*.

59. Cf. 1 Peter 5:7.

60. I have offered a parallel argument about self-forgiveness (as not necessarily excluding self-reproach, but rather not allowing self-reproach to become debilitating) in Lippitt, *Kierkegaard and the Problem of Self-Love*, chapter 8.

61. Bøgeskov, "Joy."

62. Kierkegaard puts it starkly: "What is anxiety [*Angest*]? It is the next day" (CD, 78; SKS 10:87).

63. George Pattison glosses this "acquired originality" (WA, 38; SKS 11:42) that the lily and bird teach as "a return to our original self-being . . . the being-present-to-oneself-in-the-moment that is the essence of joy" (Pattison, "The Joy of Birdsong, or Lyrical Dialectics," p. 122).

64. One way of living for "today," it might be thought, is in the old saying "Let us eat and drink, because tomorrow we shall die" (1 Cor. 15:32; Isaiah 22:13). But Kierkegaard rejects as fake the joy such hedonism might appear to commend (particularly if we add merrymaking to the list). Far from transcending worries about "tomorrow," such an attitude is entirely within the grip of "tomorrow": the remark "echoes with the anxiety about the next day, the day of annihilation, the anxiety that insanely is supposed to signify joy although it is a scream from

the abyss. He is so anxious about the next day that he plunges himself into a frantic stupor in order, if possible, to forget it" (CD, 77; SKS 10:86). Thus what appears to take pleasure in "today" is in fact firmly in the grip of "tomorrow"—and so its claim to be enjoying today rings hollow.

65. Luke 2:22–40.

66. Especially Hermann Olshausen, who here follows Calvin more than Luther; see Lee C. Barrett, "Simeon and Anna: Exemplars of Patience and Expectancy," in *Kierkegaard Research: Sources, Reception and Resources, Vol. 1, Kierkegaard and the Bible, Tome II: The New Testament*, Lee C. Barrett and Jon Stewart, eds. (London: Ashgate, 2010), pp. 4–7.

67. Since the legal custom of the time left her free to remarry, we should note that this was a freely chosen, giving love (cf. Barrett, "Simeon and Anna," p. 11).

68. Roberts, "The Virtue of Hope in *Eighteen Upbuilding Discourses*," p. 187. On the importance of hope at times of spiritual trial, in the face of anxiety and potential despair, see Kierkegaard's early sermon at JP § 3915/*Papier* III C 1.

69. A key theme of this discourse is faith's ability to conquer the anxieties engendered by doubt.

70. Kierkegaard's text here glosses victory as "that all things must serve for good those who love God" (EUD, 19; SKS 5:28), an echo of Romans 8:28.

71. "One who prays aright struggles in prayer and is victorious—in that God is victorious," the last of the *Eighteen Upbuilding Discourses*. On the "center of gravity" point, see Daphne Hampson, *Kierkegaard: Exposition and Critique* (Oxford: Oxford University Press, 2013), p. 22.

72. I have recently argued that such hope is at work in the Abraham of *Fear and Trembling*; see Lippitt, "Learning to Hope: The Role of Hope in *Fear and Trembling*," in *Kierkegaard's Fear and Trembling: A Critical Guide*, Daniel W. Conway, ed. (Cambridge: Cambridge University Press, 2015), from which some of the material in this section is derived.

73. Jonathan Lear, *Radical Hope: Ethics in the Face of Cultural Devastation* (Cambridge, MA: Harvard University Press, 2006), p. 92.

74. Lear, *Radical Hope*, p. 94, my emphasis.

75. John Macquarrie, *Christian Hope* (Oxford: Mowbray, 1978), p. 53.

76. As Lear puts it of Plenty Coups, "There is no implication that one can glimpse what lies beyond the horizons of one's historically situated understanding. There is no claim to grasp ineffable truths. Indeed, this form of commitment is impressive in part because it acknowledges that no such grasp is possible" (Lear, *Radical Hope*, p. 95). Compare here Kierkegaard's 1850 journal remark that "the concept of the absurd is precisely to grasp the fact that it cannot and must not be grasped" (JP § 7; *Papirer* X 2 A 354).

77. Consider here the image of turning one's back on "the next day" just as a rower turns his back to the direction of travel (CD, 73; SKS 10:82).

78. Barrett, "Simeon and Anna," p. 13.

79. Barrett, "Simeon and Anna," p. 13.

80. Cf. Pattison, *Kierkegaard's Upbuilding Discourses*, p. 50.

81. An earlier version of this article was presented as an invited keynote paper at a workshop on "Kierkegaard and Ethical Theory" at the University of Antwerp in February 2015. I am grateful to the organizers, Rob Compaijen and Johan Taels, and to the other participants for discussion on that enjoyable occasion.

7 The Heart of Knowledge: Kierkegaard on Passion and Understanding

Rick Anthony Furtak

Søren Kierkegaard's signed, pseudonymous, and personal writings all suggest that some questions are so urgently relevant to us that we cannot think about them, while being aware of ourselves *as* existing human beings to whom they pertain, without becoming passionate. Why is it that unemotional contemplation of these philosophical or existential matters is equivalent to not truly thinking about them at all? In this chapter, I focus on the role of our affective feelings—our passions or emotions—in enabling us to apprehend significant truths. This will illustrate the relevance of Kierkegaard's work to the problem of how we can attain knowledge of reality from a specifically human viewpoint. Furthermore, since the themes on which I am focusing appear throughout Kierkegaard's writings, from the texts written during the summer of 1835 through the great works of his middle period, *Works of Love* and the *Concluding Unscientific Postscript*, and well into the early 1850s, an investigation of these themes promises to shed light upon a theme that is central to the entire Kierkegaardian corpus.

In the *Postscript*, Johannes Climacus argues that certain existential questions are so urgently pertinent that "it is impossible" to reflect on them, while being conscious of oneself as an existing human being to whom such questions are relevant, "without becoming passionate": thus, to contemplate them "without passion . . . is not to think of them at all" (*Postscript*, 293–294). Readers of Kierkegaard's *Nachlass* will recognize this as a familiar theme in his journals, notebooks, and other unpublished writings. In his own voice, Kierkegaard speaks about the importance of "interested cognition" (as opposed to disinterested or dispassionate thought), and he carries out a polemical campaign against the preponderance of "objective thinking," which fails to take account of the thinker as a person involved in living a human life. He claims that modern philosophers have too often posited impersonal objectivity as a general standard of truth, regarding our subjective comportment toward the world as a distorting influence, even after Kant's discovery that *what* we know is conditioned by *how* we are able to know. In the following pages, I will focus on Kierkegaard's moral psychology of epistemological experience, or (what might be called) his phenomenology of our knowledge and our beliefs about the world. The world that concerns us is objectively "there" to be met with outside of our minds; at the same time, it is also conditioned by our subjective constitution to a significant degree.

When Kierkegaard writes, in a notebook entry, that philosophers ought to conceive of objectivity as that which "takes shape in a corresponding subjectivity," he makes a strong claim about how pervasively our sense of outward reality depends on how we are inwardly disposed (*Papirer* X 1 A 146; JP § 6360). And when, in a related passage, he indicates that our feelings about the meaning of reality are closely bound up with our affective or emotional disposition, he argues that our understanding of life is largely a passionate matter (*Papirer* X 2 A 355; JP § 4554). This is a radical thesis, and one whose implications have not been fully recognized, despite the widespread recognition that truthfulness in Kierkegaard's work has something to do with passion and subjectivity.[1] In fact, I can think of no better reason to characterize him as a "thinker the full scope of whose thought has yet to be appreciated."[2] Kierkegaard's conception of *passionate understanding* ["*lidenskabelige Forstaaelse*"] offers an alternative to a long line of arguments that oppose feeling and knowing—some modern philosophers have classified the emotions as confused thoughts or inadequate ideas, which allegedly obscure the truth; they have also claimed that the passions do not represent anything, and that feelings lie outside our intellectual faculty altogether—even that affective sensitivity is the sign of a diseased mind.[3] (A contemporary descendant of this view is the theoretical position that our emotions are non-cognitive states.) Yet the result of factoring out the passionate aspect of human consciousness may be that we fail to understand either the subject or the object. This would be a serious failure of post-Kantian philosophy on its own terms. The question of how we can attain reliable knowledge of reality from a specifically human viewpoint remains a major one in current philosophy, one that concerns many leading thinkers. So if Kierkegaard offers a more promising alternative, if he suggests a better way of thinking about passion, subjectivity, and truth, then it seems that we have not fully appropriated his insights, because we have not yet learned how to think in this way.

As I mentioned above, the family of themes on which I'm focusing recur throughout Kierkegaard's writings—published and unpublished, signed and pseudonymous—from early to late in his career.[4] For this reason, his reflections on these topics might collectively provide us with a way of illuminating his entire corpus, in addition to being of interest in their own right. So I hope to explain how an author who portrayed himself as a "kind of poet" could also be a "kind of epistemologist": something like a moral epistemologist, that is, even if he is not preoccupied with all the traditional problems of epistemology.[5] Perhaps Kierkegaard could be interpreted as a sort of poetic epistemologist, along the lines suggested by those who assign to poetry the role of disclosing the meaningful or affectively felt dimension of existence, because Kierkegaard is clearly attentive to the truths that might be disclosed through mood, feeling, and other potentially reasonable and perceptive forms of emotional intentionality. He credits the "poets" with recognizing that it is rare to cultivate one's own loving subjectivity (or one's passionate outlook) rather than divesting oneself of this in order to become "objective" (JP § 4537); and in *Repetition*, the "young man" is described by Constantin Constantius as "a poet" because he is especially receptive to significant passionate impressions (R 1946, 159).[6] In each of these cases, the sort of insight associated with poetry or poets offers us a glimpse of some truth about the world or about human existence; yet this mode of reason differs from logical calculation that is relatively neutral, without either musical resonance or personal meaning.

Poetic thought may serve us better as a point of reference than any other mode of cognitive activity that can be distinguished from theoretical knowledge, such as "know-how" (skillful coping), knowledge by acquaintance, knowing "what it's like," or the kind of practical reason that is involved in knowing what to do and being normatively moved to do it. Each of these bears some resemblance to what I am characterizing as "passionate understanding" in Kierkegaard's thought, but none of them adequately captures what is distinctively affective, passionate, or emotional about it. When Kierkegaard states that "feeling, imagination, and passion" are what one needs in order to grasp the ethico-religious (*Papirer* X 2 A 193; PJS, 442)[7]—that is, to comprehend matters of moral and spiritual concern—I think we should take his words at face value. By the same token, when he asserts that "to love and to know" are "essentially synonymous," I think he is really talking about *love*, that "passion of the emotions," *and* that he means to identify it with a certain type of knowing (*Papirer* IX A 438; JP § 2299).[8] It may differ from what we ordinarily have in mind when we talk philosophically about knowledge, but this is one sign that our standard epistemological vocabulary ought to be modified.

As Kierkegaard claims in a discourse from 1845, when we hold opinions about "remote events" or "scholarly works," our beliefs can be assessed for objective accuracy, which is one condition of their being true. Yet, as he explains, there is another aspect of the truth, one that we often fail to take into consideration, namely "whether one actually does have the opinion" or "whether it is just something one is reciting" (TDIO, 99). He continues,

> Yet this other side is just as important, because not only is that person mad who talks senselessly, but the person is fully as mad who states a correct opinion if it has absolutely no significance for him. . . . Alas, . . . it is so easy, so very easy, to acquire a true opinion, and yet it is so difficult, so very difficult, to have an opinion and to have it in truth. (TDIO, 99–100)

He proceeds to note the difference between endorsing a correct belief that has absolutely no significance for us and, on the other hand, assenting to a conviction and being quite earnestly convinced of its truth. We can accurately state the fact that we ourselves are mortal and going to die someday, or we can vocally affirm the proposition that someone we love has just died, without feeling emotionally moved by either of these thoughts. *Or*, by contrast, we can more passionately feel a sense of what it means that we will die, or that the other person has passed away. In the former cases, we are lacking in truthfulness of a subjective kind, because we are not wholeheartedly acknowledging the significance of what we are saying: our statement is true, but *we are not fully aware of what it means.*[9] Being gripped by the significance of our own mortality, or registering the loss of a beloved friend, is not the same as intellectually assenting to the fact that we (like all human beings) are mortal, or accurately reporting our friend's recent death without being moved by this information (which may not have "sunk in" yet). Merely dispassionate "knowledge" that X is the case is something less than full "consciousness" or awareness that X is true.[10] To me it matters greatly that my friend has died, and to register the significance of such a loss is to be grieved; so until I begin to feel grief, my understanding of what has taken place is lacking *because* I am not passionately agitated in the appropriate way. We do not "actually" *believe* that someone has died if we are just "reciting" this fact without feeling convinced of its truth; in this case, we are "far from having grasped" what we claim to know (TDIO, 99–100).[11] And if we do not *truly believe* that a person has died, then in an important sense we do not *know* that they are dead. As Sartre initially stated after hearing about the sudden death of Camus, "I do not believe it." He did not mean that the funeral at which he was speaking was an elaborate hoax, but that he had not fully processed or *acknowledged* the disturbing fact that Camus had been killed in an accident. This was not a remote event, but it had not yet hit home.

In the absence of the deeply upsetting feelings associated with grief (which may include a sense of disorientation without the lost person, rage and wonder at the tragic fragility of human life, or despair over what it all means), the belief that this person is permanently gone has more the nature of a tentative hypothesis that one has barely acknowledged, as opposed to a profound conviction or even a vivid perceptual impression. All of these are cognitive states, but cognitive states take many different forms. If I nominally affirm the proposition, "I will die one day," I could "believe" it in a variety of ways. I might dispassionately endorse it, but I also might be filled with a sense of existential dread and helplessness when giving assent to the prospect of my ultimate demise. So do I truly *believe* it in the former case?[12] I think we must answer: not in the strongest sense of the word. In this example, a passionate mode of apprehension is the experience of truth that phenomenologically embodies *more* awareness than *mere* reason.

Kierkegaard's discussion of the many ways in which *what* we apprehend can vary, in accordance with *how* we are emotionally disposed,[13] also anticipates the later investigation of these themes by phenomenologists such as Maurice Merleau-Ponty, who claims that we "do not understand the absence or death of a friend" until his loss is palpably felt—for instance, at the moment when "we expect a reply from him" and are shaken with the realization "that we shall never again receive one."[14] We think by feeling, and only through the feeling of upheaval that constitutes our grief is this feature of reality revealed; namely, that someone whom we have loved is gone from the world. This appears to be the kind of truth that we can grasp only *because* we are loving beings, and only *through* our emotional responses. If we were not already bound to the world of others by something deeper than reason—deeper than dispassionate rationality, at least—then we would suffer an even more comprehensive loss. The truly irrevocable loss, Kierkegaard suggests, is that loss of the world to which we condemn ourselves if we are impervious to the influence of love (WL, 5–6). Our emotional "hold" on the world is dependent upon "an adherence that knows itself to be beyond proofs," as Merleau-Ponty writes, and our conviction that the world exists has its foundation in emotion or feeling.[15] What both of these phenomenological authors are talking about are the passionate convictions that sustain our life in the world, and which have the nature of an axiomatic premise rather than the outcome of a deductive proof.

Let's take another example: a depressive or melancholy state can have a pervasive influence on a person's way of interpreting the world. It is not merely that one draws different inferences from an experience that contains the same phenomenal content as it would if one were not feeling depressed or melancholy—instead, one actually experiences things differently, and one's sense of reality is not the same. Possibilities that are usually appealing seem to hold no value; as far as one can tell, the world really *is* weary, stale, and flat. In this way, our whole conception of the surrounding world, our view of "how things are going," can depend upon how we are inwardly disposed. This is why Kierkegaard says that all understanding of what happens in life is conditioned by our state of mind, our way of taking things in: just after introducing this claim, he adds by way of example that we experience things differently depending upon whether our disposition is more trusting and faithful, or whether our mood is *tungsindig* (melancholic) (*Papirer* X 2 A 355 (JP § 4554); SKS 23:24–25).[16] This passage may need to be unpacked and spelled out further, but Kierkegaard clearly means to suggest that our understanding of life is based on how we are inwardly disposed—and especially on how we are affectively or emotionally disposed. This gives some indication of what it could mean to talk about objective reality taking shape in a corresponding subjectivity, or to say that how the observer is constituted has a "decisive" impact on what is observed.[17] Even a more generalized affective feeling, one that is not obviously directed toward any particular object, can still have "intentionality" in the sense that it permeates the world, as an atmosphere through which everything is experienced. Our background feelings thus influence our convictions about what is happening around us, and in this respect our understanding of life *is* a passionate matter.

We should keep in mind that "subjectivity" and "inwardness" are not utterly private, isolated conditions to which the ostensibly self-contained conscious mind has introspective access; rather, these terms refer to our passionate interest *in* and orientation *toward* the world, a mode of engagement that is highly personal and intersubjective at the same time. It should not be difficult, then, to see how an inner state could shape our sense of external reality—especially when the inner state is a diffuse mood, a pervasive sensibility, or another kind of affective orientation. And even melancholy is not simply a distorting lens that clouds and obfuscates: insofar as life is not only replete with appealing possibilities but also filled with imperfection, tragedy, and sorrow, there are truths about existence of which we are more aware when we are feeling melancholy or depressed.[18] The same is true of anxiety. Irony also might attune us to certain kinds of truth at the expense of others, and similarly with other moods: each of them puts a different aspect on the face of things. Because of the way that every mood can highlight or illuminate the world for us in a particular way, one American poet-philosopher has noted that "our moods do not believe in each other"; indeed, Emerson even goes so far as to say that we are "always insincere" by virtue of "always knowing there are other moods," and that any mood we inhabit will make us highly aware of certain things yet largely insensible of others.[19] When it comes to *"concerned truths,"* which pertain directly to the life of the individual, we should realize according to Kierkegaard that the "individual's particular condition"—whether one is "happy or dejected," for instance—is far from being a matter of indifference (EUD, 233). If we link the presence of the divine with the significance of things, as Kierkegaard does, then the feeling that one is "bored with all [of] life" is equivalent to living "without God in the world": the only truth of which one is aware in a mood of boredom is that God has withdrawn, a sacred radiance has vanished from the face of things—in short, nothing matters (TDIO, 78).[20] Needless to say, such questions as whether anything matters, what does matter, and how it matters, concern us greatly: that is why boredom is not just a blank tranquil emptiness, but rather a deeply unsettling feeling, a state of discontentment in which we do not wish to remain. We cannot grasp the meaning of anything without the appropriate mode of passionate understanding; therefore, we can only *know* in a diminished sense that anything is meaningful when we are unable to *feel* that it is. If affective feelings are the key to grasping the worth of anything, then if the feeling is deficient, then the grasp will be inadequate as well.

Human existence is not indifferent to a person who loves, and loving trust is therefore the inward affective disposition that allows us to experience life as meaningful and worth living. Our sense of value or meaning depends comprehensively on this "fundamental impulse," as Arne Grøn calls it, which is always already present at the ground of our being.[21] I have said more about this elsewhere, so I will not go much further into it now. At the moment I am emphasizing just one element of this theme: namely, that there is something belief-like about our basic affective orientation toward the world. In *Works of Love*, Kierkegaard claims that "the individual first begins his life with 'ergo,' with *belief*," and he adds that love "believes all things"—suggesting that the natural attitude of trust, after all, might be a state worth preserving and broadening (WL, 230).[22] Once we have discovered the possibility of skeptical doubt, we can recognize the possibility of believing in the world's reality and significance even though we lack certainty with respect to our most important convictions. That is, in matters of "existential knowledge," we rely on a feeling of assurance that cannot be entirely justified: "The passionate, the inward, . . . is just what a firm conviction is. . . . As when a lover says, 'She is the one I love,' and doesn't go on about it . . . or talk of his reasons for loving her" (*Papirer* X 1 A 481; SKS 22:107–109).[23] The kind of conviction to which he refers is not akin to a belief formed based on the outcome of a proof, and this is why Kierkegaard suggests that we cannot simply reason ourselves into such a feeling of belief. Far from being irrational, however, it does have a "logic" of its own, as evidenced by the fact that it is a *conviction*, a passionate disposition that enables us to *know* significant truths that would otherwise be inaccessible. As Kierkegaard states early in *Works of Love*, we can be deceived by *not* believing what *is* true; in other words, if our passionate attunement is too guarded or distrustful, then some things will remain beyond the reach of our awareness.

There is no absolute vantage point available to us from which we could apprehend a "true world" against which our sense of reality could be measured for its accuracy. This is why Kierkegaard's writings attempt to "reopen the whole question of the meaning of truth," and to redefine objective reality as that which takes shape in relation to human subjectivity.[24] If we appreciate the degree to which our *affective* constitution plays a role in constituting the world that we know, we should not be surprised to find that feelings can reveal the world— instead, we should be wondering how the world could be revealed to us *except* through our feelings. We should not underestimate how much is at stake in our emotional orientation; it is nothing less than our sense of reality. The solidity and weight of the world, what it is and what it means, are disclosed to us in accordance with our affective disposition. This includes everything from protracted moods and abiding passionate enthusiasms to episodes of grief, gratitude, and other distinct types of emotion; it also includes feeling gripped by doubt in a particular moment, or by a feeling of conviction, as opposed to merely doubting "on paper" or saying that one believes (CUP, 266, 341). It includes the idiosyncratic way in which all of these dimensions of our affective life combine to form a person's temperament or sensibility—that complex basis upon which our sense of the world rests.

Kierkegaard's identification of consciousness and "interest," in the *Johannes Climacus* narrative, signals that we must be at least minimally interested in any object in order to feel aware of its existence at all (JC, 170–171).[25] Our more intense passions, moreover, are correlated with what we perceive as axiologically salient: that is, whatever stands out in our awareness due to its value, meaning, or significance. These are the qualities of reality with which our passions are associated, and compared to other aspects of the world (such as its bare physical existence), they are particularly difficult to account for in any ontology of "objective" being. In order to explain the reality of values, a philosopher might argue that they are a subjective projection onto a world that is "really" value-neutral, or perhaps that they are "constructed" by social consensus. But the notion that the real world is axiologically vacuous is itself philosophically problematic if not incoherent, and quite contrary to how we experience things; meanwhile, a socially based explanation attains coherence by sanctioning only what is *least* distinctive to individual subjectivity, what can be confirmed by a community of like-minded others. And, as Kierkegaard points out of "passionate understanding," people "differ greatly in this" (*Papirer* IX A 365; PJS, 338); distinctive individuality is a "presupposition for loving," and the more distinct loving subjectivities there are in the world, "the more knowers there are," at least (he adds) in the personal, "Hebraic" sense of knowing (*Papirer* VIII 1 A 462; JP § 2003).[26] The drift of these remarks is that every person's emotional orientation toward the world, by virtue of their individual differences and not in spite of them, allows the truth to be disclosed.

So how could the passionate subjectivity of each human being put us epistemically in touch with the world, allowing us to make experiential contact with reality beyond ourselves? Well, consider who it is that apprehends most truthfully the worth of a person's life or the magnitude of that person's death. Needless to say, it is not the observer who stoically or skeptically doubts that such values really exist, on the grounds that the worth of a person cannot be conclusively demonstrated anyway. These intellectual commitments are the sort that would condemn us to *not* acknowledging much that *is* true. A vague, generalized sense that all human life has value, in the disinterested onlooker with no particular attachment to *this* person's life, also falls well short of a full awareness of what it means that *he* has died in a car accident. The significance of this fact is grasped more adequately by the mourners who knew and loved him, each of whom appreciated *his* unique and unrepeatable existence in their *own* distinctive way. This is why, as Mooney says, each person's "*particular* outlook or vision" is regarded by Kierkegaard as being of "irreplaceable importance."[27] Each one of us can only know so much significant truth, for the same reason that we can only have so many close friends. What we can know through our emotions, the "objective reality" that is available to us as it takes shape through our passionate interest, is limited by how much we can wholeheartedly feel aware of and concerned about. It is not only that one person at the funeral is occupied with lamenting the unfinished work and fatherless children left behind by our deceased friend while another is focused with indignation on the other driver's responsibility for the accident that killed him. No two people at the funeral could appreciate quite the same features of the one who has died, or not exactly in the same way, even if both of them are feeling the same type of emotion. Each of them therefore has a different sense of what has been lost. We are only sensible of so many aspects of reality, and our awareness of some will inevitably preclude others from our view—if only because our minds are finite and not everything is visible from a single vantage point. The reason why more significant truth can be known by a plurality of subjects, perhaps, is that each of us can passionately grasp only *some* of that which is there to be discerned. Only part of the truth is "imparted" to each of us, and this *partial* truth is what we must appropriate and take to heart. Instead of seeking comprehensive knowledge or lamenting its inaccessibility, therefore, we should on Kierkegaard's view trust that our specific vantage point, "including our emotional 'take' on the world,"[28] is capable of revealing something true that could not be perceived from elsewhere or from nowhere.

We can now see why Kierkegaard links individual subjectivity with truthfulness, and also how the remarks in the *Concluding Unscientific Postscript* and elsewhere, eulogizing the Greek philosophers as passionate thinkers interested in existence, are more than a rhetorical flourish.[29] Furthermore, since Cartesian philosophy stipulates that all knowledge worthy of the name must be *impersonal* and *dispassionate*, and that it must strive for *certainty*, we should also be able to follow the main lines of Kierkegaard's polemic against early modern epistemology. Passionate understanding is the mode of thinking appropriate to matters that concern us personally and that are somewhat uncertain. Indeed, it may be that the kind of convictions we rely upon in making sense of the world in its meaning can be formed *only* in relation to matters of objective uncertainty. In any case, our most existentially relevant beliefs cannot be proven either logically or empirically, but according to Kierkegaard this is no reason for entirely suspending judgment. And it is not as though our only options in the face of uncertainty are either comprehensive skepticism or mindless faith. Kierkegaard's writings explore the question of how we might comport ourselves with reference to those significant yet uncertain matters[30] that we cannot honestly regard with indifference, and which we cannot even think about without becoming passionate. When I am passionately agitated about the question of *what my life means*,

I realize that I would be dissatisfied if I tried to remain agnostic and believe nothing whatsoever about a matter that interests and concerns me so personally. Hence, I must find a way of holding some view about the meaning of my life while striving to clarify and refine my conception of this.

When Kierkegaard refers to an inner *"imperative of knowledge"* that would lead him not to indifferent truth but to "understanding my destiny," he is pointing out how our passionate subjectivity might be cultivated and maintained (*Papirer* I A 75; PJS, 32–33, emphasis in original). Needless to say, abstracting away from our emotions will not bring us closer to the type of awareness he is talking about. If we are interested in the sort of knowing that pertains to human life, we cannot dismiss our affective feelings as phenomena that lie outside the domain of understanding.[31] This would excuse us from the difficult task of examining the passionate convictions that define who we are and shape our view of the world. Once again, we see here how intimately the subjective and the objective are knit together, as the affective dimension of human existence defines my identity and determines what is real to me. A "concern" about the meaning of life is simultaneously about "what the world means" and about "what [one's] life means for the world" (EUD, 86), in much the same way that love enables us to become who we are by virtue of being "for others" (WL, 223).[32] Like a poet who "opens up to receive, in a flood of emotion, the being of the thing [she] sees," the person who loves "finds the truth of [her] own being" by discovering, and becoming interested in, the world of others.[33] Each passionate subjectivity plays a role in revealing the meaning of existence, not because our emotions *make* life significant, but because affective receptivity is a condition for apprehending significance and value—which must take shape in a corresponding subject if its objective reality is to be disclosed. Just as we can appreciate or fail to take notice of another person, in the same way the meaning of a human situation, an event, or an idea is something of which we can be more or less aware. Remember what Kierkegaard says about the biblical passage in which David listens to a story told by Nathan but fails to listen in such a way that "his personality (subjectivity)," is engaged, hearing only "impersonally (objectively)" what the narrative means. He needs to be told, "You."[34] That is, *you*, David, are the one to whom this story pertains, for you are guilty of the same outrage as the person in the story. As Ted Cohen writes, about the same biblical tale,

> What has happened is something like this. David's anger and moral outrage at the rich man have been transferred to himself. Nathan says "You are the man," which is essentially "You, David, are the rich man who has taken a poor man's only ewe lamb," and David connects. . . . Perhaps . . . Nathan does tell something new to David. He tells David that it is possible to see—that indeed Nathan does see—David in his treatment of Uriah and Bathsheba as a rich man taking a poor man's only ewe lamb; and when the story has been

told, David himself sees David in that way. When David sees himself in that way, his sense of himself is changed. Feelings about himself arise that had not arisen before.[35]

Only when David realizes emotionally that he is *not* a disinterested observer does he fully grasp the significance of the narrative. His passionate upheaval places him in touch with a significant, and disturbing, truth about what he has done. We are personally implicated by significant truths in ways that we often fail to acknowledge, and the difference between perceiving them without fully grasping their meaning and actually being conscious of their significance is a matter of passionate apprehension.[36] There is a difference between the type of so-called knowledge that is involved in the instance where we lack a sense of personal relevance, and the state of emotional knowing in which we do feel personally and passionately involved. This difference is like that between the thinker who professes to doubt in a disinterested mood and the one who is truly gripped by skeptical doubt regarding issues that are of serious concern to him or her.

One question that we might raise, in which something both momentous and uncertain is at stake, is whether one's entire life in the world is *good*, and worth living.[37] In an 1849 sermon on the "bird of the air," Kierkegaard asks us whether we can feel gratitude for our existence, including such ordinary facts as "that you exist, that *today* you receive what is necessary for life," and so forth, continuing to list many other unexceptional gifts (WA, 39). He calls our attention to simple abilities that we often take for granted, saying, "Bear in mind that you can see, that you can hear, that you can smell, that you can taste, that you can feel, that the sun shines." All of these are facts that we would feel emotional about if they ceased to be true, for instance when the sun is not shining or if our hearing were to become impaired. We are more inclined to notice what is not right, while not being so conscious of things that are more or less as we might wish them to be. It is almost as if we are "wired" in such a way as to be disposed toward ingratitude, whereas we must actively cultivate a sense of appreciation for whatever good may exist in life. Another way of saying this is that some qualities of the world would be lost on us if we lacked the capacity for gratitude, or if we did not employ this capacity. In order to apprehend meaning and goodness in the world, one must develop the right kind of affective receptivity. The "glow of gratitude," in other words, has an "intentional content," since it is an experience in which an aspect of the world is "registered in an affectively toned appreciation."[38] As I have suggested, such an emotion can provide us with a kind of understanding that is not available in any other way, making us aware of things that could not otherwise be known by us. When we feel a sense of comprehensive gratitude for existence, even in spite of all the pain and suffering that it also contains,[39] we experience a conviction that life is worth living.

To feel *that* one's life is good, and that it is worth living, is a kind of apprehension in which something is tangibly evident. On the other hand, the value of existence is not apparent to us when our emotional disposition is radically different: sometimes it is taken for granted, and sometimes (in certain states of mind, not only morbid ones) it is palpably in doubt. A different inward outlook permits us to see a different aspect on the face of things, conveying a felt sense of reality that is very much *of reality* and yet also relying upon *our own* sensibility. We fail to understand all of Kierkegaard's emphasis on passion and subjectivity if we omit either side of the story: when he says that what we see depends on how we see, the subjective "how" is correlated with an objective "what," and both are essential sides of the equation, so to speak.[40] Yes, there *is* a truth that is not invented or fabricated by us; and yet this does not entitle us to fall back on a conventional notion of "objective" truth, if (as Kierkegaard claims) our mode of access to such truth as we can know is through passionate subjectivity. On the contrary, if Kierkegaard is right, then getting our own individual temperament "out of the way" will *not* help us to discover the truth. To accept that our affective dispositions can enable us to know, we must revise not only our ideas about knowing, but also our ideas about being.

The capacity for passionate understanding is one whose importance could hardly be exaggerated, and Kierkegaard's writings could help us to better appreciate it, as I have been attempting to (begin to) explain. So how is it, for example, that "a truth about the nature of reality" can "be understood only in a spirit of gratitude,"[41] as I have suggested? Feeling grateful for what one has been given is not the same as believing that one has received something good, according to one's prior conception of the good. It is not a matter of having everything happen exactly in the way that one would have wished for in advance. Just as we could not persuade ourselves to feel convinced of a "truth" that we had merely "constructed," we would not be emotionally convinced by a world of consistent wish-fulfillment—as Kierkegaard proposes in the following passage from 1847: "Imagine that you possess . . . every possible good fortune and along with them the taste and genius to utilize them. . . . What would you lack? Perhaps you are thinking I will say: You lack someone with whom to share your happiness. By no means, this is granted to you as well." (*Papirer* VII 1 A 678; JP § 1511).

Casting himself as a genie with the power to indulge our every wish, Kierkegaard continues: let us imagine that "you have a beloved, the epitome of charm," as lovely and captivating as Scheherazade in the tale of the *Arabian Nights*. We also, he asks us to imagine, have admiring friends visiting from all distant lands. Now, he asks again, What do you lack? Perhaps we feel insecure now, fearing a change of fortune for the worse, or perhaps we are disturbed only by the prospect of death. Offering an impossible guarantee, he asks us to imagine that we are "absolutely assured" of holding onto all of these good things throughout a long life. So, he asks, "What now do you lack?" And his answer is that we lack a sense of "wonder" over what God has granted us—"because, after all," he says, "you are the architect of your own fortune, you are your own providence" (*Papirer* VII 1 A 678; JP § 1511).[42]

If the nature of our life were such that we really were "making it up as we go," we would not be able to appreciate it. Our well-being depends on many conditions, both internal and external, over which our power is limited. But if we can to some degree attend to our emotional disposition, and if we have some ability to influence it, then we will also be attending to and influencing our sense of the world. When we are moved by those existential questions about meaning and value that we cannot think about without becoming passionate, we are dealing with matters grasped through passionate understanding. These are matters about which *what is the case* cannot be established with "objective certainty"—because it is ambiguous, because it is perspectival, *and* because it cannot be neatly distinguished from *how we feel*.

RICK ANTHONY FURTAK is Associate Professor of Philosophy at Colorado College. His published works include *Wisdom in Love: Kierkegaard and the Ancient Quest for Emotional Integrity*.

Notes

1. Arnold B. Come notes that the importance of "passion" in Kierkegaard's thought "cannot be overstated," because "it takes us to the very heart" of what is meant by the assertion that "subjectivity is truth" (*Kierkegaard as Humanist* [Montreal: McGill-Queen's University Press, 1995], p. 100). On subjective truth, which is "essentially related to the essence of an individual's existence," see also the discussion of this theme by M. G. Piety in "The Epistemology of the *Postscript*," in *Kierkegaard's Concluding Unscientific Postscript: A Critical Guide*, Rick Anthony Furtak, ed. (Cambridge: Cambridge University Press, 2010), pp. 197–200.

2. David Walsh, *The Modern Philosophical Revolution: The Luminosity of Existence* (Cambridge: Cambridge University Press, 2008), p. 394. In the next sentence, I translate a term from *Papirer* IX A 365; SKS 21:132.

3. The vast number of texts to which I cryptically allude here share a family resemblance in their apparent dismissal of affective experience, and they stretch from early modern thinkers such as Descartes, Leibniz, and Spinoza through Hume, Kant, and even Schopenhauer. Unwittingly echoing Kierkegaard, Quentin Smith contends that "passionless" rationality is actually the "degenerate" and "epistemically unsound" type of cognition. See *The Felt Meanings of the World: A Metaphysics of Feeling* (West Lafayette, IN: Purdue University Press, 1986), pp. 88, 96–107.

4. I mentioned above the Gilleleje writings from 1835; the later works that are pertinent include, for instance, *For Self-Examination* and numerous journal and notebook entries from the early 1850s.

5. Robert L. Perkins, "Kierkegaard, a Kind of Epistemologist," *History of European Ideas* 12 (1990): pp. 7–18. Cf. Edward F. Mooney, *On Søren Kierkegaard* (Burlington, VT: Ashgate, 2007), p. 184n.

6. As Constantin writes, "At the first glance I saw that he was a poet," if only because "an occurrence which, if it had happened to a commonplace man would quietly have come to nothing, assumed in his case the proportions of a cosmic event" (R 1946, 159).

7. We should keep in mind that "practical reason," in the most narrow sense of the term, is only part of what is included under the heading of "subjective thinking," since this category must encompass any and all reflective thought that is somehow relevant to human existence in one's own case.

8. It is in *Works of Love* that Kierkegaard describes love as a "passion of the emotions" (WL, 112).

9. The earnest thought of death, that definite end to which we will come at some uncertain point, could lead us to reflect upon our finitude and "to form a good intention for the whole of life," but one could also give speeches about this without an understanding (that is, a passionate understanding) of what it means—as is proposed in CUP (pp. 139–140).

10. As Kierkegaard claims in CD (p. 194), "Personal consciousness" requires "that in my knowledge I also have knowledge of myself and my relation to my knowledge." Granted that a person's death matters to us, the "acknowledgment" of the fact that this person has died "cannot be made with equanimity," as I explain in *Wisdom in Love* (Notre Dame, IN: University of Notre Dame Press, 2005), p. 15.

11. I am now reformulating Kierkegaard's point in light of this new example. On how a person can have all kinds of dispassionate knowledge about death without having grasped this, see CUP, p. 143. A person who "knows" that a friend has died, or that they will die someday, but does not entirely "believe" it yet, has not "subjectively appropriated" this truth—as we might say, in the language of Johannes Climacus; see, for example, CUP, 171.

12. Cf. Matthew Ratcliffe, *Feelings of Being* (Oxford: Oxford University Press, 2008), p. 160.

13. See, for example, EUD, 59: "What one sees depends upon how one sees," because "observation is not just a receiving . . . but also a bringing forth, and insofar as it is that, how the observer himself is constituted is indeed decisive."

14. Maurice Merleau-Ponty, *Phenomenology of Perception*, trans. Colin Smith (New York: Routledge, 2002), pp. 93–94.

15. Maurice Merleau-Ponty, *The Visible and the Invisible*, trans. Alphonso Lingis (Evanston, IL: Northwestern University Press, 1968), p. 28.

16. That he has in mind what we would call a "mood" is evident by the nearby term *nedbøiet* (bowed, downcast, weighed down, low, dejected, or in a funk). With this term, he refers to states in which we were feeling this way: dejected, depressed, and so on. On this set of affective conditions, see also Vincent A. McCarthy, *The Phenomenology of Moods in Kierkegaard* (The Hague: Martinus Nijhoff, 1978), pp. 53–56.

17. Again, see Kierkegaard, EUD, 59–60. This is his discussion of how "what one sees" depends upon "how one sees," or in other words, on the state of one's "inner being." Regarding what follows, see Dan Zahavi, *Self-Awareness and Alterity* (Evanston, IL: Northwestern University Press, 1999), pp. 125–126.

18. Volume 1 of *Either/Or* presents melancholy primarily as a danger, a type of spiritual desolation, but this is not the whole story. Kierkegaard refers to his own melancholy as an "intellectual power" of great benefit, a proclivity by virtue of which he is or can be in the hand of a "higher power," part of his "genius" as a "poet." See *Papirer* X 1 A 421 (from 1849).

19. From "Circles" and from "Nominalist and Realist," respectively in *Essays: First Series* and *Essays: Second Series*. For citations of Emerson's *Collected Works*, see John Lysaker, *Emerson and Self-Culture* (Bloomington: Indiana University Press, 2008), p. 43.

20. This is why one must be "attentive to and capable of seeing God" in the world. "God is not there," but when we have the appropriate inward attunement, then we find it "possible to see God everywhere," as Climacus says (CUP, 204–207).

21. Arne Grøn, *The Concept of Anxiety in Søren Kierkegaard*, trans. Jeannette Knox (Macon, GA: Mercer University Press, 2008), p. 136. On the relation of love to the question of whether life is worth living, see WL, 38, 375.

22. On being deceived "by not believing what is true," see WL, 5.

23. On "existential knowledge" (or "existential science," in Hannay's translation), as opposed to logical fields in which absolute certainty, or unity between thought and being, is attainable, see *Papirer* IV C 100, in *PJS*, 178.

24. William Barrett, *Irrational Man: A Study in Existential Philosophy* (New York: Anchor Books, 1990), p. 152.

25. Patrick Stokes, while noting that "consciousness *per se* is interested" distinguishes himself from those who take "interest" (*interesse*) and "passion" (*lidenskab*) to be "broadly coterminous"; see *Kierkegaard's Mirrors: Interest, Self, and Moral Vision* (New York: Palgrave Macmillan, 2010), pp. 49–53. Merold Westphal is an advocate of the view that passion and interest are indeed broadly coterminous; see *Becoming a Self* (West Lafayette, IN: Purdue University Press, 1996), p. 138. While I am not suggesting that we can *equate* passion with interest, I read Kierkegaard's account of consciousness-as-interested as an indication that "interest" and "passion" are *continuous*, in the sense that interest is a minimal affective condition of awareness, although in everyday language such a low-level emotional arousal would not be enough to qualify as "passionate."

26. Here I am citing two remarkable passages from 1848 and 1847, respectively. On how "personal knowledge" puts us "passionately" in touch with reality, enabling us to develop a "vision" of a world that is nonetheless "not made but discovered," see Michael Polanyi, *Personal Knowledge* (Chicago: University of Chicago Press, 1962), p. 64.

27. Edward F. Mooney, *Selves in Discord and Resolve* (London: Routledge, 1996), p. 8.

28. C. Stephen Evans, *Kierkegaard: An Introduction* (Cambridge: Cambridge University Press, 2009), p. 64.

29. "Christianity rests on the idea that the truth is the single individual" (SKS 23, NB 19:70 *Papirer* X 3 A 231, from 1850). Climacus remarks upon how a Greek thinker was someone "impassioned by his thought" by virtue of his passionate interest in existence; see CUP, 258.

30. Kierkegaard's understanding of subjectivity places uncertainty at the heart of reason. For instance, we must hold views about "how the world stands" and "how I stand in relation to it"—in other words, *how things are* and *what my life means*—in order to live and act, rather than being paralyzed by doubt; see Stokes, *Kierkegaard's Mirrors*, p. 150. See also Piety, "The Epistemology of the *Postscript*," pp. 193–195.

31. Cf. Hilary Putnam, *The Collapse of the Fact/Value Dichotomy and Other Essays* (Cambridge, MA: Harvard University Press, 2004), pp. 43–44: "It is much easier to say, 'that's a value judgment,' meaning, 'that's just a value of subjective preference,' than to do what Socrates tried to teach us: to examine who we are and what our deepest convictions are and to hold these convictions up to the searching test of reflective examination."

32. On the sense in which love clarifies our identity while defining the contours of our engagement in the world, see also Lambert Zuidervaart, *Artistic Truth* (Cambridge: Cambridge University Press, 2004), pp. 39–43.

33. J. Hillis Miller, *The Disappearance of God* (Urbana: University of Illinois Press, 2000), p. 321; Albert Hofstadter, *Truth and Art* (New York: Columbia University Press, 1965), pp. 175–76.

34. II Samuel 12, discussed by Kierkegaard in FSE, 38–39. David is plainly capable of sympathy and of poetic imagination, as Kierkegaard points out, and he is also a man of passionate subjective faith; yet "even a man like" David is still capable of failing to respond adequately.

35. Ted Cohen, *Thinking of Others: On the Talent for Metaphor* (Princeton, NJ: Princeton University Press, 2008), p. 21.

36. Stokes would say that the apprehension embodied in "passionate imagination" involves a "non-thetic self-referentiality," a tacit sense of how one is implicated in what one perceives; see *Kierkegaard's Mirrors*, pp. 87–89.

37. Climacus names this as an example of a question that calls for subjective thinking: namely, what it means to be grateful to God for whatever good one has been given in life; see CUP, 148–150.

38. Mark Wynn, *Emotional Experience and Religious Understanding* (Cambridge: Cambridge University Press, 2005), pp. 91–92.

39. Quentin Smith discusses "appreciative knowledge of the world," which is available to us through affective feelings such as gratitude and awe; see *The Felt Meanings of the World*, pp. 22–28.

40. See *Papirer* X 2 A 299; PJS, 449–450.

41. Furtak, *Wisdom in Love* (Notre Dame, IN: University of Notre Dame Press, 2005), p. 117.

42. On Kierkegaard's opposition to the view that "the world offers no meaning except that which one arbitrarily gives it," and on his belief that we "can only subjectively accept meaning which is given as a gift," see K. Brian Soderquist, *The Isolated Self* (Copenhagen: C. A. Reitzel, 2007), pp. 52, 199.

8 From Hegel to Google: Kierkegaard and the Perils of "the System"

Christopher B. Barnett

The name "internet" first achieved currency in the mid-1980s. A shorter, more graceful version of the term, "internetwork," it came to be applied to the medium by which computers from around the world are connected. Thus the internet is, by definition, a *global* instrument, facilitating the exchange of information between computer systems and those who use them. At first, this exchange was as clumsy as it was limited; however, technological advancement has increased its accessibility and its rapidity. No enterprise better represents this development than Google.

Google is a multinational corporation whose eponymous search engine has revolutionized the way in which internet users seek and process information. According to its company homepage, "Google's mission is to organize the world's information and make it universally accessible and useful."[1] But is this goal *actually* desirable? Indeed, might it be dangerous?

The task of this essay is to think through these issues, drawing, above all, on the thought of Søren Kierkegaard. It will proceed in two main ways. First, it will sketch how the question concerning Google harks back to the kind of questions Kierkegaard raised about Hegelianism in his day. In turn, it will analyze Google's mission (or business model) and show how it recalls what Kierkegaard saw as the trouble with Hegelian thinking—namely, a tendency toward speculation that encourages an abstract relation to existence and, with it, a diminished interest in ethico-religious engagement. The claim here, then, is *not* that Google was founded on Hegelian principles per se; still less is it a straightforward identification of the two. Rather, the point is that, from a Kierkegaardian perspective, Hegel and Google stand in an analogous relation to one another: both promote the systematic collection and distribution of knowledge at the expense of concrete human flourishing.

Second, it will argue that Kierkegaard's brush with Hegelianism disposed him to extol and to foster a different way of thinking—*Betragtning* or "contemplation," which centers the existing person and so is propaedeutic to an earnest engagement with reality. If Google harvests information at a rate heretofore unseen, Kierkegaard suggests that one should not conflate its task with think-ing as such. In the end, then, to read Kierkegaard is a kind of *therapy*, not only redressing philosophy's tendency toward abstraction, but also anticipating the same (and more pervasive) propensity in technology.

The Rise of Google

In his 2008 book *Against the Machine: Being Human in the Age of the Electronic Mob*, Lee Siegel quips that "popularity is Web culture's Holy Grail."[2] His com-plaint, in particular, is directed at the internet's prioritization of popularity over expertise—a tendency that he likens to a high-school "class clown," who "[trans-forms] his very self . . . into a product that [fits] the needs of others."[3] What he fails to note is that this is precisely what the founders of Google, Larry Page and Sergey Brin, foresaw when they started the company in 1998. Recognizing the staggering proliferation of sites on the web, they sought a means to "evaluate and rank the value of all the pages on the Web."[4] The result was a new search engine, which today has become the chief mediator of data on the internet.

As a search engine, Google is designed to receive requests for information and, in seconds, to return pertinent results. With informational pages on the internet numbering in the billions, this is no easy task. Google copes by indexing the frequency with which a search result is recognized (or "clicked"), provid-ing, in turn, an unparalleled ability to manage a "a seemingly infinite amount of information."[5] The more clicks, the higher a given page is ranked—and the more Google collects in advertising fees.

It is, doubtless, a shrewd moneymaking program, garnering the company assets in the vicinity of 100 billion dollars. Yet Google insists that it is a force for the common good. A few reasons account for this fact. First, Google has imposed order on that which was once thought "ungoverned and ungovernable,"[6] namely the internet. Siva Vaidhyanathan even compares the search engine to Julius Caesar, whose Roman dictatorship was a welcome change to the "state of chaos and civil war"[7] that preceded it. Second, by collecting hard data about user pref-erences and by conducting psychological research,[8] Google has become adept at *directing* the way individuals interface with the web. As Eric Schmidt, then CEO of Google, put it in 2010, "[People] want Google to tell them what they should be doing next. . . . We know roughly who you are, roughly what you care about, roughly who your friends are."[9] Like a trusty guide, Google knows how to get people where they want (or think they want) to go. Third, and follow-ing on from the previous point, Google styles itself as a progressive, democratic institution that puts science in service to human productivity—an approach that recalls many of the great inventions of the Industrial Revolution, only now the product is *knowledge*. "In Google's view, information is a kind of . . . utilitarian resource,"[10] whose excavation and efficient distribution is the foundation of constructive thinking.

But what effect does Google and its services have on its customers—that is to say, on the millions of persons (including this one) who use it every day? It is at this point that Kierkegaard's critique of Hegelianism—limited here to his 1846 text *Concluding Unscientific Postscript to Philosophical Fragments*—is worth remembering. After all, in this critique, Kierkegaard not only questions but even warns against a number of features that would come to characterize Google over a century later, from the prioritization of objective knowledge to the construction of a "system" to which all knowledge is subordinated. Of course, this critique cannot be taken as an indictment of Google per se; indeed, some commentators have even wondered if it is a fair critique of Hegel himself.[11] At the same time, however, the lack of a clear-cut historical referent should not discredit the position sketched in the *Postscript*, for, as will be seen, the book's concerns about Hegelianism anticipate the era of Google in striking fashion. One might even wonder if Google does not epitomize the "system" and its dangers better than Hegel (or, for that matter, nineteenth-century Danish Hegelianism) ever could.

Johannes Climacus and the Perils of the System

Before discussing the *Postscript* and its critique of Hegelianism, it is worth surveying G. W. F. Hegel and how his thinking relates to the rise of modern technology. Hegel is typically regarded as one of the leading figures of absolute idealism—a post-Kantian movement in philosophy that sought "to penetrate existence to find the rational, conceptual truth, which is its core or kernel."[12] This ambitious task is already manifest in the extensity of Hegel's philosophical output; he composed treatises on logic, nature, and spirit [*Geist*], among others. Just as the young Hegel admired Napoleon—whom he called a "world-soul," unafraid of "reaching across the world and ruling it"[13]—so did he seek to master the history and scope of the philosophical enterprise. That this objective would come to overlap with the rise of modern technology may seem surprising. However, as will be seen, Hegel himself realized that the development and application of technology goes hand in hand with the progress of philosophy.

Hegel, Technology, and the "Systematic Exposition of Philosophy"

In his well-known work *The Technological Society* (1964), Jacques Ellul claims that one of the defining traits of the modern West is a "clear technical intention"—that is to say, "a mass intention, clearly understood and deliberately guiding the whole society in a technical direction."[14] For Ellul, this phenomenon arose by "historical coincidence."[15] On the one hand, a variety of special interests, each pursuing the most efficient way to accomplish its objectives, collectively rendered technology

dominant in Western society; these interested parties included industrial capital-
ists, the state, and the bourgeoisie. On the other hand, there was a philosophical
or theoretical impetus behind this change. Here, according to Ellul, a number
of figures and issues might be named, but Hegel garners explicit mention as one
who "reinforced" this technical intention.[16]

Precisely how Hegel reinforces the dominance of technology in the West
is not addressed in *The Technological Society*, though it is clear that, for Ellul,
Hegel's importance lies in his connection to Karl Marx. It was Marx, he notes,
who argued that technology's influence must proceed according to Hegelian
dialectic. Whereas the proletariat had once endured "the hardships of technical advance without sharing in the triumphs," Marx predicted that the ongoing
development of technology "would automatically bring about the collapse of the
bourgeoisie and of capitalism."[17] In this way, thesis would yield to antithesis, and,
following Hegel, a synthesis would emerge—namely, a society lacking in class
and wealth distinctions.

And yet, Marx's appropriation of Hegelian dialectic notwithstanding, there
is actually a significant difference between the two thinkers on technology. As
Stephen Houlgate argues, Marx understands "technological change, change in
the material forces of production, as the primary determining factor in history."[18]
In other words, for Marx, a given culture's intellectual, political, and religious life
ultimately stems from its technological development and skill. But Hegel takes
just the opposite approach. On his reading, "what is primary in a society is its
general character of 'spirit', and the development of the technological power of
a culture or society itself stems from the kind of character the society has."[19]
Hence, for Hegel, society's *Geist* orders its technology, not the other way around.
The value (or lack thereof) of an innovation or a tool is established by the way that
it is seen or understood in a civilization.

Hegel illustrates this point in *The Philosophy of History*. In discussing the
development of the "Oriental World," he notes,

> [The Chinese] knew many things at a time when Europeans had not discov-
> ered them, but they have not understood how to apply their knowledge: as *e.g.*
> the Magnet, and the Art of Printing. But they have made no advance in the
> application of these discoveries. In the latter, for instance, they continue to
> engrave the letters in wooden blocks and then print them off: they know noth-
> ing of movable types. Gunpowder, too, they pretended to have invented before
> the Europeans; but the Jesuits were obliged to found their first cannon. As
> to Mathematics, they understand well enough how to reckon, but the higher
> aspect of the science is unknown.[20]

In contrast, Hegel sees in the "German World"—whose "Spirit is the Spirit of the
new World"[21]—as one developing "in the direction of *Science*."[22] By "science" he
does not merely mean the investigation of the natural world through empirical

research; rather, he is referring to something more encompassing, namely, "development of Thought—the abstractly Universal."[23] In other words, the modern Germanic world is no longer content to think along the lines of "that elder scholastic theology"—namely, in focusing on "the doctrine of the Church"—but instead unfolds toward an ever-expanding "Universality."[24] Reason has become conscious of itself as universal, as that which is "immanent within the world and so . . . genuinely objective."[25]

In this scenario, writes Hegel, an "interest in the contemplation and comprehension of the present world" becomes paramount.[26] The world appears to reason as knowable, as searchable: "that which is diverse from [the pure Ego], sensuous or spiritual, no longer presents an object of dread, for in contemplating such diversity it is inwardly free and can freely confront it."[27] Human thinking stands confident before the world of knowledge, "challenging the external world to exhibit the same Reason which Subject [the Ego] possesses."[28] Here, indeed, empirical science emerges as "the science of the World," inasmuch as its commitment to view phenomena in terms of "Sorts, Genera, Power, Gravitation, etc." comes to characterize the relation of the human subject to the external object.[29] The goal is now to understand the world as a "system of known and recognized Laws," wherein "that only passes for truth in which [Man] finds himself at home."[30] This is as true for "the Spiritual side of things" as it is for the physical;[31] even "man's eternal destiny [his spiritual and moral position] must be wrought out *in himself* [cannot be an *opus operatum*, a work performed *for him*]."[32] In modernity, human knowledge and human autonomy have come to reinforce one another, and that is precisely why, for Hegel, the Germanic world stands as an advance over previous civilizations. As Houlgate puts it, "Hegel understands human beings to be *essentially* self-determining."[33]

This turn to the abstractly universal forms the basis of Hegel's own well-known "System" [*Das System*]. In his first major work, *Phenomenology of Spirit* (1807), Hegel writes that his aim is to make philosophy scientific—that is to say, systematic. As he explains, "The true shape in which truth exists can only be the scientific system of such truth. To help bring philosophy closer to the form of Science, to the goal where it can lay aside the title "*love* of knowing" and be *actual* knowing—that is what I have set myself to do. The inner necessity that knowing should be Science lies in its nature, and only the systematic exposition of philosophy itself provides it."[34]

This search for actual or absolute knowledge means that truth cannot just be sought here and there; rather, it "involves grasping the way [the truth's] various components contribute not only toward constituting the whole but each other as well."[35] In other words, the true philosophy is the one that, quite literally, *comprehends* the historically evolving consciousness of truth, thereby becoming a "single unity-in-diversity, a single dialectical system, which will constitute a 'systematic science'."[36]

This is, doubtless, an ambitious task. Yet, for Hegel, it is an ambition consonant with its place in history, and so it should not frighten but inspire. In his inaugural lecture in Berlin, Hegel speaks of the need to pursue knowledge with boldness, even to pry open the very mystery of the universe: "The courage of truth, faith in the power of mind is the first condition of philosophical studies; we should honor ourselves and hold ourselves worthy of the highest. We cannot think highly enough of the greatness and power of mind; the hidden essence of the universe possesses no power in itself to resist the courage of knowledge; it must open itself to us, placing its riches and depth before our eyes for our enjoyment."[37]

According to Merold Westphal, this passage epitomizes the "spirit" of Western philosophy, which, since the time of Plato, has stressed a "technical interpretation of thinking."[38] Such, indeed, was the reading of Martin Heidegger, whose 1957 seminar[39] on Hegel's *Science of Logic* identified Hegel as a "prime instance of onto-theological thinking" and therefore of the "rationalist demand for total intelligibility."[40] Yet, for Heidegger, it is just this kind of thinking that undergirds modern technology. As Westphal adds, "What Heidegger calls calculative thinking (and the Frankfurt school calls instrumental reason) is thought in the service of technology."[41] To be sure, there is a line from metaphysics to science to technology—a line that, as has been seen, Hegel himself recognized. And this point leads to a key conclusion: modern technology is not a historical accident but, rather, the fruit of (Western) philosophical *development*.

Of course, in recent decades, Heidegger's "The Question Concerning Technology"[42] has become almost obligatory reading in the philosophy of technology. However, long before Heidegger's critique of Western metaphysics, there was Kierkegaard's own multifaceted response to modernity, which raised a number of concerns about Hegel's role in the formation of Western thinking. These concerns are found throughout Kierkegaard's authorship, though they receive particular (and pointed) emphasis in *Concluding Unscientific Postscript*.

Climacus Against the System

Attributed to the pseudonym Johannes Climacus, the *Postscript* takes aim not only at Hegel's "System" but, indeed, at the very notion of philosophy as *Wissenschaft*. As Climacus sees it, Hegel's attempt to comprehend existence systematically is speculative and, therefore, problematic on a number of fronts. For one thing, the System fails to distinguish between thinking *about* existence and existence as such. The former may strive for philosophical closure—for a totalizing grasp of knowledge—but the latter rules out this possibility in advance. After all, the one who is existing cannot transcend that which is still unfolding; namely, one's existence: "Whoever is himself existing cannot gain . . . conclusiveness outside existence, a conclusiveness that corresponds to . . . eternity" (SKS 7:114; CUP, 118–19). To think otherwise, Climacus jokes, is not only "a false presupposition but a comic presupposition, occasioned by . . . a kind of world-historical absentmindedness [of] what it means to be a human being" (SKS 7:116; CUP, 120). It follows that truly systematic thinking requires a being who "in his eternity is forever concluded and yet includes existence within himself" (SKS 7:115; CUP, 119), and only a deity could be described in such terms. Thus self-deification emerges as the gravest danger facing not only Hegelian philosophy but in fact all who crave systematic clarity and total knowledge. As Westphal notes, it "is as producers and consumers of the system that Hegelian humanity takes itself to be divine."[43]

Of course, it would be one thing if such ambition promoted human flourishing; however, Climacus "sees it as pure loss, the loss of our humanity, our true self."[44] Indeed, herein lies the second overarching problem with the System: it mistakes the accumulation of knowledge with human well-being, which, in truth, is always bound up with particular concerns and needs. In other words, even if one were able to systematize all knowledge, the complete *application* of that knowledge would remain an unattainable horizon, ever frustrating the System's pretensions of closure. With this in mind, Climacus makes note of the irony that "through Hegel a system, the absolute system, was brought to completion—without having an ethics" (SKS 7:115; CUP, 119). Climacus does not attribute this absence to an oversight on Hegel's part. Rather, it is a consequence of his project as such, which prescinds from the concrete and, thereby, adopts a disembodied vantage point: "This objective thinking has no relation to the existing subjectivity, and while the difficult question always remains—namely, how the existing subject gains entrance into this objectivity in which subjectivity is pure abstract subjectivity (which again is an objective qualification and does not signify any existing human being)—it is certain that the existing subjectivity evaporates more and more. "(SKS 7:118–119; CUP, 123.)

All of the information in the world, if it is abstracted from actual existence, amounts to nothing, and so the thinker disposed to objective knowledge "becomes something infinitely great and nothing at all" (SKS 7:119; CUP, 124). She has an untold expanse of data but no concrete life in which to make it meaningful. Of course, one may object that such data is fascinating, *intéressant*. Climacus would even grant the point.[45] But life, he insists, is far more than amusement: "To be simply and solely a human being means something more than playing party games this way" (SKS 7:120; CUP, 124).

This problem only deepens when the possibility of transcendence is introduced. After all, no matter how glittering its results, the system is framed by human knowledge, and, precisely for that reason, it is discontinuous with transcendence. In contrast, as Climacus points out, "Christianity wants to give the single individual an eternal happiness," and this hope "wants to intensify passion to its highest, but passion is subjectivity and objectively it does not exist at all" (SKS 7:122–123; CUP, 130–131). Thus human beings nurtured on the system will lack passion precisely to the extent that they are preoccupied with immanent objectivity. They "have" the truth but relate to it the wrong way or, even worse, fail to relate to it at all. That is why Climacus eulogizes the epistemological humility of Gotthold Lessing, who contended that relating to the truth is as much about the *how* as the *what*: "Lessing speaks of a striving for truth; and he uses a peculiar phrase regarding this urge for truth: *den einzigen immer regen Trieb* [the one and only ever-striving drive]" (SKS 7:105; CUP, 108). And yet, if the pursuit of truth is *immer regen*, then the very notion of an objective system falls into contradiction, though Climacus quips that there nevertheless may be good reasons for calling it such: "Perhaps the systematician thinks this way: If on the title page or in the newspaper I call my production a continued striving for the truth, alas, who will buy it or admire me; but if I call it the system, the absolute system, everyone will buy the system" (SKS 7:105; CUP, 108).

This is a particularly relevant passage, for it implies that information, when packaged a certain way, can be commodified. Indeed, as Climacus sees it, Hegel's system is a prime example of how information can be sold, bought, and finally consumed in order to "*demonstrate, rationally,* the superiority of [a given] system and to demand everybody's support."[46] This is what Ellul calls "propaganda."[47]

Of course, by now, Climacus's reproach of Hegel has become part of philosophical lore, and, to put it in broader terms, the Hegel–Kierkegaard divide has emerged as one of the great fault lines in modern ideas. As Jon Stewart puts it, scholars "seem to assign the two thinkers to opposite ends of the philosophical spectrum."[48] And yet, as is often the case, the notoriety of such a dispute belies its ongoing importance. Even if, following Stewart,[49] Kierkegaard's relation to Hegel is more complicated than often assumed, their respective philosophical approaches have significance well beyond the history of ideas. At stake here is a timeless (and therefore all too timely) question about how persons ought to interact with human knowledge, which never emerges *ex nihilo* but, rather, bears a number of presuppositions and implications, whether anthropological, sociological, or theological. That Kierkegaard recognized this fact distinguished his response to Hegel. Moreover, it renders his views germane when considering what may be the greatest information system ever devised—Google.

A Kierkegaardian Critique of Google

Earlier in this chapter, it was noted that Google "rose to the top of the technological heap by tackling the challenge of the era—too much information."[50] However, to note this fact is to say nothing about the significance of a surfeit of information. What end, if any, does it serve? And how does Google's systematic mastery of so much knowledge affect our perception of the company? After all, if Google is able to encompass our relation to virtually all extant knowledge, then is it not, in Hegelian terms, the apex of all intellectual enterprise—the technological embodiment of what Hegel calls "the courage of knowledge"?

That such questions can be asked of Google is, in one sense, ironic. Brin and Page hardly set out to exemplify the Hegelian system; they simply wanted to facilitate the finding of information on the internet.[51] Theirs was not a mission of authority but of service—an objective that, quite literally, received mathematical expression in an algorithm designed "to recognize the sources and pages that informed what was popular [on the web]."[52]

And yet, it is just here that a Kierkegaardian critique of Google might begin. For Brin and Page *assume* that more information distributed to more people is more useful. Peter Barron, Google's head of communications for Europe, the Middle East, and Africa, puts it like this: "Google starts from a position that we seek to make information available to the widest number of people. Google is built on free expression."[53] To use Google, then, is to tap into the values hailed by Hegel as hallmarks of the Germanic world—namely, reason and freedom. Google expresses reason's consciousness of its own utility, of its ability to transform the world by answering the questions (however trivial, however profound) that beguile us. What's more, this ability is no longer confined to the ideas or innovations of a particular thinker but, rather, is mediated digitally as a kind of collective genius, unfettered by the limitations intrinsic to a given person's intellect. Through Google, notes Vaidhyanathan, "I have access to more information than I could ever know what to do with. So it feels somewhat liberating that I don't have to remember very much."[54]

Still, in the *Postscript*, Climacus cautions against such assumptions. First, he points out that information, in and of itself, is not a good. That is to say, it always arrives already conditioned by extrinsic factors. For example, the vehicle for a piece of information influences the way in which one receives it. Climacus makes this point clear in his critique of Hegel's system. Hegel implies that his thought, *qua* system, is "positive," possessing a secure basis in "sensate certainty, historical knowledge, [and] speculative result" (SKS 7:80–81; CUP, 80–81). And yet, snaps Climacus, "all of this positive fails to express the state of the knowing subject in existence; hence it pertains to a fictive objective subject" (SKS 7:81 / CUP, 81). Thus the *form* of Hegel's system belies its *content*. That which is presented as objective is, in truth, "approximation-knowledge" (SKS 7:81; CUP, 81), since its positivity is abstracted from the existing subject, who in turn "comes to know much about the world, nothing about himself" (SKS 7:81; CUP, 81). The upshot is an "illusion" wherein the person perceives that she knows more, even as she really knows less (SKS 7:81; CUP, 81).

Something very similar could be said of Google. It does not just deliver information but also shapes the way persons relate to it; it is a medium that, as Marshall McLuhan famously observed,[55] becomes the message. Recall that Google responds to queries in two main ways: (1) by determining how often search results are clicked, and (2) by ranking these results from most to least popular. What the user receives, then, is not necessarily the best piece of information, still less something akin to wisdom. It is simply what is popular or "trending," filtered, moreover, according to "the identity, history, and location of the user."[56] This *modus operandi* is no secret, but Google's reputation for scientific rigor, not to mention financial heft, lends it an air of authority. The reality, however, is that Google only provides what Climacus calls "approximation-knowledge," not just in terms of the veracity (or lack thereof) of the information it locates, but also inasmuch as its provision of objective information "pertains to a fictive objective subject, and to mistake oneself for such a subject is to be fooled and to remain fooled" (SKS 7:81; CUP, 81). In other words, Google may strive to resolve our questions, but, for Climacus, this ambition itself is problematic: there are no final answers in human existence, for at the core of human existence is a contradiction, namely that the self is a "synthesis" of the eternal and the temporal and therefore finds rest in neither alone (SKS 7:81–82; CUP, 82)[57]—and so the true teacher "keeps open the wound of negativity" and indicates that genuine learning consists of "continually striving" (SKS 7:84; CUP, 85). This is a far cry from Google's unqualified language of "search results" and "useful" information.

Thus Google, as an efficient digital system designed to distribute putatively objective information to existing subjects, is based on a flawed premise that has the potential to mislead persons about the nature of knowledge and its relation to human existence. But this concern only involves the systematic propagation of information as such. There is also a concern about how *much* information Google mediates to us. As Vaidhyanathan puts it, "Google puts previously unimaginable resources at our fingertips—huge libraries, archives, warehouses of government records, troves of goods, the comings and goings of whole swaths of humanity."[58] In this way, Google is a virtual apotheosis of Enlightenment thinking, positioning every aspect of human life under the watchful eye of impersonal reason. The step from Hegelian *Vernunft*[59] to the "Googlization of 'everything'"[60] is surprisingly short.

But herein lies a problem. As Climacus sees it, "the very home of existence" does not lie in thought but instead in ethics, not in the accumulation of knowledge but rather in a "continued striving" by which the "existing individual . . . directs all his attention to the actuality that *he* is existing" (SKS 7:116; CUP, 121). But one can only enter into actuality when abstract reflection stops; otherwise one will end up like Trop—a character in J. L. Heiberg's 1826 vaudeville, *The Critic and the Beast* (*Recensenten og Dyret*), who brags that his studies have led him to *almost* take the bar exam on numerous occasions. "Everyone laughs at this," notes Climacus, "but when one chatters speculatively in the same manner in the realm of truth, in the shrine of science and scholarship, then it is good philosophy—genuine speculative philosophy" (SKS 7:111; CUP, 115). The joke, then, is on those who prioritize reflection over action. But if one wants to break the cycle of reflection—and, for Climacus, this move is necessary if one is to flourish as a human being—then reflection *must* come to a stop. But how? Objective data itself cannot halt reflection. The opposite is rather the case: the more information, the more reflection. Part of Climacus's critique of Hegel is that *das System* does not adequately address this problem and, instead, relies on glib obfuscations such as "in logic . . . reflection is stopped by itself and . . . doubting everything flips over into its opposite by itself" (SKS 7:111–112; CUP, 115).

Yet if Hegelianism fails on this point, one can be sure that Google, whose *raison d'être* is to disseminate information, does so as well. After all, the company's profitability is tied to an oversupply of data, since its search results always include advertisements, thereby making Google the world's "most efficient (and valuable) advertising delivery service."[61] It would be bad business, then, for Google to restrict the flow of information, regardless of the effect on the user. To be sure, popular lingo suggests that people "surf" the internet, but in truth, they face a "sheer avalanche of choices [that] can inhibit [them] from taking action."[62] Moreover, and perhaps just as dangerously, too much information renders the acquisition of knowledge routine, even uninspiring. As David Shenk puts it, "Information, once rare and cherished like caviar, is now plentiful and taken for granted like potatoes."[63] When information arrives disconnected from one's concrete existence, it becomes superfluous—a mere matter of course or, at best, an idle curiosity, which may help pass the time but neglects to encourage a transition to the ethical life.[64]

With this sort of scenario in mind, Climacus insists that the only solution lies with the single individual, who must refuse to participate in an otherwise interminable flirtation with objective data. As he goes on to explain,

> If the individual does not stop reflection, he will be infinitized in reflection, that is, no decision is made. By thus going astray in reflection, the individual really becomes objective; more and more he loses the decision of subjectivity and the return into himself. Yet it is assumed that reflection can stop itself objectively, whereas it is just the other way around; reflection cannot be stopped objectively, and when it is stopped subjectively, it does not stop of its own accord, but it is the subject who stops it. (SKS 7:112; CUP, 115–116)

Within the context of the *Postscript*, these comments are directed toward the would-be philosopher, who does "not want to become a ludicrous creature by being transmogrified—*eins, zwei, drei, kokolorum* [one, two, three, hocus pocus]—into speculative thought" (SKS 7:113; CUP, 117). Otherwise, he will see neither himself nor his interlocutors as human beings, flesh and bone; otherwise, philosophy will become a mere game in which parties "make sport of each other" (SKS 7:105; CUP, 109).

However, as I have discussed elsewhere,[65] Kierkegaard would expand on these insights in his next work, *A Literary Review*. There he argues that, via the print media, this philosophical problem has reached sociocultural proportions. In turn, he abandons Climacus's humor and adopts a far more austere tone: "the present age" *in toto* has embraced reflection and, with it, a skeptical relation to authority, tradition, and ultimately God himself. In this context, utility trumps truth, and so the arbiters of utility—from the inventors of technological devices to the shapers of public opinion—are confused with the truth. They have become what, in an older theological parlance, are termed *idols*.

There is a connection, then, between systematic thinking and deification. According to Climacus, it follows from the notion of system itself. Whereas concrete human existence is limited, often messy, and constantly subject to change, the system is ostensibly abstracted from these conditions, providing access to objective knowledge. Such knowledge is thought to be clear, reliable, and therefore conclusive, even as human existence is anything but that. Indeed, if there *were* an existing being whose knowing is transparently and steadfastly conclusive, it would have to be a divine one. As Climacus argues,

> Whoever is himself existing cannot gain this conclusiveness outside existence, a conclusiveness that corresponds to the eternity into which the past has entered. . . . [T]hat he himself is existing implies the claim of existence upon him and that his existence, yes, if he is a great individual, that his existence at the present time may, as past, in turn have the validity of conclusiveness for a systematic thinker. But who, then, is this systematic thinker? Well, it is he who himself is outside existence and yet in existence, who in his eternity is forever concluded and yet includes existence within himself—it is God. (SKS 7:114–115; CUP, 118–119)

Of course, Climacus's point here is that, to the extent that Hegelian thinking is understood as system, it is confused with divine thinking. This confusion forgets that, like all human thinking, the Hegelian system was developed *in* time and consequently bears the limitations of temporality. To neglect this fact is comical at best, perilous at worst. It either renders Hegel a "ludicrous" creature, who thinks that he is something he is not, or "the good Lord" himself, in which case his thinking is taken as the *summum bonum* (SKS 7:115; CUP, 119).

This line of reasoning shifts the focus back to Google, for, as Nicholas Carr writes, Google has emerged as "the Internet's high church," which has a "messianic" sense of purpose.[66] Vaidhyanathan agrees, adding that "Google's appeal is almost divine," enrapturing its votaries with apparent "miracles" while concealing "the ways in which [it] exerts control over its domain."[67] Yet, in the wake of Kierkegaard's insights, this should come as no surprise. Google's goal is to organize—indeed, to systematize—human knowledge. It is an ambitious objective, so much so that "Page and Brin put forth ten commandments to guide Google's ethos."[68] The wisdom once received in the cloud on Mount Sinai (Exodus 24: 15–18) is now promulgated from the glass-encased buildings of Silicon Valley.

Of course, Google's use of a decalogue[69] might be seen as little more than an ironic twist on the vision statements often issued by corporations. And yet, at the very least, the similarity does suggest that the founders of Google grasp the precariousness of their project, that the very attempt to order human knowledge is a risk of, quite literally, biblical proportions. As one Google employee has remarked, "We try really hard not to be evil. But if we wanted to, man, could we ever."[70] Part of this power derives from the confidence, or faith, that people invest in knowledge-brokers—a point that Climacus raises vis-à-vis the Hegelian system and one that Detweiler reiterates in relation to Google:

> Our faith in Google's answers is nearly absolute. We rarely question their algorithmic authority. In fact, we imbue it with an almost mystical power. Type a few letters into its search engine, and Google will fill in the blanks, anticipating our intentions. It autocompletes us—in almost any language. With the rise of personalized search, Google seems to do more than half the thinking for us. So how should we think about Google? Have we defaulted to blind faith in the wisdom of their engine?[71]

As Climacus long ago realized, the underlying question here is that of authority. On what grounds does a human-engineered system merit our faith? Does the matter of existence not throw a spanner in the works of systematic projects, no matter their relative value? Nevertheless, with Google's influence (and revenue) increasing at almost exponential rates,[72] consumers are apparently ignoring these questions and, in effect, deifying Google. As Detweiler quips, "'I saw it on Google' [has] become a twenty-first equivalent to 'God said it, I believe it'."[73] Googling, one might very well conclude, is the new praying.[74]

If such concerns seem removed from the conscious experience of most users of Google, there are more mundane problems as well. Clinical studies have now confirmed that using Google alters brain functioning.[75] It presents persons with a glut of information and, in neurological terms, overloads the working memory, making it "harder to distinguish relevant information from irrelevant information, signal from noise."[76] As a result, attention is divided and meaningful activity hindered.[77] It is the extensity of information, rather than the intensity of thought, that now characterizes our intellectual *habitus*. As Carr puts it, "We are evolving from being cultivators of personal knowledge to being hunters and gatherers in the electronic data forest."[78] But that is not Google's problem. The more information it provides, the more it fulfills its mission. Indeed, if "the medium is the message," Google conveys that knowledge is there to be sold, bought, consumed. "The last thing it wants is to encourage leisurely reading or slow, concentrated thought. Google is, quite literally, in the *business* of distraction."[79]

Here, again, Carr effectively reiterates Climacus's concerns about system-building and, in turn, traces a Kierkegaardian critique of Google. As with previous systems, Google cannot help but divert persons from ethico-spiritual exigencies. It does not orient learning toward wisdom about oneself but, instead, treats it as a means to an external end, whether the rapid assimilation of knowledge for the sake of social productivity or the simple satisfaction of idle chatter. In short, Google molds its users into fetishizers of information, who prefer to browse and to manipulate data rather than to apply it.[80]

What, then, are persons to do? Certainly many answers might be ventured here. Consideration, however, will be given to Kierkegaard, who strives to counteract systematic thinking with a marked emphasis on *Betragtning* or "contemplation." As will be seen, where Google ties one up in the abstract assessment of information, Kierkegaard promotes a way of thinking that centers the existing person.

Betragtning as Therapy in the Age of Google

The word *Betragtning* appears, in one variation or another, over one thousand times in Kierkegaard's authorship. Similar to the German *Betrachtung*, it can be translated in a number of ways, including "consideration," "meditation," and "contemplation." The latter seems particularly apt, as the verb *betragte* means "to look at" or "to regard." This optical connotation dovetails nicely with the typical English usage of "contemplation," defined as "thinking in a concentrated manner about something." People often speak of contemplating a beautiful landscape or a religious icon. Thus it is a matter of attending to, but never dominating, a given object.

In Kierkegaard's authorship, the meaning of *Betragtning* becomes clearer when it is contrasted with two other terms that turn up in his writings— *Spekulation* and *Reflexion*. The former, naturally, is translated as "speculation," and, though it too bears visual connotations, it tends to imply a disconnection from what is at hand. To speculate, as *Webster's* defines it, is to "review something idly and inconclusively." In the *Postscript*, Climacus's frequent criticisms of *Spekulation* echo this meaning, since, as has been seen, the trouble with the System is precisely that it weakens an earnest engagement with reality.

Reflexion is a more ambiguous term. Although a topic that outstrips the present discussion, Kierkegaard's use of the term varies across contexts. Importantly, however, his most famous utilization of *Reflexion* comes in another 1846 text, *A Literary Review*, which lambasts the reflection of the present age for imprisoning persons in a state of ethical lassitude, wherein the good is pondered but not acted upon (TA, 68–76). This application of the term is etymologically correct, for the Latin cognate literally means "to bend back." *Reflexion*, then, suspends the individual in thought. It is a necessary exercise at times, but, for Kierkegaard, it is "not the kind [of thinking] that springs from and reinforces any deep, demanding commitments on the part of the individual."[81]

In contrast, Kierkegaard treats *Betragtning* as a mode of thought that grounds the existing person. To contemplate is to focus on those questions that underpin human life. Who am I? Why am I here? Why is anything here? What is the good life? What happens after death? Who (or what) is God? How can I relate to God? Thus contemplation correlates with "earnestness" (*Alvor*), which Kierkegaard defines as "the relationship to the eternal" (SKS 21, NB 8:12; JP § 235). Together they are essential precursors to existential growth.

This link between contemplation, earnestness, and self-development is, perhaps, best seen in Kierkegaard's various upbuilding discourses—a series of writings that foster *Betragtning* in two main ways. First, Kierkegaard's upbuilding discourses implore the reader to practice contemplation. Indeed, it is noteworthy that *Two Upbuilding Discourses* of 1843—the collection that inaugurates Kierkegaard's cycle of upbuilding writings—begins by recommending contemplative practice. As he writes in the opening prayer of "The Expectancy of Faith," the book's first discourse,

> When in mournful moments we want to strengthen and encourage our minds by contemplating those great men, your chosen instruments, who in severe spiritual trials and anxieties of heart kept their minds free, their courage uncrushed, and heaven open, we, too, wish to add our witness to theirs in the assurance that even if our courage compared with theirs is only discouragement, our power powerlessness, you, however, are still the same, the same mighty God. (SKS 5:17; EUD, 7)

Kierkegaard does not use *betragte* here but, rather, the more informal phrase, "by the thought of" (*ved Tanken om*). Nevertheless, the Hongs rightly translate it as "contemplating," since that term more fully conveys Kierkegaard's meaning. After all, he is extolling an earnest consideration of these biblical icons, not a fleeting or frivolous thought. In doing so, he also implies that his own authorship is a means to that end—a place where such figures can be encountered and pondered.[82]

Unsurprisingly, then, contemplation surfaces elsewhere in his upbuilding writings. In 1847's "What We Learn from the Lilies in the Field and from the Birds of the Air," Kierkegaard urges the reader to contemplate nature for the sake of spiritual growth. In fact, as he sees it, created things such as flowers and birds are ideal for contemplative practice. While human teachers instruct with words and stand against their interlocutors, the lilies and the birds are silent, beckoning. In this way, they function in the manner of icons. As Kierkegaard explains:

> Out where the lily blooms so beautifully, in the field, up there where the bird is freely at home, in the heavens, if comfort is being sought—there is unbroken silence; no one is present there, and everything is sheer persuasion.
> Yet this is so only if the person . . . actually gives his attention to the lilies and the birds and their life and forgets himself in contemplation of them and their life, while in his absorption in them he, unnoticed, by himself learns something about himself—unnoticed, since there is indeed sheer silence, no one present. The . . . person is free of any and all co-knowledge, except God's, his own—and the lilies'. (SKS 8:261; UDVS, 161–162)

This call to contemplation, Kierkegaard adds, is implicit in Jesus's own words, "'*Look at* [*betragter*] *the lilies in the field*,' look at [*betragt*] them—that is, pay close attention to them, make them the object—not of a fleeting glimpse in passing but of your contemplation [*Betragtning*]" (SKS 8:262; UDVS, 162, my translation). Thus Kierkegaard suggests that his discourse is a contemplative aid: it is tendered for "properly looking at" the lilies and the birds (SKS 8:261; UDVS, 162).

And yet, Kierkegaard does more than *exhort* the reader to practice contemplation. Rather, as George Pattison has argued, his use of language epitomizes as well as induces something akin to contemplation. In particular, the rhetoric employed in Kierkegaard's upbuilding literature seeks "to construct an ethical and religious appeal to the reader," albeit in such a way that one is persuaded, rather than pressured, to adopt a "determinate response."[83] By addressing the reader in a conversational, inquisitive fashion and by presenting "an array of personified subjunctive possibilities," the discourses commend not only values such as love and patience but also, in Pattison's words, "the inner dialogue of the self with itself."[84]

Thus Pattison reinforces the notion that Kierkegaard does not merely endorse *Betragtning* but, quite literally, fosters it. The upbuilding discourses require the reader to slow down, to concentrate, and to open himself or herself up to the presence of the eternal, both in the world and in the self. In this way, they become occasions for self-actualization and, hopefully, for a relationship with the divine—a relationship that is irreducibly mysterious, always grounded in the here-and-now (what Kierkegaard refers to as *Øieblikket* or "the moment"),[85] and, therefore, qualitatively different than the abstracted information tendered by Google.

Intriguingly, Carr himself suggests that a return to such a way of thinking is critical if human beings are to avoid losing "our humanness . . . the very qualities that separate us from machines."[86] But this resistance cannot be done *for* human beings. It is not a matter of finding the right piece of information, still less of downloading an app for enhanced productivity. Rather, it involves the cultivation of alternative habits and practices. Carr mentions "self-awareness" and "courage,"[87] and Neil Postman urges that persons must become more "conscious" of their interaction with media, lest the "spiritual devastation" of "the age of advanced technology" catch them unawares.[88] Persons may be willing to fight physical oppressors, but, Postman goes on, "what if there are no cries of anguish to be heard? Who is prepared to take arms against a sea of amusements?"[89]

This is a decisive question, because it hits on the fact that the struggle against technology—against the instrumentalizing frame of the system—is ultimately an internal struggle. After all, even if persons *wanted* to eliminate modern technology, technology would be required in order to carry out the task: "Detechnologizing would paradoxically confront us with one of the greatest technological challenges of all."[90] What is needed, then, is a spiritual revolution, yet it is precisely here that Postman despairs: "I fear that our philosophers have given us no guidance in this matter."[91] Indeed, while intellectual attention is diverted to either abstract problematics or overt threats, "public consciousness has not yet assimilated the point that technology is ideology," since "no *Mein Kampf* or *Communist Manifesto* announced its coming."[92]

On this point, however, Postman is not exactly right. It is true, of course, that modern technology has not arrived with the thunderous menace of a Hitler or a Stalin, but, then, it is doubtful whether such a comparison is even apt. For that reason, it may very well be that the best responses to technology will not come from tracts seeking to "overcome" its threat but, rather, from those that cultivate a different way of thinking about and participating in reality. Put in concrete terms, taking a walk in the woods or praying may very well be more important in this area than any particular philosophical or sociological retort. And it is just here that Kierkegaard's authorship stands out. For Kierkegaard did not only realize this point—he made it central to his literary task.

Conclusion

Google has come to rule the internet because it organizes data at a rate heretofore unseen. Yet, as a manifestation of the human desire to create an absolute system of knowledge, it is hardly the first of its kind. The Googles of the world will always be with us.

However, precisely for that reason, Kierkegaard remains (and will remain) an important figure. A self-styled "corrective," he stands as a reminder that the glittering results of Google ought not be confused with thinking itself. Moreover, his upbuilding writings serve as apertures for contemplation—a mode of thought that centers the existing person and, in turn, prepares the way for an earnest engagement with the whole of reality. Perhaps *that* is why Heidegger, himself concerned with the obtrusive nature of technical thinking, once famously observed, "There is more to be learned philosophically from [Kierkegaard's] 'edifying' writings, than from his theoretical ones."[93]

CHRISTOPHER B. BARNETT is Associate Professor in the Department of Theology & Religious Studies at Villanova University. He is author of *Kierkegaard, Pietism and Holiness* and *From Despair to Faith: The Spirituality of Søren Kierkegaard*, as well as the coeditor of *Theology and the Films of Terrence Malick*.

Notes

1. See "About Google," https://www.google.com/intl/en/about/. Accessed March 25, 2017.
2. Lee Siegel, *Against the Machine: Being Human in the Age of the Electronic Mob* (New York: Spiegel & Grau, 2008), p. 86.
3. Siegel, *Against the Machine*, p. 88.
4. Nicholas Carr, *The Shallows: What the Internet Is Doing to Our Brains* (New York: Norton, 2011), p. 154.
5. Carr, *The Shallows*, p. 154.
6. Siva Vaidhyanathan, *The Googlization of Everything (and Why We Should Worry)* (Berkeley: University of California Press, 2011), p. 13.
7. Vaidhyanathan, *The Googlization of Everything*, p. 13.
8. Carr, *The Shallows*, p. 150.
9. Quoted in Vaidhyanathan, *Googlization*, p. 200.
10. Carr, *The Shallows*, p. 152.
11. See, for example, Jon Stewart, *Kierkegaard's Relations to Hegel Reconsidered* (Cambridge: Cambridge University Press, 2003). Stewart's basic premise is that Kierkegaard's polemics against Hegel are better understood as polemics against Hegelianism, particularly as expressed in the works of some of Kierkegaard's Danish contemporaries, such as Johan Ludvig Heiberg and Hans Lassen Martensen.
12. T. Z. Lavine, *From Socrates to Sartre: The Philosophic Quest* (New York: Bantam, 1984), p. 208.
13. Quoted in Lavine, *From Socrates to Sartre*, p. 202.
14. Jacques Ellul, *The Technological Society*, trans. John Wilkinson (New York: Vintage, 1964), p. 52.
15. Ellul, *The Technological Society*, p. 52.
16. Ellul, *The Technological Society*, p. 52.
17. Ellul, *The Technological Society*, p. 54.
18. Stephen Houlgate, *An Introduction to Hegel: Freedom, Truth and History* (Oxford: Blackwell, 2005), p. 10.
19. Houlgate, *An Introduction to Hegel*, p. 10.
20. Georg Wilhelm Friedrich Hegel, *The Philosophy of History*, trans. John Sibree (New York: Dover, 1956), p. 137.
21. Hegel, *The Philosophy of History*, p. 341.
22. Hegel, *The Philosophy of History*, p. 397.
23. Hegel, *The Philosophy of History*, p. 397.

24. Hegel, *The Philosophy of History*, pp. 438–439.

25. Houlgate, *Hegel*, p. 78.

26. Hegel, *Philosophy of History*, p. 439.

27. Hegel, *The Philosophy of History*, p. 439.

28. Hegel, *The Philosophy of History*, p. 439.

29. Hegel, *The Philosophy of History*, pp. 439–40.

30. Hegel, *The Philosophy of History*, p. 440.

31. Hegel, *The Philosophy of History*, p. 440.

32. Hegel, *The Philosophy of History*, p. 441.

33. Houlgate, *Hegel*, p. 22.

34. G. W. F. Hegel, *Phenomenology of Spirit*, trans. A. V. Miller (Oxford: Oxford University Press, 1977), p. 3.

35. John W. Burbridge, *Historical Dictionary of Hegelian Philosophy*, 2nd edition (Lanham, MD: Scarecrow Press, 2008), p. 179.

36. Lavine, *The Philosophic Quest*, p. 219.

37. Hegel, *Werke in zwanzig Bänden*, Eva Moldenhauer and Karl Markus Michel, eds. (Frankfurt: Suhrkamp), Vol. 10 (1970), p. 404; quoted in Merold Westphal, *Transcendence and Self-Transcendence: On God and the Soul* (Bloomington: Indiana University Press, 2004), p. 33.

38. Westphal, *Transcendence and Self-Transcendence*, p. 32.

39. The gist of this course has been preserved in lecture form. See Martin Heidegger, "The Onto-Theo-Logical Constitution of Metaphysics," in *Identity and Difference*, Joan Stambaugh, ed. (Chicago: University of Chicago Press, 1969), pp. 42–76.

40. Westphal, *Transcendence and Self-Transcendence*, pp. 18–19.

41. Westphal, *Transcendence and Self-Transcendence*, p. 23.

42. Martin Heidegger, "The Question Concerning Technology," in *Basic Writings*, David Farrell Krell, ed. (London: Routledge, 1993), pp. 311–341.

43. Merold Westphal, *Becoming a Self: A Reading of Kierkegaard's Concluding Unscientific Postscript* (West Lafayette, IN: Purdue University Press, 1996), p. 83.

44. Westphal, *Becoming a Self*, p. 83.

45. See, for example, SKS 7:91–92 (CUP 93), where Climacus links objective thought with a fantastical relation to reality, arguing that the one "who in all his thinking can forget to think conjointly that he is existing . . . makes an attempt . . . to become a book or an objective something that only a Münchausen can become."

46. Jacques Ellul, *Propaganda: The Formation of Men's Attitudes* (New York: Vintage Books, 1973), p. 84.

47. Admittedly, the word "propaganda" carries negative connotations that exceed the scope of the present discussion; however, Ellul's treatment of the issue sums up Climacus's point nicely. After all, the word "propaganda" is derived from the Latin *propagare* ("to set forth," "to extend"), and its present meaning—"information propagated to further an ideology"— reflects Climacus's criticism of Hegel, not to mention related criticisms broached elsewhere in Kierkegaard's corpus.

48. Stewart, *Kierkegaard's Relations to Hegel Reconsidered*, p. 2.

49. See, for example, Stewart, *Kierkegaard's Relations to Hegel Reconsidered*, p. 13ff.

50. Craig Detweiler, *iGods: How Technology Shapes Our Spiritual and Social Lives* (Grand Rapids, MI: Brazos, 2013), p. 107.

51. Randall Stross, *Planet Google: One Company's Audacious Plan to Organize Everything We Know* (New York: Free Press, 2008), p. 9.

52. Detweiler, *iGods*, p. 109.

53. Quoted in Vaidhyanathan, *Googlization*, p. 110.

54. Vaidhyanathan, *Googlization*, pp. 174–175.

55. See, for example, Marshall McLuhan, *Understanding Media: The Extensions of Man* (Cambridge, MA: MIT Press, 1994), p. 7.

56. Vaidhyanathan, *Googlization*, p. 70. Personalized searching would seem to reflect Google's respect for individuality. Local news and sports scores, for example, are increasingly proffered in accordance with the user's location. But this trend entails some disconcerting consequences. As Eli Pariser explains, "Our media is [becoming] a perfect reflection of our interests and desires. By definition, it's an appealing prospect—a return to a Ptolemaic universe in which the sun and everything else revolves around us" (Eli Pariser, *The Filter Bubble: How the New Personalized Web Is Changing What We Read and How We Think* [New York: Penguin, 2012], p. 12). Furthermore, such personalization only doubles down on one's subservience to Google: inasmuch as the latter is the medium through which the user receives pertinent information, this information is objective and eo ipso abstracted from the sorts of metaphysical and ethical questions that Climacus deems essential to human flourishing. Google, therefore, does not so much "personalize" one's experience on the internet as assume that all persons want the same kind of experience—namely, that of consuming data.

57. As is well known, Kierkegaard would go on to develop this understanding of the self in *The Sickness Unto Death* (1849).

58. Vaidhyanathan, *Googlization*, p. 2.

59. For Hegel, it is "reason" (*Vernunft*), rather than "understanding" (*Verstand*), that enables one to transcend abstract conceptual definitions and, in turn, to view ideas in a more nuanced fashion, first with regard to "those contrary terms that are needed to define [their boundaries]" and second "in a unified perspective [that] articulates both the positive and the negative features of their relationship" (Burbridge, *Hegelian Philosophy*, p. 152). The former is known as dialectical reason, the latter as speculative reason. The point here, however, is just that Hegel envisions a depth—or, perhaps even better, a comprehensiveness—to *Vernunft* that has an analog in Google's own approach to information.

60. Burbridge, *Hegelian Philosophy*, p. 152.

61. Detweiler, *iGods*, p. 120.

62. Detweiler, *iGods*, pp. 120–121.

63. David Shenk, *Data Smog: Surviving the Information Glut* (San Francisco: Harper Edge, 1997), p. 11.

64. For a contemporary application of this problem—which is startling in its relevance to various trends in higher education—see Mark Bauerlein, *The Dumbest Generation: How the Digital Age Stupefies Young Americans and Jeopardizes Our Future (Or Don't Trust Anyone Under 30)* (New York: Tarcher, 2009).

65. See, for example, Christopher B. Barnett, *Kierkegaard, Pietism and Holiness* (Farnham: Ashgate, 2011), especially chapter 5.

66. Carr, *The Shallows*, pp. 150, 152.

67. Vaidhyanathan, *Googlization*, p. 14.

68. Detweiler, *iGods*, p. 115.

69. See "What We Believe: Ten Things We Know To Be True," http://www.google.com /about/company/philosophy/.

70. Quoted in Detweiler, *iGods*, p. 115.

71. Detweiler, *iGods*, p. 117.

72. For example, Google's fiscal results for the third quarter of 2014 indicated consolidated revenues of nearly seventeen billion dollars, up 20 percent from the same quarter in 2013.

Patrick Pichette, Google's CFO, said that further growth is expected, particularly in advertising and in "emerging businesses." See "Google Inc. Announces Third Quarter 2014 Results," Google Investor Relations, http://investor.google.com/earnings/2014/Q3_google_earnings.html.

73. "Google Inc. Announces Third Quarter 2014 Results."

74. If this claim seems hyperbolic, it is worth underlining that there is, in fact, a Reddit community known as the Church of Google, whose members adhere to the following creed: "We at the Church of Google believe the search engine Google is the closest humankind has ever come to directly experiencing an actual God (as typically defined). We believe there is much more evidence in favour of Google's divinity than there is for the divinity of other more traditional gods." The Church of Google even boasts a collection of prayers, including one that mimics the Lord's Prayer: "Our Google, who art in cyberspace, / Hallowed be thy domain. / Thy search to come, / Thy results be done, / On 127.0.0.1 as it is in the Googleplex." There is clearly an element of parody here, but the community does insist that to use Google is akin to prayer: "Google answers prayers. One can pray to Google by doing a search for whatever question or problem is plaguing them." See http://www.churchofgoogle.org. Accessed March 25, 2017.

75. Carr, *The Shallows*, p. 121.

76. Carr, *The Shallows*, p. 125.

77. Carr, *The Shallows*, pp. 125–126. Intriguingly, Kierkegaard anticipated this turn of affairs in *A Literary Review*.

78. Carr, *The Shallows*, p. 138.

79. Carr, *The Shallows*, p. 157, emphasis added.

80. Of course, there are contrary readings—and not just among technophiles. For example, Hubert Dreyfus has argued that Wikipedia counterbalances Google's "syntactic" approach to web-based information and, in turn, ensures that "the judgment calls of human encyclopedists and librarians" remain relevant in the digital era (Hubert L. Dreyfus, *On the Internet*, 2nd edition [London: Routledge, 2009], p. 128). For that reason, he concludes that "pessimism is no longer the order of the day" (Dreyfus, *On the Internet*, p. 128.) vis-à-vis fears about Google's ostensible elimination of qualitative interaction with data. Yet Carr's findings, at the very least, challenge Dreyfus's sanguinity, since they suggest that Google's delivery of information literally alters the way that our brains make judgments, even if Google does not eliminate judgment altogether. Moreover, from Climacus's perspective, Wikipedia can hardly be said to solve the problems raised by Google, because it too makes the crucial mistake of objectifying information, fostering reflection, and ultimately diminishing existential earnestness. More will be said about these problems below.

81. Merold Westphal, "Society, Politics, and Modernity," in *The Oxford Handbook of Kierkegaard*, John Lippitt and George Pattison, eds. (Oxford: Oxford University Press, 2013), p. 322.

82. I have treated this issued in greater detail elsewhere; see Christopher B. Barnett, *From Despair to Faith: The Spirituality of Søren Kierkegaard* (Minneapolis: Fortress Press, 2014).

83. George Pattison, *Kierkegaard's Upbuilding Discourses: Philosophy, Literature and Theology* (London: Routledge, 2002), p. 143.

84. Pattison, *Kierkegaard's Upbuilding Discourses*, p. 164.

85. For Kierkegaard, "the moment" is not just a measure of time. Rather, when an existing person consciously and in faith relates himself or herself to the eternal, it is a synthesis of temporal and eternal, finite and infinite. This latter understanding of *Øieblikket* is reserved for concrete individual experience and therefore takes Christ—who, in "the fullness of time"

(Galatians 4: 4), incarnates the eternal—as its exemplar *par excellence*. Yet, if this is true, then time has a qualitative, subjective depth that cannot be addressed by Google or by other information systems. On the contrary, time is to be fulfilled in ethico-religious practice, which, as Christ himself displays, always already includes *Betragtning*.

86. Carr, *The Shallows*, p. 207.

87. Carr, *The Shallows*, p. 207.

88. Neil Postman, *Amusing Ourselves to Death: Public Discourse in the Age of Show Business*, 20th Anniversary Edition (New York: Penguin, 2005), pp. 155, 162.

89. Postman, *Amusing Ourselves to Death,* p. 156.

90. George Pattison, *Thinking about God in an Age of Technology* (Oxford: Oxford University Press, 2005), p. 2.

91. Postman, *Amusing Ourselves to Death*, pp. 156–157.

92. Postman, *Amusing Ourselves to Death,* p. 157.

93. Martin Heidegger, *Being and Time*, trans. John Macquarrie and Edward Robinson (San Francisco: Harper & Row, 1962), p. 494.

9 An Ethics for Adults? Kierkegaard and the Ambiguity of Exaltation

Stephen Minister

> When the child is to be weaned, the mother has stronger sustenance at hand so that the child does not perish. How fortunate the one who has this stronger sustenance at hand.
>
> Søren Kierkegaard, *Fear and Trembling*

> The adult's God is revealed precisely through the void of the child's heaven.
>
> Emmanuel Levinas, *Difficult Freedom*

Both Kierkegaard and Levinas were interested in religious development and through their writings challenge us to replace religiously immature beliefs and practices with what Levinas called "A Religion for Adults."[1] Both thought their respective religious communities had settled for a complacent, illusory, juvenile religious life and were in desperate need of this challenge. Both believed that religious maturity was not about beliefs or rituals, but rather about how we live our lives, how we treat others, and how we engage with society. For both, religious maturity is a matter of ethical existence.

While this claim is obviously true for Levinas, some might be more skeptical about its veracity for Kierkegaard. After all, a longstanding interpretation claims that his work either lacks an ethics or is positively unethical.[2] However, the last few decades of Kierkegaardian scholarship have thoroughly undermined this interpretation, primarily by drawing from Kierkegaard's later writings, in which ethical existence is central to his notion of religious maturity.[3] So far from an individualistic religious duty displacing interpersonal obligations, Kierkegaard's work contains robust ethical and social responsibilities that are intimately connected to his religious commitments.

Though this recent scholarship offers a better interpretation of Kierkegaard's work, this essay suggests a few caveats or concerns about the ethical vision in his later works. I will draw out these concerns by considering how Kierkegaard's religious ethics can respond to the critique of Christianity found in Levinas's account of religious maturity. The crux of Levinas's criticism is that Christianity's focus on the spiritual, transcendent, and eternal creates confusion about the significance of social, material, historical existence. As he puts it, the "ambiguity of exaltation" makes possible "abnegation and cruelty."[4] This essay shows that though Kierkegaard's account of religious maturity recognizes the significance of social, material, and historical existence, at times he traffics in precisely the sort of ambiguity about which Levinas is concerned.[5] The goal of this analysis is not to revive the discredited interpretation of Kierkegaard as unethical, but instead to point out ways in which the ambiguity of exaltation becomes an obstacle to religiously mature ethical existence. Other essays in this volume demonstrate the value of Kierkegaard's theological commitments for ethical thought and practice. This essay serves as a reminder of the ethical risk that accompanies some of those commitments.

The Ambiguity of Exaltation and Levinas's Ethical Religion

In *Difficult Freedom*, Levinas attempts to articulate the meaning of Judaism in the contemporary world and the view of religious maturity it recommends. Writing primarily to the Jewish community in France, he expresses concern about some of the ways that Christianity has influenced Jewish life.[6] Though Levinas is keen to fend off the "Christianization" of Judaism, his account of the relationship between Christianity and Judaism is not simply antagonistic.[7] At times he even demonstrates deep admiration for Christianity. Levinas's complex response to Christianity was shaped by his personal experiences of World War II and the Holocaust. On the one hand, during the war many Christians reached out to Jewish refugees with kindness and shelter, sometimes at great risk to themselves. A group of Christian nuns hid Levinas's wife and daughter in their convent during the war, an act for which Levinas was profoundly grateful.[8] So Levinas knows that Christianity has the power to inspire the sort of responsible, caring action that he sees as the heart of mature religious existence.

On the other hand, Levinas suggests that the coexistence of the rise of National Socialism and the Holocaust with Christianity's dominance in Europe for nearly two millennia should provoke a deep suspicion of Christianity. If the rise of National Socialism were an isolated incident, such suspicion might be unfounded, but as Levinas reminds us, this is just the latest and most shocking example of centuries of violence. Levinas does not claim that Christianity encouraged or sanctioned the violence of European society, though going at least as far back as Constantine, Christianity has at times been used for this purpose. Instead, he claims that Christianity, in its focus on transcendence and personal salvation, tends to devalue materiality and social justice, thereby allowing material history to be dominated by the selfish and violent impulses of those with power. Violence is made possible not so much by what Christianity affirms as by what it fails to clearly and unequivocally affirm: the task of working for social justice in the here and now. In the hour of political violence, one needs strong principles in order to resist. Because of Christianity's ambiguity regarding material, human society, it does not always provide these.

Levinas's account of religious maturity is developed in large part as a response to this problem. Whereas he thinks Christianity emphasizes inwardness over action, transcendence over materiality, and love over justice, Levinas emphasizes the latter in each of these pairs as the site in which the former is genuinely expressed or concretized. As such, there can be no ambiguity about lived, material, social existence. To adequately understand Levinas's critique of Christianity, let us consider each of these pairs.

Inwardness and Action

Levinas rejects the idea that religious inwardness or spirituality could have priority over our relations to others, since he thinks that religion and spirituality cannot exist independent of those relations. He writes, "Every situation in which humanity recognizes its religious progress finds in ethical relations its spiritual meaning—that is to say, its meaning for an adult."[9] Since spiritual meaning comes solely from ethical relations to others, Levinas rejects both the possibility and the necessity of a spiritual connection to God independent of our relations to others. "No relation with God is direct or immediate. The Divine can be manifested only through my neighbor."[10] Neither a direct spiritual relationship with God nor a unique incarnation of God are necessary, since the divine always already calls out to me, is always already incarnated, in the others around me. The "face of the other" is the primary site of the revelation of God. The ethical responsibility it signifies is not a corollary or consequent of the manifestation of God—it is that very manifestation.

This account of God renders superfluous much Christian metaphysical theology, a theology based on what Levinas characterizes as "the realist affirmation of irrational facts."[11] For Levinas, such realist affirmations not only violate human reason but also have become increasingly implausible given the advances of modern science. In contrast to this metaphysical theology, Levinas claims that "the attributes of God are given not in the indicative, but in the imperative."[12] Thus, the true religious meaning of the claim "God is merciful" is the ethical command to be merciful to each other. This translation of a theological claim into the ethical register is representative of Levinas's view that religious maturity is not about what people believe, but what they do. A religion for adults is not a religion of theology, but of action.

Transcendence and Materiality

When Levinas turns to criticism of specific tenets of Christian theology, it is not surprising that it regularly takes the form of contrasting Christianity's spiritual, metaphysical claims with Judaism's focus on material realities. In the essay "Place and Utopia," Levinas argues that Christianity's obsession with the transcendent, eternal, and perfect amounts to daydreaming about utopia. As such it is a flight from the concrete, tangible responsibilities of the material world. By contrast, Levinas claims, Judaism is focused on place, the particular location at which one finds oneself and from which any ethical action must proceed. Such action "does not tackle the Whole in a global and magical way, but grapples with the particular. . . . It is historical, it exists in time. History is not a perpetual test whose goal is the diploma of eternal life, but the very element in which the life of the spirit moves."[13] Levinas rejects the Platonism that infuses much of the Christian tradition, degrading materiality to an inferior status as impure and illusory. Instead, it is precisely in the material world, in the face of an embodied other with tangible material needs, that we encounter the divine, the call to ethical responsibility. The material world is not a propaedeutic for or prefiguration of the hereafter, but is precisely that in which we live and move and have our being.

For Levinas, there is another way in which the Christian conception of the material world discourages us from recognizing both the possibility and the necessity of practical ethical action. He writes, "Christianity simultaneously overestimates and underestimates the weight of the reality which it wants to improve. It overestimates it because it sees in it a total resistance to human action. The relationships that man entertains with himself and his neighbors seem to him fixed, unalterable, eternal. He underestimates it, for he hopes that a miraculous intervention on the part of divinity will transfigure this brutal weight."[14]

On the one hand, Christianity overestimates the weight of reality, which Levinas elsewhere links to its doctrine of original sin. To see human relations as unavoidably trapped in the chains of sin can diminish our sense of our ability to work for positive change. The inevitability of sin risks providing an excuse for the acceptance of violence. If sin is inevitable, then the violent will always be with us. Though Levinas never denies the human propensity toward selfishness, this is always secondary to the non-allergic relation of responsibility toward others. Human society does not proceed from a war of all against all, which naturalizes violence, but from the call to responsibility, which legitimates the work of social justice. "History flows not from sin, but from humanity's creation."[15] We *can* make the world a better place, even if not a utopia. On the other hand, for Levinas, it is only we, only human beings, who can do this. We underestimate the weight of reality when we expect God to come and fix our problems. That such an expectation is futile and even dangerous should be abundantly clear in the aftermath of the Holocaust. In response to the puerile view that a loving God will intervene to protect the innocent, the Holocaust reveals "the void of the child's heaven."[16] The responsibility to intervene is ours alone.

Rather than focusing on this responsibility, Levinas is concerned that Christianity encourages us to attend to our own eternal souls. In so doing, Christianity is turning its back on its common heritage with Judaism. As Levinas points out, "Moses and the prophets preoccupied themselves not with the immortality of the soul but with the poor, the widow, the orphan and the stranger. The relationship with others in which contact with the Divine is established is . . . manifested, tested and accomplished in a just economy."[17] Levinas is not adverse to speaking of salvation or even the possibility of a hereafter, but for him these notions are always linked to the ethical responsibility of the here and now. So Levinas suggests that the uniqueness of Judaism is found in its unwillingness to separate the notion of "personal salvation" from "the redemption of the visible world."[18] Hence, Levinas is very suspicious of the Christian account of "salvation by faith" made possible by the forgiveness of sin.[19] The emphasis on an interior faith rather than the concrete work of ethics, and on God's forgiveness rather than human reparation and reconciliation, makes possible the evasion of responsibility. No doubt because of his life experience, Levinas is particularly critical of the Christian notion of forgiveness. "Evil is not a mystical principle that can be effaced by a ritual, it is an offence perpetrated on man by man. No one, not even God, can substitute himself for the victim. The world in which pardon is all-powerful becomes inhuman."[20]

Love and Justice

While implicating Christianity in the violence of Europe, Levinas recognizes that Christianity also contains a strident call to ethical responsibility toward others. Indeed, he acknowledges that there is much in the New Testament—his favorite passage is the parable of the sheep and the goats in Matthew 25—that he finds inspiring. He even allows that in a certain sense Christianity takes up the ethical call of Judaism and intensifies it, but with a significant modification.[21] Christian ethics is centered on the command to love one's neighbor, but for Levinas there are two weaknesses with the notion of love: it is too sentimental and too private. As sentimental, love is subject to the contingencies of emotion, which contrasts with the necessity of ethical responsibility. Since responsibility calls us not to certain feelings but to action, emotion is not the heart of the matter. Further, love is typically taken to characterize a private relationship rather than a social order. Though for Levinas the call to responsibility is rooted in the interpersonal encounter of the face-to-face, it must immediately move to the level of the social. "To see a face is to hear 'You shall not kill,' and to hear 'You shall not kill' is to hear 'Social justice.'"[22] The "You shall not kill" is fulfilled not simply when I refrain from murder, but instead when no innocents are killed in or by my society. The significance of this distinction is clear in the context of the aforementioned heroic acts of Christian love during World War II. Levinas praises without qualification the private rescue of Jewish refugees, but such works of love were only necessary because of the glaring absence of social justice. These works of love were truly awe-inspiring, but social justice would have been better. To focus on neighbor-love over and above social justice is to misplace our ethical, and so religious, priorities.

The difference between focusing on justice and focusing on love is so stark for Levinas that he concludes that "justice and charity [i.e., love] designate two diverging tendencies."[23] Levinas sees Christianity's tendency to focus on the latter as a result of its separation of transcendent, eternal goodness from the sinful, fallen world. For Christianity, goodness can make brief, fleeting appearances in the world through acts of love, but true peace and justice will be accomplished in the hereafter. This renders ambiguous the task of working for justice here and now, handing society over to the powers that be. As Levinas puts it, "The faith that moves mountains and conceives of a world without slaves immediately transports itself to utopia, separating the reign of God from the reign of Caesar. This reassures Caesar."[24]

It is clear that Levinas's concern is not that Christianity recommends violence or neglect, but that by focusing on inwardness, transcendence, and love, it creates ambiguity about action, materiality, and social justice. This ambiguity creates confusion about our responsibilities toward others, which are the heart of religious maturity for Levinas. Can Kierkegaard's religious ethics respond to such criticisms?

Kierkegaard's Religious Ethics

Inwardness and Action

When we turn to Kierkegaard's later work, what stands out is the great extent to which he shares Levinas's concerns about society broadly and Christian culture specifically. Similar to Levinas, Kierkegaard is critical of the transformation of Christianity into a theology that becomes a matter of private belief. He repeatedly rejects the notion that Christianity is an "objective doctrine" (FSE, 131) or a "teaching" to be comprehended (PC, 141). While he makes this same point in *Concluding Unscientific Postscript* in order to bring out the way in which truth requires subjective appropriation, in later writings his point is to contrast internal beliefs with external action. He even criticizes the notion of "hidden inwardness," for which he argued so strenuously in previous works. He chastises Christendom, which has "relegated being a Christian to inwardness" (PC, 215), and claims that the true Christian "refuses to let Christianity be something one supposedly should only have hidden in one's innermost being—perhaps so well concealed that it is not there at all" (PC, 197). This criticism is not a refutation of his earlier work, but an acknowledgement that hidden inwardness is not the whole story. The emphasis of the later works is that for mature Christianity, inwardness must express itself in external action.

Kierkegaard diagnoses a variety of strategies within Christendom to avoid such action, again anticipating some of Levinas's concerns. Key among these strategies is the use of the notion of salvation by faith to get oneself off the hook for acting as Christianity demands. However, Kierkegaard does not reject this notion. He writes,

> Lutheran doctrine is excellent, is the truth. With regard to this excellent Lutheran doctrine, I have but one misgiving. It does not concern Lutheran doctrine—no, it concerns myself: I have become convinced that I am not an honest soul but a cunning fellow. Thus it certainly becomes most proper to pay a little more attention to the minor premise (works, existence, to witness to and suffer for the truth, works of love, etc.), the minor premise in Lutheran doctrine. (FSE, 24)

The problem for Kierkegaard is not salvation by faith, but our tendency to interpret and apply this doctrine in self-serving ways. For Kierkegaard, we can counteract this tendency by attending to both the historical and theological context of this doctrine. He argues that Luther's emphasis on faith was justified by the historical context in which the focus on works had eclipsed the centrality of faith. However, Luther did not dismiss the significance of works to which both his life and the "minor premises" of his theology attest. Kierkegaard's sense that his contemporaries have widely embraced the doctrine of salvation by faith while happily forgetting its context inspires the central preoccupation of his later writings, namely, the essentiality of action to religious maturity.

Kierkegaard further argues that even seemingly devout practices can be strategies for evading Christian maturity. One strategy he is sharply critical of is the "admiration" of Christ. For Kierkegaard, admiration is a form of worship that keeps Christ at a distance, focusing on the eternal, transcendent loftiness of Christ, rather than Christ's concrete embodiment, which calls for imitative action, not admiring worship (PC, 233). Like Levinas, Kierkegaard is concerned that focus, even worshipful focus, on the transcendent and eternal, while generating pleasant thoughts and feelings, can be a way of evading the need for action in the here and now. To avoid this pitfall, Kierkegaard stresses the importance of loving (i.e., imitating) the mundane, material Jesus more than loving (i.e., admiring) the lofty, transcendent Christ. We could perhaps read this as a Christian translation of Levinas's provocative title "Loving the Torah More Than God." As with Levinas, the highest expression of religion is not contemplative experience but ethical action. Kierkegaard suggests that in emphasizing admiration and de-emphasizing imitation, Christendom has transformed Christianity into "a pleasant, a sentimental paganism" (PC, 143). A Christianity for adults must challenge us to act.

Transcendence and Materiality

So far, so good. But we must ask, what does this imitation really look like? How did Jesus really live? It is here that Levinas's concerns about Place and Utopia reemerge, as there is a longstanding debate about the relative weight Kierkegaard places on material, earthly, temporal matters and transcendent, spiritual, eternal matters in regard to loving others. To what degree should my love of another focus on her material existence, and to what degree her spiritual existence? Straight away, we must recognize that Kierkegaard's conception of the human as a synthesis undermines any sharp distinction between the material and the transcendent, the temporal and the eternal. Hence, any claim that Kierkegaard focuses on one side of this distinction to the exclusion of the other can be rejected forthwith. Nonetheless, the ability to conceptually distinguish these aspects makes possible the sort of uneven emphasis, ambiguity, and confusion of which Levinas is critical. And indeed, when Kierkegaard writes that "truly to love another person is . . . to help the other person to love God or in loving God" (WL, 114), critics raise the accusation that Kierkegaard emphasizes the transcendent to the detriment of the material. Even if love requires concrete action, it seems that actions are only loving if they are directed toward others as spiritual and eternal beings.

An important response to this accusation appears in Jamie Ferreira's *Love's Grateful Striving*, a lucid and helpful commentary on *Works of Love*. Ferreira takes a twofold approach to defusing this concern. First, she argues that in interpreting what it would mean to help another to love God, we must recall that it is a basic point of Kierkegaard's ethics that to love God is to love other people. Hence, to help another to love God simply means helping her to love other people. Ferreira goes so far as to say that "when we help others to love God . . . we are pointing them away from God to their neighbor."[25] So far from an obsession with the transcendent and eternal, this is a very earthly task. Second, Ferreira points to the many ways Kierkegaard endorses giving material help to others. Her primary examples are Kierkegaard's use of scripture passages like the Good Samaritan and Matthew 25, as well as a quotation from Kierkegaard's journals in which he notes the variety of ways Jesus gave material aid to others. She concludes, "We could say that Kierkegaard upholds a version of the proverb to which Levinas alludes . . . 'the other's material needs are my spiritual needs'."[26] My spiritual need to love others finds its fulfillment in responding to the earthly, temporal needs of others.

At times, Kierkegaard undeniably recognizes the importance of responding to the material needs of others, and Ferreira is right that his critics do not give him enough credit for this. However, Ferreira's Levinasian reading of Kierkegaard's ethics does not quite fit with his other work. If our duty to love others means pointing them away from God and toward their neighbors, then it is hard to make sense of Kierkegaard's first authorship, which does not have this focus. Moreover, if the goal is to point us away from God and toward our neighbors, must we not conclude that Levinas's work accomplishes this more directly and clearly than Kierkegaard's? Why do we need Kierkegaard's God-talk or the paradox of the God-man for this?

John Davenport has expressed similar concerns about Levinasian readings of Kierkegaard. He writes, "If an ethical standpoint that respects individual uniqueness above universal law is what's central to Kierkegaardian religiousness, why not develop this idea without the 'baggage' from revealed religion."[27] As an example Davenport notes Levinas's ability to reach this ethical conclusion without an account of salvation. Instead, Levinas pushes in the direction of universalism by claiming that the call to ethical responsibility and the possibility of responsible action are open to all. But surely Kierkegaard is pushing in the opposite direction, toward Christian particularity, by claiming that the paradox of the God-man and the imitation of Jesus are utterly unique revelations. In defense of Kierkegaard, Davenport argues that the Christian account of salvation offers a vital support to neighbor-love by giving us the "eschatological hope that our moral efforts are not ultimately fruitless or without eternal significance" and "the belief that striving for ethical ideals need not all be *for naught* in the final scheme of things."[28] While this defense offers a possibility for the practical ethical value of Kierkegaard's Christian commitments, it does so by regarding the significance of material concerns as secured only by reference to transcendent, eternal realities. But this reinstates the supremacy of the transcendent to the detriment of the material. Why does correcting an injustice or providing food for one who is hungry need eternity to secure its significance? Why aren't they significant as such? If the material lives of others truly matter, then responsible action here and now will never be "for naught," regardless of the "final scheme of things."

Merold Westphal offers a different interpretation of Kierkegaard's ethics that attempts to respond to the criticism that it is too focused on the transcendent. Westphal draws inspiration from the story in which Jesus is asked what the single greatest commandment is and responds, oddly, with two commands: to love God and to love our neighbors (Matt. 22). Westphal suggests that Kierkegaard's first authorship generally points us toward a loving God-relation, which legitimately includes the hope of eternal salvation, while his second authorship generally focuses on the call to love our neighbors. The key to properly understanding these two themes is to see them, as in Jesus's response, as distinct but inseparable.[29] Contrary to Levinas, the first command should not be reduced to the second, because a direct relationship with God and the non-egoistic hope of salvation are, for Westphal, valid in their own right. Nonetheless, the second command, to love our neighbors, which includes lending material aid to those in need, should not be made "secondary" or "less important" than the first.[30] There is significance in both the material and the transcendent, and so for Kierkegaard we cannot justify the neglect of either. While Westphal finds this position theoretically defensible, he recognizes the practical risk it entails. He writes, "Levinas's concern that hope of eternal happiness may lead me to neglect the widow, the orphan, and the stranger points to a very real danger in the Kierkegaardian position, one not entirely absent from Christian history."[31] Though Kierkegaard's texts are, in Westphal's judgment, "as pure as the driven snow," they could in practice be misused if we invest our time and resources disproportionately in an inward relation to God to the detriment of concrete action to love our neighbors. He concludes that Levinas's criticism of Kierkegaard "may be unfair to the text, but it is the ever-needed reminder that pure texts are not the same as pure hearts nor profession the same as practice."[32]

The position that Westphal defends contains a plausible balance of the material and the transcendent and is the position that Kierkegaard suggests, some of the time. However, other times the inseparability and equality of these two commands is compromised as Kierkegaard becomes intoxicated with the loftiness of the transcendent and eternal and disdainful of the corruption of material, earthly life. This equivocation results in an ambiguity about the material world, justifying Levinas's concern. To see this, consider how Levinas and Kierkegaard write about material, earthly goods. When Levinas is questioned as to where the radical responsibility he describes is ever enacted, he points to the mundane: saying "after you" at an open door.[33] For Levinas, the call of ethical responsibility is not a call to abandon or even criticize the goods of the world, but to extend them to others in everyday situations. This is the significance of the proverb Ferreira quotes from Levinas. My spiritual needs refer directly to securing normal material goods for others.

For Kierkegaard, my spiritual needs introduce a fundamentally different type of good, namely "eternal happiness as the absolute good" (PC, 111). This relativizes all material goods, thereby justifying material deprivation for the sake of eternal happiness. Kierkegaard is so intent on establishing this hierarchy that he goes to extremes in devaluing material help. He writes that Jesus invites "the poor and sick and suffering to come—and then [is] able to do nothing for them, but instead of that promise them the forgiveness of sins . . . 'And when a human being is almost starving to death, then to say to him: I promise you the gracious forgiveness of your sins—this is outrageous'" (PC, 61). Yes, one can hear Levinas saying, it is outrageous, but this should not be credited to it as righteousness.

This theme is further evinced in Kierkegaard's suggestion that mature Christians should reject worldly goods including basic material goods, relational goods, and our own good actions. As an illustration of his claim that "the essentially Christian . . . [has] not a shred of the things of this earth," Kierkegaard describes the situation Jesus chose for his disciples as he sent them out: "The disciple, however, is unconditionally in poverty; he is literally indigent when it comes to life's primary necessities, a cup of water—and he has no money, he has nothing, nothing to give for it . . . Well, it is true that he has a check drawn on heaven, and properly viewed . . . that is worth more than all the glories of this world" (FSE, 162). For Kierkegaard, the disciple cannot even give the bread from his own mouth to satisfy the hunger of another, since he has no bread. One might be inclined to read this figuratively or as an exaggeration, or perhaps as the point that we should be willing to give everything, whether or not we actually do. But Kierkegaard forecloses such readings by indicating that the disciple is "literally indigent." Would it not be better to use our resources to strive for a world where no one is impoverished, rather than striving for literal poverty ourselves? Does not this focus on our own suffering obscure the point about our duty to love the temporal, material others around us? So far from being a mere side effect of following Jesus, Kierkegaard takes this indigence to be necessary. "Christ knew he had to make these men as unhappy and miserable, humanly speaking, as human beings could be, 'the most wretched of all'—if they were to belong to him" (FSE, 203). At times Kierkegaard even criticizes a concern for such suffering, as when he dismisses "all the dangers and suffering of this life as child's play and a half-hour prank" (PC, 229). The Holocaust, a half-hour prank?

Kierkegaard also at times suggests that Christianity is incompatible with normal earthly human relationships. He points out that Jesus as the prototype rejected family and marriage (FSE, 170) and elsewhere comments that "Christianity has an uneasiness about marriage . . . [because along with it] come all the weaker, softer elements in a person" (PC, 117). Precisely because friends often try to protect us from suffering, Kierkegaard says that if one truly wants to be a Christian, one must "above all exercise caution not to have a friend" (PC, 118). He even condemns "human compassion" as an "offense" that one must "crucify" (PC, 119, 137). The reason that Kierkegaard criticizes these notions is because they can distract from true service to God, including truly loving other people. Levinas too is suspicious of the way that close relationships can woo people into a clandestinity that is forgetful of others, but he does not on that account disparage marriage or friendship.

Kierkegaard counsels us to regard even our works of love with disdain. He claims that we should take these actions "and deeply humbled before God [see] them transformed into something miserable and base—this is what it is to worship God—and this is a lifting up" (FSE, 154). He goes on to suggest that what actually makes such actions Christian is not simply that they are loving toward others, but that they result in one's own suffering and rejection. His emphasis on such suffering in his later writings is surely a useful provocation for those living contented lives within Christendom; however, he sometimes goes so far with this idea that it detracts from focus on the neighbor. For example, he writes that were one to live a life serving God, this would be piety, but "in the strictest sense this is still not Christianity; it is really Jewish piety. What is crucial in Christianity is not manifested here at all: to suffer because one adheres to God" (FSE, 187).[34] Kierkegaard justifies this by reference to Jesus's awareness that he would suffer for his ministry, which he now reads as the true essence of Christian action. If you love others but do not suffer for it, then it is not truly religious; it is merely human ethics, merely being "Jewish."

The devaluing of material life in the light of eternity reaches an extreme in a passage that Levinas, given his life experience, would surely find quite shocking:

> I completely agree with Luther . . . that a person who countless times, if that were possible, countless times every day for a lifetime, had committed all the most horrible crimes—but still has the one comfort of saying to God: God, be merciful to me a sinner—that he may count himself indescribably happy compared with the person who, making every sacrifice for the truth in greatest possible self-denial for an entire lifetime, for one single moment made the mistake of thinking he had merit before God. (FSE, 198)

The criminal may be happy and saved, but where is the consideration for the victims of his horrible crimes? What becomes of the criminal's responsibility for the suffering he has caused? Moreover, what is so terrible about thinking, just once, that one had merit before God? Such a thought may be mistaken, and even Levinas is quite critical of this sort of self-satisfaction. Nonetheless, is momentarily taking up such a disposition really indescribably worse than committing countless horrible crimes? Kierkegaard's conclusion here seems to betray a severe devaluation of material existence and provide evidence for Levinas's concern that "the world in which pardon is all-powerful becomes inhuman."

This view is also a part of Kierkegaard's mixed record on the question of whether historical life is simply a "perpetual test whose goal is the diploma of eternal life." On the one hand, Kierkegaard is critical of the escapist mentality that fantasizes about eternity as "the craftiness of a sick soul that wants to sneak out of life" (EUD, 259). Rather than religious maturity, this mentality is merely superstitious. On the other hand, Kierkegaard is perfectly happy embracing the language of testing: "This earthly existence of ours is indeed a real test, a time of testing. This is a teaching of Christianity and what Christian orthodoxy has therefore always acknowledged as its view. To be a human being, to live here in this world, is to be tested" (PC, 183). When one teaches to the test, it is all too easy to lose sight of the intrinsic value of the content, in this case neighbor-love, as it becomes merely instrumental to the goal of achieving a passing grade. Kierkegaard seems to betray this shift in focus when a few pages later, considering the consequences of Christian suffering, he writes nothing about how others may be helped, but rather that the one who suffers "has become stronger" and "passed his test" (PC, 191). This passage is all too typical, as throughout *For Self-Examination* and *Judge for Yourself,* Kierkegaard's account of suffering for the truth focuses not on help-ing others but on the resistance of worldly society, the voluntary nature of the suffering, the narrowness of the way, and the eternal reward to be had.

Since suffering and social rejection are a necessary part of the Christian test, earthly historical society must always remain essentially opposed to Christianity. Kierkegaard claims that "if it ever is the case that indeed all are in truth Chris-tians, then this life is no longer a time of testing" (PC, 222), and consequently it would be impossible to be a Christian. If it could ever happen that most people became true Christians, then God did not plan properly. Given God's omni-science, that cannot happen, and so it must be that "it has been Governance's idea . . . that it will never be the case that at a given time all or even the major-ity become true Christians" (PC, 222). Is this not a piece of the mythology that presents material reality as, in Levinas's words, a "brutal weight" that provides "total resistance to human action"? So far from personal salvation being linked with the redemption of the material world, for Kierkegaard, personal salvation requires the non-redemption of a majority of other persons. It is in this context that Kierkegaard brings in the idea of "eternal damnation" (WL, 196) or "eternal punishment" (PC, 229). Kierkegaard's claims that what those with power regard as good is actually evil and that they will pay for this mistake with eternal damna-tion are uncomfortably reminiscent of the resentment of a Nietzschean priest.[35] Does not all this call into question whether Kierkegaard's texts (and heart) are really as pure as Westphal would have us believe?

Love and Justice

Despite his earlier reputation, recent scholarship has established that Kierkegaard is not a radical individualist or an asocial, apolitical thinker. Though he empha-sizes the individual, his intent is primarily to shake people out of their compla-cency and get them to take responsibility for their lives and decisions. Levinas is also at work on this task, and surely he is no individualist. In fact, Kierkegaard's address of his work to the single individual seems to parallel Levinas's claim that the face addresses itself uniquely to me. For both thinkers, I have an escapable responsibility to act in an inherently social and relational context. So this sec-tion will not take its direction from the discredited myth of individualism in Kierkegaard, but instead from the question Levinas poses for Christian social ethics: is there a place for social justice or only love?

As we saw, Levinas favored the idea of justice over love because he conceived of love as too sentimental and too private to adequately fulfill our responsibility to others. While Kierkegaard readily prefers the language of love to that of jus-tice, does he too conceive of love as sentimental and private? With regard to the first concern, the answer is clearly no. In fact, in *Works of Love* he goes to great lengths to distinguish neighbor-love from any sort of sentiment-based love since, like Levinas, he is concerned that sentiment-based love is too contingent for the commanded nature of neighbor-love. To turn to Levinas's second concern, are Kierkegaard's works of love merely private? Here we run into ambiguity again.

On the one hand, Kierkegaard's work shows a clear concern for the state of society and argues that religious practice should be socially disruptive. Like Levinas, Kierkegaard thinks that Christendom has domesticated religion and that this domestication serves the deification of the state. Interestingly, for Kierkegaard, the domestication of religion happens not by the privatization of religion, as it does for Levinas, but by the subsumption of religion into the state. Kierkegaard thinks Hegel's view of the state as the source of people's ultimate beliefs and values is all too true all too much of the time. Kierkegaard regards the Hegelian endorsement of this situation as "the smug invention of the lazy, secular human mentality that wants to settle down and fancy that now there is total peace and security, now we have achieved the highest" (PC, 88). The driving motive in the deification of the state is the desire to reassure ourselves about the rightness of our way of life, to remain comfortably and securely at home with ourselves, *chez soi* as Levinas would say. Achieving this requires the corresponding de-deification of God and the obscuring of our need for ongoing Christian becoming. Kierkegaard's work is thus inherently socially engaged, as it challenges this modern tendency to deify contemporary society and envisions Christian life as a resistance to this tendency.

This line of reasoning is taken up by Westphal, who acknowledges that in some of Kierkegaard's pseudonymous works, the "preoccupation with the eternal is so complete that . . . his knights of hidden inwardness will be unconcerned about social exploitation."[36] For Westphal, Kierkegaard's later development of Religiousness C, with its call to imitate the earthly life of Christ, fills this gap. As Westphal points out, Jesus's life, as a life of love, was one of perpetually challenging the powers that be, religiously, socially, legally, and politically. So far from being politically quietistic, Jesus's life was so threatening that the powers that be arranged his death. Westphal concludes that the sort of love the Jesus exhibits demonstrates that "merely to preach that God is on the side of the poor and oppressed is to engage in ideology critique, to challenge the theological, political and economic metanarratives that make it possible to identify a class-structured society with the Kingdom of God."[37]

This is a legitimate point and is consistent with the way Kierkegaard presents religious maturity, some of the time. But the emphasis is different in his presentation of the offense Jesus causes in *Practice in Christianity*. There Kierkegaard points out that it is not uniquely Christian for an individual to challenge the established order on the basis of a higher authority. Socrates also does that. What is uniquely Christian is the conflict between the established order and an individual who claims to be God despite living a lowly, abased life. As Westphal recognizes, this latter notion contains within it a challenge to a variety of social theologies—for example, that material success is an indication of divine favor. Such a challenge would no doubt be embraced by Levinas, for whom the revelation of God in the face of the other attaches especially to the needy, the vulnerable, and the powerless. However, the fact that Levinas could concur on this point suggests that it misses something essential to Kierkegaard's specifically Christian ethics. For Kierkegaard, Jesus was not merely a social activist preaching about the injustice of the powers that be, but the God-man who presented himself as such. He did not get himself killed by supporting higher taxes on the rich and more social services for the poor, but by claiming to be divine.

As we have already seen, when focused on Jesus's salvific task, Kierkegaard's concern for material needs tends to fade. This is true of his social justice concerns as well. When discussing the passage Levinas alluded to, in which Jesus says we should "render to Caesar the things that are Caesar's" (Luke 20:25), Kierkegaard claims that Jesus shows "infinite indifference" to Caesar and the governmental circumstances of the day (PC, 169). Kierkegaard's concern here is to distinguish between religious responsibility and governmental authority, a distinction he thinks is much needed in Christian Denmark. Nonetheless, in making this distinction, Kierkegaard undercuts the idea that religious duty could be relevant to the political realm and claims that to try to make it so is to "secularize" God (PC, 170). "[Jesus] makes the distinction, the infinite distinction, makes paying tax to the emperor a matter of the greatest indifference, which means something one must do and not waste one word or one moment on talking about it—in order, then, to have more time to give to God what is God's" (PC, 170). "One must" pay taxes unquestioningly to an oppressive, imperial, military government so that we have more time to focus on religious responsibility. But if religious maturity requires concern for the concrete, material conditions of people's lives, how can supporting such a government be a matter of infinite "indifference"? Kierkegaard justifies the infinite indifference of Christ since "he wanted only one thing—to save humankind," not apparently from poverty and oppression, but from sin (PC, 170).

Elsewhere, having argued that true Christianity "places infinite emphasis" upon eternal life, Kierkegaard explicitly disparages an interest in "civic justice" as rooted in Christendom's mistaken idea that "there is no infinite contrast between what is Christian and what is secular" (PC, 111). A similar dismissal of social justice shows up in the infamous cases of the charwoman and the wife in *Works of Love* (WL, 136–139). These cases argue for an abstract notion of equality, unequivocally rejecting any need to reform a patently unequal social order, the merely secular. The tendency to forget the significance of social exploitation when writing about the eternal is not just a fault of the pseudonyms, but at times surfaces even in Kierkegaard's explicitly ethical works.

Two Accounts of Divine Presence

Perhaps it is telling that Kierkegaard opens section 3 of *For Self-Examination* and section 1 of *Judge for Yourself* with references to the Pentecost story in Acts 2. Pentecost takes place during a Jewish festival celebrating God's giving of the law to the Israelites through Moses. It is during the giving of the law that the infamous episode with the golden calf occurs. Moses, who had been the people's conduit to God, has been up on Mount Sinai for some time, and the people get nervous that he might not come back. Seeking reassurance of divine presence, they entreat Aaron to make an image of God, and he duly obliges, fashioning the golden calf. This is not what God has in mind for them, and so God sends Moses down to stop it, armed with the tablets of the law. The people want to experience divine presence, and God gives them the law. As Levinas writes, "In the Holy Ark from which the voice of God is heard by Moses, there are only the tablets of the Law."[38] God's presence is to be found in a just society.

In Acts 2, the disciples are gathered, similarly missing their leader and direct link to God. In this story, what is given to them is not law but the Holy Spirit, miraculously inspiring each of them to speak in other languages. The happenings are so crazy that some of the people witnessing this presume that the disciples are drunk. Peter speaks up, defending their sobriety—it is only nine o'clock in the morning, after all—and gives a speech proclaiming Jesus as the messiah and the key to salvation. Here the transcendent God is present directly, providing personal inspiration to preach about salvation. "The apostles, on Pentecost Day, were never more sober than when . . . they were simply instruments for God—what Christian sobriety" (FSE, 103)!

Kierkegaard and Levinas both recognize the risks of law becoming legalism and inspiration becoming a cover for self-serving intoxication, even as they diverge over which side to come down on. Perhaps these inevitable risks only underscore our need to imitate both Kierkegaard and Levinas in critically analyzing our own contemporary religious practice, attempting to discern the ways in which it keeps us from living loving and just lives. For as Kierkegaard tells us, religious maturity entails an "honest distrust" of oneself, treating oneself as a "suspicious character" (FSE, 44). Surely Levinas would have no argument there.

STEPHEN MINISTER is Clara Lea Olson Professor of Ethical Values and Associate Professor of Philosophy at Augustana University in South Dakota. He is author of *De-Facing the Other: Reason, Ethics, and Politics after Difference.*

Notes

1. Levinas, *Difficult Freedom: Essays on Judaism*, trans. S. Hand (Baltimore: Johns Hopkins University Press, 1990), p. 11.

2. See Theodor W. Adorno, "On Kierkegaard's Doctrine of Love," *Studies in Philosophy and Social Science* 8.3 (1939): pp. 413–429; and Knud Ejler Løgstrup, *The Ethical Demand*, trans. T. I. Jensen and G. Puckering (Notre Dame, IN: University of Notre Dame Press, 1997).

3. See, for example, M. Jamie Ferreira, *Love's Grateful Striving: A Commentary on Kierkegaard's Works of Love* (New York: Oxford University Press, 2001).

4. Levinas, *Difficult Freedom*, p. 49.

5. This essay will not attempt a comparative analysis of Kierkegaard and Levinas, as there is already a large literature devoted to that task. See, for example J. Aaron Simmons and David Wood (eds.), *Kierkegaard and Levinas: Ethics, Politics, and Religion* (Bloomington: Indiana University Press, 2008); and Merold Westphal, *Kierkegaard and Levinas in Dialogue* (Bloomington: Indiana University Press, 2008).

6. Though Levinas tends to use the term "Christianity" in an undifferentiated way, I do not think a unified Christianity, a single "Christianity in itself," exists. Consequently, I will not herein consider whether Levinas's account of Christianity is "accurate." Suffice it to say, most of Levinas's criticisms apply to some influential interpretations of Christianity. It would, however, be a mistake to take these interpretations as the only interpretations of Christianity. For example, liberation theology offers an interpretation of Christianity that shares many of Levinas's concerns.

7. For extended consideration of Levinas's relationship to Christianity, see Kevin Hart and Michael A. Signer (eds.), *The Exorbitant: Emmanuel Levinas between Jews and Christians* (New York: Fordham University Press, 2010).

8. Levinas, *In the Time of Nations*, trans. M. B. Smith (Bloomington: Indiana University Press, 1994), p. 163.

9. Levinas, *Difficult Freedom*, p. 4.

10. Levinas, *Difficult Freedom*, p. 159.

11. Levinas, *Difficult Freedom*, p. 3.

12. Levinas, *Difficult Freedom*, p. 17.

13. Levinas, *Difficult Freedom*, p. 100.

14. Levinas, *Difficult Freedom*, pp. 99–100.

15. Levinas, *Difficult Freedom*, p. 141.

16. Levinas, *Difficult Freedom*, p. 143.

17. Levinas, *Difficult Freedom*, pp. 19–20.

18. Levinas, *Difficult Freedom*, p. 21.

19. Levinas, *Difficult Freedom*, p. 49.

20. Levinas, *Difficult Freedom*, p. 20.

21. Levinas, *Difficult Freedom*, p. 159.

22. Levinas, *Difficult Freedom*, pp. 8–9.

23. Levinas, *Difficult Freedom*, p. 126. Levinas's preference for social justice over love may come as a surprise to those who are under the sway of what Simon Critchley calls the "angelic reading" of Levinas. On this view, Levinas rejects the totality of the social order in favor of private acts of love for individual others. This reading is based on a fundamental misunderstanding of Levinas's work, as has been shown in Simon Critchley, *The Ethics of Deconstruction* (Edinburgh: Edinburgh University Press, 1992); and Stephen Minister, *De-Facing the Other: Reason, Ethics, and Politics after Difference* (Milwaukee, WI: Marquette University Press, 2012).

24. Levinas, *Difficult Freedom*, p. 101.

25. Ferreira, *Love's Grateful Striving*, p. 81.

26. Ferreira, *Love's Grateful Striving*, p. 83.

27. John J. Davenport, "What Kierkegaardian Faith Adds to Alterity Ethics: How Levinas and Derrida Miss the Eschatological Dimension," in Simmons and Wood, eds., *Kierkegaard and Levinas*, p. 175.

28. Davenport, "What Kierkegaardian Faith Adds to Alterity Ethics," pp. 178–179.

29. J. Aaron Simmons, in *God and the Other: Ethics and Politics after the Theological Turn* (Bloomington: Indiana University Press, 2011), argues for a similar reading of Kierkegaard's ethics, attributing to it the notion of a bidirectional responsibility.

30. Merold Westphal, "The Many Faces of Levinas as a Reader of Kierkegaard," in Simmons and Wood, eds., *Kierkegaard and Levinas*, pp. 31–32.

31. Westphal, "The Many Faces of Levinas as a Reader of Kierkegaard," p. 31.

32. Westphal, "The Many Faces of Levinas as a Reader of Kierkegaard," p. 31.

33. Emmanuel Levinas, *Ethics and Infinity*, trans. R. A. Cohen (Pittsburgh: Duquesne University Press, 1985), p. 89.

34. Given the manifold historical sufferings of Jewish communities at the hands of purportedly Christian ones, surely Levinas would not miss the terrible irony of this distinction.

35. "The difference between secularity and Christianity is not that the one has one view and the other another—no, the difference is always that they have the very opposite views, that what the one calls good the other calls evil" (FSE, 96).

36. Merold Westphal, *Becoming a Self: A Reading of Kierkegaard's Concluding Unscientific Postscript* (West Lafayette, IN: Purdue University Press, 1996), p. 195.

37. Westphal, *Becoming a Self*, p. 199.

38. Levinas, *Difficult Freedom*, p. 17.

PART III

Existence Before God

10 Difficult Faith and Living Well

Edward F. Mooney

W<small>HAT WOULD MAKE</small> for a good life—a life well lived despite its considerable detours, difficulties, and disasters? Kierkegaard is usually taken to focus more on life's difficulties and anxieties than on what a well-lived life might look like. There's even something bourgeois about the concept "a well-lived life"—a successful career, comfort, good money, and family. This would be exactly the sort of complacent life Kierkegaard spent his lifetime criticizing. So if I try to elaborate the theme of "a life well lived" as *compatible* with faithful living, I will have to distinguish "living well" from what town folk would call "success."

For Kierkegaard faith is a deep and often silent presence in a well-lived life. The knight is often invisible. But Kierkegaard also makes him, it seems, terrifyingly visible, as in the case of Abraham climbing Mt. Moriah to sacrifice Isaac. At least he's visible to readers—apparently. No one else saw his climb or descent, horribly visible. We have to make out how the exemplary knight of faith in *Fear and Trembling*—Abraham on his way to Moriah to sacrifice his son—can be understood to be "living well." There are numerous other treatments of a deep and silent faith, but *Fear and Trembling* is a kind of touchstone for non-specialists' impressions of Kierkegaard's faith, so it behooves me to start with that classic text.

The challenge, then, is to probe how it can be that the knight of faith in *Fear and Trembling* can be "living well." If we fixate on Abraham on Moriah, faith and living well seem to be on a collision course. An added dimension of the difficulty of linking faith and "flourishing" or "living well" to faith in *Fear and Trembling* is the repugnant—or at least very strange—role of God in the account. How does God contribute to the structure of a life well lived in *Fear and Trembling*? Is God whimsical in demanding Isaac? Does faith require believing in a whimsical or tyrannical God? Divinity seems to instigate trouble and turmoil rather than underwrite anything we'd immediately recognize as a life well lived. How could the God who orders Abraham to the mountain have any part in fashioning a well-lived life for Abraham?

Fear and Trembling

Fear and Trembling offers not one but many sketches of faithful living. Abraham is not the centerpiece throughout. One sketch of faithful living seems to directly undermine the prominence of Abraham as a knight of faith. A quarter of the way into the text, we find a contrasting paradigm of faith and faithful living. We encounter an unassuming burgher strolling home from work at the office. He is both a faithful townsman and living well. What is the mark of his faith (as Johannes *de silentio*, the pseudonym in charge of *Fear and Trembling*, portrays it)? He wonders what his wife has in store for dinner. It might be roast lamb, or it might be nothing. It's an ironic or even comic counterpoint to Abraham, as if Abraham thinks on the way up the mountain, "Well, God might have in store a lamb to replace Isaac, or he might not—I'm okay with it either way." Once we take in this bizarre parallel, we could conclude that faithful living is compatible with living well, and both require being able to take what comes one's way with ease and fortitude and grace.

Another set of sketches that challenge the centrality of Abraham's terrible burden depict a mother weaning her infant. If we're baffled by the insertion of a burgher's return home for lamb dinner as an instance of faithful living, we should be baffled by the insertion of four sketches of a nursing mother, too. I will return to these milder, motherly, or pedestrian knights of faith. For the moment, though, I simply wish to underline that aligning "living well" with the silent faith of the weaning mother or with that of the burgher strolling home has a far better chance of success than immediately trying to align living well with the trudge of Abraham up the mountain.

Let me turn to more general features of Kierkegaard's evocations and analyses of faith in *Fear and Trembling*, features that are usually overlooked.

We might think that any discussion of faith or faithfulness needs to begin with the nature of God and the detail of creeds, doctrine, and traditions. Doesn't faith begin with belief in something, in something divine, and the heartfelt endorsement of practices and creeds linked up to divinity? Strikingly, these issues or topics are *not* up for discussion in *Fear and Trembling*. Johannes *de silentio* is strangely silent about what a person of faith should believe about God or about conduct (rules for faithful living) or about specific faith traditions—say, Jewish or Lutheran. We don't find any abstract theological discussion about whether God exists, or whether he commands what's best, or whether obeying God is always a good thing.

The focus in *Fear and Trembling* remains exclusively on portraits of human beings. The portraits provide *clues* to living faithfully but no explicit formulae. In real life it is hard, if not impossible, to know if a neighbor, or someone in the news, is *really* a person of faith, once we go beyond conventional indicators like church or synagogue attendance. Johannes *de silentio*, with his opening Abraham portraits, illustrates the difficulty. It's not enough that Abraham starts up the mountain with Isaac. Each portrait of Abraham gives us a sketch that is *suggestive* of faith but is not the real thing. We have images only of "faith" that is *flawed*. Once we rule out avowed creeds and church or synagogue attendance, what could be the *unmistakable* marks of faithful living? How to *picture* faithful living—faith in action and passion, in joy and consternation, in crisis and pedestrian affairs—is the question that motivates the improvising thought experiments we find in the first half of *Fear and Trembling*.[1]

The uphill challenge of the present essay is to clear away the misconception that Kierkegaardian faith is blind obedience to divine commands, or is in some way wedded to creeds, doctrines, or cultural practices. More positively, the challenge is to show how the strenuous interior demands of faith can contribute to, or underwrite, a satisfying life—a well-lived life rather than a disastrous one.[2] This happens, when it does, by harboring certain virtues, some requiring striving, some requiring patience.[3]

Faith and Difficult Reality

Faith is a way of living that faces up to the inescapable incongruities of life, the clashing push-and-pulls that confront us. Cora Diamond refers to such practice as facing "difficult reality."[4] On the one hand, *Fear and Trembling* often leaves us with the sense that faithful living is groping in the utter darkness of difficult reality. That seems to be Abraham's plight. On the other hand, the faithful burgher whistling on his way home to dinner seems well out of the dark. In any case, faith does not remove difficulties but seems to be what, in retrospect, and in part, provides the assurance and trust that get us *through*—whether the difficulties are salient and catastrophic, as with Abraham, or all but invisible, as with the burgher knight of faith.

Faith will be an embodied *openness* to those trying circumstances that instill fear and trembling and, simultaneously, an embodied *poise, trust, and assurance* that gets us through those inescapable difficulties. And if we are lucky enough to escape monstrous circumstances, faith will be the *openness, poise, trust, and assurance* that more quietly permeate a largely uneventful life. Living faith underwrites our capacity to take a next step joyfully, confidently, *despite* fear and trembling.

On this account, faith—absurdly—is both cause and cure of trouble. *Openness and clear-sightedness* make us aware of, and hence vulnerable to, troubles to which a less faithful person could remain blind or closed. Tunnel vision and rule-bound living can blot out life's subtle and not-so-subtle hurts and troubles. To be aware of, and open to, suffering within and around one's life can *increase* one's quota of suffering relative to someone who is closed to life's difficulties. As if in recompense for the pain of openness, faith's *trust and assurance* help us weather rough spots or catastrophes. *Faith helps us through difficulties that only faith makes us alert to.* It can seem absurd, but faith is both cause and cure of trouble. It's mixed with fear and trembling (the downside) but also with joy and delight (the upside). Johannes *de silentio* puts this in the idiom of God's intrusions: "Isn't it true that those whom God blesses he damns in the same breath?" (FT, 94).

I've claimed that faith for Kierkegaard is not based on the sort of formulae one can post on the cathedral door or recite before dinner. If someone asks a knight of faith *what* his faith is, there will be little he or she can say. To point to a creed or to answer, "I'm Lutheran," "I'm Sufi," or "I'm Russian Orthodox" just won't tell us whether the person before us qualifies as a bona fide knight of faith. Kierkegaard turns to sketches of *near*-knights of faith, but there are inherent difficulties in rendering a full and accurate portrait. Portraits, even the cleverest ones, always fall short. There's a reason, and it's connected with the sublimity of faithful living.

Kierkegaard speaks in this text of "finding the sublime in the pedestrian" (FT, 70). The phrase arises in the context of sketching a pedestrian burgher, strolling miles from any crisis on Moriah (it seems). If encountering faith is akin to encountering "the" sublime, then we'll necessarily fail in attempts to represent the sublime—even the pedestrian sublime. The sublime has dimensions that escape a painter's or poet's attempt at description. It has shimmering excess, an overflow of energy that is larger and wider than the bare outline of the storm or mountain peak depicted. Attempts to represent the dual presence of fearsomeness and attractiveness are attempts to represent the unrepresentable. The analogy would be attempting to believe in a contradiction. Efforts to represent this shimmering and contradictory excess necessarily break down.

In his multiple stories, the narrator of *Fear and Trembling* enters the sector of life we should attend to while leaving intact the unrepresentable and paradoxical. The difficulty of describing faith is the difficulty of having faith; its vectors seem to be at cross-purposes: the joy and delight of faith run counter to its fear and trembling. Our moral terror at witnessing Abraham runs counter to our gripping fascination. Johannes *de silentio*'s stories, parables, or reveries boil over with an excess that escapes direct telling, even though the tellings sharpen our perceptions of this inscrutable domain. The writer's quixotic aim is to stay faithfully open to achieving a better, less distorting sketch or portrait of faith while consciously withholding prospects of a definitive portrait.

Lyrical Dialectics

Fear and Trembling calls itself lyrical and dialectical. We find three main inhabitants to reckon with in the lyrical pursuit of faith: Abraham, the *father* of faith; second, an anonymous *mother* of faith smuggled in as Abraham's counterpart; and third, an utterly worldly chap, as unlikely and unassuming as a tax collector or shopkeeper would be.[5] The figure who might be a shopkeeper is a domesticated, citified Abraham, a father of faith without fangs. The mother is Abraham as maternal, a soft source of nurture. She's meditative, tender, and private, not whistling jauntily down the street.

These figures carry something sublime, something of electric allure allied with fear and danger, a combination that resists full representation. Too much stress on the danger depletes the allure; too much stress on the allure depletes the danger. The typical instances of eighteenth-century sublimity cited by Kant and Burke are starry heavens, raging seas, or precipitous mountain cliffs. Abraham's trudge, knife and child in hand, God looming over it all, exemplifies a grandiose sublime. The grand scale of fearfulness and potential for death wedded to its supreme attractiveness defies full representation.

The mother and shopkeeper exemplify a miniature sublime of understatement. Their situations are fraught but on a smaller scale than Abraham's and also largely invisible. This sublimity is on the scale of nursing mothers and of a baby's soft coo, or on the scale of a faithful shopkeeper's anticipation of roast lamb and green peas. Abraham may lose his child, the mother may lose the trust of her infant, the shopkeeper may find his roast lamb isn't there, and perhaps his wife will be absent, too. These latter two near-knights of faith find "the sublime in the pedestrian" (FT, 70; SKS 4:136). The sublime here is the tremulous and attractive found in the everyday—not high in the heavens or in raging seas. Both mother and shopkeeper play *simple virtue* against Abraham's extravagant heroics. We can conclude that it's a *mistake* to model faith on melodramatic *outward* heroics. When the matter is a small wonder and not monstrous or grandiose, fear is scaled down, and only minor tremors of disquietude speak. Nursing mothers and burghers on the way home teach by embodying the trusting openness of faith despite undergoing what appear to be only small-scale, minor crises.

In the persons of the mother, "shopkeeper," and Abraham, we have three improvisations on faith.[6] This makes for contingency of meaning or interpretation. Grant that each exemplifies a trusting openness. What do we make of their obvious differences? There's a contingency that surrounds who is a *person* of faith, and also around who is the *author* of these sketches of faith. Is it Kierkegaard speaking, or is it *de silentio*? And if the latter, why trust a writer whose code name is "silence," who loudly sings and argues about silence and faith, and who frankly confides that he *can't understand* the faith of Abraham?

The text lacks a stable figure of faith, a stable author, and a stable register, style, or tonality. Style and genre set the aims and moods of writing. Lyric is one mode of writing, and dialectic, another; yet we're told on *Fear and Trembling's* title page that we hold a "Dialectical Lyric." We also have burlesque, fairy tale, and fable; satire, farce, and tragedy; the grotesque and the sublime. We have the antinomian and apophatic and what has been dubbed the eucatastrophical (a tale with an unexpected finish that's marvelously good).[7] There are scenes that approach slapstick: Johannes mentions the possibility of Isaac being killed at home (Abraham could skip the bother of a climb); or the possibility of having a parishioner run from the sermon, knife in hand, to corner his own son; or of having the burgher stop to watch rats scamper, or of having his wife serve him lamb. And then there are the four mothers balancing the quartet of terrifying Abraham portraits. Under what genre do *they* belong? Tragedy? Comedy? Farce? Abraham holds a knife. A mother weans her child. This four-part improvisatory installation has no center. How can such an unstable *divertimento* illuminate faith?

The *Preface* doesn't prepare us for a killing scenario, and the opening "*Attunement*" (meant to set a mood for thinking) lets us mull wistfully or daydream. There's a pervasive tone of fantasy and "what if" afoot. What *if* we take Abraham (or the nursing mother, or the figure who could be a shop owner) to be a figure of faith? *Fear and Trembling* begins as if a fairy tale were being dreamily retold: "*Once there was a man who recalled . . .*" And the would-be fairy tale is about a man who had a *daydream*, who remembered "a beautiful childhood tale."[8] This is decidedly *not* the tonality of considering would-be child-sacrifice. There is absolutely *nothing* dreamy, nostalgic, or beautiful about *that*. It's as if Johannes wants to *suspend* stark, bare-bones realities.

Even a monstrous Abraham, the father with knife in hand, might be a diversion from the truth, for the knife *blinds*, doesn't it? Think of Chagall's dreamy version of the scene, so unlike Caravaggio's hyperrealistic rendering. Chagall has Abraham almost whimsically floating among stars, angels, and lambs.

Improvisation and fantasy complement Kierkegaard's aversion to doctrinal disputation and academic contention. Look again at the titles of the two books universally taken as the core of his philosophy: *Philosophical Fragments* and *Unscientific Postscript*. These titles are shorthand tags, not the full titles. The little book knows as *Fragments* in full regalia is *Philosophical Crumbs, or Scraps of Philosophy*. Its follow-up, known as *Postscript*, is a 600-page afterthought or appendix to the diminutive *Fragments*. In full regalia it is *Concluding Unscholarly Postscript to Philosophical Crumbs: A Mimic-Pathetic-Dialectic Compilation—an Existential Contribution*. Is this sober scholarship, technical philosophy, or perhaps theology? Perhaps it's kitsch, but if not, the *Postscript* is surely the most comical paraphilosophy ever—infinite in scope, and infinitely becoming.

Let's say we've established that *Fear and Trembling* is a text of diverse and indeterminate tonal register, genre, and authorship that gives us not just Abraham on Moriah, but also a mixed crew of faith's near-exemplars. If we grant all this, why should we think that *Fear and Trembling* is a guide to a stable conception of faith?

Here are three answers.

First, we are shown over and over what faith is *not*. This clears the board for what faith might be. Second, by rummaging through candidates that turn out not to pass muster, we get habituated to *precisely the difficulty of faith*—of tracking it and of *living* by it, through trial and error. The difficulty and temptations of the terrain are replicated, testing our acuity and resolve. Third, there is what we could call the "positive theme," that faith is *trusting openness* modulated as *giving up* (or resignation) and *getting back* (the world or love or faith as a gift).

Let me pause on the second sort of teaching that the book affords: the way we are led to insights through the *difficulties* of tracking faith. Working through the conundrums of the text, seeing how faith as open trust permeates the comportment of Abraham, of the mother, of the burgher, is seeing how faith might permeate any number of lives. The indeterminacy of faith is the indeterminacy and contingent variation found in any lives that can be animated by faith.

We learn what faith is, while avoiding the back-and-forth of theological thesis and antithesis. Johannes *de silentio*'s multiple images, styles, and figures recapitulate our experience in a world of multiple strands of faithful living. By practicing his knack of tracking faith's varied embodiments, in women sewing or in mothers weaning their infants, grooves will be laid down in the heart and mind that deepen our capacity to follow the dispersion of faith through any number of persons, and to avoid identifying faith with churchgoers or creedal confessions.[9] A knack for following the text becomes a knack for seeing faith outside the text. It is a knack for embodying trust and openness in the interpretation of life's experiences and ambiguities as both flow through the present.

Insofar as we give ourselves to indeterminacies in this way, we inoculate ourselves against the strident singleness of vision so characteristic of self-deception. The self-deceiver needs to bolster self-esteem and reduce complexity. He'll feel better about himself (he thinks) if he simplifies and purifies his sense of the world, if he buries distasteful things outside explicit consciousness. Faith is an *expansion* of virtue—self-deception, a lethal *contraction*. I'll return to this.

Weaning, Mortality, Natality

Here are two enigmatic pronouncements: "Only one who descends to the underworld saves the loved one" (FT, 57; SKS 4:123). But we might ask why the lover and beloved are charged with descending into the nether regions. Is all love an infernal *ordeal*? Here is a second pronouncement: "The one who works will give birth to his own father" (FT, 57; SKS 4:123). This echoes the psychological truth that acknowledging our ancestors, inheriting them properly, starting with my father, is work, spiritual labor. Linking the two gives us a compound enigma: a descent in the name of love into the nether regions of unclarities is a prerequisite to fixing one's paternity, and hence one's birth, or rebirth. Go down, and then come up, reborn.

Fear and Trembling is a kind of motley or medley; a quilt or collage, many panels and squares stitched loosely together, scene after scene; a carnival and horror show, a Chagall-like, *dreamy* sort of art.[10] Abraham first appears in "a beautiful dream" of an old man remembering a childhood story. Giving up waking life for a dream—and then getting waking life back, dream included—is entering the giving up and getting back of faith.

Cycling in and out of imagination can be radically transformative. We redo our past by such cycles, and so redo our present as an offspring of the past. As in a dream, oracle, or prophecy, *de silentio* whispers that the faithful *give birth to their fathers*.[11] Such is the power of imaginative transformations. In a simple biological sense, mothers give birth to their children from the womb, and in a more complex imaginative sense, they give birth to an infant's growing independence in weaning. If we are beings toward death, as Heidegger learns from Kierkegaard, we are equally beings from birth, as Arendt learns from Kierkegaard. Birthing ourselves is modeled on birthing our children. We are mother and father to ourselves, giving (imaginative) birth to our fathers and mothers in practices of self-nourishment and earning inheritance or legacy.

Most readers skip over the motif of birth and weaning in *Fear and Trembling*. Levinas sees only the monstrosity of Moriah, with its apparent invitation to killing. He misses these quiet images of faith as natality or birth.[12] A mother weaning or a shopkeeper watching rats scamper under gutter planks is an image of a tender attention to, and acceptance of, life.[13] The denial of the maternal in philosophical thinking is pervasive. To account for its repression would be a long story, but a colleague puts the issue this way: "As philosophers, we have engaged in self-deception in order not to 'messy' the waters of philosophical investigation by recognizing the voice of the maternal. Doing so would complicate an otherwise tidy, 'single-vision' view of the world." And she adds, "Leaving out the maternal closes off a morally essential reality."[14]

In addition to a view of natality, *de silentio*'s writing provides numerous other glancing perspectives: a critique of bourgeois market society (*Preface*); a critique of direct communication (*Epigraph*); a critique of religion as bible-based hero-worship (*Speech in Praise of Abraham*); an attack on rule-based and bureaucratic conventional morality (*Problema*); an appreciation of domesticity (mothers weaning, shopkeepers strolling home for dinner, a woman sewing). In addition, the little tome provides a slightly pornographic peephole into dreamlike blood-and-violence, as well as a critique of the spectacular city. It provides a range of polyphony (the voice of terror, of praise, of detached analysis) and a startlingly imaginative array of thematic variations on the theme: Abraham might have dallied there, rushed there, stabbed himself, asked God to do it, refused outright, done it in despair or in deception. All this occurs in a little non-book by a non-author.[15]

It's remarkable that Don Quixote can belong in this varied troop of knights of faith—perhaps even being *de silentio*'s inspiration![16] The merchant-like fellow will not *immediately* bring to mind the mad Spanish knight, but imagination can mark links. Quixote was living Christianly and erratically in a world that took him to be mad; yet he was more Christian than they. The apparent merchant is living Christianly but not erratically, not madly; yet he is more Christian than they. How? Well, he refuses the ethics of convention that guarantees that a wife shall not leave her husband without dinner. He will be free of resentment should the meal not be there; he'll feel perfectly at ease. There is a notable delight and a freedom from presumption or moralism. He shows delightful assurance paired with cognitive, moral, and spiritual humility. All these traits make this sane fellow a likely knight of faith.

The pattern of faith in *Fear and Trembling* is an assured stance amid threatening contingency. Now we can add that this faith is lived out in *giving up and getting back*, being quieted then receiving, suffering then celebrating, moment by moment over time.[17] Is this what the poet Yehuda Amichai has in mind in his title *Open Closed Open*?[18] Abraham opens to God, closes down in fright, hand closed on the knife, then opens to a transformed world as the angel speaks. The nursing mother opens her breast to her infant, closes it off in blackening the breast, and then opens the infant to a new, more independent world. The shopman opens to the world, imagining even a roast head of lamb awaiting him at home, finds that possibility perhaps closed, but gets his world back, as fresh as before. Job is wonderfully open, then horribly closed in his anger and grief, then wonderfully silenced, opened, by the gift of new worlds. Faith is this pattern of giving up Isaac and getting him back.

Self-deception vs. Faith

Self-deception is defense against threats to moral self-image or integrity. Faithful living is an antidote to self-deception, and hence an ingredient in good living. But how does self-deception work?

You might lie to a thief to protect your daughter. That would be deception but not *self*-deception. To protect yourself, you might lie to your friends, but if you know you adopt the tactic of lying, that is not self-deception either. In self-deception, I want to *hide my lying from myself*, and hide from myself the threatening facts that *need* to be hidden to protect my moral self-image. As Melville has it, "When a man suspects any wrong, it sometimes happens that if he be already involved in the matter, he insensibly strives to cover up his suspicions even from himself."[19] In faith I hide nothing from myself. That's how it defies self-deception and furthers living well.

Sartre and others have wondered how self-deception is possible. If I do the deceiving, I must know I'm deceiving; but if I successfully deceive myself, I can't know I've deceived myself.[20] Which is it? Do I know or not know what I'm doing?

Well, when I skillfully apply my brakes while driving, I knowingly, skill-fully act, yet I don't have to advance any belief, or have any belief about what I know. If someone asks, "Do you know how to brake?" it suffices to say, "I do it all the time." The proof is in a way of acting (braking), not in holding a belief or in knowing that something is so. I can know how to deceive (how to keep a straight face when lying, say) without knowing explicitly what goes into doing this successfully. The paradox of knowing and not knowing is only apparent. "Knowing" can mean that I know how to do something skillfully—say, how to negotiate complex situations where cognitive uptake is essential. Just as I know how to correct my imbalance as I'm about to slip on ice, so I know how to cor-rect psychic imbalance as something transpires that wounds my self-image. In this sense, I can know how to hide hurtful things from myself, and how to hide that process of hiding from myself. The net result is that I can avow sincerely in some circumstances that I am not hiding things from myself when in fact I am doing precisely that. Children of five or six can be enormously skillful in evading damage to their self-image—"Mom, I didn't steal the cookies from Jane" (said in worked-up but "real" sincerity).

I tell myself a lie (knowingly making myself unknowing) in order to restore balance to my reigning self-conception. Self-deception works "out of sight" in the way catching one's balance works out of sight. It's a kind of "learned instinct" to recapture one's balance, whether on ice or when one has "slipped up" in main-taining the moral ground upon which one hopes flawlessly to tread. Yet we also have instincts that oppose the mechanisms of self-deception. With luck and com-panionable mentors and friends, we learn to catch those moments when our first impulse is to cover up. But often the instinct of wanting to be better than we are wins out, and we kid ourselves, shamelessly.

As we drive home, I mention that I feel sorry about your daughter's "bad luck" in an advanced geometry class. You protect your self-image by passing off what you know full well is her poor performance, by protesting that she didn't perform *that* poorly—and by venturing that her bad grade will almost certainly be overlooked by the teacher in the long run. You skillfully give a tilt to whatever evidence and interpretation can boost your self-image as a successful parent of a successful child—and you cover up the rest with aplomb and finesse. You sense my mild skepticism and so work harder to make your character—and hers—spotless. She didn't do *that* poorly, you repeat, raising your voice in irritation. You close yourself to hard truths, to full realities, to painful ambiguities, persuading yourself that contingencies are in your control when they aren't. You have no faith, for faith is living without despair and transparently, hiding nothing from yourself, in circumstances that threaten your sense of moral viability. Being of faith is maintaining the fragile stance or mood of *transparency* toward oneself. It is akin to *receiving* yourself, acknowledging who you are and your position, with full knowledge that brutal, unexpected, inescapable contingency could destroy the self you now are.

Imagine that the weaning mother is self-deceptive, without faith. She has (let's imagine) an investment in thinking of herself as never causing worry or pain to her child. Even as she blackens her breast, she tells herself that her infant "won't notice a thing"—a tremor in her hand betrays the contrary: she fears her infant will be pained. A friend tactfully asks about her trembling hand. She hides the truth from herself, saying she shakes from too much caffeine. She has no faith, for she can't brook the contingency that her infant will be harmed.

This imagined mother is faithless because she knows implicitly that contingency can befoul her dearest wish (that her child not be harmed). And she manages to deny to herself that such a contingency might occur. Her body shows fear and trembling not simply because of objective circumstance, but also because she is in the risky project of lying to herself in hope of self-protection. Living faithfully with uncertainty and contingency rules out self-deception.

Contingencies or troubling disruptions in mood and situation threaten to defeat the natural desire to avoid or deny the uncertainties that constitute rich life. To live faith's wild, tender, and pedestrian unfurling is to be open to such contingency and trouble. Love, wonder, and grief are responsive to fragility. To protect my investments in power and efficacy, I may come to deny the uncertain and fragile, against which I am ultimately powerless. I bury this denial from myself in order to shore up commitments to things I control: critique, discipline, technique, or efficacy. But then I forfeit those humane responses that presuppose vulnerability. To relentlessly assert prerogatives of the mastering, executive self strips the world of the background against which humane response shimmers. Of course to understand is to master, and Johannes admits he cannot understand Abraham; he can only be amazed in his presence.[21] He's not an object to be studied, but rather a marvel to behold.

Yielding to Contingency and Affliction

The nursing mother is not self-centeredly wrestling with a problem, gathering her resources to master it. The world presents issues: the child must be weaned, set free. The mother, we surmise, realizes that how the weaning goes is not totally in her control. If she is of faith, she awaits her time, the child's time, and doesn't cast blame if her timing is off. The infant speaks its comfort (or discomfort) to the listening mother. We remember the "shopman knight of faith" jauntily returning home, expecting that his good wife has a meal waiting. He realizes, we surmise, that how his dinner goes is not totally in his control. He awaits his time and will accept the world, come what may. Rats scamper under gutter boards or not; the table is set or not. The evening meal declares its presence (or absence). Both nursing mother and strolling burgher listen willingly, patiently to an outer, intimate world. Those of little faith try to wrestle the world to submission, to make it answer their needs and aspirations. Those of faith realize that veiled contingencies may eventuate, and they will be patient—not attack the veiling or contingency to eliminate it.[22] The minute either of them attempts to wrestle ambiguity or contingency to the mat, they will have lost faith.

When I turn to technique to skirt or subvert obstacles that confront me, I become, for the moment, a technocrat, not a person of faith. Yet love, death, grief, shame, and birth are matters to which we are existentially subject, and not at all amenable to diminishment, enhancement, or administration by technique, by tools I might wield, or by tools others might offer me: "Don't cry, take a walk, you'll get over it, trust in the Lord, don't probe, answers are at hand, be a grownup." All too readily, we are offered psychological, doctrinal, rabbinical, or ministerial nostrums, tools to lean on and apply. But these are not ultimately effective—*nothing graspable is*—and they are often little more than superficial and condescending diversions.

Death, love, and grief are not problems to solve with appropriate tools, nor will knowing more about them help to manage or corral them. Knowing more about delights (in love) or aches (in grief, death, or love) only deepens our appreciation of their elusiveness, their bottomless mystery—veiled and shifting, alluring and repelling. Enigmas don't retreat but expand and fan out as we dwell on, as we experientially undergo, the multifold meanings of grief, innocent delight, vulnerability and love.

As thinkers who by profession are trained to attack and subdue the ambiguous and problematic, we take offense at those regions where faith is at home, and we seek to drain any need or trace of it. Pervasive commitments to rational progress, whether Hegelian, Analytic, or Marxist, aim to disenfranchise and bury patience with inexpugnable darkness. We wield dialectics meant to subdue. But ultimate vulnerability and contingency disarm us—and not always when we're in the vicinity of faith. When this disarming is devastating, we have what Simone Weil calls *affliction*.[23]

Afflictions are contingencies that are disturbing, harmful, painful--that we *suffer*. She writes, "To acknowledge affliction means saying to oneself: 'I may lose at any moment, through the play of circumstances over which I have no control, anything whatsoever I possess, including those things which are so intimately mine that I consider them as being myself'."[24] Stanley Cavell sees that the loss of self might be a condition of gaining a self. As he puts it, "The possessing of a self is not—is the reverse of—possessive; . . . it is the exercise not of power but of reception."[25] Faith, then, is the vulnerable condition under which a self is transparently received, with full knowledge that at any moment it might be taken, that contingency could destroy it, or that one could have to relinquish the self one now is.

Faith is first a trusting openness or transparency. It can now be further specified as a *giving up* (as in Job or Abraham or a weaning mother) and a *getting back*, a receptivity, openness, to a return of the world, return of the son, return of the nursing infant. Giving up and getting back is the double movement of faith in *Fear and Trembling*.[26] Self-deception is willfully, strategically engineering a clean bill of moral health, which means willfully dismissing the verdicts of our own experience. We would masterfully take possession of the self we would be. But that mastery is denied us. To avoid self-deception, to abide in faith, the trick is to remain open to the world despite the contrary desire to master it, to close in on it, take possession of it. Yet affliction speaks only to a vulnerable, less than lordly self, only to a soul. Only less than a lordly, masterly soul can muster a true response.

Faith is at risk from several corners, not least our fear of the evident fragility of life. Love and faith reside amid acknowledged vulnerability to contingency. They are a type of undergoing that is neither uniform nor transparent but eccentrically, enigmatically open-closed-open, without rules for when to hold or when to let go—when to relinquish, when to welcome, arms open.

Deadly Ideals vs. Openness, Love, Trust

I've said we deceive ourselves in order to crudely simplify and violently purify our virtue—which makes of our virtue a vice. Faith, in contrast, is a subtle twofold (or multifold) vision or mood, a yielding relinquishment of will-to-power, a willingness to await reception, and a ready responsiveness to what may be given. Faith is a giving up and getting back that *sustains without simplification* what emerges as a veiled and vulnerable complication and expansion of virtue in a difficult reality.

Self-deception is a killing *contraction* of virtue. Single vision is subject to hyponomia, a compulsive adherence to narrow rules, to artificially constrictive and inflexible norms. Its rigid focus blocks out a saving modulation that could be provided by an openness to complex and multivalent circumstance. Such openness shows up in acknowledgement of contrary-tilting norms embedded in one's circumstance. Kindness can conflict with truth, mercy with justice, strength with humility, and so on. Rather than shutting it down, an expansive virtue listens to increasing complexity. Kierkegaard is right to link faith to objective uncertainty, to a self striving in darkness to become itself, to the possibility that ordinary ethics, as simple commonplace rules, might have to be suspended. And Kierkegaard is right to highlight the terror that accompanies radical suspension of rules in the name of deeper connections to difficult realities.

When we simplify in order to preserve a single constricted and violently "purified" virtue, we sacrifice what does not fit, creating, as I mentioned, from virtue what is surely a vice.[27] Sometimes the self kills itself, sacrifices itself, in the name of a radically "purifying" *nomos*. A soldier commits suicide because he can't live up to the categorical and pure demand that because others in his unit died for him, he must die for them. His survival profanes the nobility of their sacrifice, and so he must not survive. A celebrity singer, in her own eyes only a would-be beauty, takes her life because she lets her vision of superlative beauty become isolated from all other value, and demands categorically that she be an instance of "pure beauty." She excludes herself from being *ordinarily* beautiful, or simply attractive.

Sometimes the narrow self of constricted vision kills others, sacrificing them as scapegoats in the name of "purifying" the social landscape by installing a restrictive ideal or archetype: the pure Aryan; the pure Christian; the pure male, the male who must despise any hint of heterodox sexuality (it's all brotherhood and guns); the pure female, who must be sexy, striking, and poised. Many, if not all, of our ideals or aspirations can slip in a moment from legitimacy to poison: "No one's better than anyone else!" "You're mine, my dear!" "Anything less than winning is losing!" "The unexamined life is not worth living!"

A colleague reminds me how it can be that neither "know thyself" nor faith's "allegiance to openness" is exempt from poisonous descent: "Couldn't faith's 'I hide nothing from myself' be denatured into a perverse nepsis, a remorseless, light-glaring-in-the-face interrogation of the self, distorted and distorting?"[28] Knowing oneself, or wanting to be faithfully open, requires a certain gentleness toward oneself. He adds,

> It strikes me that living by faith . . . is so to live that faithfulness itself is rarely dwelt upon and certainly does not become overtly programmatic in the faithful person's life. Faith-fullness is an unforced, active, inward and sympathetic attention to what is uncertain and contingent, even while it is acknowledged to be uncertain and contingent. But it is not, or not often, attentive to itself. (Perhaps this is, phenomenologically, part of the experience of faith as a gift, a theological [and not a cardinal] virtue.)

I find this very helpful.

If self-deception closes off morally essential realities, faith opens *to* them— ever more opens to ever *more of* them. It is the opposite of an embrace of a dogma. Love, too, opens endlessly, shifting between relinquishment and embrace. Although I can't make the case here, I'll stand by the equation *what goes for faith goes for love*. And what goes for Kierkegaardian faith is the utter absence, the ultimate impossibility, of anything like self-deception. Whether mortals can attain or receive such faithfulness, and what the odds are, is quite another matter.

Equilibrium, Groundlessness, Rebirth

The book's "dialectical" sections pit ethics (which includes many beliefs about right and wrong, better and worse) against God's command to Abraham. Can he believe that it's wrong to sacrifice his child yet believe that it's right to obey God? Is it right to offer up Isaac as a sacrifice? But even here, the issue seems to be less about *belief* than about how one can *trust* ethics, and *trust* God, when these trusts collide. If Abraham suffers a collision of trusts, the question is how he weathers that collision, how he proceeds without betraying one trust or the other, his trust in God and his trust in ethics, how he maintains openness and poise in a situation that is catastrophic. The question is not to decide what propositions to believe or to recite as a creed. In *Fear and Trembling*, it is whether a particular person, Abraham, can weather the conflict that is his dark reality, whether he can emerge unbroken.

An unbroken Abraham will come through with a love of the world (rather than a hatred of it) and a trust in the world (rather than a despairing mistrust). Love and trust are neither propositional beliefs nor creeds to nail on the cathedral door. They become an achieved stance or equilibrium, always potentially on trial, and so an achievement under constant renewal. Athletic excellence is like that, and love and trust are as well. They are difficult virtues that require hard work and a readiness to accept both gifts bestowed and gifts withheld. Love and trust inform Abraham's climb through doubt and terror. They underwrite his poise, his unbrokenness in the face of an unaccommodatingly harsh, even brutally unspeakable, reality.

Keeping faith—a way of living infused by love, trust, and openness to hard realities—is compatible with being quite *agnostic* about what propositions might *ground* one's achieved and ever-renewed assurance or poise. The conduct of life is rooted in primitive assurances rather than foundational tenets. At some point reasons for what we do, or for what stance we assume, run out. We discover and affirm what we love, where we abide, what moves us. This is the antifoundationalism of Wittgenstein, Heidegger, and pragmatism.[29] The moment reasons run out can be one of despair and skepticism, or of trust that we can nevertheless go on, and the world will be with us. Of course, a faithful stance is not beyond critique. It may be ill-advised, foolish, infantile, or self-destructive. But a stance is not shattered or defeated in the way an assertion is. A person does not fall apart or regain poise the way propositions do. There can be no requirement that I ground every stance from which I live in an explicit propositional belief. Life would stop dead in its tracks if that requirement were in force. My stance is *here* in my living with poise and openness—or not. Snow is *here* to grace the limbs of my trees—or not. I live from the poise and openness of faith, or I don't. Snow is a present illumination that graces my life, or it isn't. I won't attempt to *ground* my faith in a tenet any more than I'll attempt to ground the grace and illuminations of snow.

And how do the dynamics of faithful living eventuate in a life better lived? At the least, an undeceived life will be an improvement over a self-deceived one, and a life of trust and openness will be an improvement over a life of mistrust and refusal of others and the world. A life of trust, assurance, and poise is several notches above one of mistrust, self-doubt, and erratic unease and fearfulness. Furthermore, a willingness to undergo the giving up and getting back of faith leaves one accessible to rebirth, which must be a boon to hopes for a life well lived. Faithful living can be welcomed as flowing with virtues constituent of a life well lived, able to weather disruptions and to stay open to marvels.

EDWARD F. MOONEY is Professor Emeritus in the Departments of Religion and Philosophy at Syracuse University. His publications include *On Søren Kierkegaard: Dialogue, Polemic, Lost Intimacy and Time* and *Recovering Personal Philosophy from Thoreau to Cavell.*

Notes

1. I often get a stare of disbelief when a new acquaintance hears that I write about Kierkegaard's *Fear and Trembling.* Doesn't it champion faith as blind obedience to God? Startled, she wonders if I've converted to the worst kind of fundamentalism—and politely holds her tongue.

2. I limit my discussion to the improvisational sketches in *Fear and Trembling.* Of course the theme of faithful living crisscrosses the Kierkegaardian corpus, first to last. However, looking for a generic or composite account of faith is as flawed as looking for a generic "Bach Theme." There's no substitute for listening attentively to particular Bach passages—whether culled from arias, suites, or full Passions. Just so, there is no substitute for listening attentively to particular Kierkegaard phrases, passages, and lyrical improvisations of the sort we find so artfully rendered in *Fear and Trembling.*

3. A critic has noted that elsewhere Kierkegaard suggests, often indirectly, that faith is not a virtue. It is certainly not a cardinal virtue. But this opens too large a topic for this paper. I restrict my attention to faith as it is displayed and discussed in *Fear and Trembling*, not as it might appear in the authorship elsewhere or as a whole.

4. Cora Diamond, Stanley Cavell, John McDowell, Ian Hacking, and Cary Wolfe, *Philosophy and Animal Life* (New York: Columbia University Press, 2008).

5. The man "looks just like a tax-collector" (FT, 68).

6. Agnes (in the third *Problema*) also wrestles with faith.

7. John Davenport picks up Tolkien's discussion of the eucatastrophical and deploys it in "Faith as Eschatological Trust in *Fear and Trembling*," in *Ethics, Love, and Faith in Kierkegaard: A Philosophical Engagement,* Edward F. Mooney, ed. (Bloomington: Indiana University Press 2008), pp. 196–233.

8. I follow Hannay's translation, rendering the title of this opening section, *"Stemning,"* as "attunement."

9. "The secret in life is that everyone must sew it for himself, and . . . a man can sew it as well as a woman" (FT, 74).

10. For *Fear and Trembling* as depicting spectacle and carnival that diverts us from faith, see my *On Søren Kierkegaard: Dialogue, Polemics, Lost Intimacy, and Time* (Burlington: Ashgate, 2007), chapter 8.

11. No doubt this echoes Eckhart. I discuss *de silentio*'s allusion to giving birth to one's father, of being mother to one's father, and hence to oneself, in my *Knights of Faith and Resignation: Reading Kierkegaard's Fear and Trembling* (Albany: SUNY 1996), p. 40. In the Book of Job, Elihu tells us that we are instructed spiritually by dreams, suffering, and songs in the night. To have access to "dreams, suffering, and songs in the night" is a condition of access to faith and its gifts.

12. See my discussion of George Pattison on natality, "The Intimate Agency of Death," *Kierkegaard and Death*, Patrick Stokes and Adam Buben, eds. (Bloomington: Indiana University Press, 2011), pp. 136–138.

13. I pass on a caution first raised by Patrick Stokes (in personal correspondence). "I think we [must] face the question of how some of *de silentio*'s rather domestic pictures of modern knights of faith cohere with Kierkegaard's later writings, particularly the 1855 writings."

14. Jennifer Lemma, in personal correspondence; she adds, "There is an innate philosophical value to Kierkegaard's faith as it pertains to the population of women who are mothers and because of this, it deserves to be recognized as an integral part of ethical, philosophical discourse." See note 15, below.

15. I consider what lies behind philosophy's neglect of the feminine and maternal in my "Gender, Philosophy, and the Novel," *Metaphilosophy* 5, no. 3 (1987): 241–252; and in "Birth, Love, and Hybridity: *Fear and Trembling* and the *Symposium*" (with Dana Lloyd), *Cambridge Critical Studies, Fear and Trembling,* Daniel Conway, ed. (Cambridge: Cambridge University Press, 2015).

16. See Eric Ziolkowski on Cervantes in *The Literary Kierkegaard* (Evanston: Northwestern University Press, 2011).

17. See my extended discussion of this "double movement" in *Knights of Faith.*

18. Yehuda Amichai, *Open Closed Open* (New York: Harcourt, 2000).

19. Herman Melville, *Moby-Dick* (New York: Penguin 2001), chapter 20, p. 106.

20. See Herbert Fingarette's classic analysis, *Self-Deception* (Berkeley: University of California Press, 2000).

21. FT, 66. There is an ongoing critique in *Fear and Trembling* of lecturers who expound on matters of faith in the classroom while being studiously oblivious to any possible relevance of their lectures to their lives; they remain far from "the convulsions of existence" (p. 91).

22. See Sheridan Hough on how the "shop man" lives with contingency: "Silence, 'Composure in Existence,' and the Promise of Faith's Joy," in *Why Kierkegaard Matters,* Marc A. Jolly, ed. (Macon, GA: Mercer University Press, 2010), pp. 147–157.

23. Simone Weil, "Human Personality," in *The Simone Weil Reader,* George A. Panichas, ed. (New York: David McKay, 1977), p. 332.

24. Weil, "Human Personality," p. 332.

25. Stanley Cavell, "Thinking of Emerson," in his *The Senses of Walden* (Berkeley: North Point Press, 1981), p. 135.

26. Edward Mooney, *Knights of Faith and Resignation,* chapters 3–6. I have recently heard the suggestion that Luther's notion of baptism (a cleansing that removes the old life, and the reception of new life) and the death and resurrection of Christ are also movements of giving up (life) and getting it back.

27. Some of these formulations follow the reflections of Andy Martin, in "Winehouse, Breivik and Deadly Ideals," The Opinionator, *New York Times*, July 26, 2011, written only days after the Oslo massacres. Of course, not all self-deception leads to violence; and not every attempt to save face is an instance of self-deception. Retrieved March 24, 2017, from https://opinionator.blogs.nytimes.com/2011/07/26/winehouse-breivik-and-deadly-ideals/?_r=0.

28. Kelly Jolley (in correspondence).

29. See Lee Braver, *Groundless Grounds: A Study of Wittgenstein and Heidegger* (Cambridge, MA: MIT Press, 2012).

11   Kierkegaard and the Early Church on Christian Knowledge and Its Existential Implications[1]

M. G. Piety

ALL THE ESSAYS in this volume make clear that both love and faith are essential to Kierkegaard's conception of the good life for a Christian. Only Rick Anthony Furtak dares to argue directly that knowledge is similarly essential. This relative neglect of the role of knowledge in Kierkegaard's thought is explicable, I believe, as consequence of the fact that faith is often considered to be opposed to knowledge. Furtak is correct, however. Kierkegaard's is not a noncognitivist fideism. Faith serves as a means, according to Kierkegaard, through which Christian knowledge is attained, knowledge that is crucial to the good life for a Christian.

Kierkegaard refers frequently, and approvingly, to what he calls "original Christianity"[2] precisely because of the emphasis he believed it placed on the existential implications of religious knowledge. Kierkegaard's account of Christian knowledge is strikingly similar, in fact, to the positions of two of the earliest church fathers, Irenaeus and Clement of Alexandria—so similar that it is not unreasonable to assume that the similarity is the result of Kierkegaard's attempt to develop an epistemology that was consistent with the doctrines of the early church. The purpose of this essay is to provide a sketch of Kierkegaard's view that Christian knowledge cannot be separated from a way of life that is itself an expression of Christian truth, and to show the similarity of this view with the views of Irenaeus and Clement.

Knowledge of God

In *Fear and Trembling*, Kierkegaard refers to human beings as having an "eternal consciousness" that he associates with the love of God (FT, 48).[3] It would appear that Kierkegaard believes the idea of God is built into human consciousness. Precisely how this is so is something he doesn't directly address. It may be that it is simply part of the way consciousness is constructed,[4] or it may be associated with a person's appreciation that his is a finite, or limited, form of rationality.

Kierkegaard asserts in *Philosophical Crumbs* that "one does not *believe* that there is a God, even though one assumes that there is." He continues, "This is a misuse of language. Socrates did not have faith that there was a God. What he knew [*vidste*] about God he achieved through recollection" (*Crumbs*, 153). This reference to "recollection" recurs in Kierkegaard's journals, where he observes that both proving that there is a God, and being convinced of this by proofs, are "equally fantastic,"

> for just as no one has ever proven it, so has there never been an atheist, even though there certainly have been many who have been unwilling to let what they knew get control of their minds. . . . With respect to the existence [*Til-værelsen*] of God, immortality, etc., in short with respect to all problems of immanence, recollection applies; it exists altogether in everyone only he does not know it. (JP, 3:3606)

It makes sense that Kierkegaard would have felt no need to defend the view that the idea of God is included in the contents of human consciousness. This view is part of the earliest Christian orthodoxy and was very likely a part of Kierkegaard's theological studies at the University of Copenhagen. Close examination of the writings of Irenaeus, one of the earliest of the early church fathers, reveals that he also believes that the idea of God is built into human consciousness. God, according to Irenaeus,

> confers on all a great mental intuition and perception of His most mighty, yes, almighty greatness. Therefore, though "no one knows the Father except the Son, nor the Son except the Father, and those to whom the Son has revealed Him" (cf. Matt. 11:27), yet *all beings* know this fact at least [i.e., that there is a God] because reason, implanted in their minds, moves them, and reveals to them that there is one God, the Lord of all.[5]

Irenaeus appears, actually, to employ a primitive argument from design. He writes, for example, that

> [c]reated things, in their great number and diversity, fit beautifully and harmoniously into the creation as a whole. And yet, when viewed individually, they appear discordant and opposed to each other, just as the sound of the lute makes a single harmonious melody out of many and opposite notes by means of the intervals between them. The lover of truth must not be deceived, therefore, by the intervals between the different notes, nor imagine that this note was the work of one artist or another, and that note due to another, nor think that one person fitted the treble, another the bass, and yet another the tenor strings. He must not forget that one and the same Artist was responsible for the wisdom, justice, goodness, and munificence of the whole work. And those who listen to the melody ought to praise and glorify the Artist, and admire the tension of some notes, appreciate that relaxation in others, enjoy the moderation of those between the two extremes. Recalling that some things are

symbols, they will consider what it is that each thing points to and what causes it. But they will never alter the rule, nor stray from the Artist, nor abandon faith in the one God who made all things, nor blaspheme our Creator.[6]

That is, "[c]reation," according to Irenaeus, "shows its Creator, and what is made suggests its Maker."[7] One need only be a "lover of truth," according to Irenaeus, in order to see this.

To the extent, however, that reason reveals to the individual that there is a God, knowledge that God exists does not require the assistance of the kind of revelation that Christianity is chiefly concerned with. That is, knowledge that there is a God is not specifically Christian. It is tempting to conclude, given Kierkegaard's skeptical leanings, that there is no specifically Christian knowledge on his view. It's clear, however, from Kierkegaard's remarks in his journals that such a conclusion would be mistaken.

Christian Knowledge

Christian knowledge comprises both what philosophers traditionally refer to as "acquaintance knowledge" and "propositional knowledge," where the former is the source of the latter, just as our acquaintance with the objects of our experience is the source of our propositional knowledge of them. And just as our knowledge of empirical reality dictates to us a certain manner of navigating our way through this reality, so does our knowledge of religious truth, according to Kierkegaard, dictate to us a certain manner of navigating our way through the moral landscape.

Christian knowledge is a subset of what Kierkegaard refers to as "essential knowledge,"[8] and essential knowledge is "essentially related to existence." But this does not signify, explains Kierkegaard, "that abstract identity mentioned above between thought and being; nor objectively does it mean that knowledge corresponds to something that is there as its object. It means that knowledge relates to the knower, who is essentially someone existing, and that for this reason all essential knowledge essentially relates to existence and to existing" (*Postscript*, 166).

"Everything Is New In Christ," observes Kierkegaard in his journals. "This will be my position for a speculative Christian epistemology" (JP, 2:2277). Christian knowledge is a product of revelation, and the specific revelation with which Kierkegaard is concerned can be characterized as an encounter with Christ, or as contemporaneity with Christ, as Kierkegaard expresses it in *Philosophical Crumbs*.[9] "Christ is the truth," according to Kierkegaard, hence to know Christ is to know the truth (*Crumbs*, 205).

But what does it mean to know Christ? Epistemologists are interested primarily in propositional knowledge. It appears, however, that in every instance where Kierkegaard refers to "knowledge" of Christ, the Danish expression is either *"Kjendskab"* or some form of the verb *"kjende,"* and these terms refer to acquaintance knowledge rather than propositional knowledge.[10] There is even at least one place where Kierkegaard alters the then–current Danish translation of the New Testament by replacing the expression "know" (*kiende*), in connection with the truth of Christianity, with "experience" (*erfarer*).[11] The reference is from his papers, where he quotes John 7:17 as "If anyone's will is to do my father's will, he shall experience whether the teaching is from God or on my own authority" (JP, 2:1881).[12] This substitution is important. It provides us with a key to understanding an early journal entry in which Kierkegaard asserts that "[t]he historical anticipation of and also the position in human consciousness[13] corresponding to the Christian '*Credo ut intelligam*' [I believe in order that I might understand] is the ancient *Nihil est in intellectus quod non antea fuerit in sensu* [There is nothing in the intellect that has not previously been in the senses]" (JP, 2:1098). That is, a person meets Christ, according to Kierkegaard, in the moment of faith. This meeting yields acquaintance "knowledge" of Christ. If there is Christian knowledge in the propositional sense, this acquaintance knowledge of Christ both precedes it and provides the foundation for it. To become acquainted with Christ is an experience that is related to the intellect in a manner analogous to the way *sensory* experience is related to the intellect.

Experience, according to Kierkegaard, belongs to the realm of existence, or actuality. It becomes knowledge, or a candidate for knowledge, only when it is brought into relation to ideality in the intellect. Hence, for Kierkegaard, Christian knowledge, in the propositional sense, is a *consequence* of—rather than, as some have argued, *equivalent* to—Christian experience.[14] "Knowing the truth," argues Kierkegaard in *Practice in Christianity*, is not equivalent to being the truth, but instead is something that "*follows* of itself from being the truth" (PC, 205, emphasis added).

But what does it mean to be the truth? Christianity posits that people are sinful. Even the believer is still a sinner. To be sinful, explains Kierkegaard in *Crumbs*, is to be essentially outside the truth. To be outside the truth in this way is to be incapable of understanding it, or of becoming properly related to it on one's own, because if this were possible, then in an important sense, one could not really be said to be outside it. To be essentially outside the truth, according to Kierkegaard, is to need assistance to gain a proper understanding of it, or to be put into the proper relation to it. Such assistance, he argues, can come only from the truth itself.[15]

This is the difference between what Kierkegaard refers to as "guilt consciousness"[16] and "sin consciousness."[17] A person's understanding of himself as sinful is inseparable from his understanding the truth, in that sin is what separates him from the truth. If a person is essentially ignorant of the truth, then the truth can be called "the unknown" (*Crumbs*, 111–118), Thus Climacus argues that

> the individual, if he is truly to come to know something about the unknown (God), must come to know that it is different from himself, absolutely different. The understanding cannot come to know this by itself (because, as we have seen, this is self-contradictory). If it is to come to know this, it must come to know this through God ... One needs God simply in order to come to know God is the different, and now comes to know that God is absolutely different from himself. But if God is absolutely different from human beings, this cannot have its basis in what human beings owe to God (for to this extent they are related), but in what they are themselves responsible for, or what they have themselves earned. What then is the difference? What else could it be but sin. (*Crumbs*, 119)

"Christianity," asserts Kierkegaard in *The Sickness Unto Death*, "assumes that neither paganism nor the natural man knows what sin is; yes, it assumes there must be a revelation from God to reveal what sin is" (*Sickness*, 89).

According to Kierkegaard, a person does not come to know that sin is the difference between himself and God, or himself and the truth, as a result of his own efforts to understand this difference. He comes to know this as a result of having been transformed in a manner that makes such knowledge possible.[18] This transformation can be brought about only by God.[19]

A person cannot come to know the truth in the sense of what sin is, or that it is sin that separates him from God, on his own, because if he could, he would essentially possess this knowledge even if he happened, accidentally, to be unaware of it. The truth must come to the sinner. Eternal ethical-religious truth must come to be in time. Kierkegaard refers to this intersection of the temporal and the eternal as a "paradox."[20] But it is not primarily the difficulty of conceiving a synthesis of temporality and eternality that presents an obstacle to the understanding, according to Kierkegaard. Indeed, he defines human beings as such a synthesis.[21] The difficulty is rather that a person's own eternal consciousness, or understanding of the truth, is supposed to come to be through his relation to this paradox, which is to say, through his encounter with the god in time. What a person comes to know, through his encounter with the god in time, is not that he must conform his concrete existence to abstract ethical-religious ideality. This is something that he is presumed already to know, to the extent that he is innately conscious that there is a God who is not only the creator of the universe, but also the author of the moral law that he is aware of through the medium of his conscience. What he comes to know, as a result of this encounter, is that he is essentially incapable of doing what he is eternally responsible for doing.

Such knowledge cannot help but be offensive, and the knower naturally rebels against it. It is offensive in that it is self-contradictory to propose that a person could be eternally responsible for doing something he is essentially incapable of doing. It's an offense to reason, in that it is incoherent; and it's an offense to a person's innate moral sense, in that it is obviously unjust. To the extent that this is the message of the god in time, a person will be unable to get this message into his head, so to speak.[22] How then, asks Kierkegaard,

> does the learner come to an understanding with this paradox . . . It happens when the understanding and the paradox meet happily in the moment, when the understanding sets itself aside and the paradox gives itself; and this third thing, in which this happens (because it happens neither through the understanding, which is excused, nor through the paradox which offers itself—but *in* something), is the happy passion we will now give a name . . . We will call it: *faith*. (*Crumbs*, 128–129)

To learn the truth, according to Kierkegaard, is thus to become a believer. A person becomes a believer when, after having surrendered his reason to the paradox, he receives the condition for understanding the truth.[23]

One might wonder why Kierkegaard would refer to a person's belief that he is a sinner as a "happy passion." The answer is that sin is only half of what a person is expected to believe as a Christian. Grace is the other half, and grace relieves the impression of guilt, which, according to Kierkegaard, is omnipresent in human consciousness. Hence Kierkegaard argues, "The hope of the life-giving Spirit is against the hope of the understanding" (FSE, 82–83). A person can understand guilt. What he cannot understand without divine assistance is that, in the eyes of the eternal, he is forgiven.[24]

The forgiveness of sins is thus "the absurd" (JP, 2:1215).[25] It is absurd in the sense that, from the perspective of the sinner (i.e., from the human perspective) it seems impossible. "[W]hen the believer has faith," asserts Kierkegaard, however, "the absurd is not the absurd—faith transforms it. . . . The passion of faith is the only thing capable of mastering the absurd rightly understood" (JP, 1:10). Faith transforms the absurd because faith is an expression of a person's encounter with the infinite. A person understands the forgiveness of sins to the extent that he encounters God's love in the passion of faith, the "love" that, according to Kierkegaard, "hides a multitude of sins" (EUD, 78).

A person who has encountered God's love is thus able to understand both that he is a sinner and that his sins are forgiven. Not only is he able to understand these things; he is able to achieve certainty, in the psychological sense, that this conception of himself and his relation to God corresponds to reality.[26] According to Kierkegaard, such an individual is immediately related to the reality of God's love in this encounter.[27] Since the reality of God's love is presumably that his sins are forgiven, he can be said to appreciate this forgiveness through an insight into the essence of this love made possible by his immediate relation to it. The reality of the forgiveness of sins is fundamentally subjective, in that it can be said to be equivalent to the sinner's appreciation that his sins are forgiven, which appreciation he gains through his encounter with God's infinite love. The forgiveness of sins, according to Kierkegaard, is not something that awaits one in eternity. "The forgiveness of sins," he argues, "means to be helped temporally" (JP, 2:1123) in that it represents liberation from the feeling of guilt that is omnipresent in human consciousness.[28] To the extent, however, that the knowledge in question is subjective, the truth to which it is related cannot be a property of thought but must be instantiated in the existence of the knower. This truth is the knower's *acceptance* that his sins are forgiven.[29]

A person's knowledge that his sins are forgiven is contingent on his having faith. As soon as "the enthusiasm of faith" (CA, 27) disappears, argues Kierkegaard, the lower nature, or "cunning prudence," will assert itself by endeavoring to engage the knower in the dialectic of self-deception in order to "escape the knowledge of sin" (CA, 27). That is, a person can know that his sins are forgiven, in the sense that he has a concept of such forgiveness of whose correspondence to reality he is certain, only while he is in the passion of faith, which is to say, only while he is in contact with God's infinite love. The passion of faith cannot be sustained indefinitely, however, but is something at which a person can only repeatedly arrive.[30]

Faith is what Kierkegaard calls "the risky venture." Before a person has made this venture, he continues, "he can understand it only as madness . . . and when he has taken the risk he is no longer the same [person]" (*Postscript*, 355). It is through this risky venture that a person is "infinitized" (*Postscript*, 355). That is, one first comes into contact with God's infinite love, or first comes to feel "in kinship with God," in faith (*Sickness*, 120n).

The experience of faith thus provides the foundation for Christian knowledge, just as sensory experience provides the foundation for empirical knowledge. It's tempting to conclude that while Christian knowledge may initially be a result of Christian experience, once it has been attained, it determines, for the knower, appropriate Christian behavior such that, from that point on, Christian experience, in terms of right action, is either indistinguishable from Christian knowledge or follows immediately and unproblematically from it. If this were the case, then knowing the good would be indistinguishable from doing the good. But to know the good, according to Kierkegaard, is not necessarily to do it. This is apparent in the following passage from one of Kierkegaard's religious discourses:

> The double-minded person did have a *knowledge of the good* . . . *Alas* contemplation [*Betragtning*] and the moment of contemplation, despite all its clarity, easily conceals an illusion, because its moment has something in common with the counterfeited eternity. There is a foreshortening that is necessary in order

for the contemplation to come about; it must shorten time considerably . . . In this it is something like the work of an artist in drawing a map of a country. The drawing . . . cannot be as large as the country . . . but it also becomes all the easier for the viewer to survey the outlines of that country. And yet if that viewer were suddenly set down in the actuality of that country, where the many, many miles have all their force, he very likely would not be able to recognize the country . . . or as traveler to get his bearings in it. The same thing will also happen to the double-minded person. His knowledge has certainly been an illusion. What was compacted airtight, as it were, in the completeness of contemplation must now be stretched out to its full length. (UDVS, 72)

It's important to appreciate two things here. The person in question is described as having "knowledge of the good." The problem was not an inadequacy in his conception of the good, but instead an inadequacy in his character—that is, he was double-minded. Such an inadequacy in character is not restricted, according to Kierkegaard, to certain people; it is an expression of sin, which is universal. We are all double-minded, according to Kierkegaard, and living as a Christian means striving to purge ourselves of this double-mindedness, or to purify our will.[31]

It's for this reason that Kierkegaard asserts that the life of a Christian only "approaches" the truth. The being of truth, for the Christian, he asserts, "*approaches* [*tilnærmer*] truth in the striving for it" (PC, 205).[32] Only in Christ, according to Kierkegaard, are truth and existence combined in such a way that they are indistinguishable from each other.

Knowledge of the truth of Christianity appears equivalent, according to Kierkegaard, to knowledge that Christianity "is not a doctrine" but instead "a believing and a very particular kind of existing [*Existeren*] corresponding to it" (JP, 2:1880),[33] where this kind of existing is one that takes Christ's life as a model for one's own. But while there is clearly such a thing, according to Kierkegaard, as Christian knowledge in this sense,[34] he argues that Christian truth, or the truth of Christianity, when viewed *merely* as knowledge (i.e., as an idea or concept) abstracted from any existential situation, is untruth.[35] One can see, asserts Kierkegaard, "what a monstrous mistake it is, almost the greatest possible, to didacticize Christianity, and how altered Christianity has become through this continual didacticizing is seen in this, that now all expressions are formed according to the view that truth is cognition [*Erkjendelsen*], knowledge [*Viden*] (now one speaks continually of comprehending, speculating, observing, etc.), whereas in original Christianity all the expressions were formed according to the view that truth is a [way of] being." (PC, 206.)

Christian knowledge is possible as something that follows from Christian experience, and it is reasonable to assume that it was this knowledge to which Kierkegaard referred when he said he could conceive of a specifically Christian epistemology, the development of which, he asserted, could be undertaken only after a person had become a Christian.

But what is the content of Christian knowledge? We've already seen that Christian knowledge, according to Kierkegaard, includes the appreciation of the believer that his sins are forgiven. To the extent that this knowledge is indistinguishable from the appreciation that God is love, the latter too may be understood to be known by the believer in the moment of faith. To these two sorts of knowledge we may now add the knowledge that Christianity itself is neither the doctrine that one's sins are forgiven nor the doctrine that God is love, but instead a way of life. That is, Christianity is the process of a person's striving to bring his existence into conformity with ethical-religious ideality, which is characterized by his belief that the activity itself is pleasing to God and that God does not hold against him his failure to establish perfect conformity.

There may be a great deal more that could be placed under the heading of Christian knowledge according to Kierkegaard. Whatever Christian knowledge comprises, however, it cannot include a knowledge that God came into being in the person of Christ, because all knowledge, according to Kierkegaard, is either of the eternal, which excludes the temporal, or of the historical. No knowledge, he explains in *Crumbs*, can have for its object that the eternal came into existence (*Crumbs*, 131).

There is a reference to "knowledge [*Viden*] of Christ" in *The Sickness Unto Death* (*Sickness*, 113), but the context of the reference makes it clear that it is not a reference to knowledge that Christ was God. That is, this knowledge is later referred to as a representation (*Forestilling*), which exists in the knower to a greater of lesser degree. "[T]he more conception [*Forestilling*] of Christ," asserts Kierkegaard, "the more self" (*Sickness*, 113). That is, the more complete the concept is that one has of what ethical-religious ideality would look like if it were expressed in the life of a particular person,[36] the more self that one has.

Specifically Christian knowledge, like all other knowledge, according to Kierkegaard, is either knowledge of eternal truth, or it is historical knowledge. It does not include knowledge that the eternal became historical. A person's knowledge, for example, that he is a sinner and that his sins are forgiven is historical knowledge. Sin is not a part of a person's eternally established essence, according to Kierkegaard, but was freely appropriated at some point. To the extent that a person was not always a sinner, his sins cannot for all eternity have been forgiven. Both a person's concept of himself as a sinner and his belief that his sins are forgiven concern historical truths. Knowledge that there is a God, on the other hand, is knowledge of an eternal truth.

Kierkegaard refers in his journals to "knowledge of the paradox" where he argues, in a draft of the *Postscript,* for example, that "Christian knowledge is not knowledge of the paradox, but knowledge of it in passion and the knowledge of the wise that it can be known only in passion."[37] If we interpret "paradox" to stand for the idea that one's sins are forgiven, then the meaning of the claim is clear: Knowledge of the paradox is a passionate grasping of the truth that one's sins are forgiven. If, on the other hand, "paradox" refers to the claim that God became man in the person of Christ, then it would appear that what Kierkegaard means is that "objectively there is no truth, for an objective knowledge of the truth, or truths, of Christianity is precisely untruth. To know a declaration of faith by rote is paganism, because Christianity is inwardness" (*Postscript*, 188).

Christian knowledge proper is not "knowledge" of what has historically been referred to as Christian doctrine, or, more specifically, "knowledge" that the proposition that God became man is part of this doctrine. Christian knowledge proper is a grasp of this doctrine in the sense of "the objective uncertainty maintained through appropriation in the most passionate inwardness" (*Postscript*, 171), as well as the wise person's insight that the only way one can properly relate to this "knowledge" is subjectively, in the passion of faith.

Kierkegaard and Orthodox Epistemology

I began this essay with the assertion that Kierkegaard's views on the substance of Christian knowledge placed him squarely within the tradition of the early Christian church. Now that we've examined Kierkegaard's views in some detail, it's time to compare those views with the views of some of the church fathers. It is difficult to determine the extent of Kierkegaard's familiarity with the views of the church fathers. Some study of their thought, as I observed above, was very likely a part of Kierkegaard's theological studies at the University of Copenhagen. There are several references to various church fathers, including Tertullian, Clement of Alexandria, and Irenaeus, in Kierkegaard's works. There are three references to Clement of Alexandria in Kierkegaard's works: one in *Repetition* (op. cit., 76), another in an unpublished polemic against Heiberg (SKS 15:66), and a third in Kierkegaard's journals and papers (SKS 24:259). There is apparently only one reference to Irenaeus in all of Kierkegaard's works, published and unpublished. It is in his journals and papers (SKS 24:269). The presences of references to these two thinkers, scant though they are, at least serve to show that Kierkegaard was familiar with their thought.

We saw in the first section that Kierkegaard's view that knowledge of God, or more correctly, the knowledge that there is a God, agreed with the views of Irenaeus on this issue. Such knowledge is not, however, specifically Christian, so we must see now whether what Kierkegaard considers specifically Christian knowledge agrees in substance with the views of the church fathers.

It's possible, according to Kierkegaard, to know the truth, or to recognize Christ as the truth. God, he observes, did not take on human form "to ridicule human beings. His intention cannot thus be to go through the world in such a way that not a single person ever came to know [*vide*] it. He does indeed want something of himself to be understood [*forstaae*]" (*Crumbs*, 126).

The claim that knowledge of God is possible through an encounter with Christ may seem heretical to those who view Christianity as a religion based on faith. This passage from *Crumbs* is strikingly similar, however, to Irenaeus's claim in *Against the Heresies* that "the Lord did not say that the Father and the Son could not be known at all [μη γινωσκεσθαι] for in that case his coming would have been pointless."[38]

Irenaeus is specifically concerned here with rejecting the claim of the Gnostic Valentinus that the message of the incarnation was God's inaccessibility to human knowledge. "What the Lord really taught," asserts Irenaeus, "is this: no one can know God unless God teaches him; in other words, without God, God cannot be known [ἄνευ Θεοῦ μὴ γινώσκεσθαι τὸν θεόν]. What is more," continues Irenaeus, "it is the Father's will that God be known [αὐτὸ δὲ τὸ γινώσκεσθαι τὸν Θεὸν, θέλημα εἶναι τοῦ Πατρός]."[39]

Man's imperfection, or sin, is, for Irenaeus, the obstacle to his attaining specifically Christian knowledge. "[T]he Word of the Father [i.e., Christ]," asserts Irenaeus, "and the Spirit of God [i.e., faith in Christ], united to the ancient substance of Adam's formation [i.e., man], made man living and perfect capable of knowing the perfect Father."[40] But sinful man is no longer perfect and hence is incapable of knowing God without the intermediacy of Christ. Thus Irenaeus asserts that "no one can know God unless God *teaches* him."

Can "the truth be taught?" asks Kierkegaard in *Crumbs* (88). His answer, of course, is yes—if God *himself* teaches it. In other words, Kierkegaard's claim in *Crumbs* that union with God is necessary in order for specifically Christian knowledge to be possible echoes exactly Irenaeus's claim in *Against the Heresies* that "no one can know God unless God teaches him."[41]

The view that knowledge of God is attained through Christ is also central to the doctrines of Clement of Alexandria. Clement, like Kierkegaard, refers to God as a "teacher."[42] Both Irenaeus and Clement were concerned with opposing the doctrines of the Gnostics. This does not mean, however, as one might be tempted to suppose, that they rejected the possibility of Christian knowledge.

"The most important aspect of Clement's philosophy," writes Salvatore R. C. Lilla in his book *Clement of Alexandria: A Study in Christian Platonism and Gnosticism,* "is represented by the idea of *gnosis*." But he continues, "[T]he idea of *gnosis* is, in Clement's thought, closely connected with that of *pistis* [i.e., faith]."[43] Clement was concerned not merely with discrediting the Gnostics, who, in Lilla's words, "sharply distinguished the *pistis* of the common believers from the higher *gnosis* which, according to them, was a natural gift bestowed as a privilege to only a very few persons, the πνευματικοί,"⁴⁴ but also with defending Christianity against the accusations of Greek philosophers that it represented an *irrational* faith, a faith that offered no higher knowledge of the truth.

Man's aim, according to Clement, "is to know God, to have knowledge of God (γνῶσις τοῦ θεοῦ): 'We call upon man'," writes Clement, "'who was made for the contemplation of heaven, and is in truth a heavenly plant, to come to knowledge of God (*Protr.* 100.3)'."⁴⁵ The foundation of such knowledge, according to Clement, however, is faith-πίστις. "[T]he two cannot be separated: 'Now neither is knowledge without faith, nor faith without knowledge' (ἤδη δὲ οὔτε ἡ γνῶσις ἄνευ πίστεως οὔθ' ἡ πίστις ἄνευ γνώσεως) (*Stromata.* 5.1.3)."⁴⁶ Or as Wilhelm Scherer expresses it, "Ihm steht es von vornherein fest, das sich die Ergebnisse des Gnosis nicht von der Regel des Glaubens entfernen können."⁴⁷

What distinguishes Irenaeus and Clement from the Gnostics is thus not that the latter believed in the possibility of knowledge of God whereas the former did not. What distinguished them was that instead of relegating gnosis to a select few, they emphasized that gnosis, or Christian knowledge, was possible for *everyone* who had *pistis* (i.e., faith). "The reason," writes Henny Fiskå Hägg in *Clement of Alexandria and the Beginnings of Christian Apophaticism*, "that knowledge is not in everyone is simply that not all men have faith (*Strom.* 5.1.); but those who seek Him 'after a true search (κατὰ τὴν ζήτησιν τὴν ἀληθῆ) . . . shall be filled with the gift that comes from God, that is, true knowledge (τῆς γνώσεως)' (*Strom.* 5.12.2)."⁴⁸

According to Kierkegaard, again, a person meets Christ in the moment of faith. This meeting is what is meant by "knowledge" of Christ; hence *acquaintance* knowledge of Christ precedes genuine *Christian* knowledge in the propositional sense. This position is reflected in the view of Clement of Alexandria that an "august knowledge of the truth" may be built "on the foundation of faith" (*Strom.* V, Chapter 1).⁴⁹ The view that acquaintance with Christ is an experience that is related to the intellect in a manner analogous to the way sensory experience is related to the intellect is not original to Kierkegaard, as one might suppose. It was part of the earliest Christian orthodoxy in that it agrees in substance with Clement's view of the relation between Christian experience and Christian knowledge.

But what does it mean to be acquainted with Christ? God in the person of Christ is, to use Kierkegaard's own expression, "indistinguishable" [*ikke til at skjelne*] from other people (*Crumbs*, 126). He cannot be known immediately,⁵⁰ but he can be "seen" only in the metaphorical sense, which is to say, only with "the eyes of faith" (*Crumbs*, 134).

According to Arkadi Choufrine in *Gnosis, Theophany, and Theosis,* this is also Clement's position.⁵¹ That is, Clement refers to what he calls "the visual faculty of the soul" (*Strom.* V, Chapter 1). It is with this faculty, or, as Clement goes on to explain, with the love that "allies" the faithful through the agency of "divine love to God in the person of Christ," that we are able to "see" (*Strom.* V, Chapter 1) that Christ is the truth.

Knowledge of the truth, according to Kierkegaard again, *follows* from being the truth, which is to say that it follows from the belief that God is love, which belief is itself an expression of love, or of gratitude toward God for the revelation that one's sins are forgiven. This is also Clement's position, according to Choufrine. "The starting point for *Gnosis*," Choufrine explains, "is *gnosis*: a direct and sudden experience of redemption, which has been neither felt as needed, nor contemplated as a goal, but is a realization of an absolutely unknown possibility."[52]

Knowledge of the truth, for both Clement and Kierkegaard, is a product of faith, or of a faithful life. Hence Hägg argues that for Clement, "a gnostic is a person whose gnosis is demonstrated through his activities: 'The gnostic . . . being on the one hand not without a knowledge of God (or rather being known by him) and on the other hand showing the effects thereof . . . For works (τὰ ἔργα) follow knowledge as the shadow the body' (*Strom.* 7.82)."[53]

Knowledge is *distinguished* from the truth itself, or from a way of being. To argue, however, that knowledge is distinguishable from the activity that makes it possible does not mean that it may be separated from this activity. Specifically Christian knowledge, like all of what Kierkegaard refers to as "subjective knowledge,"[54] is essentially prescriptive. It is impossible to separate it from a certain way of life. The same, again, is true for Clement. According to Hägg, gnosis, for Clement, "may be seen as a twofold thing: it is on the one hand, a subject matter and, on the other, a way or process. . . . [Hence] [t]o have knowledge of God is to be part of a *process*, leading from faith via gnosis to the love of God. Faith and love represent the beginning and the end of this *process*."[55] Or as Kierkegaard expresses it, "The being of truth is not the *direct* redoubling of being in relation to thinking, which gives only thought-being . . . [I]t is the redoubling of truth within yourself, within me, within him, so that your life, my life, his life . . . is approximately [*Tilnærmelsesvis*] the being of truth in the striving for it" (PC, 205).

Neither Kierkegaard nor the church fathers were epistemologists. This does not, however, lessen the importance of the role that knowledge plays in their thought. Both religious knowledge in general and Christian knowledge in particular are essential for all these figures for achieving what one could call authentic Christian existence. Kierkegaard never explicitly developed a Christian epistemology, because although knowledge figures prominently in his works, it is not knowledge, even of the Christian sort, that was his primary interest. He argues, for example, that knowledge exists in a "spurious eternity of the imagination," and hence that the knower develops "double-mindedness" if knowledge is not "slowly and honestly earned by the will's purity" (UDVS, 74).[56] Christianity, according to Kierkegaard, is essentially oriented toward the will rather than toward knowledge.[57] It is thus the will, or human psychology, that primarily interests him. Willing, according to Kierkegaard, is a more basic activity than knowing, and this is part of the reason it is so significant with respect to issues in epistemology.[58]

Kierkegaard is concerned with the difficulties involved in being a Christian, or in trying to live a Christian life. "Just when one has understood the truth best," he observes, "the old suddenly crops up again. The infinite, the eternal, hence the true, is so alien to the natural man that with him it is as with the dog, which can indeed learn to walk upright for a moment but yet continually wants to walk on all fours" (WL, 244).

There is indeed Christian knowledge according to Kierkegaard, in the sense that it is possible to have an intellectual grasp of the "truths" of Christianity. But possession of this "knowledge" is not sufficient to make a person a Christian. "If the rights of knowledge are to be given their fair due," he argues in keeping with Clement's emphasis on "activities," "we must venture out into life, out upon the ocean, and scream in the hope that God will hear . . . only then does knowledge acquire its *official* registration" (JP, 2:2279). "Here in the world of knowledge," he observes, "there rests upon the human being a curse (blessing) which bids him eat his bread in the sweat of his brow" (JP, 2:2274).[59]

A "completely human life," according to Kierkegaard, is not merely one of knowledge, because the medium of knowledge is thought, or ideality, whereas a human being is an *interesse* between thought and being, or between ideality and reality. A completely human life consists of action as well as thought, and to be really complete, the action in question should represent the efforts of the individual to bring the actuality of his existence into conformity with ethical ideality.

To meet Christ, according to Kierkegaard, in the passion of faith, is to come to know that God is love, that love is a living, dynamic force, not a mere fact, and that Christian truth is a way of living rather than a set of propositions. To meet Christ in the moment of faith is to come into contact with the reality of God's love. The knower is said to be certain that the resultant idea that "God is love" corresponds to reality because he has "the certainty, which can be had only in infinitude" (*Postscript*, 68); that is, "the certainty of faith" (*Postscript*, 48). The difficulty, however, is that faith is not something a person can attain once and for all. The contact established, through faith, with God's infinite love cannot be indefinitely sustained. This infinitude, according to Kierkegaard, is something in which a person cannot, so long as he exists, rest, but to which he can only repeatedly arrive.[60]

Conclusion

I began this paper with the assertion that knowledge was central to Kierkegaard's conception of "the good life" for the Christian and that, in this respect, it was essentially in continuity with the thought of some of the earliest of the early church fathers: Irenaeus and Clement of Alexandria. There are relatively few references to either Irenaeus or Clement in Kierkegaard's works, so while it is clear that he had at least a passing familiarity with these thinkers, it is impossible to establish with certainty whether Kierkegaard was deliberately attempting to develop an epistemology that was consistent with their thought. There cannot be any question, however, that it is. Both Irenaeus and Clement emphasize not merely that knowledge can come from faith in Christ, but also that this knowledge cannot be separated from a life that can be said to be an expression of Christian truth. This is "the good life" for the Christian: a life that is an expression of Christian truth. Kierkegaard's position on the nature of Christian knowledge and its role in the life of the Christian places him firmly in the tradition of orthodox epistemology.

M. G. PIETY is Professor of Philosophy at Drexel University. She is author of *Ways of Knowing: Kierkegaard's Pluralist Epistemology* and the translator of Kierkegaard's *Repetition and Philosophical Crumbs*.

Notes

1. I'd like to thank Joseph Gulka of the Advanced Judaic Studies Library at the University of Pennsylvania for his help in locating the relevant passages in the confusing *Sources Chrétiennes* (the references to which in Balthasar's translation of Irenaeus's *Against the Heresies* include volume but not tome numbers). I'd also like to thank my research assistant, Douglas Stafford. Doug's help has been invaluable in many ways. Finally, I would like to thank Brian J. Foley, whose feedback on earlier versions of this essay was enormously helpful and who proofread the present version, as he does all my essays.

2. See, for example, PC, 206.

3. See also Arild Christensen, *Efterskriftens Opgør med Martensen* (the confrontation with Martensen in the *Postscript*), *Kierkegaardiana* 4 (1962): 45–62, 59.

4. See, for example, *Sickness*, 13; *Crumbs*, 153.

5. Irenaeus, *The Scandal of the Incarnation: Irenaeus Against the Heresies*, selected and Introduced by Hans Urs von Balthasar, trans. John Sayward (San Francisco: Ignatius Press, 1990), p. 32, emphasis added.

6. Irenaeus, *Against the Heresies*, p. 41.

7. Irenaeus, *Against the Heresies*, p. 33.

8. See, for example, *Postscript*, 166.

9. See *Crumbs*, 138–139 and 167–168.

10. See, for example, EUD, 325–326; and *Crumbs*, 136–137.

11. The Greek is γνώσεται.

12. I have altered the translation here slightly because the Hongs do not take account of the substitution of *"erfarer"* for *"kiende."* The Greek term in question is *gnosetai*, which is related to the noun *gnosis*. There is also another passage in Kierkegaard's journals and papers where Kierkegaard translates the Greek expression for "know" in the inscription over the oracle at Delphi, *gnothi seauton*, as *"kjende,"* which supports the view that Kierkegaard considered *gnosis* to be knowledge of the substantive, or acquaintance, sort.

13. I have altered the Hongs' translation of *"Bevidsthed"* from "knowledge" to "consciousness" because the former is not an acceptable translation of *"Bevidsthed"* (see *A Danish-English Dictionary*, eds. James Stephen Ferrall and Thorleifr Gudmundson Repp (Copenhagen: Gyldendal, 1845), *Dansk Ordbog, Anden forøgede og forbedrede Udgave*, ed. Christian Molbech (Copenhagen: Gyldendal, 1859), and *Dansk-Engelsk Ordbog, Anden reviderede of udvidede udgave*, eds. Hermann Vinterberg and C.A. Bodelsen (Copenhagen: Gyldendal, 1966)).

14. Contra Steven N. Emmanuel, "Kierkegaard on Faith and Knowledge," *Kierkegaardiana* 15 (1991): 136–146, 139.

15. See, for example, *Crumbs*, 92–93.

16. See, for example *Postscript*, 440.

17. See, for example, *Postscript*, 445.

18. See EUD, 303; *Postscript*, 325, 355; and JP, 3:3109.

19. Thus Kierkegaard asserts that "truth is a snare: you cannot get it without being caught yourself; you cannot get the truth by catching it yourself but only by its catching you" (JP, 4:4886.

20. See JP, 3:3085. The references to "paradox" in the pseudonymous works are too numerous to list. Most occur, however, in the *Crumbs* and the *Postscript*.

21. See, for example, *Postscript*, 49, 253.

22. See *Crumbs*, 124.

23. Thus David Wisdo argues that "Kierkegaard's analysis of faith appeals to *non-epistemic* factors; namely Grace and will" ("Kierkegaard on the Limits of Christian Epistemology," *International Journal for Philosophy of Religion* 29, no. 2 (1991): 97–112, 100).

24. See *Postscript*, 189.

25. See also *Postscript*, 188.

26. I am thus taking exception to Benjamin Daise's claim that "truth," in the context of the *Crumbs*, "does not have any epistemological significance" ("The Will to Truth in Kierkegaard's *Philosophical Fragments*," *Philosophy of Religion* 31 (1992): 1–12, 2).

27. See Martin Slotty's observation that, according to Kierkegaard, "Christ is the only past actuality that can continue to be present to anyone whatever" (*Die Erkenntnislehre S. A. Kierkegaards* [The epistemology of S. A. Kierkegaard], diss., Friedrich-Alexanders-Universität [1915], p. 70); and also Anton Hügli's observation that "in belief in Christ, the individual has the eternal in time, present in every moment" (*Die Erkenntnis der Subjektivität und die Objektivität des Erkennens bei Søren Kierkegaard* [Knowledge of subjectivity and the objectivity of knowing in Søren Kierkegaard] [Basel, Switzerland: Editio Academica, 1973], p.223).

28. See JP, 2:2249. Thus Alastair Hannay argues that, according to Kierkegaard, the truth of Christianity is "appropriated in feeling" rather than in thought (*Kierkegaard* [London: Routledge & Kegan Paul, 1982], p. 173).

29. Thus Hügli argues, "I could no more receive certainty concerning my [true] determination without the free act of belief, than I could receive certainty that I could swim without risking going into the water" (*Erkenntnis*, p. 132).

30. See, for example, *Postscript*, 48, 68–69.

31. This is the theme of Kierkegaard's discourse entitled "Purity of Heart" (UDVS, 5–155).

32. Emphasis added. I have altered the Hongs' translation slightly by replacing their "approximately" with "approaches," because this is a better translation of *"Tilnæremer"* than is "approximate."

33. See Wisdo, "Kierkegaard on the Limits of Christian Epistemology, p. 97.

34. See JP, 1:653; and Hügli, *Erkenntnis*, p. 169.

35. See PC, 206.

36. That is, Christ's life, according to Kierkegaard, is essentially eternal truth that has come to be in time. It is because Christ's life is essentially eternal truth, however, that everyone can be contemporary with it, according to Kierkegaard (see PC, 64).

37. The wording here is from volume II, page 50 of the Hongs' translation of the *Postscript*. It seems likely that the ambiguity of the reference to "knowledge of the paradox" is the reason Kierkegaard omitted this reference from the final version of the *Postscript*.

38. Irenaeus, *Against the Heresies*, p. 45.

39. Irenaeus, *Against the Heresies*, p. 45.

40. Irenaeus, *Against the Heresies*, p. 57.

41. The similarity in language between certain parts of *Crumbs* and passages from Irenaeus's *Against the Heresies* supports, I believe, the translation of *læres* at the beginning of chapter 1 in *Crumbs* as "be taught" (see *Crumbs*, 88 and the note to p. 88 on p. 183).

42. See *Strom.* iv 162. 5 (ii. 320. 19–20), v. I. 3 (ii. 326. 10–11), v. I. (ii. 326. 13), vi. 122 I (ii. 493. 6–7), vi. 123. I (ii. 493. 30–31). All direct quotations to the *Stromata* cited here can be found at *New Advent*, available online at http://www.newadvent.org/fathers/0210.htm, accessed March 30, 2017. The original translation from which this online resource is drawn is Ante-Nicene Fathers, *Vol. 2*, trans. William Wilson, eds. Alexander Roberts, James Donaldson, and A. Cleveland Coxe. (Buffalo, NY: Christian Literature Publishing Co., 1885). Revised and edited for *New Advent* by Kevin Knight.

43. Salvatore R. C. Lilla, *Clement of Alexandria: A Study in Christian Platonism and Gnosticism* (Oxford: Oxford University Press, 1971), p. 119.

44. Lilla, *Clement of Alexandria*, pp. 118–119; see also *Strom.* Ii. 10. 2 (ii. 118. 13–17).

45. Henny Fiskå Hägg, *Clement of Alexandria and the Beginnings of Christian Apophaticism* (Oxford: Oxford University Press, 2006), p. 151.

46. Hägg, *Clement of Alexandria*, p. 151. All of Hägg's references to the *Stromata* are from: Clemens Alexandrinus, vol. ii: *Stromata I-VI*, ed. Otto Stählin, GCS 15 (Leipzig: Hinrichs, 1906), and Clemens Alexandrinus, vol. iii: *Stromata VII, VIII, Excerpta ex Theodoto, Eclogae propheticae, Quis dives salvetur, Fragmente*, ed. Otto Stählin, GCS 17 (Leipzig: Hinrichs, 1906).

47. Wilhelm Scherer, *Klemens von Alexandrien und seine Erkenntnisprinzipien* (München, 1907), p. 70.

48. Hägg, *Clement of Alexandria*, p. 152.

49. See, *New Advent*, available online at http://www.newadvent.org/fathers/0210.htm - accessed March 30, 2017.

50. See *Crumbs*, 132.

51. See Akadi Choufrine, *Gnosis, Theophany, Theosis: Studies in Clement of Alexandria's Appropriation of His Background* (New York: Peter Lang, 2002), pp. 113 and 116.

52. Choufrine, *Gnosis, Theophany, Theosis*, p. 36.

53. Hägg, *Clement of Alexandria*, p. 152. It is important to appreciate that "gnostic," in this context, refers to a person who has genuine knowledge of God, not to a member of the heretical sect against which, Irenaeus, for example, polemicized.

54. See, for example, *Postscript*, 169.

55. Hägg, *Clement of Alexandria*, p. 151.

56. I have given the page reference here to the Hongs' translation because it is the most readily available. The wording I've used here, however, is from Douglas V. Steere's earlier translation. I've chosen this wording because I believe it is generally superior to the Hongs'. See PH, 117.

57. See JP, 2:1202; JP 4:4953; JP, 6:6966; and Hügli, *Erkenntnis*, p. 161 and p. 210.

58. Knowledge is always the result of willing. A person has to will to know even what he is inherently capable of knowing without assistance. This is true not merely with respect to

scholarly and scientific knowledge, but also with respect to knowledge of immanent metaphysical truths, although it is less apparent with respect to the latter.

59. Compare this with the assertion of Kierkegaard's pseudonym Johannes *de silentio* in *Fear and Trembling* that "there is a knowledge that presumptuously wants to introduce into the world of spirit the same law of indifference under which the external world sighs. It believes that it is enough to know what is great—no other work is needed. But for this reason it does not get nourishment [*Brød*]; it perishes of hunger while everything changes to Gold" (FT, 27–28).

60. See *Postscript*, 68.

12 Thunderstruck: Divine Irony in Kierkegaard's Job

Grant Julin

Of the major religious figures addressed in Kierkegaard's works, Job has received little attention in comparison with Abraham, Paul, and Christ. Yet there is good reason to reconsider Kierkegaard's treatment of Job, whom he describes as "a teacher and guide for all humankind" (EUD, 109). What does Kierkegaard mean by this, and in what ways does Job embody Kierkegaardian philosophy? This chapter draws attention to the significance of Job as an exemplar of Kierkegaardian philosophy through a comparative analysis of *Repetition* (1843) and *Eighteen Upbuilding Discourses, The Lord Took Away* (1843). Contra conventional interpretations that read the Book of Job as a Judeo-Christian theodicy, Kierkegaard's Job is presented as an examination into the moral psychology of human suffering. For Kierkegaard, the true significance of Job's trial is found in its embattled protagonist who loses and then regains himself in a violent psychic rupture. This chapter examines Job's rupture and the ironic consciousness that helps him persist through his trial.

Job: The Prototype of Suffering

In his self-penned *Upbuilding Discourse* from 1843 "The Lord Gave, and the Lord Took Away," Kierkegaard remarks that Job is a great teacher of humankind. However, Job for Kierkegaard is not a teacher in the sense of having a specific truth or knowledge that can be passed down to others. Instead, Job "left humankind only himself as a prototype, his life a guide for everyone." Like Socrates, Job's greatness is not for what he said *but for what he did* (EUD, 109). Job's wisdom *is* his individual concrete existence—a model and guide that has "accompanied" all generations battling "the oppression of suffering" (EUD, 110). Job is a guide that "comforts," "secures," and "encourages." This comfort, Kierkegaard tells us, is not a security that guarantees victory over one's particular trial, but one that merely asserts "that the horror has been suffered, the horror has been experienced, the battle of despair has been fought" (EUD, 110).

Job, for Kierkegaard, is not merely a guide; he is a "prototype" (EUD, 109). In the upbuilding discourse, Kierkegaard characterizes Job as an "unfailing spokesman for the suffering," "the oppressed," and "the down-trodden" and a guide for all "those who are being tried" (EUD, 109). Kierkegaard has good reason to consider Job, above all other Judeo-Christian exemplars, as the archetype of human suffering, for no other pious figure suffers so unjustly at the hand of Yahweh. The old man from Uz, we are told, was the most pious of Yahweh's followers: an "upright," "blameless," and "god-fearing" man who "set his face against wrongdoing" (Job 1:1).[1] Suggesting to Yahweh that Job is only pious because he has lived a prosperous life, ha-Satan proposes a test: Take away Job's family and wealth "and see if he will not curse you to your face" (Job 1:11). Yahweh agrees to the test; he obliterates Job's wealth and murders his children. Though upset, pious Job rips his cloak, shaves his head, and falls to the ground in prayer:

> Naked I came from the womb,
> naked I shall return whence I came.
> The Lord gives and the Lord takes away;
> blessed by the name of the Lord. (Job 1:21)

When Job does not curse Yahweh, ha-Satan encourages him to afflict Job's health, at which point Yahweh allows him to attack Job's body, "only sparing his life" (Job 2:6). Inflicted with painful, festering sores, Job persists and does not curse Yahweh. Though steadfast in this faith, Job's psyche is weakened. When Job's three friends arrive to console him, they "did not recognize him." As Job lay on the ground suffering silently for seven days and seven nights, "none of them spoke a word to him, for they saw that his suffering was very great" (Job 2:13). It is this spiritually wounded Job that interests Kierkegaard the most—the Job whose sickened body and shattered psyche thrashes on the ground before an absent God.

Kierkegaard makes clear that, unlike Christ, Job's suffering was not sacrificial. Where the God of the New Testament sacrificed his son to atone for the sins of humankind, Job's suffering was not that he "suffered once and for all what would never be suffered again" (EUD, 110). Instead, Kierkegaard remarks that Job's suffering was "for his own rescue" (EUD, 110). What did Job, the most pious of humans, need to be rescued from? Why does Kierkegaard seem to suggest that Job's trial was necessary for his own well-being? Did Job need to undergo a major trial himself before becoming the prototype of human suffering?

The Courage of a Roaring Lion

In *Repetition* (1843),[2] written by the pseudonymous Constantin Constantius, Kierkegaard's paean to Job is voiced through the Young Man, who, in his letters to Constantin, depicts Job as the "poetic" embodiment of human suffering, remarking that "nowhere has the passion of pain found such expression" (R 2009, 63–64). For the Young Man, Job's greatness is not merely that he suffered such a trial, but also that he was capable of persisting through such adversity. The Young Man is amazed with Job's integrity and the fact that he "sticks to his position" (R 2009, 66). Job is all too aware that he does not deserve his suffering and that he is in the right, even though "all of existence seems to refute him" (R 2009, 65). After the second "thunder strike," when Job's wife remarks, "Do you still persist in your integrity? Curse God and die" (Job 2:9), Job maintains his (and God's) innocence (Job 2:10). When his three friends Eliphaz, Bildad, and Zophar arrive to comfort him, their conclusion is clear: "that he should see that he is being punished" (R 2009, 67). Yet Job's "cries of pain" grow "louder and louder in proportion to his friends' protests" (R 2009, 67) as he maintains his innocence and challenges his friends and their "false poultices."

Of importance for the Young Man is that Job's integrity is not that of an obstinate, self-righteous zealot. Though steadfast in his position, Job's own conscience is "tempted" by his friends and their solution to the problem—*that he should repent*. Despite this temptation, Job possesses the power to reject their account of his trial and "frighten" and "challenge" his own self (R 2009, 66). Consequently, Job's integrity withstands the challenges of not only his wife and his friends, *but even more importantly, himself*: "If he lacked the strength or ingenuity to try his conscience and frighten his soul, lacked the imagination to become afraid for himself, for the guilt and transgressions that might hide in the innermost reaches of his self, then his friends help him with their clear allusions, their offensive acusations, which, like envious divining-rods, are supposed to be able to call forth what lies most deeply hidden" (R 2009, 66). Had Job merely resigned himself to the fact his friends were right, he would have bypassed the paradox at the heart of his ordeal. Instead, Job takes the absurdity of his ordeal head-on and fights it out alone. For the Young Man, this is Job's true significance: "that the disputes at the boundaries of faith are fought out in him, that this tremendous insurrection of passion's desire and combative force is presented here" (R 2009, 67).

The Young Man associates Job's integrity with a "superhuman soul strength"—a courage like no other. Job has the courage to stand up not only to his spouse and friends, but also to "the highest tribunal as unafraid as a roaring lion" (R 2009, 59) and to go to "battle" and "quarrel with God" (R 2009, 58). Though Job does not curse God's name, he is unafraid to express his grievances, which, initially indirect[3] and to himself,[4] increase in directness and tone the longer they go unanswered.[5] The Young Man praises Job for his courage to complain to God in a day and age when many are so cavalier in their faith: "I need you, a man who knows how to complain loudly, so that it echoes in heaven, where God consults with Satan concerning His plans for a person" (R 2009, 59). Lamenting that people have stopped complaining to God, the Young Man himself cries out, "Does one no longer dare to complain to God? Has the fear of God, or merely fear and cowardice in general, become greater?" (R 2009, 58–59). For Kierkegaard, Job's integrity represents a courage that transcends human nature and raises himself above humanity.

Ironic Elasticity

What is the nature of the "soul-strength," this "courage," this "integrity" that allows Job to persist through his ordeal? In both *Repetition* and "The Lord Gave," Kierkegaard argues that Job's strength is a courage based in a certain type of consciousness; that is, a consciousness capable of holding together two seemingly irreconcilable ideas—*that both he and God are right*. "He claims that he and God are on good terms, that he knows that he is innocent and pure in his innermost heart where, in addition, he knows this with God, and yet all of existence seems to refute him" (R 2009, 65). The "secret," "the vital force," the core of the Book of Job is that Job knew he was in the right (R 2009, 65), a firm fact of the Job narrative corroborated by both its author[6] and Yahweh.[7] At the same time, Job and the reader are confronted with the troublesome fact that it was God that was the cause of Job's suffering.[8] Job "traced everything back to God" (R 2009, 121), and he knew this right away (EUD, 121). To make matters worse, not only did God consent to ha-Satan's plan, but the first wave of sufferings were brought about by God's hand alone.[9] Kierkegaard knew all too well that it was God's "thunder" (R 2009, 59) that caused the murder of his children and the obliteration of all of his material possessions. Yet how can Job maintain that both he and God are innocent while simultaneously knowing that God willfully brings about Job's suffering so unjustly?[10] It is on this question—and not issues regarding God's justice—that Kierkegaard's analysis of the text is centered. For Kierkegaard, Job's consciousness of this antinomy is the basis of the fortitude underlying his tremendous integrity—a consciousness that allows him to persist through the absurdity of his trial *in spite of its inherent paradox*.

The idea of paradox is essential to Kierkegaard's understanding of faith in his *Fear and Trembling* (1843), where we are told that Abraham is a "knight of faith" because of his ability to resign himself to the loss of Isaac while simultaneously maintaining belief in his son's return through the grace of God. Like Job, Abraham persists in the face of paradox (FT 1993, 48). However, unlike Abraham, we are told in *Repetition* that Job *is not* a "hero of faith" (R 2009, 67, 68) and does not comfort as such. Although Job is ultimately rewarded twofold at the end of his trial, he neither hopes for nor expects this.[11] After the second thunderstorm, his skin afflicted with painful, burning sores, it is clear that Job, cursing his life and calling for his death,[12] has lost all hope (R 2009, 69). In addition, the entire point of "The Lord Gave" is based on the fact that Job expects nothing from God. Even though he was eventually rewarded, Job is fully aware that God is capable of taking everything away again, and to suggest that Job, the most pious of humans, would find resolve in the mere return of material possessions seems unlikely. Finally, Job's faith at the apex of his suffering reflects a complete lack of confidence in God's benevolence, justice, and intelligence. Job's faith is important, but Johannes *de silentio*, reminds us in *Fear and Trembling* that Abraham's "act of resignation does not require faith, but to get the least little bit more than my eternal consciousness requires faith, for this is the paradox" (FT, 42). Hence, Job's consciousness seems more foundational than the paradox of faith, for he seems to understand that not only God, *but all of existence*, is abounding with paradox. As I propose, this deeper paradoxical consciousness for Kierkegaard is based not in faith but in *irony*.

Kierkegaard and Irony

Kierkegaard's indirect method of writing and his pseudonymous authorship were spurred by his fascination with irony, which he favored as a tool because of its duplicitous powers. Through irony one can say one thing while meaning another, and the pseudonymous authorship, which allowed Kierkegaard to entertain views that were not his own, functions in this manner. Kierkegaard's use of irony as a literary device was heavily influenced by the philosopher he considered a master ironist, Socrates. In *The Concept of Irony with Continual Reference to Socrates* (1841), Kierkegaard attributes the origin of irony to Socrates.

Much of the first part of the *Concept of Irony* is devoted to his analysis of Socratic irony, which Kierkegaard depicts as being simultaneously "constructive" and "destructive." Generally speaking, the negative component of Socratic irony pertains to the methodology of elenchus, which stimulates self-knowledge by means of rejecting conventional norms and "truths." Socrates was charged with corrupting the youth and not believing in the gods of Athens—charges that depict Socrates as a dissident and a blasphemer. Irony for Kierkegaard is subversive, having the power to negate "the phenomenal, conventional, socially determined world of actuality (which is usually the socially accepted world of overt behavior and ordinary language use)" and "the views of public common sense."[13] Kierkegaard argues that Socratic irony is a negation of all absolutes, "a corrosive cutting away of pretension, comfortable certainty, and what might be called sophistic extremism (e.g., in the cases of Thrasymachus and Callicles)."[14]

This rejection leads to the constructive component of Socratic irony for Kierkegaard—the self-knowledge or consciousness instigated by the maieutic. However destructive, Socratic irony has the power to facilitate self-knowledge through the individual's break from conventional norms and commonly accepted beliefs. For Kierkegaard, the break provides an opportunity for the individual to gain concrete existence through examining oneself as a singular existing being apart from the universal. As such, irony is essential to the development of self, which is why Kierkegaard remarks, "Irony is a qualification of subjectivity" (CI, 262). Consequently, irony is not merely a literary device for Kierkegaard; it is a type of consciousness required for self-knowledge and authentic subjective existence.

Even though Kierkegaard alludes to a constructive component of elenchus, he simultaneously doubts whether Socratic irony truly offers anything constructive in place of the destruction it causes. Socratic irony is negative for Kierkegaard, in that Socrates maintains his ignorance while simultaneously offering no solution for the problems he poses. "It is negativity, because it only negates; it is infinite, because it does not negate this or that phenomenon; it is absolute, because that by virtue of which it negates is a higher something that still is not" (CI, 261). Although the negative ironist is liberated from the tyranny of objective norms and hence not bound by the ideas of others (CI, 228), in lacking a position, the negative ironist is incapable of making concerted decisions and hence rendered inert: "In irony, the subject is negatively free, since the actuality that is supposed to give the subject content is not there. He is free from the constraint in which the given actuality holds the subject, but he is negatively free and as such is suspended, because there is nothing that holds him" (CI, 262).

Unless Socratic irony is accompanied with convictions upon which to base one's actions, the Socratic ironist will be "suspended" and unable to act. As Söderquist remarks, Socrates's lack of specificity "leaves Socrates and his disciples in an existentially difficult position: his irony deprives them of the comfort of immediate ethical guidelines and goals—and he stops right there, leaving them all directionless."[15] Hence, Kierkegaard argues that the Socratic ironist is "negatively free"; though conscious of his existential freedom, he lacks direction required for action.

Controlled Irony

In the final pages of *The Concept of Irony*, under a section entitled "Irony as Controlled Element, the Truth of Irony," Kierkegaard sketches out for the reader what he conceives to be a proper philosophical understanding of irony. In contrast to the rudderless Socratic ironist, Kierkegaard points the reader to a "controlled" or "mastered" irony.

> As soon as irony is controlled, it makes a movement opposite to that in which uncontrolled irony declares its life. Irony limits, finitizes, and circumscribes and thereby yields truth, actuality, content; it disciplines and punishes and thereby yields balance and consistency. Irony is a disciplinarian feared only

by those who do not know it but loved by those who do. Anyone who does not understand irony at all, who has no ear for its whispering, lacks eo ipso what could be called the absolute beginning of personal life; he lacks what momentarily is indispensable for personal life; he lacks the bath of regeneration and rejuvenation, irony's baptism of purification that rescues the soul from having its life in the finitude even though it is living energetically and robustly in it. He does not know the refreshment and strengthening that come with undressing when the air gets too hot and heavy and diving into the sea of irony, not in order to stay there, of course, but in order to come out healthy, happy, and buoyant and to dress again. (CI, 327)

Though Kierkegaard warns us of the destructive and corrosive power of the Socratic ironist, he considers controlled irony a requisite for "the absolute beginning of personal life" (CI, 326). In contrast to the stagnation and aimlessness of negative irony, Kierkegaard's positive irony is a type of strength and even courage[16] that helps one not merely to persist, but also to become refreshed and strengthened in one's trials, emerging "healthy, happy, and buoyant and to dress again" (CI, 327).

Positive Irony

Kierkegaard's most complete account of irony sees a reassessment of his early work through Johannes Climacus in the *Concluding Unscientific Postscript* (1846), which questions the original account of Socrates in *Concept of Irony* (CUP, 503). Climacus's conclusion suggests that there is indeed a positive component to the Socratic ironist. Where the Socrates of *Concept of Irony* never fully transcended the aesthetic—that is, remaining suspended between the aesthetic and the ethical—the later Kierkegaard revises his account of the Socratic ironist, suggesting that Socrates is an "ironist who is really [an] ethicist who uses irony as his incognito."

> The irony emerges by continually joining the particulars of the finite with the ethical infinite requirement and allowing the contradiction to come into existence. The one who can do it with proficiency and not let himself be caught in any relativity, in which his proficiency becomes diffident, must have made a movement of infinity, and to that extent it is possible he is an ethicist. . . . He is an ethicist only be relating himself within himself to the absolute requirement. Such an ethicist uses irony as his incognito. In this sense Socrates was an ethicist, but, please note, bordering on the religious. (CUP, 502–503)

In contrast to the one-sided reading of Socrates as a negative ironist who is suspended in the immediacy of the aesthetic, the later Kierkegaard makes the case that Socrates is indeed an ethicist. That Kierkegaard upgrades Socrates from an aesthetic figure to an ethical one is no small matter, for the "leap" from the aesthetic into the ethical marks the beginning of selfhood in Kierkegaard's philosophy. Because the aesthete neglects the "infinite" component of human existence and remains in the immediacy of the aesthetic (i.e., the finite), he will have no identity, given the fact that he is relegated to living from moment to moment and lacks a persisting individual existence. The ethicist, on the other hand, is capable of "continually joining the particulars of the finite with the ethical infinite requirement and allowing the contradiction to come into existence" (CUP, 502). Kierkegaard is arguing that the ethicist gains an identity through relating to the absolute, which he does by "relating himself within himself to the absolute requirement." Kierkegaard feels that one carves out an identity for one's self in the conflict between the infinite and finitude, *but this requires irony*. In an 1845 journal simply entitled "Definition of Irony," Kierkegaard affirms this point: "Irony is the unity of ethical passion, which in inwardness ethically accentuates one's own I, and cultivation, which in outwardness (in associating with human Beings) infinitude abstracts from one's own I. The result of the latter is that no one notices the former—that is where the art of the matter resides, and this is what makes possible the true infinitization of the former" (JN 2:223).

Kierkegaard's irony is related to the ethical because its paradoxical nature allows for a moment when the I and the infinite collide in a moment of unity, when the infinite is abstracted in one's character. The aesthetic worldview is incapable of persisting through the paradoxes of existence because it has yet to understand the conflict underlying becoming ethical and the general paradox of existence. Until one has truly embraced and understood this conflict, she cannot transition into the ethical. In short, the ability to understand paradox for Kierkegaard marks a qualitative shift from the purely aesthetic to the aesthetic-ethical worldview, which for Kierkegaard marks the beginning of selfhood. It is for this reason that Kierkegaard remarks in the postscript, "Irony is the *confinium* between esthetic and the ethical" (CUP, 501–502).

Ethical consciousness requires the development of an ironic mood or "formation"—an acceptance of the absurdity of the existence; that is, an "ironic elasticity" that is necessary for the preservation and enduring of the self through the existential struggle that is subjective becoming. For Kierkegaard, such an irony is to be acquired through the negation of the objective world and made manifest in the passion and enthusiasm to continue to press forward in life through one's trials and tribulations, despite the absurdity of the human condition. "The ethicist who uses irony as his incognito has what is, in Climacus' schema, a more complete picture: he is aware of, and is continually appropriating, the ethical's demand. This realization of the ethical's demand is his 'way out'."[17] Unlike the absolute infinite irony, positive irony for Kierkegaard provides a stability that the negative ironist lacks.

Although Kierkegaard had not yet fully developed his notion of positive irony in his early authorship, his comments in the *Postscript* and in his *Journals* help to clarify his early remarks on irony, which will be beneficial for our analysis of Kierkegaard's Job. Positive irony, for Kierkegaard, is consciousness that can free one from the inertia of negative irony and provide "a way out" for the individual who is striving through the paradox or antinomy of the paradox of existence.

Job's Irony

The Book of Job is built around the theme of paradox, and its poet author, like Kierkegaard, plays with irony's duplicitous powers.[18] Job's complaints in the second part are saturated in irony, which may be his only means of defense.[19] Kierkegaard likewise saw the irony in the Book of Job and the complete paradox of Job's trial. Although references to *The Concept of Irony* are scant in his account of Job, a close reading of both *Repetition* and *Eighteen Upbuilding Discourses* reveal Kierkegaard's ironic approach to Job's trial.

Gaining Oneself Back

The Young Man in *Repetition* is troubled. Having broken with his fiancée, he consults Constantin in his despair through a series of letters. In these letters, the Young Man compares his trial to that of Job's. Like Job, the Young Man's trial sends him into an existential crisis where everything falls into a state of uncertainty.

> I am at the end of my rope. I am nauseated by life; it is insipid—without salt and meaning . . . One sticks a finger into the ground to smell what country one is in; I stick my finger into the world—it has no smell. Where am I? What does it mean to say: the world? What is the meaning of that word? Who tricked me into this whole thing and leaves me standing here? Who am I? How did I get into the world? Why was I not asked about it, why was I not informed *of the rules and regulations but just thrust into the ranks* as if I had been bought from a peddling shanghaier of human beings? How did I get involved in this big enterprise called actuality? Why should I be involved? Isn't it a matter of choice? And if I am compelled to be involved, where is the manager—I have something to say about this. Is there no manager? To whom shall I make my complaint? (R 2009, 200)

The Young Man's heartbreak may seem like a poor analog to Job's trial. However, as the Young Man himself remarks, one does not have to "feel as if he has lost sons and daughters," for the heartbroken individual "can also feel as if he has been struck down with sores, he who has lost this honour and pride, and with them meaning and the will to live" (R 2009, 59). Both Job and the Young Man suffer in different ways, yet in their trials both express a loss of self resulting from an inability to make sense of the world.

At the beginning of *Repetition*, our author Constantin remarks that the Young Man's soul is too delicate, and that he does not possess the "ironic elasticity" (R 2009, 8) that would help him to persist through his trial. As both Constantin and Kierkegaard tell us, Job is the only figure in *Repetition* truly to "repeat," which would lead us to believe that Job *does* possess the requisite ironic elasticity. Evidence for Job's ironic mood can be found in his ability to embrace the primary paradox at the heart of his trial—that both he and God are in the right—a consciousness that Kierkegaard associates with irony. Important for Kierkegaard is that Job's capacity to join these two seemingly irreconcilable ideas is not a matter of intellectual laziness or ideological stubbornness, for throughout the three cycles of speeches between Job and his friends, he continually challenges much of what he had previously considered true. Carl Jung remarks in his *Response to Job* that, prior to his trial, Job believed in "a 'good' God, or . . . a benevolent ruler and just judge" and that "he had imagined that a 'covenant' was a legal matter and that anyone who was party to the contract could insist on his rights as agreed; that God would be faithful and true or at least just, and, as one could assume from the Ten Commandments, would have some recognition of ethical values or at least feel committed to his own legal standpoint."[20]

Both Jung and Kierkegaard rightly acknowledge that, throughout his suffering, Job undergoes a major shift in his worldview. Prior to the storm, Job perceives God as someone who is just and does not punish the innocent. However, toward the end of the first cycle of speeches, Job entertains the possibility that God "destroys blameless and wicked alike" (Job 9:22). The fundamental belief underlying Job's conviction, that God is just and does not punish the innocent, is clearly challenged in Job's complaints, but in a way that seems to *strengthen*, and not weaken, his integrity. Of course, maintaining all these paradoxes while simultaneously positing that "God is one" is no easy task for Job, who

> cannot give up his faith in divine justice, it is not easy for him to accept the knowledge that divine arbitrariness breaks the law. On the other hand, he has to admit that no one except Yahweh himself is doing him injustice and violence. He cannot deny that he is up against a God who does not care a rap for any moral opinion and does not recognize any form of ethics as binding. This is perhaps the greatest thing about Job, that, faced with this difficulty, he does not doubt the unity of God.[21]

Jung, like Kierkegaard, situates Job's greatness in his ability to hold together the antinomy at the heart of his ordeal, all the while never once doubting God's unity.

In addition, Job's ironic mood is demonstrated not merely by his holding together paradoxical ideas, but also by his *persisting in his integrity in spite of its absurdity*. Even though Job knows that he and God are both right, he nonetheless complains to God throughout his trial, while fully aware that such complaints are entirely futile. "The Lord has no fear of complaints . . . Speak, lift up your voice, speak loudly, God can always speak more loudly—after all, he has thunder" (R 2009, 59). In addition, the very nature of his trial is absurd for the very reason that "no one can win his case against God" (Job 9:2). Although he continually expresses his desire to bring his trial before the Almighty (Job 13:3; 13–28; 23:3–7), to challenge God and make a case for his innocence (Job 19:23–29; 31:1–40), Job sees himself as a plaintiff in a trial for which no ruling can be made, for there exists no court beyond God capable of judging such a trial.[22] Finally, the very nature of a trial where God is on the stand as a defendant, with the human interrogating God, subverts the relationship established through the covenant. In short, the very idea of summoning God to court is absurd, and Job knows this. Despite these facts—that Job is powerless before God and cannot win, that his complaints will have no effect on God, and that the very nature of the trial is absurd—Job nonetheless complains and "summons him to court" (Job 9:16).

That Job possesses the requisite Kierkegaardian "ironic elasticity" that the Young Man lacks is clear, for unlike aesthetic figures like the Young Man, who lacks "the endurance to think through a thought when the world thought the opposite" (R 2009, 65), Job's ability to persist through his trial despite its paradox demonstrates the requisite elastic ironic consciousness that Kierkegaard deemed necessary for persisting through the absurd trials of existence.

In the Eye of the Storm

Two final questions remain in our analysis: What type of irony does Job possess (positive or negative), and where did it come from? Though we sympathize with Job, it is clear that, in the second part of the Job narrative, after the second thunder-strike, when his body is afflicted with painful, burning boils, Job's reactions are demonstrative of the negative irony that Kierkegaard attacks in the first part of *Concept of Irony*. First, Job's irony is entirely reactionary, in that it subverts conventional understandings of God. Though the pre-thunderstorm Job embraces the idea of a loving God that rules and judges from a divine position, the Job of the second part of the book challenges these convictions while simultaneously subverting the theological power structure. Job's arguments are negative in the Socratic sense, in that they are corrosive and destructive to the conventional norms—and Job's questioning of God's benevolence is clearly indicative of this. Second, it is clear that Job's cries in the second part of the book are indicative of the "infinite absolute" of the Socratic ironist who lacks a position. Job's comments are erratic and inconsistent, wavering between a rational humility one moment to complete hopelessness and despair the next.

Similarly, the Young Man in *Repetition*, Job's literary analog, suggests that he might have "lost his mind," stating, "At one moment I am so tired, so dulled, it is as if I had died of indifference. The next moment I am raving mad, travelling from one end of the world to the other in search of someone on whom I could vent my rage" (R 2009, 60). The Young Man mimics Job's moods, vacillating between thoughts of suicide and spiritual bliss. Though it is clear that Job is not an aesthetic figure, his erratic moods throughout the second part of his trial are demonstrative of a figure who is neither aesthetic nor ethical but instead—like (the young Kierkegaard's) Socrates, Constantin, and the Young Man—a boundary figure who straddles both. Job knows that he is right, but without a solid foundation on which to base this, he remains "negatively free." Of course, it is understandable why Job lacks a position, for his entire worldview has been shattered. Though Job has his integrity, the foundation of that integrity—the belief in a just God who practices retributive justice—has been challenged.

After the Storm

Though it is clear that the Job of the second part of the narrative is indicative of negative irony, what of the Job of the third part of his chronicle, who, Kierkegaard tells us in the *Upbuilding Discourse*, emerges "victoriously" from his trial (EUD, 123, 111)? For many, the key to unlocking the meaning of the Book of Job rests in the final section of the text, where after three cycles (and thirty-seven chapters) of philosophical and theological wrangling, Yahweh emerges from the "whirlwind" to respond to Job's plea (Job 38-42). This response, which comes in the form of two separate speeches, provides no retort to Job's original complaints, but instead points to Job's lack of divine understanding: "Who is this who darkens counsel with words devoid of knowledge? Brace yourself and stand up like a man . . . Where were you when I laid the earth's foundations?" (Job 38:3–4). Job's response to Yahweh is debated—much of this debate a result of the final line of Hebrew text, "Therefore I yield, repenting in dust and ashes" (Job 42:6).[23] As Edward Mooney remarks in his treatment of Kierkegaard's Job, "In Job the question of God's acquittal before the highest court remains unresolved."[24] In short, if there is a resolution in the final section of the Book of Job for Kierkegaard, it is not theological in nature.

Kierkegaard's commentary on the final and most controversial aspect of the Book of Job is conspicuously missing. Though the upbuilding discourse devotes itself to the prologue of the Book of Job, and *Repetition* to the poetic Job of the second section who first sits and then emerges from this silence through his impassioned complaints, little is said in Kierkegaard's writings regarding those final controversial chapters. Before we hastily accuse Kierkegaard of the negative absolute infinity of the Socratic ironist, we should not be surprised that

Kierkegaard's analysis, which is focused exclusively on Job as sufferer, says little regarding the troublesome part of the text when the suffering is lifted. As stated previously, even though he was rewarded twofold, this event seems irrelevant to Kierkegaard's Job, who is fully aware that God is just as capable of taking every-thing away again. The true significance of this trial for Kierkegaard is not in God's angry retort, but instead in those moments when Job goes to battle with God in his demand for justification. It is only then that Job is thrown upon himself and forced to question his understanding of God as the foundation of his integrity. Further, Kierkegaard's glaring omissions in his account of Job are entirely consis-tent with his method of indirect communication, which directs (albeit indirectly) the reader toward self-knowledge. The Book of Job for Kierkegaard is a work that instigates self-knowledge, a book with more problems than answers, a book that he believed needed to be read again and again. As the Young Man remarks, "Even though I have read the book again and again, each time every word is new to me" (R 2009, 64). In short, to expect Kierkegaard to provide answers in a book marred by ambiguity is to misunderstand Kierkegaard's philosophical methodology; we learn more about Kierkegaard's Job not through what is said but instead through what is not said, for "Kierkegaard's telling of the story is as remarkable for what it omits as for the simple power of what it says."[25]

Job's Victory

Despite this glaring omission in Kierkegaard's account of the Book of Job, Kierkegaard does say one thing about the controversial final section—*Job emerges victoriously.* But what kind of victory can we imagine this to be? Although Kierkegaard does not directly answer this question, an examination of the Young Man's failed victory indirectly discloses one way of interpreting Job's victory in his philosophy. The Young Man initially suggests that Job's repetition occurs when "the Lord gave Job twice as much as he had before" (R 2009, 69), but later he acknowledges the paltry nature of a "repetition of worldly goods, which have no meaning in relation to spiritual matters" (R 2009, 75). True repetition, the Young Man argues, is not a return of worldly goods but a return of oneself, which he experiences after his own storm has passed: "I am back to my old self. This self, which another would not pick up off the street, is mine again. The schism in my being has been removed. I am whole again. The anxieties of sympathy, which my pride nourished and supported, no longer force splits and separations" (R 2009, 74).

Because we are told that Job is the only person in *Repetition* to truly repeat, we can take this to mean that Job's true repetition arises when, after his rup-ture, he *regains* himself as a singular individual. Consequently, the significance of the third part of the Book of Job for Kierkegaard (and the victory that Job experiences) does not pertain so much to a resolution between Job and God as to *a resolution within Job's own spirit*.

We learn more about Job's victory through Constantin's account of the Young Man's failures:

> If he had had a more devoutly religious background he would have become a poet. He would then have acted with an entirely different iron-like consistency and firmness. He would have gained a fact of consciousness he could have stuck with, and because he would have established it himself by virtue of a relationship to God. In the same instant the whole question of finitude would become insignificant; genuine actuality would, in a deeper sense, make no difference to him. He would have religiously exhausted every possible horrific consequence of the situation. Whether things turned out to be other than he had thought would not disturb him at all. Even if the worst had happened, this could not have frightened him any more than it already had. (R 2009, 80)

Corroborated by Constantin, the Young Man's failure to repeat is based in his lack of a position. He lacks the "iron-like consistency" and "firmness" that would help him to persist through his trial. In the same way that the negative ironist lacks a position that would allow him to make a decision to overcome his trial, the Young Man's "mind has become paralysed" (R 2009, 60). He is rendered inert, standing "suspenso grandu [immobilized] . . . without moving a foot or making one single movement" (R 2009, 214). The Young Man has been waiting for a resolution to his ordeal, but one that *would happen* to him, a "thunderstorm," as opposed to a resolution that he would actively bring about through his own free will. Because the Young Man is not free and he will not choose, others will make his choices for him, which in this case is his betrothed's decision to marry another.

In the Job narrative, it is clear that, unlike the Young Man and his negative irony, Job not only has a position (one that is "fundamentally religious") but is also clearly free. Though Job gains a position through a relationship with God, it is on Job's terms—not God's—for Job establishes this relationship "himself by virtue of a relationship to God" (R 2009, 80). We are told throughout that Job does not let his "consciousness" and "freedom" get crushed by his suffering, does not apathetically resign himself to the conventional in a way that prevents him from having to act. "This is what is great in Job, that the passion of freedom in him is not quelled or calmed through a false expression" (R 2009, 65). For Kierkegaard, Job's freedom is the one thing that God cannot take away from him: "Job's noble human boldness . . . [f]rom the perspective of freedom is something great, has a consciousness that not even God, though He gave it, can wrest from him" (R 2009, 66). As Mooney remarks, "Job's freedom is not diminished by some tyrannical power play from above. He rises up, tears his robe, and shaves his head. In these responsive gestures, in his latter bitter interrogations of the

Lord, and in his final recognition of his blindness, his "repentance" in dust and ashes, we have Job's free responsiveness, not blunt obedience to coercive power."[26] At each stage of the way, we see Job questioning not only God but also himself, actively employing his free will throughout his trial.

We have concluded, through Kierkegaard's indirect method, the following about Job's victory: Job has a position, he is resolutely committed and hence freely engaged in his trial, and he possesses a certain type of consciousness that Kierkegaard associates with a strength that lets him persist. From Kierkegaard's own account of irony, it is clear that Kierkegaard's Job does ultimately possess the positive irony, or is the "ethicist who uses irony as his incognito" (CUP, 503). Unlike the Young Man, Job possesses a particular consciousness and "ironic elasticity" that allows him to think through the paradox of his situation and its possible "horrific" consequences. If the Young Man had the capacity to think through his paradox, if he had "the endurance to think through a thought when the world thought the opposite" (R 2009, 65), it is likely that he could have emerged victoriously from his trial.

Of primary concern for the Young Man in *Repetition* is whether or not Job possessed his "ironic elasticity" prior to his tempest, or if it was acquired in the process: "When all existence collapsed upon you and lay like broken pottery around you, did you immediately have this suprahuman self-possession, did you immediately have this interpretation of love, this cheerful boldness of trust and faith?" (R 2009, 197). The answer to this question is no small matter and has great implications for those looking to Job for existential comfort. If Job's suffering requires a preexisting soul strength, it is likely that his "door is closed to one who is grief-stricken" (R 2009, 58), for unlike the majority of humans, Job is truly pious. If, however, Job's soul-strength was acquired *during his rupture*, when his psyche shattered in the thunderstorm, there is hope that each individual can not only persist through *but also become strengthened in a trial*. Kierkegaard's conclusion seems to be the latter. Though Job is clearly "developed" prior to his trial, Kierkegaard makes clear that nothing could prepare Job for the magnitude of this suffering and that Job's reflection is "deepened in his suffering" (R 2009, 67). In addition, we are told in the upbuilding discourse that Job "discovered" his "truth" and was "redeemed it by" through his "unflagging toil" (EUD, 109). Consequently, it is only when his psyche is pushed to its limits—that is, when everything "went to pieces" (R 2009, 58)—that Job reaches the ironic consciousness and soul-strength that allow him to persist through and emerge victoriously from his trial.

Though the upbuilding discourse "The Lord Gave" is devoted to the prayer that Job utters in the aftermath of his tragedy, and the humility that it portrays, *Repetition* is based on the observation that the prayer was not repeated after the second wave of sufferings: "What is great about Job is therefore not that he said: 'The Lord gave and the Lord took away, praised be the name of the Lord', which he said at first, but not later repeated" (R 2009, 67). Though we know that Job was truly pious, Kierkegaard's emphasis on the fact that Job did not repeat the prayer suggests a pre-thunderstorm Job who is, though incredibly pious, perhaps slightly naive. After the first wave of suffering, he prays, but his heart is already shattered. After the second wave of suffering, when everything "went to pieces," Job undergoes a transition. As Mooney remarks, "As Kierkegaard has it, Job's soul, through his suffering and rebellion, becomes fertile soil receptive to new growth."[27] The change in Job's soul that allows for "new growth" is a consciousness akin to positive irony in Kierkegaard's philosophy, a consciousness that guides and directs without stifling or restraining the subject, a consciousness that allows for the individual to persist "energetically" and "robustly" through the trials of existence in a way that *edifies and strengthens one's identity as it breaks forth in the existential dialectic of subjective becoming.*

In the upbuilding discourse on Job, Kierkegaard discusses how so few are capable of understanding the meaning of Job's prayer. Though the child and the youth may have a "faint presentiment" (EUD, 111–112) of the wisdom of Job's words, they do not truly understand Job, "since what he does not grasp is all the distress and misery in which Job was tested." Even if the adult can understand such distress and misery at the heart of Job's trial, still "he may not understand Job, because he cannot understand how Job was able to say it" (EUD, 111). For Kierkegaard, "Only the person who has been tried and who tested the saying in being tested himself, only he rightly interprets the saying in being tested himself, only he rightly interprets the saying" (EUD, 112). Yet we know that Job himself had not been tried up to that point—the basis of ha-Satan's challenge to Job's piety in the first place. Consequently, there is good reason to believe that Kierkegaard's Job, who was also young once, did not fully understand the meaning of his prayer until his religiosity was tested after the second wave of suffering. "Then the silence is broken and Job's tormented soul breaks forth with powerful cries. These I understand. I make these words my own. In the same instant I feel the contradiction and smile at myself as one smiles at a child who has put on his father's clothes" (R 2009, 65). In the same way that the Young Man gains an understanding of Job's meaning only after going through his own trial, we similarly imagine Kierkegaard's Job emerging from his silence as a youth in grownup clothing, swimming around in the sea of paradox that is his ordeal. In the subsequent chapters, as we watch the great complainant go to battle with forces far greater than him, we imagine Job slowly growing into his adult clothes as he comes to understand the absurdity of the human condition revealed in his trial—a wisdom that is simultaneously the underlying strength that allows him to persist through it.

GRANT JULIN is Associate Professor of Philosophy at St. Francis University.

Notes

1. All references to the bible come from the *Oxford Study Bible* (New York: Oxford University Press, 1992), annotated edition.

2. *Repetition* was published four months prior to his upbuilding discourse on Job and on the same day as *Fear and Trembling*.

3. "I would speak to the Almighty, and I desire to argue with my case with God" (Job 13:3).

4. "My soul is weary of my life; I will leave my complaint upon myself; I will speak in the bitterness of my soul. I will say unto God, Do not condemn me; shew me wherefore thou contendest with me. Is it good unto thee that thou shouldest oppress" (Job 10:1–4).

5. "Will you not look away from me for a while, let me alone until I swallow my spittle? . . . Why have you made me your target? Why have I become burden to you?" (Job 7:19–20); "I cry to you and you do not answer me; I stand and you merely look at me. You have turned cruel to me, with the might of your hand you persecute me [to the point where] my skin turns black and falls from me, and my bones burn with heat" (Job 30:20–21, 30).

6. Job 1:1.

7. When God finally emerges from the whirlwind, he defends Job's integrity and uprightness, at one point saying that Job has "spoken truly" when condemning his friends and their conventional belief that Job must have sinned (Job 38).

8. Both Job (Job 1:21; 2:10; cf. 12:9; 19:21) and the narrator (Job 42:11) attribute Job's suffering to God alone.

9. "While he was still speaking, another messenger arrived and said 'God's fire flashed from heaven, striking the sheep and the shepherds and burning them up; only I have escaped to bring you the news'" (Job 1:16).

10. Job is fully aware that he has been tried unjustly—"Though I am in the right, he condemns me out of my own mouth though I am blameless, he makes me out to be crooked" (Job 9:20)—and at times suggests that God is wicked: "He destroys blameless and wicked alike" (Job 9:22).

11. The Young Man remarks that Job does not hope for "a repetition to the point of excess" (R 2009, 69).

12. "Why did I not die at birth, come forth from the womb and expire? . . . Why is light given to one who cannot see the way, whom Yahweh has fenced in? . . . What I dread befalls me, I am not at ease nor am I quiet" (Job 3:11, 23, 25–26).

13. George Stack, *Kierkegaard's Existential Ethics (Studies in the Humanities, no. 16)* (Tuscaloosa, AL: University of Alabama Press, 1977), p. 7.

14. Stack, *Kierkegaard's Existential Ethics*, p. 7.

15. Brian K. Söderquist, "Irony," in *The Oxford Handbook of Kierkegaard*, John Lippitt and George Pattison, eds. (New York: Oxford University Press, 2013), p. 354.

16. Kierkegaard compares irony to a type of courage: "It takes courage not to surrender to the shrewd or sympathetic counsel of despair that allows a person to erase himself from the number of the living . . . It takes courage when sorrow would delude one, when it would reduce all joy to sadness, all longing to privation. So it is also with irony. Even though one must warn against irony as against a seducer, so must one also commend it as a guide" (CI, 327).

17. John Lippitt, *Humour and Irony in Kierkegaard's Thought* (New York: Palgrave Macmillan, 2000), p. 145.

18. Martin Buber remarks on the "frequent repetition" of the Hebrew verb *berekh* (see Job 1, 5, 11; 2, 5, 9), "which means both real blessing and also blessing of dismissal, departure" (*The Prophetic Faith* [New York: Harper & Row, 1949], p. 190). Though its authors did not want its readers to translate *berekh* into the blasphemous "curse God," the duplicity of the phrase

suggests both, with most modern translations only using the latter: "Curse God and die" (Job 2:9).

19. Many of Job's responses to his friends are explicitly ironic: "What a help you have been to one without resource! What deliverance you have brought to the powerless! What counsel you offer to one bereft of wisdom" (Job 26:1–3).

20. Carl Jung, *Answer to Job (Jung Extracts)* (Princeton, NJ: Princeton University Press, 2012). Kindle edition, p. 21.

21. Jung, *Answer to Job*, p. 7.

22. "God is not as I am, not someone I can challenge, and say, 'Let us confront one another in court'." (Job 9:32).

23. Though most scholars argue that Job's final lines to God indicate repentance, J. B. Curtis reads *nhm* as "to be sorry" in the context of "man in his utter frailty before the divine," and not "to repent" ("On Job's Response to Yahweh," *Journal of Biblical Studies* 98, no. 4 (1979): 497–511, 500–501). This interpretation depicts a spiteful and loathsome Job who rejects God: "Therefore I feel loathing contempt and revulsion (toward you, O God); and I am sorry for frail man" (Curtis, pp. 497–511).

24. Edward F. Mooney, *Selves in Discord and Resolve: Kierkegaard's Moral-Religious Psychology from Either/or to Sickness Unto Death* (New York: Routledge, 1996), p. 37.

25. Stephen Crites, "The Blissful Security of the Moment: Recollection, Repetition, and Eternal Recurrence," in *The International Kierkegaard Commentary, Vol. 6*, Fear and Trembling and Repetition, Robert L. Perkins, ed. (Macon, GA: Mercer University Press, 1993), p. 255.

26. Mooney, *Selves in Discord*, p. 35.

27. Mooney, *Selves in Discord*, p. 33.

13 Kierkegaard and Pentecostal Philosophy

J. Aaron Simmons

TRADITIONALLY, KIERKEGAARD'S THOUGHT has been a key resource for debates concerning religious epistemology,[1] divine command theory,[2] and the problems and possibilities of existentially oriented faith.[3] More recently, it has also been used by philosophers working on issues related to political theory,[4] postmodern philosophy,[5] and deconstructive ethics.[6] Given Kierkegaard's expansive authorship and his deep religious concerns, such widespread appropriation within the philosophy of religion and related fields is not surprising. Nonetheless, in this chapter, I will consider a topic that has not been the focus of much, if any, philosophical debate within the Kierkegaardian scholarship, and has only recently begun to receive any attention within contemporary philosophy more broadly: Pentecostalism.

One might legitimately ask, then, given the lack of *philosophical* attention to Pentecostalism, why consider it here?[7] Moreover, why consider it in relation to the decidedly *Lutheran* Kierkegaard? In response to the first question, let me point to James K. A. Smith's recent argument for the importance of "pentecostal philosophy" for contemporary philosophy in general.[8] In response to the second question, we should remember that Kierkegaard wrote an upbuilding discourse entitled "It Is the Spirit Who Gives Life," which he offers on the occasion of Pentecost—included as part 3 of *For Self-Examination*. Moreover, in *Judge For Yourself!*, Kierkegaard includes the lengthy discourse "Become Sober," which also directly engages the narrative of Pentecost recorded in Acts 2. Those particular Kierkegaardian "Pentecost" discourses, as it were, have not received much direct engagement, and, even in those essays that do consider them, the role of the Holy Spirit has rarely been the primary focus of concern.[9]

In this chapter, then, I will explore the possible Kierkegaardian resources for the contemporary philosophical project of what Smith refers to as "thinking in tongues." Ultimately, I will argue that Kierkegaard's thought can be productively appropriated for those working in contemporary pentecostal philosophy for two reasons. First, it displays many of the key aspects of a pentecostal "worldview," or "social imaginary," as laid out by Smith. Second, when reading Kierkegaard's

Pentecost discourses in light of Smith's framework, they can plausibly be viewed as much more important to Kierkegaard's overall philosophy of religion than is often claimed.

I will proceed as follows. First, I will lay out the broad strokes of Smith's account as a possible lens through which to consider Kierkegaard's Pentecost discourses. Then, I will turn to Kierkegaard and show how themes in his discourses resonate nicely with much of Smith's proposal. Finally, I will offer some suggestions on what such a "pentecostal" reading of Kierkegaard might offer to the contemporary debates in both the philosophy of religion and Kierkegaardian scholarship.[10]

James K. A. Smith's Account of Pentecostal Philosophy

Smith sets out to "sketch how we might articulate a uniquely Pentecostal philosophy, and [show] what that Pentecostal philosophy has to offer broader conversations."[11] Smith begins by laying out two important stipulations for his overall project—one is linguistic and the other is conceptual. First, by "pentecostal" he does not mean anything narrowly circumscribed, but instead uses the term as broadly as possible such that classical Pentecostals, charismatics, and third-wave or neo-pentecostals are all included.[12] Thus, he uses the lower-case "pentecostal" to refer to this big-tent approach.

In addition to his inclusive understanding of pentecostalism, Smith also notes that he is not defining pentecostalism "theologically" (viz., as a matter of doctrinal specificity)[13] but instead approaches it as a "spirituality" that displays a determinate "worldview" or "social imaginary."[14] "Because pentecostalism is primarily a spirituality," Smith claims, ". . . a pentecostal worldview is not a set of doctrines or dogmas. Instead, latent, implicit theological and philosophical intuitions are embedded within, and enacted by, pentecostal rituals and practices."[15] Smith's focus on "rituals and practices" is important because it underlies one of his basic methodological commitments: "Pentecostalism is not first and foremost a doctrinal or intellectual tradition; it is an affective constellation of practices and embodied 'rituals'."[16] As Smith puts it, pentecostalism is appropriately described as what Ludwig Wittgenstein would term a "form of life."[17] Despite articulating it as decidedly pentecostal, one might take issue with the assertions of the "distinctiveness" and "uniqueness" of the perspective that Smith articulates.[18]

Setting aside some reservations I have about Smith's account, I want to outline what he takes to be the determinate five aspects of pentecostalism in order then to consider Kierkegaard's thought in light of them: (1) radical openness to God, (2) an "enchanted" theology of creation and culture, (3) a nondualistic affirmation of embodiment and materiality, (4) an affective, narrative epistemology, and (5) an eschatological orientation to mission and justice.[19] Smith takes these five characteristics to "resonate" with what Amos Yong describes as the "pneumatological imagination"[20] that defines pentecostal existence.[21] Respectively, we might say that the five aspects Smith highlights serve to illustrate the ways in which pentecostalism is able to speak into debates concerning existential theology, ontology and anthropology, philosophy of mind, epistemology, and ethics and political theory.

(1) Radical Openness to God

Smith's account of radical openness might be seen as quite close to open theism,[22] in that the openness about which he speaks seems to be dually referred both to the future and also to God. Given that one can't predict how God will work in the world, the future is a horizon of hope, rather than knowledge; of confident trust, rather than determinate expectation. For Smith, pentecostal models of God require expecting the unexpected such that we must "forsak[e] existing, status quo ideas and expectations of how God works."[23] Being open to divine surprise amounts to fundamental receptivity as an existential attitude. Accordingly, Smith sees possible links between pentecostal philosophy and continental discussions of alterity offered by such thinkers as Emmanuel Levinas,[24] Jacques Derrida,[25] and John D. Caputo.[26]

When radical alterity is an essential part of a philosophical system, the *system* begins to break down. For pentecostals, this point gets cashed out in terms of *divine* personality. Pentecostal models of God are decidedly personal and, accordingly, appreciate the dialogical aspects of faith.[27] Relating to God as a person demands that God not be absolutely predictable, and, as such, pentecostal notions of a personal God locate trust and risk as central to religious life.[28]

(2) An Enchanted Theology of Creation and Culture

Being radically open to God entails a belief that God is still working in history in a variety of ways: healing, restoring, helping, revealing, encouraging, and so forth. Smith will refer to this belief as the sense of "enchantment" that pervades pentecostalism.[29] Smith explains that the belief in God's continued working in the world leads to a "deep sense of the Spirit's immanence" within pentecostalism.[30] Importantly, though, the enchantment of the world also underlies the notion that there are more spirits at work in the world than God's Spirit. As Smith explains, "pentecostal spirituality is also deeply attentive to what we might describe as the mis-enchantment of the world by other spirits."[31]

Though the affirmation of an essentially spirited reality certainly can invite ironically reductionistic explanations of phenomena, Smith does not understand enchantment to be reducible to a problematic belief in "magic," say.[32] Rather, Smith charitably reads pentecostal spirituality as consistently expressing the conviction that a belief in Spirit should invite an openness to belief in spirits working at counter-purposes to God. In this way, pentecostals are open to the fact that there might be more going on in reality than it seems. Smith rightly understands that being radically open to the surprise of divine personality faces difficulty if one, then, mechanistically shuts down the range of possibilities for *how* God might surprise us. In particular, Smith suggests that reductive physicalisms (whether concerning cosmology or philosophy of mind, etc.) would be problematic.

As a helpful illustration of this point, consider the "didactic little story" offered by David Foster Wallace in his commencement address to the Kenyon College graduating class of 2005,[33] which was then published as a short book titled *This Is Water*. His main point is that taking things to be obvious can often get in the way of our being open to the meaningful realization that things could be otherwise. Norms that are invisible are the most dangerous because they are the ones that do not result from intentional endorsement, but merely tacit approval. Pentecostalism similarly invites what I would term an *epistemic humility* about the way in which the world works precisely because of a *faithful confidence* (though not philosophical or theological certainty) in God's continued working in the world. This is not a humility that leads to wishy-washy indifference, though. Instead, pentecostal epistemic humility/faithful confidence occurs as a result of an existential investment in God's relational benevolence.

(3) A Nondualistic Affirmation of Embodiment and Materiality

Given Smith's suggestion that pentecostalism resists reductive physicalistic explanations of existence, it might seem odd that Smith then describes pentecostal spirituality as being "nondualistic." Yet this need not seem strange at all when one understands Smith's stipulative definition of "dualism" as a view that sees material reality as "fundamentally bad or evil."[34] In this way, Smith's suggestion of nondualism is offered as ethical insight into the way in which pentecostalism should not be understood as a *theological escape plan*, as it were, but instead as a *robust theological entanglement with physical reality as always already "spirited."* Resulting from an affirmation of an enchantment is the rejection of the idea that creaturely physicality is something to be overcome in the name of true spiritual identity. Poetically, we might say that living in haunted houses (and churches) changes things.[35] Accordingly, Smith presents an implicit philosophical anthropology as part of an explicit theological ontology. Smith takes the rejection of dualism to yield not only theological results, such as beliefs and practices concerning divine healing, but ethical and political results as well: "Inchoately embedded in this central affirmation that God cares about our bodies is a radical affirmation of the goodness of creation that translates (or *should* translate) into a radical affirmation of the goodness of bodies and materiality *as such*."[36]

Indeed, affirming a nondualistic understanding of embodiment should cause pentecostals to go beyond the frequent evangelical focus on saving the soul while forgetting the body. As Smith notes, the social justice implications of pentecostalism resonate with much of liberation theology in ways that much of contemporary evangelicalism might not.[37] When lived out in community, pentecostalism should invite radical hospitality not simply to those who are seeking religious conversion, but to all those who, whether physically, emotionally, or spiritually, "are weary and burdened" (Matt. 11:28, NIV).

(4) An Affective, Narrative Epistemology

It is in the area of epistemology that Smith's notion of pentecostalism as a social imaginary really gains philosophical traction. Focusing on the role of testimony within pentecostalism, Smith suggests that testimony occurs in stories that yield "narrative knowledge."[38] Within pentecostal communities, the shorthand expression for this narrative knowledge, says Smith, is "I know that I know that I know." Let's refer to this as *IKTIKTIK epistemology*. This structure is primarily a linguistic attempt to be existentially aware. For Smith, pentecostal worship "constitutes a kind of performative postmodernism" that serves to "resist the slimmed-down reductionism of modern cognitivism."[39] Pentecostalism understands the relationship with God to operate such that religious knowledge is not a matter of objectivist verification or falsification, but instead of personal *theological* commitment and singular *existential* investment.

William J. Seymour, the African American leader of the famous Azusa Street Revival of 1906, expresses the important link between a personal relationship to God and the soteriological knowledge that one might then affirm: "Salvation is not feeling; it is a real knowledge by the Holy Spirit, bearing witness with our spirit."[40] Far from being a matter of emotive expressivism, pentecostalism eschews the suggestion that emotivism and cognitivism are an exclusive dichotomy. Instead, pentecostalism stresses the importance of *personal* transformation such that requests for external confirmation would perhaps miss the central theo-epistemological point. As Seymour explains, "Some people to-day cannot believe they have the Holy Ghost without some outward signs: that is Heathenism. The witness of the Holy Spirit inward is the greatest knowledge of knowing God, for he is invisible. St. John 14:17. It is all right to have the signs following, but not to pin our faith to outward manifestations. We are to go by the world of God."[41]

Like Smith, Seymour stresses that God's Spirit is a person and, as such, invites a different sort of relationship than one might have with an external physical object, such as a shoe or a book, say, and also that one might have with a nonphysical, but still non-personal, object such as an idea or a proposition. "The gift of the Holy Ghost," Seymour writes, "is more than speaking in the tongues.

He is wisdom, power, truth, holiness. He is a person that teaches us the truth."[42] Here, the notion of being taught by God conveys the sense that God communicates directly and personally: *Spirit to spirit*. Hence, Seymour refers to the true hope of religious life as a "real personal Pentecost," which would provide "power for service and work and for sealing unto the day of redemption."[43] This claim bridges the gap between epistemology and social justice.

(5) An Eschatological Orientation to Mission and Justice

Although pentecostalism is often characterized as being primarily about "speaking in tongues" (glossolalia), Smith rightly claims that the practice of speaking in tongues is not as important to pentecostal spirituality as an eschatological orientation to historical existence.[44] "Contrary to common assumptions about the 'otherworldliness' of pentecostals," Smith writes, there is "a commitment both to mission and to ministries of empowerment and social justice, with a certain 'preferential option for the marginalized' tracing back to its roots in the fishermen at Pentecost."[45] Concerned with issues such as racism, poverty, and violence, early American pentecostalism was, perhaps, in some respects *more* socially progressive than many of its contemporary manifestations. As an example, consider that even though, as an African American, Seymour was not allowed to sit in the classrooms of the bible school established by Charles Parham, but made to listen from the hall,[46] Seymour nonetheless explicitly affirms that pentecostalism ought to follow Christ's leading and overcome all racial exclusion:

> We want all of our white brethren and white sisters to feel free in our churches and missions, in spite of all the trouble we have had with some of our white brethren in causing diversion, and spreading wild fire and fanaticism. Some of our colored brethren caught the disease of this spirit of division also. . . . We must love all men as Christ commands (Heb. 12:14). . . . We love our white brethren and sisters and welcome them. Jesus Christ takes in all people in his Salvation. Christ is all and for all.[47]

Consider also the following from Robert Clarence Lawson: "The terrible scourge of race prejudice, like a disease, has afflicted the nations, like a mighty monster holds them in captivity. . . . We trusted that the Pentecostal people would rise to redeem man by example and precept. It is all right to sing and shout and pray and preach loud, but what this poor world is longing for is the real love of God, lived."[48] Here, Lawson displays a conception of pentecostalism as displaying what Kierkegaard would likely term "works of love."[49]

Having worked through what Smith takes to be the main five characteristics of the pentecostal social imaginary, or the pneumatological imagination, let's now turn to Kierkegaard's consideration of Pentecost and attempt to read it in light of this framework.

Living with Spirits: Kierkegaard on Pentecost

Kierkegaard's only direct considerations of Pentecost come late in his authorship. In "It Is the Spirit Who Gives Life," which is included in *For Self-Examination* (published in 1851), and "Become Sober," which is included in *Judge For Yourself!* (written in 1851–1852 but posthumously published in 1876), Kierkegaard offers a sustained reading of the Pentecost narrative provided in Acts 2. These two works represent an important moment in Kierkegaard's authorship, and Howard and Edna Hong even suggest that these two books stand as the "culminat[ion]" of Kierkegaard's second authorship.[50] Nonetheless, these works have received a mixed scholarly reception. For example, Bruce Kirmmse claims that "although not developing anything new in the theological or theoretical sense," these books "are essentially popularizations of the radical critique contained in *Training in Christianity*."[51] For Kirmmse, these books might be helpful as clarifications of other Kierkegaardian texts, but they are not necessarily important in their own right.[52] Alternatively, Paul Martens claims that these books "significantly develop the role of the Holy Spirit beyond any other works in the Kierkegaardian corpus."[53] Given that, as Martens notes, "it is impossible to miss the frequent appearance of the Holy Spirit in these later discourses," it is surprising that "most [scholars] have missed the importance of these appearances."[54]

Regardless of where one comes down on the importance of these books in the development of Kierkegaard's overall philosophical and theological views, the role of the Holy Spirit in these texts makes them distinctive. Accordingly, Martens is right to note that "it is a bit puzzling that so few have taken Kierkegaard's understanding of the Holy Spirit seriously."[55]

A variety of possible explanations for why Kierkegaard did not make the Holy Spirit, generally, and Pentecost, specifically, more common themes in his authorship might be offered. For example, Jørgen Bukdahl suggests that the absence of such themes is due to the severe influence of Kierkegaard's father on Kierkegaard's own notion of religious experience: "Kierkegaard's father's influence was obvious in the willful onesidedness with which his son embraced the New Testament command to imitate Christ and in his son's vision of the humiliated Christ, the Good Friday scene—while speaking only rarely of Easter and having no use either for Pentecost or Christmas."[56] Whether or not Bukdahl is right about the reason for the general absence of Pentecost from Kierkegaard's work, his claim only strengthens the idea that Kierkegaard's considerations of Pentecost in 1851–1852 should warrant special attention.

In what follows, then, I will look at what I think are the three most important aspects of Kierkegaard's consideration of Pentecost: (1) the importance of believing in Spirit and spirits as the first step in receiving the gifts offered by God's Spirit; (2) the notion of "dying to" as the key middle step in receiving such gifts; and (3) the existential conception of "becoming sober" as a way of relating self-knowledge and social action. I will suggest that these three aspects productively resonate with Smith's notion of enchanted reality, being open to God, and a pentecostal epistemology that is eschatologically oriented toward mission and justice.

Believing in and Speaking about Spirit

In the prayer at the beginning of *Works of Love*, Kierkegaard asks how one could "speak properly about love if you were forgotten, you Spirit of love, who take nothing of your own but remind us of that love-sacrifice, remind the believer to love as he is loved and his neighbor as himself!" (WOL, 3–4). Here we see Kierkegaard present God as the "Spirit" who makes love possible. Yet it is not clear whether this reference to God as the "Spirit of love" is any indication of Trinitarian theological commitments. Indeed, this same prayer begins with the words, "How could one speak properly about love if you were forgotten, you God of love, source of all love in heaven and on earth" (WOL, 3). Given the similarity of these two passages, it seems that the reference to the "Spirit of love" is simply a reference to God, pure and simple, and not a reference to part of the triune godhead that is distinctively present at a particular point in history: the day of Pentecost, say.

In *For Self-Examination*, though, a decidedly Trinitarian theology is arguably more clearly on display. The three sections of the book divide largely along Trinitarian lines. The prayer that begins the first discourse, "What Is Required in Order to Look at Oneself with True Blessing in the Mirror of the Word?," is addressed to our "Father in heaven." Subsequently, the second discourse, "Christ Is the Way," is addressed to the "Lord Jesus Christ." Finally, the opening prayer of the third discourse, "It Is the Spirit Who Gives Life," proceeds as follows: "O Holy Spirit, you who give life, bless also this, our coming together, the speaker and the listener. With your help this will come fresh from the heart; let it also go to the heart" (FSE, 73).

Father, Son, Holy Spirit. These are the divine persons invoked at the beginnings of the three discourses, respectively. Moreover, the reference to the "Holy Spirit" in the third discourse is not merely a stand-in for "God" but presents a distinctive aspect of God's identity: the giver of particular sorts of blessings. In this sense, the discourse certainly resonates with *Works of Love*, which identifies God as the source of love, but now love is named as a "gift of the Spirit," in a more determinate way than simply that it issues forth from a generally divine source. In *For Self-Examination*, God's Spirit is depicted in a personal, and personalist, manner: as active, engaged, and interested in the social world and one's place in it. Kierkegaard's social focus is clear from the prayer itself: it is a request that the

Holy Spirit will bless the "coming together" and will connect the "hearts" of the speaker and the listener by the words that are offered. Here, again, the personal dimension is repeated. This is not a dry sermon offered to an anonymous audience, but one that goes "from the heart . . . to the heart." Kierkegaard's prayer is for an intimate connection with others in light of the intimate personal relationship with the Holy Spirit. Simply put, he indicates that he can deliver a message from heart to heart as a result of being in a relationship of Spirit to spirit.

The scriptural passage under consideration in this discourse is the outpouring of the Holy Spirit on the day of Pentecost, as recorded in Acts 2:1–12. That the focus of Kierkegaard's comments will be the Holy Spirit is announced from the outset. Noting that nearly everyone nowadays believes in "the spirit of the age," "the spirit of the world," or "the human spirit," Kierkegaard postulates that nearly everyone, thus, "believes in spirit." Such belief should not impress us, though, since it is "not exactly something essentially high that [one] believes in" (FSE, 74). Kierkegaard's point is that, when it comes to the commonly held belief in spirit, this is not necessarily something that demands much of the believer. Indeed, it serves more as an expression of one's social identity than as a proclamation of a relationship with the divine that itself demands a singular response. As Kierkegaard asks with rhetorical effect, "As soon as the discourse is about a holy spirit, about believing in a holy spirit, how many do you think believe in that? Or when the discourse is about an evil spirit that should be renounced: how many do you think believe in such a thing? How can this be? Is it perhaps because the subject becomes too earnest when it is a holy spirit?" (FSE, 74). The notion of being "too earnest" echoes the discussion of earnestness in his earlier 1845 discourse offered "At a Graveside" (in TDIO). In that earlier text, earnestness is discussed in the attempt to stress the heightened existential relevance one faces when confronted with death. In "It Is the Spirit Who Gives Life," Kierkegaard draws upon this idea by emphasizing the importance of specificity when it comes to the idea of a "Holy Spirit." That is, the other spirits in which nearly everyone believes are general matters of being disposed to a way of speaking and thinking that is characteristic of "the present age."

Belief in a Holy Spirit that requires devotion and an evil spirit that requires renunciation is a personal matter in two senses: on the one hand, it is personal in that *I am the one* who must be devoted to the Holy Spirit and renounce the evil spirit; on the other hand, it is personal in that such spirits lay claim upon me in *their* singularity—that is, they are not to be confused with each other, but possess distinct identities and invite distinct responses. This second sense shows up when Kierkegaard claims that it is possible to "talk about, believe in, the spirit of the age, the spirit of the world, and the like" without thereby having "to think of anything specific" (FSE, 74). The first sense is, then, presented as essentially connected to the second sense. Such nonspecific notions of spirit are nonetheless a "kind of spirit, but I am not absolutely bound by what I say" (FSE, 74). Alternatively, when the spirit in which one believes is specific, one's belief is subjectively binding.

Consider that if a person claims to love "love" (in general), it is not clear that such love would require anything determinate from that person. Yet if a person claims to love "this person" (specifically), then a host of requirements follow: that the beloved be viewed, treated, and understood as distinct from all others. The beloved lays claim on the lover, and singularly so. The same is true in the realm of spirit: "One cannot speak about there being a holy spirit and about believing in a holy spirit without binding oneself by one's words, and furthermore, not without binding oneself to the holy spirit in renunciation of the evil spirit" (FSE, 75). Such specificity, in which one is "absolutely bound," is simply too "earnest" for the present age. Nonetheless, "Christianity, which requires the renunciation of an evil spirit, teaches that there is a holy spirit" (FSE, 75). As recorded in Acts 2, Pentecost is the day when "the Spirit for the first time was poured out upon the apostles" (FSE, 75). Kierkegaard then proclaims that "we should speak about this Holy Spirit today" (FSE, 75). The subtitle of *For Self-Examination*, "Recommended to the Present Age," should resound in Kierkegaard's claim here. Namely, "today" is not simply a reference to the literal day of the Church festival, but instead a statement as to the contemporary importance of the Holy Spirit in an age that lacks earnestness. For Kierkegaard, *we, today, in our age*, should speak about *this* Holy Spirit.

In light of Smith's work on pentecostal philosophy, I think that *we philosophers* should also, *today, in our age*, speak about the Holy Spirit. Smith's account of enchanted creation and culture shows up in Kierkegaard's description of the "life" given by the Spirit. Kierkegaard's account challenges any reductive physicalistic description of existence. The Spirit gives life, but "it is a new life" that is not to be confused with the life considered by biology, physiology, or neuroscience, say. Instead, it is a life that results from a death to oneself: "This life-giving in the Spirit is not a *direct* heightening of the natural life in a person in *immediate* continuation from and connection with it—what blasphemy!" (FSE, 76). Importantly, like Smith, Kierkegaard is not defending some sort of substance dualism. Rather, the Spirit opens a depth dimension of reality itself that is occluded (or rejected) by any account whereby everything that is, is a matter of *physical* explanation. Kierkegaard and Smith both introduce the possibility of a spirited reality, an enchanted creation, in which physical accounts and explanations remain in place but are not all that one can say—like David Foster Wallace, Smith and Kierkegaard both invite us to consider that things might be *more than they seem*.

The life brought by the Spirit is not a matter of one's spending more time upon the Earth, but instead a matter of living more deeply (*passionately/faithfully*) while alive. In this sense, Kierkegaard views the Holy Spirit as bringing the "abundant life" declared in John 10:10. In order to facilitate such living, the Spirit provides "gifts" that are necessary conditions of living life "more abundantly," as it were: faith, hope, and love. All three gifts of the Spirit are distinctive to the enchanted reality announced by the specificity of God's Spirit in the world. That is, faith is not simply a matter of weak knowledge, but stands "against understanding" (FSE, 82); hope is not simply a matter of expecting something that is unlikely, but is "eternity's hope," which is "hope against hope" (FSE, 82); and love is not simply a matter of desiring an object, but is the suffering stance of "loving this unloving world" (FSE, 85). "Such are the gifts," Kierkegaard proclaims, "the life-giving Spirit brought to the apostles on the day of Pentecost. Would that the Spirit might also bring us such gifts—truly they are certainly needed in times like these!" (FSE, 85).

Kierkegaard's emphasis on the importance of affirming the life-giving Holy Spirit and renouncing the evil spirit that would work at cross-purposes seems to suggest that he understands enchanted reality to involve "spiritual warfare" in much the same way as Smith. Indeed, Kierkegaard's metaphor involving a team of horses and the royal coachman can be read as illustrating the importance of being properly guided—by the spirit of the world or by the Holy Spirit. Kierkegaard views the apostles as called by God and gifted by the Spirit at Pentecost to "transform the world, and on the most appalling scale, against its will" (FSE, 86). Such transformation, however, is not going to occur by *simply* putting into place different social institutions, or even different ecclesial institutions, but will happen only by the Spirit through the action of those who are guided and gifted by the Spirit for such work. Accordingly, Kierkegaard also expresses a "deep sense of the Spirit's immanence."[57] Such immanence, for both Smith and Kierkegaard, leads to a notion of miraculous gifts that are "affirmed as operative" in one's daily life[58]—hence a transformed world as a result (FSE, 86).

"Dying To"

Anticipating Dietrich Bonhoeffer's distinction between "cheap grace" and "costly grace,"[59] Kierkegaard has no patience for those who would view religious existence as easy, comfortable, and worldly rewarding.[60] Indeed, Kierkegaard is explicit that only by "dying to" one's own interests and secular horizons of meaning could one receive the "new life" offered by the Holy Spirit. When Smith claims that "pentecostal spirituality goes all the way down,"[61] Kierkegaard might respond that it can only "go all the way" when one is willing to "die to" oneself and to the world. Death lies between natural existence and the spiritual existence offered by the Holy Spirit:

> Death goes in between; this is what Christianity teaches, you must die to. The life-giving Spirit is the very one who slays you; the first thing the life-giving Spirit says is that you must enter into death, that you must die to—it is this way in order

> that you may not take Christianity in vain. A life-giving Spirit—that is the invitation; who would not willingly take hold of it! But die first—that is the halt! It is the Spirit who gives life. Yes, the Spirit gives life—through death. (FSE, 76–77)

Kierkegaard clearly wants to be done with all sentimentality when it comes to the Holy Spirit. This is not a heartwarming story about God's love meant to make the listener feel good about things. Instead, Kierkegaard's engagement with Pentecost yields a defense of costly grace, of existential sacrifice, and of singular, risky investment. He thus reads Acts 2 as calling for heightened attention regarding the necessary condition for receiving the gifts of the Spirit: death. Just as Abraham could only truly receive Isaac as a gift from God after being willing to give up Isaac,[62] those who would receive the life given by the Spirit must die in order to be spiritually reborn.[63] "Come receive life . . . but die first"—Kierkegaard explains that this is not a message that would be celebrated by the masses, but it is a message that can transform the world.

Importantly, that to which one dies is selfishness: "You must first die to every merely earthly hope, to every merely human confidence; you must die to your selfishness, or to the world, because it is only through your selfishness that the world has power over you" (FSE, 77).

That selfishness is the key obstacle to receiving the gifts of the Spirit is helpfully considered in light of Smith's account of the pentecostal openness to God. Simply put, so long as God is expected—indeed, demanded—to work according to human categories, conceptualities, and contexts, then God is reduced to an idol of our own making. Alternatively, when one approaches God in humble confidence, while admitting that God likely ruptures the very categories we have for thinking about God, then we are transformed.

In this way, both Kierkegaard and pentecostalism reject ontotheology—whereby God is articulated according to philosophical categories rather than allowing philosophy to be radically challenged by God.[64] As Merold Westphal explains, "*God is the voice beyond my own who calls me to a life beyond my own through a promise and a command beyond any knowledge or will of my own.*"[65] We might simply say that the encounter with God is traumatic. It requires a different framework for intelligibility and meaning. Namely, it requires dying to the world and to oneself.[66]

All three of the gifts of the Spirit that are part of "new life" require death as a necessary first step. *Only when one has died to human understanding is faith possible*:

> Faith is against understanding; faith is on the other side of death. . . . It is when all confidence in yourself or in human support, and also in God in an immediate way, is extinct, when every probability is extinct, when it is dark as on a dark night—it is indeed death we are describing—then comes the life-giving Spirit and brings faith. (FSE, 82)

Only when one has died to worldly expectations is hope possible:

> In every human being there is a spontaneous, immediate hope; it can be more robust in one than in another, but in death (that is, when you die to) every such hope dies and changes into hopelessness. Into this night of hopelessness—it is indeed death we are describing—come the life-giving Spirit and brings hope, eternity's hope. (FSE, 82)

Only when one has died to love as selfish object-possession is true love as neighbor-love possible:

> Not until you have died to the selfishness in you and thereby to the world so that you do not love the world or anything in the world, do not selfishly love even one single person—not until you in love of God have learned to hate yourself, not until then can there be talk of the love that is Christian love. (FSE, 83–84)

In all three cases, "dying to" is the condition of receiving the gifts of the Spirit. This "dying to" is best thought of, though, as not simply a negation but a positive response. Dying to the world is ultimately not the stance of resignation but of receptivity. In *For Self-Examination,* and especially in *Judge for Yourself!,* "dying to" means a willingness to *"live for"* (see FSE, 101, 116, 130–132). This basic gesture presented in both texts is appropriately understood as a radical openness to God—an openness that is not merely theological (as concerns one's conception of God) but also existential (as concerns how one lives in light of the immanence of the Spirit in the world). Just as a team of horses is responsive to the leading of the royal coachman, those who would serve God in spirit and truth must allow God to set the direction of travel and then to lead them toward fulfillment.[67] Kierkegaard notes that although the apostles "were men just like us," it is crucial to realize that "they were driven well" (FSE, 87). By reading Kierkegaard in light of pentecostal philosophy, we can hear the radical openness to God advocated by pentecostalism as a call to be "driven well."

Becoming Sober

Earlier we saw that, for Kierkegaard, Pentecost announced the moment at which the apostles were gifted by the Holy Spirit in preparation for the spiritual warfare in which the whole world would be transformed. In his later works, Kierkegaard explicitly understands that such spiritual transformation is likely to yield direct conflict between Christianity and secular society. As Kirmmse explains, "In the post-1848 period, SK's assessment of the social and political state of Christendom led him to an increasingly revisionist position with respect to James and "works." SK's growing feeling that traditional Lutheran grace was being taken in vain led him to see that the normal form of Christian interaction with the social order is opposition and witness—and not the prioritarian integration which shrouds its differences with the world in hidden inwardness as a solely private matter between the individual and God."[68]

Considering that so much work has been done on Kierkegaard's complicated relation to Lutheran theology,[69] we should realize that here in the Pentecost discourses, Kierkegaard directly explains that the events of Acts 2 are *instructive not only for a proper understanding of grace, but also for present-day social engagement.* Indeed, following on the Trinitarian indications in the prayers of *For Self-Examination*, in the prayer offered at the beginning of "Becoming Sober," Kierkegaard locates "becoming sober" as the "condition for all else"— namely, it is the condition for receiving the "courage and life and power and strength" that would be of "benefit to us" (FSE, 95). It is worth noting that Kierkegaard actually has more direct references to Pentecost in this first essay in *Judge for Yourself!* than he does in "It Is the Spirit Who Gives Life."

Although taking 1 Peter 4:7 as its guiding text, Kierkegaard opens "Becoming Sober" as follows: "My devout listener. When the apostles came forward on Pentecost Day, for the first time filled with the Holy Spirit, "All were alarmed and doubted and said, 'What does this mean?' But others mocked and said, 'They are full of sweet wine'" (Acts 2:12–13) (FSE, 96).

Directly linking the first discourse in *Judge for Yourself!* with the last discourse in *For Self-Examination*, Kierkegaard uses Acts 2 to illustrate that what the world sees as "drunkenness" is, according to Christianity, actually sobriety. Depending on and deepening his earlier account of "dying to," Kierkegaard makes clear that there can be no middle way of compromise between the two viewpoints: "No, the difference is always that they have the very opposite views . . . what the one calls being drunk the other calls being sober" (FSE, 96).

Such a stark conflict is crucial to Kierkegaard's reading of Pentecost, which he references four times in "Becoming Sober" (FSE, 96, 98, 103, 114). For Kierkegaard, Pentecost is where the conflict of interpretations offered by Christianity and the world is at its most obvious. Similarly, Smith explains this conflict as owing to two rival hermeneutic frameworks: the "wine theory" as opposed to the "Spirit theory."[70] For both Smith and Kierkegaard, it is appropriate to say that "Pentecost . . . is a hermeneutic."[71] Smith specifically suggests that the pentecostal hermeneutic is "a *counter*interpretation of the world—one that counters the regnant interpretations . . . of our world and events that unfold within it."[72] Here we can see that Smith does not understand the conflict of interpretations simply to be a matter of philosophical and/or theological disagreement. Pentecost challenges the worldly power structures according to which the "wine theory" is fundamentally articulated. Similarly, when Kierkegaard puts Christianity into essential conflict with the world, he also indicates a veritable social revolution at the level of how to interpret society, truth, and power itself. At the end of "It Is the Spirit Who Gives Life," Kierkegaard calls it a "blessing" that the Holy Spirit would "take the power and give life" (FSE, 87). Rather than simply pitting power against power, Christianity shows that one can only "die to" and "become sober" when one not only admits being personally powerless, but also recognizes that *all earthly powers are powerless.*[73] To think otherwise is to be drunk (*with one's own power*).[74]

Pentecost is much more than a mere example in these discourses. It is presented as the inaugural event that explains the essential conflict between Christianity and the world. The "wine theory" and the "Spirit theory" are not merely rival interpretations of the events in Acts 2; they are interpretations of reality itself. The former rejects enchantment; the latter depends on it. Those espousing the wine theory love power and, hence, do not love. Those who espouse the Spirit theory admit of powerlessness and receive the gift of love from the Holy Spirit. Drawing on an implicit understanding of Spirit (*Pneuma*) as "breath," Kierkegaard claims that "Christianly, *inspiration* is first of all becoming sober" (FSE, 98, emphasis added). Just as a firefighter might put on an oxygen mask to avoid the poisonous fumes in a burning building, we might say that, for Kierkegaard, Christianity requires *breathing different air.*

Drunkenness is typified by not properly navigating the world around you. Hence, people who are suspected of being drunk are asked to perform such tasks as walking a straight line, repeating the alphabet, or doing simple things to demonstrate steady balance. Similarly, for Kierkegaard, those who have not received the Spirit are unable properly to navigate the world. The task is, then, to become sober: "*to come to oneself in self-knowledge and before God as nothing before him, yet infinitely, unconditionally engaged*" (FSE, 104, emphasis in original).

In this definition of "becoming sober," we can plausibly read Kierkegaard as hinting at both a pentecostal epistemology and an eschatological orientation toward mission and justice. Kierkegaard's notion of appropriately knowing oneself in self-knowledge resonates with IKTIKTIK epistemology's focus on testimony and narrative. Unlike the worldly idea in which one turns outward toward objectivity and thereby "los[es] oneself in knowing, in comprehending, in thinking, in artistic production, etc.," the Christian turns inward in self-knowledge (FSE, 105). "There is only one kind of knowing that brings a person completely to himself," writes Kierkegaard, "self-knowledge; this is what it means to be sober, sheer transparency" (FSE, 105). Kierkegaard's use of the idea of "transparency," here, echoes the beginning of *The Sickness Unto Death* where Anti-Climacus defines the "formula" that describes the self who is not in despair (SUD, 14). For Anti-Climacus and also for Kierkegaard, "transparency" names the state of exposure before God (*for Gud/coram Deo*). The self overcomes despair and achieves self-knowledge when no longer attempting to hide from God's presence. Importantly, though, when the Holy Spirit is understood as immanent in the world, then Jesus's question, "You do not want to leave too, do you?"

(John 6:67, NIV) confronts *each of us, singularly, and at every instant*. Will we turn outward toward the world and away from ourselves, standing before God? Or will we turn inward, and there find that we are always already found by God? Like Peter, Kierkegaard's Pentecost discourses suggest that the only appropriate answer is to humble oneself before God and realize that there is nowhere else to go (John 6:68).[75]

Knowing God and knowing oneself are not, then, appropriately achieved in the same way that one would know worldly externalities. One knows God through "coming to oneself as nothing" such that one's own story, one's own testimony, is all that one has. In many Pentecostal churches, one hears the phrase, "If you only knew like I knew," as a preface to claims about God's goodness and grace. Crucially, this is not meant as an epistemic disclaimer, but instead as a proclamation of the depth of relational intimacy with God shared by all in the community. Kierkegaard helps us to understand that Christian epistemology is not a matter of subjectivist knowledge, where you have your truth and I have my own. It is a matter of a shared experience of God's grace that is, nonetheless, only subjectively available: I can't tell you who you are in God; only you can "come to know" yourself before God. Ultimately, though, we both subjectively testify to the shared truth that, as Kierkegaard says in his 1843 discourse, "The expectancy of faith, then, is victory!" (EUD, 19).[76]

Christian existence is not something that invites ascetic isolation but rather demands engagement with the powers of the world. In the relation to the Holy Spirit, Kierkegaard says, "all my work oriented to knowing does not touch my life at all, its desires, its passions, its selfishness, and leaves me completely unchanged—my action changes my life" (FSE, 116). The Christian must stand publicly as a witness to the truth. For Kierkegaard, Pentecost again stands as the demonstration of this fundamental aspect of Christianity:

> When the apostles spoke on the first Pentecost Day, they were never more sober than on that very day. Their lives perfectly expressed the unconditioned; they had completely come to themselves as nothing in self-knowledge before God—that is, as mere instruments in his hand, lost to and liberated from every consideration, burned to spirit, complete sober—but mockery said, "They are full of sweet wine," and the sagacious, sensible, levelheaded, purely human point of view had to say: They are intoxicated. (FSE, 114–115)

When Peter stood up and proclaimed that the apostles were not drunk, he testified to the unconditioned: he bore witness to the demand that one is nothing before God, such that being concerned about one's worldly dignity, human wisdom, and public status is the true intoxication. Kierkegaard takes this proclamation to resound as more than merely theological truth—as an invitation to social action.

When Kierkegaard claims that the new life given by the Spirit on the day of Pentecost was able to transform the world, he means it literally: the Spirit opened not only a new way of being but rather a new world—as defined by faith, hope, and love.[77] In this sense, the justice declared by Kierkegaard is eschatological: it is not about an achieved state of affairs but instead about a deep trust in God, who is the giver of good gifts. But living a life defined by such trust demands sacrifice. Costly grace would require nothing less: "*Either* there is an actual renunciation of the things of this world in order, with sacrifice and suffering, to proclaim Christianity—this is the higher form; *or* one secures the temporal things of this world but then makes the confession that this proclamation is not really Christianity" (FSE, 135).

For Kierkegaard, there are no guarantees and assurances in religious life (FSE, 136–137). *Trust is defined by risk.* Eschatological *hope* is the space in which social justice continues to signify in a world problematically operating according to the "wine theory." For both Kierkegaard and Smith, "thinking in tongues" invites a different way of inhabiting the world and of relating to our neighbors within it.

Conclusion: Living in Haunted Houses . . . and Churches

It is important that Smith does not define "pentecostalism" according to narrow theological doctrinal commitments, but instead as a perspective that displays a broad pneumatological imagination. It is this "big tent" conception of pentecostalism that allows for the plausibility of the admittedly strange idea of bringing Kierkegaard together with pentecostal philosophy. Importantly, there are certainly objections that could be raised regarding such proximity. For example, Kierkegaard seems to be describing many charismatic and Pentecostal churches when he rightly criticizes the empty emotivism that can quickly replace Christian seriousness: "If you wish to be a success in the world with your proclamation of Christianity, it is now required that your life express the very opposite of the proclamation. . . . Weep a little about it; the Christian public will be moved to weep along with you in the quiet hour, because your life guarantees that the proclamation is an artistic work" (FSE, 138–139).

It is certainly the case that in many Pentecostal churches, displays of emotional affectivity take center stage, seemingly having asked God to wait quietly in the hall (as William J. Seymour was told to do by Charles Parham). Kierkegaard's warning not to let the intimate relation to God become a public display, such that it occludes the message of Christianity itself, is certainly one that a good many contemporary Christians would do well to heed. Indeed, the excesses of charismatic aesthetics are something about which early Pentecostal theologians were themselves worried. As we saw in Seymour's own account of Pentecostal theology, "the gift of the Holy Ghost is more than speaking in the tongues."[78]

Although Smith's expansive conception of pentecostalism is what opens space for the possible resonance with Kierkegaard, one might still object that Smith's notion is *so broad* as to include practically any religiously oriented postmodern philosophy. If Smith's account is inclusive in such ways, then it is not surprising that Kierkegaard's proto-postmodern philosophy of religion is going to resonate with some of it. Accordingly, "pentecostal" would not be a descriptor that does much philosophical work, since it could seemingly be applied to a wide variety of generally postmodern thinkers who advocate the importance of social justice, relational openness, nondualism, and narratival knowledge. While I think that there is important work yet to be done in the area of pentecostal philosophy responding to such an objection, I do not think it should threaten the idea that Kierkegaard and pentecostal philosophy can and should be read together. Again, I have not attempted to argue that Kierkegaard was himself a Pentecostal, but merely that his two Pentecost discourses are especially helpful for thinking through some of the possible characteristics of contemporary pentecostal philosophy as proposed by Smith. That non-pentecostals might share aspects of that worldview and embrace parts of that imagination is plausibly viewed as cause for optimism about the possibilities of a wide range of conversation partners for contemporary pentecostal philosophy, rather than as reason to abandon the notion of pentecostal philosophy as merely derivative. While I am sympathetic to the suggestion that pentecostal philosophy might benefit from a narrowing of its defining characteristics in various ways, Smith's strategy of starting as broadly as possible seems sensible as a first step toward a continued discussion and an expanding scholarly literature in which pentecostalism would be taken more seriously as being relevant to contemporary philosophical debates.

Ultimately, by bringing Kierkegaard's discourses into conversation with Smith's account of pentecostalism, I think we are better able to appreciate what might be right about pentecostalism in "the present age," while maintaining a critical eye toward those aspects of contemporary Pentecostal worship and social identity that have often captured popular imagination in problematic ways. In light of Kierkegaard's Pentecost discourses, pentecostal philosophy might better be able to clarify that the "actions" for which the gifts of the Spirit empower the faithful are not best thought of as self-glorifying, but instead other-serving. When a charismatic aesthetics turns the spotlight (and the attention of the crowd) toward *my* actions, I have failed to translate my self-knowledge into appropriate humble practice. Too often Pentecostal and charismatic churches think that God is served when people are talking about the awesome things going on in those churches, rather than remembering that "dying to" must precede the "new life" offered by the Spirit. Otherwise put, true self-knowledge reveals that God "must become greater; I must become less" (John 3:30, NIV). We must simultaneously embrace the Kierkegaardian insight while also appreciating the Kierkegaardian critique.

Smith claims that his account is offered as something of a research program for an "emerging generation of pentecostal philosophers."[79] While only time will tell if such a generation ends up really emerging on the philosophical scene in ways that are productive to philosophy more broadly, I hope that Kierkegaard will be viewed as a resource for such work. Although it is unlikely that Kierkegaard ever spoke in tongues, I think that he can certainly help philosophers of religion to think well about the Holy Spirit, while also encouraging us all to consider how personal identity and social existence might be enriched by "*thinking* in tongues."

J. AARON SIMMONS is Associate Professor of Philosophy at Furman University in Greenville, South Carolina. He is author of *God and the Other: Ethics and Politics After the Theological Turn* (Indiana University Press, 2011) and with Bruce Ellis Benson of *The New Phenomenology: A Philosophical Introduction*.

Notes

1. Famously such discussions have tended to focus on the issue of fideism—see, for example, Genia Schönbaumsfeld, *A Confusion of the Spheres: Kierkegaard and Wittgenstein on Philosophy and Religion* (Oxford: Oxford University Press, 2007); James Mark Shields, "Faith and the Sublation of Modernity: Kierkegaard, Quixote and the Transformation of Fideism," *Philosophy, Culture, and Traditions* 4 (2007), pp. 231–47; Terrence Penelhum, *God and Skepticism: A Study in Skepticism and Fideism* (Dordrecht: Reidel, 1983); James T. King, "Fideism and Rationality," *New Scholasticism* 49 (Autumn 1975): 431–450; Christopher Insole, "Kierkegaard: A Reasonable Fideist?" *Heythrop Journal* 39, no. 4 (October 1998): 363–378; and several works by C. Stephen Evans, see especially "Kierkegaard and Plantinga on Belief in God: Subjectivity as the Ground of Properly Basic Religious Beliefs," *Faith and Philosophy* 5, no.1 (1988): 25–39; "The Epistemological Significance of Transformative Religious Experiences: A Kierkegaardian Exploration," *Faith and Philosophy* 8, no. 2 (1991): 180–192; *Faith Beyond Reason: A Kierkegaardian Account* (Grand Rapids, MI: William B. Eerdmans, 1998); "Kierkegaard and the Limits of Reason: Can There Be a Responsible Fideism?" *Revista Portuguesa de Filosofia* 64, no. 2–4 (April–December 2008): 1021–1035. For the most comprehensive discussion of Kierkegaardian epistemology, see M. G. Piety, *Ways of Knowing: Kierkegaard's Pluralist Epistemology* (Waco, TX: Baylor University Press, 2010).

2. See especially Zachary R. Manis, "Kierkegaard on Divine Command Theory: Replies to Quinn and Evans," *Religious Studies* 45, no. 3 (September 2009): 289–307; and "Kierkegaard and Evans on the Problem of Abraham," *Journal of Religious Ethics* 39, no. 3 (2011): 474–492; C. Stephen Evans, *Kierkegaard's Ethic of Love: Divine Commands and Moral Obligations* (Oxford: Oxford University Press, 2004); Philip L. Quinn, "The Divine Command Ethics in Kierkegaard's Works of Love," in *Faith, Freedom, and Rationality: Philosophy of Religion Today*, Jeff Jordan and Daniel Howard-Snyder, eds. (Lanham, MD: Rowman & Littlefield, 1996), pp. 29–44. See also Richard H. Bell, *The Grammar of the Heart: Thinking with Kierkegaard and Wittgenstein* (San Francisco: Harper & Row, 1988).

3. See, for example, Jon Stewart, ed., *Kierkegaard and Existentialism: Kierkegaard Research: Sources, Reception, and Resources, Vol. 9* (Burlington, VT: Ashgate, 2011); Robert Merrihew Adams, "The Knight of Faith," in *The Existentialists: Critical Essays on Kierkegaard, Nietzsche,*

Heidegger, and Sartre, Charles Guignon, ed. (Lanham, MD: Rowman & Littlefield, 2004), pp. 19–32; John J. Davenport and Anthony Rudd, eds., *Kierkegaard After MacIntyre: Essays on Freedom, Narrative, and Virtue* (Peru, IL: Open Court, 2001). For examples of classical discussions of Kierkegaard and existentialism, see Lev Shestov, *Kierkegaard and the Existential Philosophy* (Athens: Ohio University Press, 1969); and Jean Wahl, *Études Kierkegaardiennes*, 2nd ed. (Paris: Librairie Philosophique, 1949). For a consideration of how French existential appropriations of Kierkegaard have affected contemporary continental readings of Emmanuel Levinas, see J. Aaron Simmons, "Existential Appropriations: The Influence of Jean Wahl on Levinas's Reading of Kierkegaard," in *Kierkegaard and Levinas: Ethics, Politics, and Religion*, J. Aaron Simmons and David Wood, eds. (Bloomington: Indiana University Press, 2008), pp. 41–66.

4. See J. Aaron Simmons, *God and the Other: Ethics and Politics After the Theological Turn* (Bloomington: Indiana University Press, 2011); Stephen Backhouse, *Kierkegaard's Critique of Christian Nationalism* (Oxford: Oxford University Press, 2011); Stephen Minister, "Works of Justice, Works of Love: Kierkegaard, Levinas, and an Ethics Beyond Difference," in Simmons and Wood, eds., *Kierkegaard and Levinas*, pp. 229–243; Mark Dooley, *The Politics of Exodus: Kierkegaard's Ethics of Responsibility* (New York: Fordham University Press, 2001); Martin J. Matuštík, *Postnational Identity: Critical Theory and Existential Philosophy in Habermas, Kierkegaard, and Havel* (New York: Guilford Press, 1993); and Matuštík's "Kierkegaard's Radical Existential Praxis, or Why the Individual Defies Liberal, Communitarian, and Postmodern Categories," in *Kierkegaard and Post/Modernity*, Martin J. Matuštík and Merold Westphal, eds. (Bloomington: Indiana University Press, 1995), pp. 239–264.

5. See Matuštík and Westphal, eds., *Kierkegaard in Post/Modernity*; and Silvia Walsh, "Kierkegaard and Postmodernism," *International Journal for Philosophy of Religion* 20, no. 2 (1991): 113–122.

6. See Simmons and Wood, eds., *Kierkegaard and Levinas*.

7. There is, of course, a significant and continually developing literature on Pentecostalism in religious studies and theology.

8. James K. A. Smith, *Thinking in Tongues: Pentecostal Contributions to Christian Philosophy* (Grand Rapids, MI: William B. Eerdmans, 2010). Hereafter cited as *Tongues*.

9. For the most sustained consideration of those Kierkegaardian texts, see Robert Perkins, ed., *International Kierkegaard Commentary, Vol. 21*, For Self-Examination *and* Judge for Yourself! (Macon, GA: Mercer University Press, 2002). For one of the very few essays that directly and extensively considers the role of the Holy Spirit in Kierkegaard's work (especially in the context of the Pentecost discourses), see Paul Martens, "The Emergence of the Holy Spirit in Kierkegaard's Thought: Critical Theological Developments in *For Self-Examination* and *Judge for Yourself!*, in Perkins, ed., *International Kierkegaard Commentary*, Vol. 21, pp. 199–222.

10. Smith, *Tongues*, pp. xv–xvi. However, I will not be suggesting that pentecostalism is an appropriate historical description of how to understand Kierkegaard's own version of Danish Lutheranism. As such, I intend this essay to be primarily philosophical, rather than primarily historical or theological.

11. Accordingly, Smith does not set out to criticize pentecostals for being anti-intellectual, as some other scholars have done (see Mark A. Noll, *The Scandal of the Evangelical Mind* [Grand Rapids, MI: William B. Eerdmans, 1994]), but rather attempts to argue for the positive contributions that pentecostalism might offer to philosophy itself. For Smith's response to Noll's charge of anti-intellectualism, see James K. A. Smith, "Scandalizing Theology: A Pentecostal Response to Noll's Scandal," *Pneuma* 19 (1997): 225–238.

12. Smith, *Tongues*, pp. xv–xvi.

13. Smith, *Tongues*, p. xvii.

14. Smith, *Tongues*, p. xviii.

15. Smith, *Tongues*, p. xix.

16. Smith, *Tongues*, p. xx. Smith is quick to clarify that he is not denying pentecostal doctrinal specificity, but instead simply not viewing doctrines as the key distinguishing feature of pentecostalism itself. As he explains, "By a 'pentecostal worldview' . . . I mean that embedded in the embodied practices and spirituality of pentecostalism are the elements of a latent but distinctive understanding of the world, an affective 'take' on the world that constitutes more of a social imaginary than a cognitive framework" (*Tongues*, p.31).

17. Smith, *Tongues*, p. 33.

18. Smith, *Tongues*, pp. xiii, xv, xxiv. Indeed, for the first three of the four areas Smith discusses (epistemology, ontology, philosophy of religion, and philosophy of language), there seem to be alternative "forms of life" that could come close to exhibiting the traits that Smith articulates as "distinctly" pentecostal. Of course, Smith might intend that the distinctiveness shows up as the result of a conjunction of such features, rather than due to the individual features themselves.

19. Smith, *Tongues*, p. 12.

20. Amos Yong, *Spirit-World-Community: Theological Hermeneutics in Trinitarian Perspective* (Aldershot: Ashgate, 2002), pp.119–149.

21. Smith, *Tongues*, p. 20.

22. I realize that in light of Smith's own Reformed perspective, this might seem an odd claim to make. For explanations of open theism, see John Sanders, *The God Who Risks: A Theology of Divine Providence*, revised edition (Downer's Grove, IL: InterVarsity, 2007); Clark Pinnock, Richard Rice, John Sanders, William Hasker, and David Basinger, *The Openness of God: A Biblical Challenge to the Traditional Understanding of God* (Downer's Grove, IL: InterVarsity, 1994).

23. Smith, *Tongues*, p. 34.

24. See Emmanuel Levinas, *Totality and Infinity: An Essay on Exteriority*, trans. Alphonso Lingis (Pittsburgh: Duquesne University Press, 1969); and *Otherwise than Being or Beyond Essence*, trans. Alphonso Lingis (Pittsburgh: Duquesne University Press, 1997).

25. See Jacques Derrida, *The Gift of Death*, trans. David Wills (Chicago: University of Chicago Press, 1995); and *Adieu to Emmanuel Levinas*, trans. Pascale-Anne Brault and Michael Naas (Stanford, CA: Stanford University Press, 1999).

26. See John D. Caputo, *Against Ethics* (Bloomington: Indiana University Press, 1993); and *The Prayers and Tears of Jacques Derrida: Religion Without Religion* (Bloomington: Indiana University Press, 1997).

27. I would argue that this underlies the practice of petitionary prayer, which is frequently found within pentecostal communities—especially as concerns prayer for divine healing. For more on how prayer functions within early Pentecostal theology, see Douglas Jacobsen, ed., *A Reader in Pentecostal Theology: Voices from the First Generation* (Bloomington: Indiana University Press, 2006).

28. Divine personalism will become especially important in Smith's subsequent conception of pentecostal epistemology, which stresses the importance of personal testimony and narratival truth, but also in the way pentecostalism invites a robust ethical engagement with the marginalized and oppressed. Elsewhere I have argued that Levinas's own philosophy might benefit from a more decidedly personalist conception of God: see J. Aaron Simmons, "In Whom, Then, Do We Put Our Trust?—Thinking About Levinas with Drew Dalton," *The Journal for Cultural and Religious Theory* 11, no. 3 (Fall 2011): 37–45.

29. Smith, *Tongues*, p. 39.

30. Smith, *Tongues*, p. 40.

31. Smith, *Tongues*, p. 41.

32. Here I am thinking of John D. Caputo's suggestion that a belief in a personal God who actively works in history is tantamount to believing in magic (*The Weakness of God: A Theology of the Event* [Bloomington: Indiana University Press, 2006], e.g., pp. 15, 18, 20). Ironically, though Caputo is one of the most prominent advocates of the intimate relation of stories and truth, which in many ways resonates with pentecostal epistemology, he constrains the way in which such stories can operate such that many pentecostals are likely to take issue with his description of a God who is miraculously active in history as akin to a "laser show at Disneyworld" (*The Weakness of God*, p. 16). Though I find Caputo to be among the most helpful of contemporary philosophers of religion for thinking about the unseen dimensions that resonate throughout existence, I worry that his otherwise deeply compelling account of a "hyper-realism of the event" ends up limiting the possible ways of relating to those dimensions. In brief, I think that he ends up being quite close to someone like Richard Rorty, who rightly appreciates the value of narrative in both moral life and religious existence but then appears to force such narratives to operate according to inherently quasi-naturalistic assumptions.

33. David Foster Wallace, *This Is Water: Some Thoughts, Delivered on a Significant Occasion, about Living a Compassionate Life* (New York: Little, Brown & Company, 2009), p. 16.

34. Smith, *Tongues*, p. 42.

35. Though I am thinking here of the way in which the Holy Spirit is sometimes referred to as the "Holy Ghost," the notion of being "haunted" is one that might further link pentecostalism with deconstructive postmodernism (e.g., consider Derrida's notion of "hauntology" [Jacques Derrida, *Specters of Marx: The State of Debt, the Work of Mourning, and the New International*, trans. Peggy Kamuf (New York: Routledge, 1994).

36. Smith, *Tongues*, p. 42, emphasis in original.

37. Smith, *Tongues*, p. 43.

38. Smith, *Tongues*, p. 64.

39. Smith, *Tongues*, p. 59. While I am certainly sympathetic to Smith's articulation of an affinity between pentecostalism and postmodernism in this way, one does not have to look to postmodern texts to find philosophical manifestations of such existentially aware narratival approaches to knowledge. Consider, for example, the debates concerning theology and falsification between Antony Flew, R. M. Hare, and Basil Mitchell (see Antony Flew and Alasdair MacIntyre, eds., *New Essays in Philosophical Theology* [London: SCM Press, 1955], pp. 96–108). Therein, a question of how personal relationships and discursive contexts might affect one's evidentiary standards is already in play, in ways that would invite comparison to IKTIKTIK epistemology. Even more appropriate might be C. S. Lewis's notion of "obstinacy in belief" (C. S. Lewis, *The World's Last Night and Other Essays* [Boston: Harcourt, 1960], pp. 13–30). For Lewis, a personal relationship with a personal God invites a shift of epistemological register such that what might have counted as evidence prior to that relationship no longer has the same epistemic weight internal to the relationship. Moreover, according to Lewis, new evidentiary sources emerge as a result of the relationship itself. From within more contemporary analytic philosophy of religion, one might also consider William Alston's account of perceiving God, Nicholas Wolterstorff's idea of the historical context in which control beliefs arise, and Alvin Plantinga's notion of religious beliefs as "properly basic" as all, in various ways, being expressions of epistemological perspectives that have at least some affinity with the sort of narratival and affective account Smith finds in Pentecostalism (see William Alston, *Perceiving God: The Epistemology of Religious Experience* [Ithaca, NY: Cornell University Press,

1991]; Nicholas Wolterstorff, *Reason within the Bounds of Religion*, 2nd ed. [Grand Rapids, MI: William B. Eerdmans, 1984]; Alvin Plantinga, *God and Other Minds: A Study of the Rational Justification of Belief in God* [Ithaca, NY: Cornell University Press, 1967]). Again, the point is not that Smith is wrong about the postmodern sensibilities of pentecostalism, but simply that were one suspicious of postmodernism, for whatever reason, there are other epistemological resources to which one might turn to make sense of pentecostal spirituality.

40. Jacobsen, ed., *A Reader in Pentecostal Theology*, p. 51.

41. Jacobsen, ed., *A Reader in Pentecostal Theology*, p. 51.

42. Jacobsen, ed., *A Reader in Pentecostal Theology*, p. 54.

43. Jacobsen, ed., *A Reader in Pentecostal Theology*, p. 49.

44. Smith, *Tongues*, p. 44.

45. Smith, *Tongues*, p. 45.

46. Jacobsen, ed., *A Reader in Pentecostal Theology*, p. 45.

47. Jacobsen, ed., *A Reader in Pentecostal Theology*, p. 53.

48. Jacobsen, ed., *A Reader in Pentecostal Theology*, p. 202.

49. For the possible connections between "works of love" and "works of justice," see Minister, "Works of Justice, Works of Love."

50. Howard V. Hong and Edna H. Hong, "Historical Introduction," in Kierkegaard, FSE, pp. vii–xvii, vii.

51. Bruce H. Kirmmse, *Kierkegaard in Golden Age Denmark* (Bloomington: Indiana University Press, 1990), p. 423.

52. Indeed, Bruce H. Kirmmse claims that they are "particularly interesting" more for their tone than for their content, which finds a middle ground between the more restrained "Open Letter" to Rudelbach and the polemical "abandon" demonstrated in the "attack on Christendom" (*Kierkegaard in Golden Age Denmark*, p. 423).

53. Martens, "The Emergence of the Holy Spirit," p. 199.

54. Martens, "The Emergence of the Holy Spirit," p. 200.

55. Martens, "The Emergence of the Holy Spirit," p. 200. Martens suggests that it seems that "we have not learned anything in this respect" (p. 200) since Jeremy Walker's 1985 admission that, "I can say almost nothing about SK's understanding of this idea. This is a serious lacuna in the present study. For presumably, the deepest of all ways of existing before God is existing in the Holy Spirit" (Jeremy Walker, *Kierkegaard: The Descent into God* [Montreal: McGill-Queen's University Press, 1985], p. 205; quoted in Martens, "The Emergence of the Holy Spirit," p. 200). As an example of the odd absence of these texts as foci of Kierkegaardian scholarship, Ronald L. Hall's excellent book *Word and Spirit: A Kierkegaardian Critique of the Modern Age*, which includes sections entitled "Spirit as Psyche" and "Spirit as Pneuma," does not list either *For Self-Examination* or *Judge For Yourself!* among the books given abbreviations due to their being "cited more than once" (Bloomington: Indiana University Press, 1993, pp. xi–xiii).

56. Jørgen Bukdahl, *Søren Kierkegaard and the Common Man*, trans., rev., and ed. Bruce H. Kirmmse (Grand Rapids, MI: William B. Eerdmans, 2001), p. 32.

57. Smith, *Tongues*, p. 40.

58. Smith, *Tongues*, p. 39.

59. Dietrich Bonhoeffer, *The Cost of Discipleship*, trans. R. H. Fuller with revisions by Irmgard Booth (London: SCM Press, 1959).

60. See Geoffrey Kelly, "The Influence of Kierkegaard on Bonhoeffer's Concept of Discipleship," *Irish Theological Quarterly* 41 (1974): 148–154; David R. Law, "Cheap Grace and the Cost of Discipleship in Kierkegaard's For Self-Examination," in Perkins, ed., *International Kierkegaard Commentary, Vol. 21*, pp. 111–142; and Murray Rae, "Kierkegaard, Barth, and

Bonhoeffer: Conceptions of the Relation between Grace and Works," in Perkins, ed., *International Kierkegaard Commentary, Vol. 21*, pp. 143–168.

61. Smith, *Tongues*, p. 39.

62. For more on the logic of gift that operates in *Fear and Trembling*, see Simmons, *God and the Other*, chapters 2 and 3.

63. Kierkegaard explicitly connects these two biblical accounts in such ways (FSE, 79).

64. For an extended consideration of ontotheology in this respect, see Merold Westphal, *Overcoming Onto-Theology: Toward a Postmodern Christian Faith* (New York: Fordham University Press, 2001). In *Transcendence and Self-Transcendence: On God and the Soul*, Westphal also argues that Kierkegaard moves beyond ontotheology ([Bloomington: Indiana University Press, 2004], chapter 8).

65. Westphal, *Transcendence and Self-Transcendence*, p. 224, emphasis in original.

66. For a helpful consideration of the link between dying to the world and self-denial, see Silvia Walsh, "Dying to the World and Self-Denial in Kierkegaard's Religious Thought," in Perkins, ed., *International Kierkegaard Commentary, Vol. 21*, pp. 169–198.

67. Such fulfillment might even be best achieved by remaining still—as seems to be the case in Kierkegaard's discussion of the coachman/horses metaphor in "Become Sober."

68. Kirmmse, *Kierkegaard in Golden Age Denmark*, p. 424.

69. I will not go into any detail on this topic here, but for more on Kierkegaard and Luther as concerns *For Self-Examination* and *Judge For Yourself!*, see Lee Barrett, "Faith, Works, and the Uses of the Law: Kierkegaard's Appropriation of Lutheran Doctrine," in Perkins, ed., *International Kierkegaard Commentary, Vol. 21*, pp. 77–110; Craig Hinkson, "Luther and Kierkegaard: Theologians of the Cross," *International Journal of Systematic Theology* 3, no. 1 (March 2001): 27–45.

70. Smith, *Tongues*, p. 23.

71. Smith, *Tongues*, p. 23.

72. Smith, *Tongues*, p. 24.

73. The notion of worldly (or we might even say "ontological") powerlessness, here, might resonate well with Levinas's notion of "substitution" (Emmanuel Levinas, *Otherwise than Being*, chapter 4).

74. Though I am not able to pursue the connections here, I think that Kierkegaard's revolutionary conception of the distinction between Christianity and the secular world has much in common with Michel Henry's distinction between the "truth of the world" and the "truth of life" (see *I Am the Truth: Toward a Philosophy of Christianity*, trans. Susan Emanuel [Stanford, CA: Stanford University Press, 2003]; *Words of Christ*, trans. Christina M. Gschwandtner [Grand Rapids, IL: William B. Eerdmans, 2012]).

75. For an extended consideration of this section of *Sickness* in relation to the notion of standing "before God," see Simmons, *God and the Other*, pp. 95–100.

76. I think that there are reasonable debates that could be had at this point about whether such "victory" is eschatologically assured, as it were, or more a matter of relational hope in light of radical openness to God and the future. For more on how Kierkegaard might understand such victory, see John Davenport, "What Kierkegaardian Faith Adds to Alterity Ethics: How Levinas and Derrida Miss the Eschatological Dimension," in Simmons and Wood, eds., *Kierkegaard and Levinas*, pp.169–196. Importantly, in light of Smith's contention that pentecostal philosophy might resonate in many ways with postmodern philosophy and alterity ethics, Davenport suggests that it is precisely the role of eschatological victory that differentiates Kierkegaard from such thinkers as Levinas and Derrida. Though I think that Davenport underestimates the eschatological dimensions in Levinas and Derrida, he is right to highlight that different eschatologies are likely to follow from personal conceptions of God as opposed

to those conceptions that suggest that God is "transcendent to the point of absence," as Levinas says (Levinas, *God, Death, and Time*, trans. Bettina Bergo [Stanford, CA: Stanford University Press, 2000], pp. 219–224). For a discussion of the difference between Kierkegaard's decidedly personal conception of God and Levinas's seeming impersonal conception, see Merold Westphal, *Levinas and Kierkegaard in Dialogue* (Bloomington: Indiana University Press, 2008).

77. Again, I think Michel Henry is an important interlocutor with Kierkegaard at this point.

78. Jacobsen, ed., *A Reader in Pentecostal Theology*, p. 54.

79. Smith, *Tongues*, p. 7.

Bibliography

Adams, Robert. *Finite and Infinite Goods*. New Haven, CT: Yale University Press, 1999.
———. "The Knight of Faith." In *The Existentialists: Critical Essays on Kierkegaard, Nietzsche, Heidegger, and Sartre*. Ed. Charles Guignon. Lanham, MD: Rowman & Littlefield, 2004, pp. 19–32.
Adorno, Theodor W. "On Kierkegaard's Doctrine of Love." *Studies in Philosophy and Social Science* 8.3 (1939): 413–429.
Alston, William. *Perceiving God: The Epistemology of Religious Experience*. Ithaca, NY: Cornell University Press, 1991.
Amichai, Yehuda. *Open Closed Open*. New York: Harcourt, 2000.
Aristotle. *Nicomachean Ethics*. Trans. Terence Irwin. Indianapolis: Hackett, 1985.
Backhouse, Stephen. *Kierkegaard's Critique of Christian Nationalism*. Oxford: Oxford University Press, 2011.
Balthasar, Hans Urs von. *The Scandal of the Incarnation: Irenaeus Against the Heresies*. Trans. John Sayward. San Francisco: Ignatius, 1990.
Barnett, Christopher B. *From Despair to Faith: The Spirituality of Søren Kierkegaard*. Minneapolis: Fortress, 2014.
———. *Kierkegaard, Pietism and Holiness*. Farnham, UK: Ashgate, 2011.
Barrett, Lee C. "Faith, Works, and the Uses of the Law: Kierkegaard's Appropriation of Lutheran Doctrine." In *International Kierkegaard Commentary, Vol. 21*, For Self- Examination *and* Judge for Yourself! Ed. Robert Perkins. Macon, GA: Mercer University Press, 2002, pp. 77–110.
———. "Simeon and Anna: Exemplars of Patience and Expectancy." In *Kierkegaard Research: Sources, Reception and Resources, Vol. 1, Kierkegaard and the Bible, Tome II: The New Testament*. Eds. Lee C. Barrett and Jon Stewart. London: Ashgate, 2010.
Barrett, William. *Irrational Man: A Study in Existential Philosophy*. New York: Anchor, 1990.
Bauerlein, Mark. *The Dumbest Generation: How the Digital Age Stupefies Young Americans and Jeopardizes Our Future (Or Don't Trust Anyone Under 30)*. New York: Tarcher, 2009.
Bauman, Zygmunt. *Liquid Love: On the Frailty of Human Bonds*. Cambridge: Polity, 2003.
Beabout, Gregory R. "The Silent Lily and Bird as Exemplars of the Virtue of Active Receptivity." In *International Kierkegaard Commentary, Vol. 18*, Without Authority. Ed. Robert L. Perkins. Macon, GA: Mercer University Press, 2007.
Bell, Richard H. *The Grammar of the Heart: Thinking with Kierkegaard and Wittgenstein*. San Francisco: Harper & Row, 1988.
Bonhoeffer, Dietrich. *The Cost of Discipleship*. Trans. R. H. Fuller with revisions by Irmgard Booth. London: SCM, 1959.

Braver, Lee. *Groundless Grounds: A Study of Wittgenstein and Heidegger.* Cambridge, MA: MIT Press, 2012.

Buber, Martin. *The Prophetic Faith.* New York: Harper & Row, 1949.

Bukdahl, Jørgen. *Søren Kierkegaard and the Common Man.* Trans. and ed. Bruce H. Kirmmse. Grand Rapids, MI: William B. Eerdmans, 2001.

Burbridge, John W. *Historical Dictionary of Hegelian Philosophy*, 2nd edition. Lanham, MD: Scarecrow, 2008.

Bøgeskov, Benjamin Miguel Olivares. "Joy." In *Kierkegaard Research: Sources, Reception and Resources, Vol. 15, Kierkegaard's Concepts, Tome IV: Individual to Novel.* Eds. Steven M. Emmanuel, William McDonald, and Jon Stewart. London: Ashgate, 2014.

Caputo, John D. *Against Ethics.* Bloomington: Indiana University Press, 1993.

———. *The Prayers and Tears of Jacques Derrida: Religion Without Religion.* Bloomington: Indiana University Press, 1997.

———. *The Weakness of God: A Theology of the Event.* Bloomington: Indiana University Press, 2006.

Carr, Nicholas. *The Shallows: What the Internet Is Doing to Our Brains.* New York: Norton, 2011.

Cavell, Stanley. *The Senses of Walden.* Berkeley, CA: North Point, 1981.

———. Cora Diamond, Ian Hacking, John McDowell, and Cary Wolfe. *Philosophy and Animal Life.* New York: Columbia University Press, 2008.

Choufrine, Akadi. *Gnosis, Theophany, Theosis: Studies in Clement of Alexandria's Appropriation of His Background.* New York: Peter Lang, 2002.

Christensen, Arild. *Efterskriftens Opgør med Martensen* [The Confrontation with Martensen in the *Postscript*]. *Kierkegaardiana* 4 (1962): 45–62.

Coe, David. "Asceticism." In *Kierkegaard Research: Sources, Reception and Resources, Vol. 15, Kierkegaard's Concepts, Tome I: Absolute to Church.* Eds. Steven M. Emmanuel, William McDonald, and Jon Stewart. London: Ashgate, 2013.

Cohen, Ted. *Thinking of Others: On the Talent for Metaphor.* Princeton, NJ: Princeton University Press, 2008.

Come, Arnold B. *Kierkegaard as Humanist.* Montreal: McGill-Queen's University Press, 1995.

Critchley, Simon. *The Ethics of Deconstruction.* Edinburgh: Edinburgh University Press, 1992.

Crites, Stephen. "The Blissful Security of the Moment: Recollection, Repetition, and Eternal Recurrence." In *The International Kierkegaard Commentary, Vol. 6, Fear and Trembling and Repetition.* Ed. Robert L. Perkins. Macon, GA: Mercer University Press, 1993.

Curtis J. B. "On Job's Response to Yahweh." *Journal of Biblical Studies* 98.4 (1979): 497–511.

Daise, Benjamin. "The Will to Truth in Kierkegaard's *Philosophical Fragments.*" *Philosophy of Religion* 31 (1992): 1–12.

Dalsgaard, Matias Møl. *Don't Despair: Letter to a Modern Man.* Trans. Patrick Stokes. London: Pine Tribe, 2014.

Davenport, John. "Faith as Eschatological Trust in *Fear and Trembling.*" In *Ethics, Love, and Faith in Kierkegaard: A Philosophical Engagement.* Ed. Edward F. Mooney. Bloomington: Indiana University Press, 2008, pp. 196–233.

———. *Narrative Identity, Autonomy, and Mortality: From Frankfurt and MacIntyre to Kierkegaard*. London: Routledge, 2013.

———. "Romantic Marriage as a Model for Ethical Will." *Klassiker Auslegen: Søren Kierkegaards Entweder-Oder* [Interpreting Philosophical Classics: Søren Kierkegaard's *Either/Or*]. Eds. Hermann Deuser and Marcus Kleinert. Berlin: Walter de Gruyter, 2016.

———. "What Kierkegaardian Faith Adds to Alterity Ethics: How Levinas and Derrida Miss the Eschatological Dimension." In *Kierkegaard and Levinas*. Eds. J. Aaron Simmons and David Wood. Bloomington: Indiana University Press, 2008, pp.169–196.

———. *Will as Commitment and Resolve: An Existential Account of Creativity, Love, Virtue, and Happiness*. Fordham, NY: Fordham University Press, 2007.

Davenport, John J., and Anthony Rudd, eds. *Kierkegaard After MacIntyre: Essays on Freedom, Narrative, and Virtue*. Peru, IL: Open Court, 2001.

Derrida, Jacques. *Adieu to Emmanuel Levinas*. Trans. Pascale-Anne Brault and Michael Naas. Stanford, CA: Stanford University Press, 1999.

———. *The Gift of Death*. Trans. David Wills. Chicago: University of Chicago Press, 1995.

———. *Specters of Marx: The State of Debt, the Work of Mourning, and the New International*. Trans. Peggy Kamuf. New York: Routledge, 1994.

Detweiler, Craig. *iGods: How Technology Shapes Our Spiritual and Social Lives*. Grand Rapids, MI: Brazos, 2013.

Dooley, Mark. *The Politics of Exodus: Kierkegaard's Ethics of Responsibility*. New York: Fordham University Press, 2001.

Dostoevsky, Fyodor. *The Brothers Karamazov*. Trans. David McDuff. London: Penguin Classics, 2003.

Dreyfus, Hubert L. *On the Internet*. 2nd edition. London: Routledge, 2009.

Ellul, Jacques. *Propaganda: The Formation of Men's Attitudes*. New York: Vintage, 1973.

———. *The Technological Society*. Trans. John Wilkinson. New York: Vintage, 1964.

Emmanuel, Steven N. "Kierkegaard on Faith and Knowledge." *Kierkegaardiana* 15 (1991): 136–146.

Evans, C. Stephen. "The Epistemological Significance of Transformative Religious Experiences: A Kierkegaardian Exploration." *Faith and Philosophy* 8.2 (1991): 180–192.

———. *Faith Beyond Reason: A Kierkegaardian Account*. Grand Rapids, MI: Eerdmans, 1998.

———. "Kierkegaard and the Limits of Reason: Can There Be a Responsible Fideism?" *Revista Portuguesa de Filosofia* 64.2–4 (April–December 2008): 1021–1035.

———. "Kierkegaard and Plantinga on Belief in God: Subjectivity as the Ground of Properly Basic Religious Beliefs." *Faith and Philosophy* 5.1 (1988): 25–39.

———. *Kierkegaard: An Introduction*. Cambridge: Cambridge University Press, 2009.

———. *Kierkegaard's Ethic of Love: Divine Commands and Moral Obligations*. Oxford: Oxford University Press, 2004.

Evans, C. Stephen, and Robert C. Roberts. "Ethics." In *The Oxford Handbook of Kierkegaard*. Eds. John Lippitt and George Pattison. Oxford: Oxford University Press, 2013.

Ferreira, M. Jamie. "Love." In *The Oxford Handbook of Kierkegaard*. Eds. John Lippitt and George Pattison. Oxford: Oxford University Press, 2013, pp. 328–343.

——. *Love's Grateful Striving: A Commentary on Kierkegaard's* Works of Love. Oxford: Oxford University Press, 2001.

——. "The Problematic Agapeistic Ideal—Again." In *Ethics, Love, and Faith in Kierkegaard: Philosophical Engagements.* Ed. Edward F. Mooney. Bloomington: Indiana University Press, 2008, pp. 93–110.

——. "Review of Sharon Krishek, *Kierkegaard on Love and Faith*." *Notre Dame Philosophical Reviews* (January 21, 2010), online. Retrieved March 24, 2017, from http://ndpr.nd.edu/news/kierkegaard-on-faith-and-love/.

Fingarette, Herbert. *Self-Deception.* Berkeley: University of California Press, 2000.

Flew, Antony, and Alasdair MacIntyre, eds. *New Essays in Philosophical Theology.* London: SCM, 1955.

Frankfurt, Harry. *The Reasons of Love.* Princeton, NJ: Princeton University Press, 2004.

Fremstedal, Roe. "The Concept of the Highest Good in Kierkegaard." *International Journal for Philosophy of Religion* 69 (2011): 155–171.

Fremstedal, Roe. *Kierkegaard and Kant on Radical Evil and the Highest Good: Virtue, Happiness, and the Kingdom of God.* London: Palgrave Macmillan, 2014.

Furtak, Rick Anthony. *Wisdom in Love: Kierkegaard and the Ancient Quest for Emotional Integrity.* Notre Dame, IN: University of Notre Dame Press, 2005.

Geismar, Eduard. *Søren Kierkegaard, hans Livsudvikling og Forfattervirksomhed* [Søren Kierkegaard, The Development of His Life and Activity as an Author] I–VI. Copenhagen: G. E. C. Gads Forlag, 1927.

Glenn, J. D., Jr. "'A Highest Good . . . An Eternal Happiness': The Human Telos in Kierkegaard's *Concluding Unscientific Postscript*." In *International Kierkegaard Commentary, Vol. 12,* Concluding Unscientific Postscript to "Philosophical Fragments." Ed. R. L. Perkins. Macon, GA: Mercer University Press, 1997, pp. 247–262.

Grøn, Arne. *The Concept of Anxiety in Søren Kierkegaard.* Trans. Jeannette Knox. Macon, GA: Mercer University Press, 2008.

Hall, Ronald L. *Word and Spirit: A Kierkegaardian Critique of the Modern Age.* Bloomington: Indiana University Press, 1993.

Hampson, Daphne. *Kierkegaard: Exposition and Critique.* Oxford: Oxford University Press, 2013.

Hannay, Alastair. *Kierkegaard.* London: Routledge & Kegan Paul, 1982.

Hart, Kevin, and Michael A. Signer, eds. *The Exorbitant: Emmanuel Levinas between Jews and Christians.* Bronx, NY: Fordham University Press, 2010.

Hegel, G. W. F. *Phenomenology of Spirit.* Trans. A. V. Miller. Oxford: Oxford University Press, 1977.

——. *The Philosophy of History.* Trans. John Sibree. New York: Dover, 1956.

——. *Werke in zwanzig Bänden.* Eds. Eva Moldenhauer and Karl Markus Michel. Frankfurt: Suhrkamp, 1970.

Heidegger, Martin. *Being and Time.* Trans. John Macquarrie and Edward Robinson. San Francisco: Harper & Row, 1962.

——. *Being and Time.* Trans. John Stambaugh. Albany, NY: State University of New York Press, 1996.

——. "The Onto-Theo-Logical Constitution of Metaphysics." In *Identity and Difference.* Ed. Joan Stambaugh. Chicago: University of Chicago Press, 1969.

———. "The Question Concerning Technology." In *Basic Writings*. Ed. David Farrell Krell. London: Routledge, 1993.

Henry, Michel. *I Am the Truth: Toward a Philosophy of Christianity*. Trans. Susan Emanuel. Stanford, CA: Stanford University Press, 2003.

———. *Words of Christ*. Trans. Christina M. Gschwandtner. Grand Rapids, IL: William B. Eerdmans, 2012.

Herdt, Jennifer A. *Putting on Virtue: The Legacy of the Splendid Vices*. Chicago: University of Chicago Press, 2008.

Hinkson, Craig. "Luther and Kierkegaard: Theologians of the Cross." *International Journal of Systematic Theology* 3.1 (March 2001): 27–45.

Hofstadter, Albert. *Truth and Art*. New York: Columbia University Press, 1965.

Hough, Sheridan. "Silence, 'Composure in Existence,' and the Promise of Faith's Joy." In *Why Kierkegaard Matters*. Ed. Marc A. Jolly. Macon, GA: Mercer University Press, 2010, pp. 147–157.

Houlgate, Stephen. *An Introduction to Hegel: Freedom, Truth and History*. Oxford: Blackwell, 2005.

Hügli, Anton. *Die Erkenntnis der Subjektivität und die Objektivität des Erkennens bei Søren Kierkegaard* [Knowledge of Subjectivity and the Objectivity of Knowing in Søren Kierkegaard]. Basel: Editio Academica, 1973.

Hägg, Henny Fiskå. *Clement of Alexandria and the Beginnings of Christian Apophaticism*. Oxford: Oxford University Press, 2006.

Insole, Christopher. "Kierkegaard: A Reasonable Fideist?" *Heythrop Journal* 39.4 (October 1998): 363–378.

Jacobsen, Douglas, ed. *A Reader in Pentecostal Theology: Voices from the First Generation*. Bloomington: Indiana University Press, 2006.

Jollimore, Troy. *Love's Vision*. Princeton, NJ: Princeton University Press, 2011.

Jung, Carl. *Answer to Job*. Princeton, NJ: Princeton University Press, 2012.

Kelly, Geoffrey. "The Influence of Kierkegaard on Bonhoeffer's Concept of Discipleship." *Irish Theological Quarterly* 41 (1974): 148–154.

King, James T. "Fideism and Rationality." *New Scholasticism* 49 (Autumn 1975): 431–450.

Kirmmse, Bruce H. *Kierkegaard in Golden Age Denmark*. Bloomington: Indiana University Press, 1990.

———. "Kierkegaard and MacIntyre: Possibilities for Dialogue." In *Kierkegaard After MacIntyre: Essays on Freedom, Narrative and Virtue*. Eds. John J. Davenport and Anthony Rudd. Chicago: Open Court, 2001.

Krishek, Sharon. *Kierkegaard on Faith and Love*. Cambridge: Cambridge University Press, 2009.

———. "The Enactment of Love by Faith: On Kierkegaard's Distinction between Love and Its Works." *Faith and Philosophy* 27.1 (2010): 3–21.

———. "In Defence of a Faith-Like Model of Love: A Reply to John Lippitt's 'Kierkegaard and the Problem of Special Relationships: Ferreira, Krishek, and the "God Filter."'" *International Journal for Philosophy of Religion* 75.2 (2014): 155–166.

Kupfer, Joseph. "The Moral Perspective of Humility." *Pacific Philosophical Quarterly* 84 (2003): 249–269.

Lavine, T. Z. *From Socrates to Sartre: The Philosophic Quest*. New York: Bantam, 1984.

Law, David R. "Cheap Grace and the Cost of Discipleship in Kierkegaard's *For Self-Examination.*" In *International Kierkegaard Commentary, Vol. 21,* For Self-Examination *and* Judge for Yourself! Ed. Robert Perkins. Macon, GA: Mercer University Press, 2002, pp. 111–142.

Lear, Jonathan. *Radical Hope: Ethics in the Face of Cultural Devastation.* Cambridge, MA: Harvard University Press, 2006.

Lewis, C. S. *The World's Last Night and Other Essays.* Boston: Harcourt, 1960.

Levenson, Jon D. *Inheriting Abraham: The Legacy of the Patriarch in Judaism, Christianity and Islam.* Princeton, NJ: Princeton University Press, 2012.

Levinas, Emmanuel. *Basic Philosophical Writings.* Eds. Adriaan T. Peperzak, Simon Critchley, and Robert Bernasconi. Bloomington: Indiana University Press, 1996.

———. *Difficult Freedom: Essays on Judaism.* Trans. S. Hand. Baltimore, MD: Johns Hopkins University Press, 1990.

———. *Ethics and Infinity.* Trans. R. A. Cohen. Pittsburgh, PA: Duquesne University Press, 1985.

———. *God, Death, and Time.* Trans. Bettina Bergo. Stanford, CA: Stanford University Press, 2000.

———. *In the Time of Nations.* Trans. M. B. Smith. Bloomington: Indiana University Press, 1994.

———. *Otherwise than Being or Beyond Essence.* Trans. Alphonso Lingis Pittsburgh, PA: Duquesne University Press, 1997.

———. *Totality and Infinity: An Essay on Exteriority.* Trans. Alphonso Lingis Pittsburgh, PA: Duquesne University Press, 1969.

Lewis, C. S. *The Four Loves.* Orlando, FL: Harcourt Brace, 1960.

Lilla, Salvatore R. C. *Clement of Alexandria: A Study in Christian Platonism and Gnosticism.* Oxford: Oxford University Press, 1971.

Lippitt, John. "Giving the 'Dear Self' Its Due: Kierkegaard, Frankfurt, and Self-Love." In *Love, Reason, and Will: Kierkegaard after Frankfurt.* Eds. Anthony Rudd and John Davenport. London: Bloomsbury, 2015.

———. *Humour and Irony in Kierkegaard's Thought.* New York: Palgrave Macmillan, 2000.

———. "Jest as Humility: Kierkegaard and the Possibility of Virtue." In *Humor, Comedy, and Laughter in 19th-Century Philosophy.* Ed. Lydia L. Moland. New York: Springer, forthcoming.

———. "Joy Beyond Worry: On Learning Humility from the Lilies and the Birds." In *Kierkegaard and Joy.* Eds. Edward F. Mooney and Carson Webb. Unpublished manuscript..

———. *Kierkegaard and the Problem of Self-Love.* Cambridge: Cambridge University Press, 2013.

———. "Learning to Hope: The Role of Hope in *Fear and Trembling.*" In *Kierkegaard's* Fear and Trembling: *A Critical Guide.* Ed. Daniel W. Conway. Cambridge: Cambridge University Press, 2015.

———. "Love's Perception: Søren Kierkegaard." In *The Oxford Handbook of the Philosophy of Love.* Eds. Christopher Grau and Aaron Smuts. Oxford: Oxford University Press, forthcoming.

———. "What Can Therapists Learn from Kierkegaard?" In *Therapy and the Counter-Tradition: The Edge of Philosophy.* Eds. Manu Bazzano and Julie Webb. London: Routledge, 2015.

Lysaker, John. *Emerson and Self-Culture*. Bloomington: Indiana University Press, 2008.

Løgstrup, Knud. *The Ethical Demand*. Trans. Theodor I. Jensen, Gary Puckering, and Eric Watkins. Eds. Hans Fink and Alasdair MacIntyre. Notre Dame, IN: University of Notre Dame Press, 1997.

MacIntyre, Alasdair. *Dependent Rational Animals: Why Human Beings Need the Virtues*. Chicago: Open Court, 1999.

Mackey, Louis. *Kierkegaard: A Kind of Poet*. Philadelphia: University of Pennsylvania Press, 1971.

———. *Points of View: Readings of Kierkegaard*. Tallahassee: Florida State University Press, 1986.

Macquarrie, John. *Christian Hope*. Oxford: Mowbray, 1978.

Manis, Zachary R. "Kierkegaard on Divine Command Theory: Replies to Quinn and Evans." *Religious Studies* 45.3 (September 2009): 289–307.

———. "Kierkegaard and Evans on the Problem of Abraham." *Journal of Religious Ethics* 39.3 (2011): 474–492.

Marino, Gordon. "A Critical Perspective on Kierkegaard's *At a Graveside*." In *Kierkegaard and Death*. Eds. Patrick Stokes and Adam J. Buben. Bloomington: Indiana University Press, 2011.

Marion, Jean-Luc. *The Erotic Phenomenon*. Trans. Stephen E. Lewis. Chicago: University of Chicago Press, 2007.

Martens, Paul. "The Emergence of the Holy Spirit in Kierkegaard's Thought: Critical Theological Developments in *For Self-Examination* and *Judge for Yourself!* In *International Kierkegaard Commentary, Vol. 21,* For Self-Examination *and* Judge for Yourself! Ed. Robert Perkins. Macon, GA: Mercer University Press, 2002, pp. 199–222.

Martin, Andy. "Winehouse, Breivik and Deadly Ideals." *The Opinionator. The New York Times*. July 26, 2011, online. Retrieved March 24, 2017, from https://opinionator .blogs.nytimes.com/2011/07/26/winehouse-breivik-and-deadly-ideals/?_r=0.

Matuštìk, Martin J. *Postnational Identity: Critical Theory and Existential Philosophy in Habermas, Kierkegaard, and Havel*. New York: Guilford Press, 1993.

———. "Kierkegaard's Radical Existential Praxis, or Why the Individual Defies Liberal, Communitarian, and Postmodern Categories." In *Kierkegaard and Post/Modernity*. Eds. Martin J. Matuštìk and Merold Westphal. Bloomington: Indiana University Press, 1995, pp. 239–264.

Mavrodes, George. "Religion and the Queerness of Morality." In *Rationality, Religious Belief, and Moral Commitment*. Eds. William Wainwright and Robert Audi. Ithaca, NY: Cornell University Press, 1986.

May, Rollo. *The Meaning of Anxiety*. Revised edition. New York: Norton, 1977.

McCarthy, Vincent A. *The Phenomenology of Moods in Kierkegaard*. Boston: Martinus Nijhoff, 1978.

McLuhan, Marshall. *Understanding Media: The Extensions of Man*. Cambridge, MA: MIT Press, 1994.

Melville, Herman. *Moby Dick*. New York: Penguin 2001.

Merleau-Ponty, Maurice. *Phenomenology of Perception*. Trans. Colin Smith. New York: Routledge, 2002.

———. *The Visible and the Invisible*. Trans. Alphonso Lingis. Evanston, IL: Northwestern University Press, 1968.

Miller, J. Hillis. *The Disappearance of God*. Urbana: University of Illinois Press, 2000.

Minister, Stephen. *De-Facing the Other: Reason, Ethics, and Politics after Difference.* Milwaukee, WI: Marquette University Press, 2012.

———. "Works of Justice, Works of Love: Kierkegaard, Levinas, and an Ethics Beyond Difference." In *Kierkegaard and Levinas: Ethics, Politics, and Religion.* Eds. J. Aaron Simmons and David Wood. Bloomington: Indiana University Press, 2008, pp. 229–243.

Mooney, Edward F. "Gender, Philosophy, and the Novel." *Metaphilosophy* 5.3 (1987): 241–252.

———. "The Intimate Agency of Death." In *Kierkegaard and Death.* Eds. Patrick Stokes and Adam Buben. Bloomington: Indiana University Press, 2011, pp. 136–138.

———. *Knights of Faith and Resignation: Reading Kierkegaard's* Fear and Trembling. Albany, NY: SUNY Press, 1996.

———. *On Søren Kierkegaard: Dialogue, Polemics, Lost Intimacy, and Time.* Burlington, VT: Ashgate, 2007.

———. *Selves in Discord and Resolve: Kierkegaard's Moral-Religious Psychology from* Either/Or *to* Sickness Unto Death. New York: Routledge, 1996.

Mooney, Edward F., and Carson Webb, eds. *Kierkegaard and Joy.* Unpublished manuscript.

Noll, Mark A. *The Scandal of the Evangelical Mind.* Grand Rapids, MI: William B. Eerdmans, 1994.

Pariser, Eli. *The Filter Bubble: How the New Personalized Web Is Changing What We Read and How We Think.* New York: Penguin, 2012.

Pattison, George. "Foreword." *Works of Love.* New York: Harper Perennial, 2009.

———. "The Joy of Birdsong, or Lyrical Dialectics." In *International Kierkegaard Commentary, Vol. 18,* Without Authority. Ed. Robert L. Perkins. Macon, GA: Mercer University Press, 2007.

———. *Kierkegaard's Upbuilding Discourses: Philosophy, Literature, and Theology.* London: Routledge, 2002.

———. *Thinking about God in an Age of Technology.* Oxford: Oxford University Press, 2005.

Penelhum, Terrence. *God and Skepticism: A Study in Skepticism and Fideism.* Dordrecht: Reidel, 1983.

Perkins, Robert. "Kierkegaard, a Kind of Epistemologist." *History of European Ideas* 12 (1990): 7–18.

———, ed. *International Kierkegaard Commentary, Vol. 21,* For Self-Examination *and* Judge for Yourself! Macon, GA: Mercer University Press, 2002.

Piety, M. G. "The Epistemology of the Postscript." In *Kierkegaard's Concluding Unscientific Postscript: A Critical Guide.* Ed. Rick Anthony Furtak. Cambridge: Cambridge University Press, 2010.

———. *Ways of Knowing: Kierkegaard's Pluralist Epistemology.* Waco, TX: Baylor University Press, 2010.

Pinnock, Clark, Richard Rice, John Sanders, William Hasker, and David Basinger. *The Openness of God: A Biblical Challenge to the Traditional Understanding of God.* Downer's Grove, IL: InterVarsity, 1994.

Plantinga, Alvin. *God and Other Minds: A Study of the Rational Justification of Belief in God.* Ithaca, NY: Cornell University Press, 1967.

Plato. *The Republic.* Trans. C. D. C. Reeve. Indianapolis: Hackett, 2004.

Polanyi, Michael. *Personal Knowledge.* Chicago: University of Chicago Press, 1962.

Postman, Neil. *Amusing Ourselves to Death: Public Discourse in the Age of Show Business.* 20th Anniversary Edition. New York: Penguin, 2005.

Potkay, Adam. *The Story of Joy: From the Bible to Late Romanticism*. Cambridge: Cambridge University Press, 2007.

Puchniak, Robert B. "Humility." In *Kierkegaard Research: Sources, Reception and Resources, Vol. 15, Kierkegaard's Concepts, Tome III: Envy to Incognito*. Eds. Steven M. Emmanuel, William McDonald, and Jon Stewart. London: Ashgate, 2014.

Putnam, Hilary. *The Collapse of the Fact/Value Dichotomy and Other Essays*. Cambridge, MA: Harvard University Press, 2004.

Quinn, Philip L. "The Divine Command Ethics in Kierkegaard's *Works of Love*." In *Faith, Freedom, and Rationality: Philosophy of Religion Today*. Eds. Jeff Jordon and Daniel Howard-Snyder. Lanham, MD: Rowman & Littlefield, 1996, pp. 29–44.

Rae, Murray. "Kierkegaard, Barth, and Bonhoeffer: Conceptions of the Relation between Grace and Works." In *International Kierkegaard Commentary, Vol. 21, For Self-Examination and Judge for Yourself!* Ed. Robert Perkins. Macon, GA: Mercer University Press, 2002, pp. 143–168.

Ratcliffe, Matthew. *Feelings of Being*. Oxford: Oxford University Press, 2008.

Roberts, Robert C. *Emotions: An Essay in Aid of Moral Psychology*. Cambridge: Cambridge University Press, 2003.

———. "Existence, Emotion and Character: Classical Themes in Kierkegaard." In *The Cambridge Companion to Kierkegaard*. Eds. Alastair Hannay and Gordon D. Marino. Cambridge: Cambridge University Press, 1998.

———. "Gratitude and Humility." In *Perspectives on Gratitude: An Interdisciplinary Approach*. Ed. David Carr. London: Routledge, 2016.

———. "Kierkegaard, Wittgenstein and a Method of Virtue Ethics." In *Kierkegaard in Post/Modernity*. Eds. Martin J. Matustik and Merold Westphal. Bloomington: Indiana University Press, 1995.

———. "Learning Intellectual Humility." In *Intellectual Virtues and Education: Essays in Applied Virtue Epistemology*. Ed. Jason Baehr. London: Routledge, forthcoming.

———. *Spiritual Emotions: A Psychology of Christian Virtues*. Grand Rapids, MI: William B. Eerdmans, 2007.

———. "The Virtue of Hope in *Eighteen Upbuilding Discourses*." In *International Kierkegaard Commentary, Vol. 5, Eighteen Upbuilding Discourses*. Ed. Robert L. Perkins. Macon, GA: Mercer University Press, 2003.

Rudd, Anthony, and John Davenport, eds. *Love, Reason, and Will: Kierkegaard after Frankfurt*. London: Bloomsbury, 2015.

Sanders, John. *The God Who Risks: A Theology of Divine Providence*. Revised edition. Downer's Grove, IL: InterVarsity, 2007.

Scherer, Wilhelm. *Klemens von Alexandrien und seine Erkenntnisprinzipien*. München: Verlag der J. J. Lentnerschen Buchhandlung, 1907.

Schönbaumsfeld, Genia. *A Confusion of the Spheres: Kierkegaard and Wittgenstein on Philosophy and Religion*. Oxford: Oxford University Press, 2007.

Shenk, David. *Data Smog: Surviving the Information Glut*. San Francisco: Harper Edge, 1997.

Shestov, Lev. *Kierkegaard and the Existential Philosophy*. Athens: Ohio University Press, 1969.

Shields, James Mark. "Faith and the Sublation of Modernity: Kierkegaard, Quixote and the Transformation of Fideism." *Philosophy, Culture, and Traditions* 4 (2007): 231–247.

Siegel, Lee. *Against the Machine: Being Human in the Age of the Electronic Mob*. New York: Spiegel & Grau, 2008.

Simmons, J. Aaron. "Existential Appropriations: The Influence of Jean Wahl on Levinas's Reading of Kierkegaard." In *Kierkegaard and Levinas: Ethics, Politics, and Religion*. Eds. J. Aaron Simmons and David Wood. Bloomington: Indiana University Press, 2008, pp. 41–66.

———. *God and the Other: Ethics and Politics after the Theological Turn*. Bloomington: Indiana University Press, 2011.

———. "In Whom, Then, Do We Put Our Trust?—Thinking About Levinas with Drew Dalton." *The Journal for Cultural and Religious Theory* 11.3 (Fall 2011): 37–45.

Simmons, J. Aaron, and David Wood, eds. *Kierkegaard and Levinas: Ethics, Politics, and Religion*. Bloomington: Indiana University Press, 2008.

Slotty, Martin. *Die Erkenntnislehre S. A. Kierkegaards* [The Epistemology of S. A. Kierkegaard]. Diss. Friedrich-Alexanders-Universität, 1915.

Smith, James K. A. "Scandalizing Theology: A Pentecostal Response to Noll's Scandal." *Pneuma: Journal of the Society for Pentecostal Studies* 19 (1997): 225–238.

———. *Thinking in Tongues: Pentecostal Contributions to Christian Philosophy*. Grand Rapids, MI: William B. Eerdmans, 2010.

Smith, Quentin. *The Felt Meanings of the World: A Metaphysics of Feeling*. West Lafayette, IN: Purdue University Press, 1986.

Soble, Alan. *The Structure of Love*. New Haven, CT: Yale University Press, 1990.

———, ed. *Eros, Agape, and Philia: Readings in the Philosophy of Love*. New York: Paragon House, 1998.

Solomon, David. "Virtue Ethics: Radical or Routine?" In *Intellectual Virtue: Perspectives from Ethics and Epistemology*. Eds. Michael DePaul and Linda Zagzebski. New York: Oxford University Press, 2003.

Spinoza, Benedict de. *Ethics*. Ed. and trans. Edwin Curley. New York: Penguin, 1996.

Stack, George. *Kierkegaard's Existential Ethics*. Tuscaloosa: University of Alabama Press, 1977.

Stewart, Jon. *Kierkegaard's Relations to Hegel Reconsidered*. Cambridge: Cambridge University Press, 2003.

———, ed. *Kierkegaard Research: Sources, Reception, and Resources, Vol. 9, Kierkegaard and Existentialism*. Farnham, UK: Ashgate, 2011.

Stokes, Patrick. *Kierkegaard's Mirrors: Interest, Self, and Moral Vision*. New York: Palgrave Macmillan, 2010.

Strawser, Michael. *Kierkegaard and the Philosophy of Love*. Lanham, MD: Lexington, 2015.

———. "Kierkegaard's Erotic Reduction and the Problem of Founding the Self." In *Narrative, Identity and the Kierkegaardian Self*. Eds. John Lippitt and Patrick Stokes. Edinburgh: Edinburgh University Press, 2015.

Stross, Randall. *Planet Google: One Company's Audacious Plan to Organize Everything We Know*. New York: Free Press, 2008.

Stump, Eleanore. "Love, by All Accounts." Presidential Address to the APA. *Proceedings and Addresses of the American Philosophical Association* 80.2 (November 2006): 25–43.

Söderquist, Brian K. "Irony." In *The Oxford Handbook of Kierkegaard*. Eds. John Lippitt and George Pattison. Oxford: Oxford University Press, 2013.

———. *The Isolated Self: Truth and Untruth in Søren Kierkegaard's* On the Concept of Irony. Copenhagen: C. A. Reitzel, 2007.

Tietjen, Mark A. "Kierkegaard and the Classical Virtue Tradition." *Faith and Philosophy* 27.2 (2010): 153–173.

———. *Kierkegaard, Communication and Virtue: Authorship as Edification*. Bloomington: Indiana University Press, 2013.

Tolstoy, Leo. "The Death of Ivan Ilyich." In *The Death of Ivan Ilyich and Other Stories*. Trans. Ronald Wilks, Antony Briggs, and David McDuff. London: Penguin Classics, 2008.

Tutewiler, Corey Benjamin. "Gratitude." In *Kierkegaard Research: Sources, Reception and Resources, Vol. 15, Kierkegaard's Concepts, Tome III: Envy to Incognito*. Eds. Steven M. Emmanuel, William McDonald, and Jon Stewart. London: Ashgate, 2014.

Vaidhyanathan, Siva. *The Googlization of Everything (and Why We Should Worry)*. Berkeley: University of California Press, 2011.

von Hildebrand, Dietrich. *The Heart: An Analysis of Human and Divine Affectivity*. Ed. John H. Crosby. South Bend, IN: St. Augustine's, 2007.

———. *The Nature of Love*. Trans. John F. Crosby with John H. Crosby. South Bend, IN: St. Augustine's, 2009.

Wahl, Jean. *Études Kierkegaardiennes*. 2nd edition. Paris: Librairie Philosophique, 1949.

Walker, Jeremy. *Kierkegaard: The Descent into God*. Montreal: McGill-Queen's University Press, 1985.

Wallace, David Foster. *This Is Water: Some Thoughts, Delivered on a Significant Occasion, about Living a Compassionate Life*. New York: Little, Brown & Company, 2009.

Walsh, David. *The Modern Philosophical Revolution: The Luminosity of Existence*. Cambridge: Cambridge University Press, 2008.

Walsh, Sylvia "Dying to the World and Self-Denial in Kierkegaard's Religious Thought." In *International Kierkegaard Commentary, Vol. 21*, For Self-Examination *and* Judge for Yourself! Ed. Robert L. Perkins. Macon, GA: Mercer University Press, 2002, pp. 169–198.

Walsh, Sylvia. "Forming the Heart: The Role of Love in Kierkegaard's Thought." In *The Grammar of the Heart*. Ed. Richard H. Bell. New York: Harper & Row, 1988, pp. 234–256.

———. "Kierkegaard and Postmodernism." *International Journal for Philosophy of Religion* 20.2 (1991): 113–122.

———. *Living Christianly: Kierkegaard's Dialectic of Christian Existence*. Philadelphia: Penn State University Press, 2005.

Weil, Simone. *The Simone Weil Reader*. Ed. George A. Panichas. New York: David McKay, 1977.

———. *Waiting for God*. Trans. Emma Craufurd. New York: Harper Perennial Classics, 2000.

Westphal, Merold. *Becoming a Self: A Reading of Kierkegaard's* Concluding Unscientific Postscript. West Lafayette, IN: Purdue University Press, 1996.

———. *Levinas and Kierkegaard in Dialogue*. Bloomington: Indiana University Press, 2008.

———. "The Many Faces of Levinas as a Reader of Kierkegaard." In *Kierkegaard and Levinas*. Eds. J. Aaron Simmons and David Wood. Bloomington: Indiana University Press, 2008.

———. *Overcoming Onto-Theology: Toward a Postmodern Christian Faith*. New York: Fordham University Press, 2001.

———. "Society, Politics, and Modernity." In *The Oxford Handbook of Kierkegaard*. Eds. John Lippitt and George Pattison. Oxford: Oxford University Press, 2013.

———. *Transcendence and Self-Transcendence: On God and the Soul*. Bloomington: Indiana University Press, 2004.

———. *Whose Community? Which Interpretation?* Grand Rapids, MI: Baker Academic, 2009.

Williams, Bernard. *Ethics and the Limits of Philosophy*. Cambridge, MA: Harvard University Press, 1985.

Wisdo, David. "Kierkegaard on the Limits of Christian Epistemology." *International Journal for Philosophy of Religion* 29.2 (1991): 97–112.

Wolterstorff, Nicholas. *Reason Within the Bounds of Religion*. 2nd edition. Grand Rapids, MI: William B. Eerdmans, 1984.

Wynn, Mark. *Emotional Experience and Religious Understanding*. Cambridge: Cambridge University Press, 2005.

Yong, Amos. *Spirit-World-Community: Theological Hermeneutics in Trinitarian Perspective*. Aldershot, UK: Ashgate, 2002.

Zahavi, Dan. *Self-Awareness and Alterity*. Evanston, IL: Northwestern University Press, 1999.

Ziolkowski, Eric. *The Literary Kierkegaard*. Evanston, IL: Northwestern University Press, 2011.

Zizioulas, John. "An Ontology of Love: A Patristic Reading of Dietrich von Hildebrand's *The Nature of Love*." In *Quaestiones Disputate: Selected Papers on the Philosophy of Dietrich von Hildebrand* 3.2 (2012): 1427.

Zuidervaart, Lambert. *Artistic Truth*. Cambridge: Cambridge University Press, 2004.

Index

Abraham, 42, 97, 113n72, 173–81, 183, 185, 187, 209, 212, 213, 238. *See also* faith, Abrahamic

action, 87, 140,153–54, 156, 157, 159, 161, 163, 164, 175, 197, 204, 214, 237; external, 157–58; moral, ix; responsible, 160; social, 234, 242. *See also* ethics, ethical action

affection, 36, 46, 52, 54, 60, 66, 69

affliction, 84, 85, 86, 87, 88, 184, 185

agape, xi, 35–36, 37, 46, 47, 48–52, 54, 55–58, 59–60, 61, 62–63, 64–66, 67–69, 70, 71, 73nn4–5, 73n9, 74n18, 74n26, 74n29, 75n31, 75n34, 76nn43–44, 81, 88, 89

Alston, William, 248n39

alterity, 47, 59, 60, 62, 63, 65, 67, 68, 69, 71, 229, 250n76

Amichai, Yehuda, 181

anthropology, 137, 229, 230

anti-theory, 80, 81

anxiety, 96, 100–101, 103, 110n25, 112n64, 119

Aquinas, Thomas, 52, 69, 72, 84, 89, 96

Arendt, Hannah, 180

Aristotle, 7, 12, 47, 64, 80, 83, 96

assurance, 120, 175–76, 181, 187, 188

atheism, 78, 81, 87, 88, 90, 192

Augustine, 35, 73n5, 80, 96

authority, 55, 138, 141, 142, 165

autonomy, 54, 55, 75n33, 81, 82, 87, 134

baptism, 85, 189n26

Barron, Peter, 138

Bauman, Zygmunt, 40, 41

Beabout, Gregory, 96

believer, the, 42–43, 194, 196, 199, 234, 235

bestowal, 67, 75n34, 10, 187, 202

Bible, the, 180; New Testament, 106, 156, 194, 210, 233; Old Testament, 106

blessedness, 25, 26

Bonhoeffer, Dietrich, 237

Brin, Sergey, 131, 138, 142

Buber, Martin, 47, 61, 63, 64–65, 69, 225n18; I-Thou relationship, 63, 64–65, 66, 69, 77n52

Bukdahl, Jørgen, 233

Caputo, John D., ix, 229, 248n32

caritas, 63, 64, 69–72

Carr, Nicholas, 141, 142, 143, 145–46

Catholicism, ix, 63

Cavell, Stanley, 184

charismatics, 228, 243, 244

charity, 36, 58, 68, 157

children, xi, 11, 14n12, 14n20, 24–25, 29n38, 33, 38, 50, 57, 58, 60, 66, 72, 100, 122, 152, 155, 178, 180, 182, 183, 224. *See also* love, parental

Choufrine, Arkadi, 202–203

Christianity, ix, xi, xviii, 58, 81, 84, 88, 97, 100, 101, 128n29, 136, 152, 153–58, 160, 161, 162–64, 165, 166, 167, 168n6, 169nn34–35, 181, 186, 191, 192, 193, 194, 195, 196, 198–204, 236, 237–38, 239, 240–41, 242–43, 250n74; Christian doctrine, 81, 90n2, 97, 102, 134, 155, 157, 174, 175, 191, 198, 199, 200, 201, 228, 247n16; Christian epistemology, xvi, 193, 242; Christian existence, 74n19, 203, 242; Christian experience, 194, 197, 198, 202; Christian knowledge, xvi, 91, 193, 194, 197, 198, 199, 200, 201, 202, 203, 204, 205; Christian orthodoxy, 163, 192, 202; Christian practice, 97, 107; Christian theism, ix, xii, 78, 81, 89–90, 229; Christian tradition, 13n6, 109n15, 155. *See also* Catholicism; humanity, and Christianity; Jesus Christ; love, Christian; truth, and Christianity; virtues, Christian

church fathers, 191, 200, 203, 205

Clement of Alexandria, xvi, 191, 200, 201–203, 204, 205

cognition, 114, 126n3, 198; cognitive limitation, 80, 81, 89

Cohen, Ted, 123

Come, Arnold B., 126n1

commitment, 48, 55, 60, 62, 66, 67, 70, 71, 95, 106, 107, 113n76, 121, 144, 152, 160, 183, 228, 231, 232; theological, 153, 234, 243

common watermark, 62, 68

compassion, 10, 50, 87, 97, 162

competition, 82, 100, 101, 108, 110n25, 110n30

conscience, 22, 48, 49, 54, 57, 58, 102, 195, 211

Lightning Source UK Ltd.
Milton Keynes UK
UKHW040857240620
365432UK00012B/195